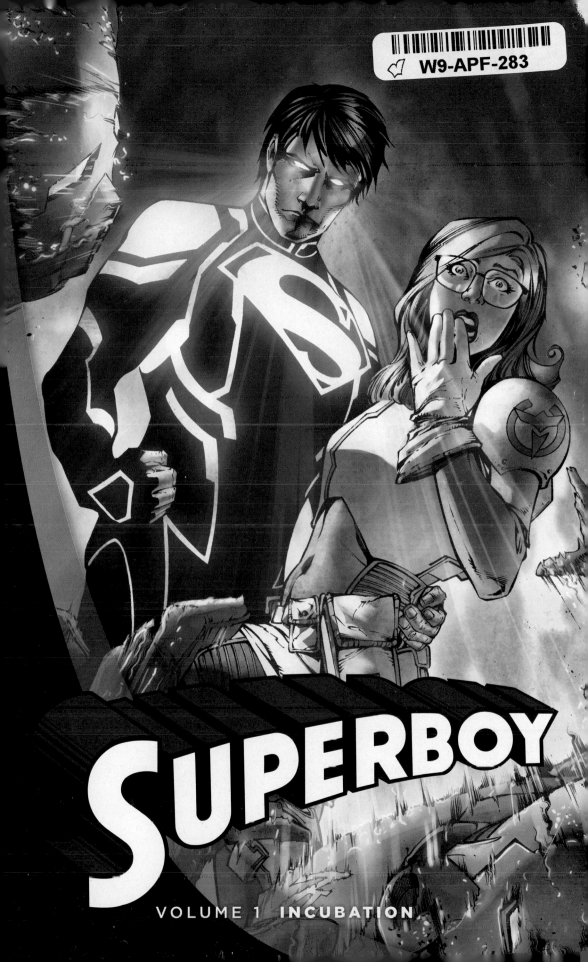

SUPERBOY

VOLUME 1 INCUBATION

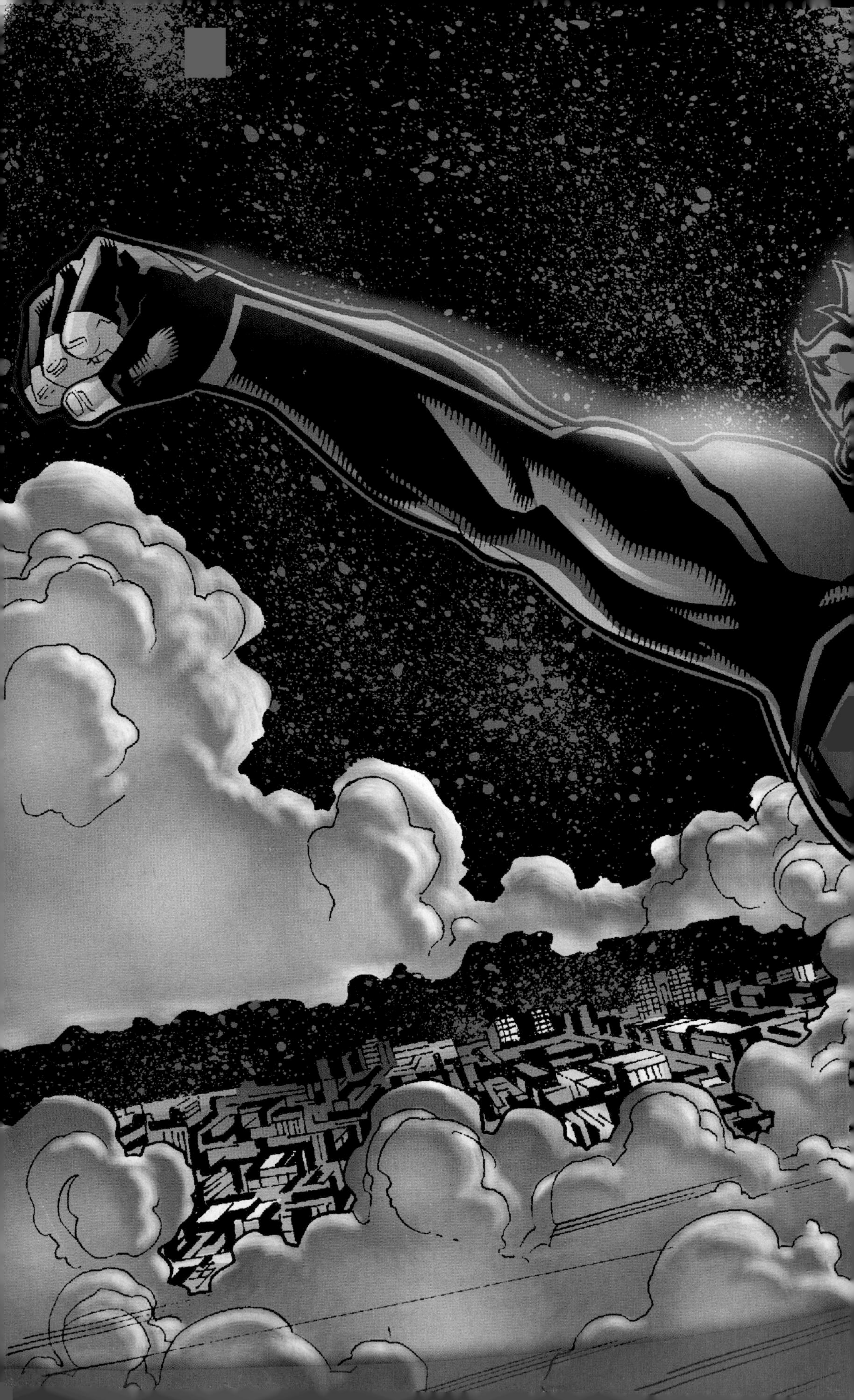

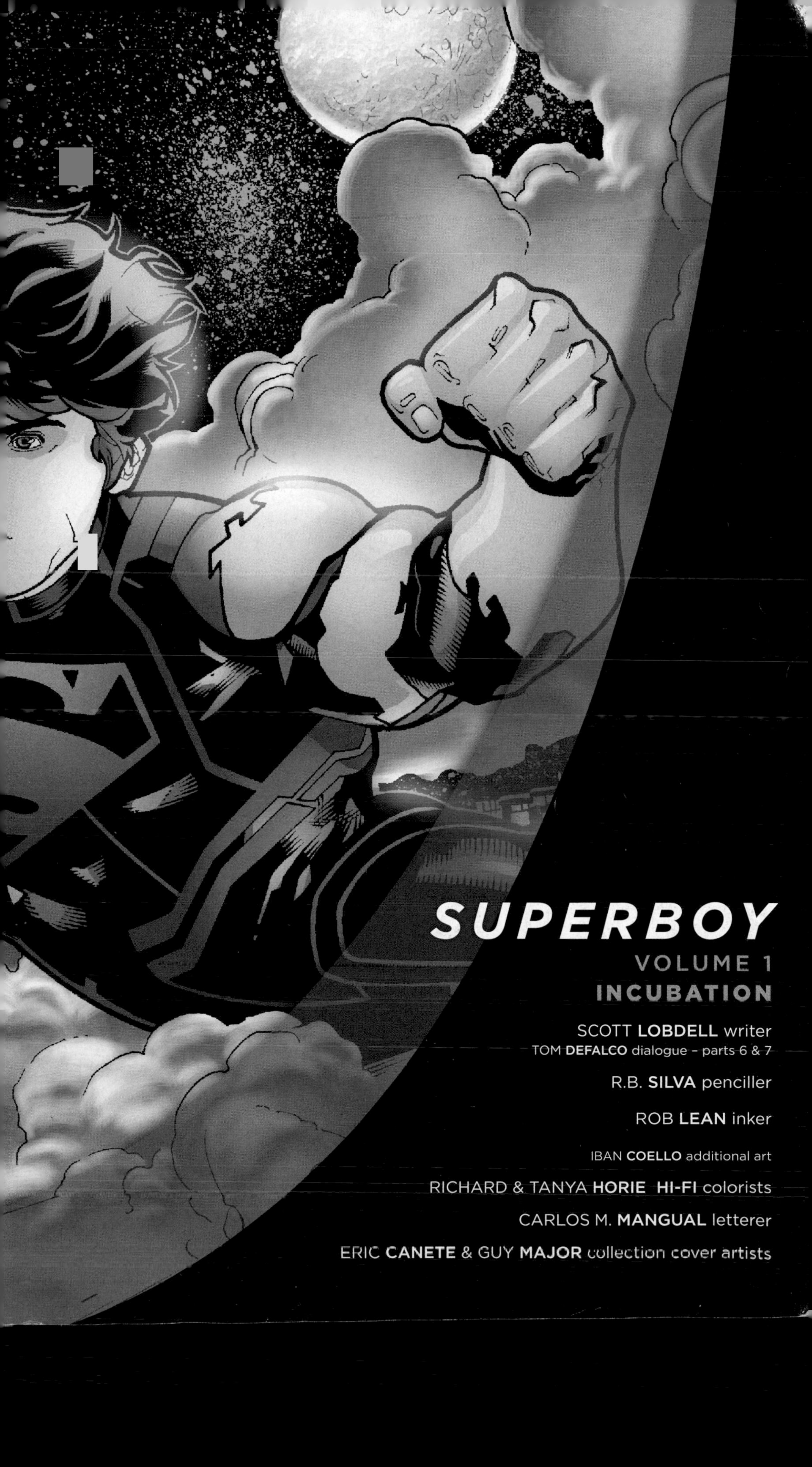

SUPERBOY

VOLUME 1

INCUBATION

SCOTT **LOBDELL** writer

TOM **DEFALCO** dialogue – parts 6 & 7

R.B. **SILVA** penciller

ROB **LEAN** inker

IBAN **COELLO** additional art

RICHARD & TANYA **HORIE** **HI-FI** colorists

CARLOS M. **MANGUAL** letterer

ERIC **CANETE** & GUY **MAJOR** collection cover artists

CHRIS CONROY Editor – Original Series ROBIN WILDMAN Editor
ROBBIN BROSTERMAN Design Director – Books ROBBIE BIEDERMAN Publication Design

BOB HARRAS VP – Editor-in-Chief

DIANE NELSON President DAN DIDIO and JIM LEE Co-Publishers GEOFF JOHNS Chief Creative Officer
JOHN ROOD Executive VP – Sales, Marketing and Business Development AMY GENKINS Senior VP – Business and Legal Affairs
NAIRI GARDINER Senior VP – Finance JEFF BOISON VP – Publishing Operations
MARK CHIARELLO VP – Art Direction and Design JOHN CUNNINGHAM VP – Marketing
TERRI CUNNINGHAM VP – Talent Relations and Services ALISON GILL Senior VP – Manufacturing and Operations
HANK KANALZ Senior VP – Digital JAY KOGAN VP – Business and Legal Affairs, Publishing
JACK MAHAN VP – Business Affairs, Talent NICK NAPOLITANO VP – Manufacturing Administration
SUE POHJA VP – Book Sales COURTNEY SIMMONS Senior VP – Publicity BOB WAYNE Senior VP – Sales

SUPERBOY VOLUME 1: INCUBATION

DC Comics, 1700 Broadway, New York, NY 10019
A Warner Bros. Entertainment Company.
Printed by RR Donnelley, Salem, VA, USA. 3/13/13. Second Printing.
ISBN: 978-1-4012-3485-0

Library of Congress Cataloging-in-Publication Data

Lobdell, Scott.
Superboy volume 1 : incubation / Scott Lobdell, R.B. Silva, Rob Lean.
p. cm.
"Originally published in single magazine form in SUPERBOY 1-7."
ISBN 978-1-4012-3485-0
1. Graphic novels. I. Silva, R. B., 1985- II. Lean, Rob. III. Title. IV. Title: Incubation.
PN6728.S87L63 2012
741.5'973–dc23
2012015242

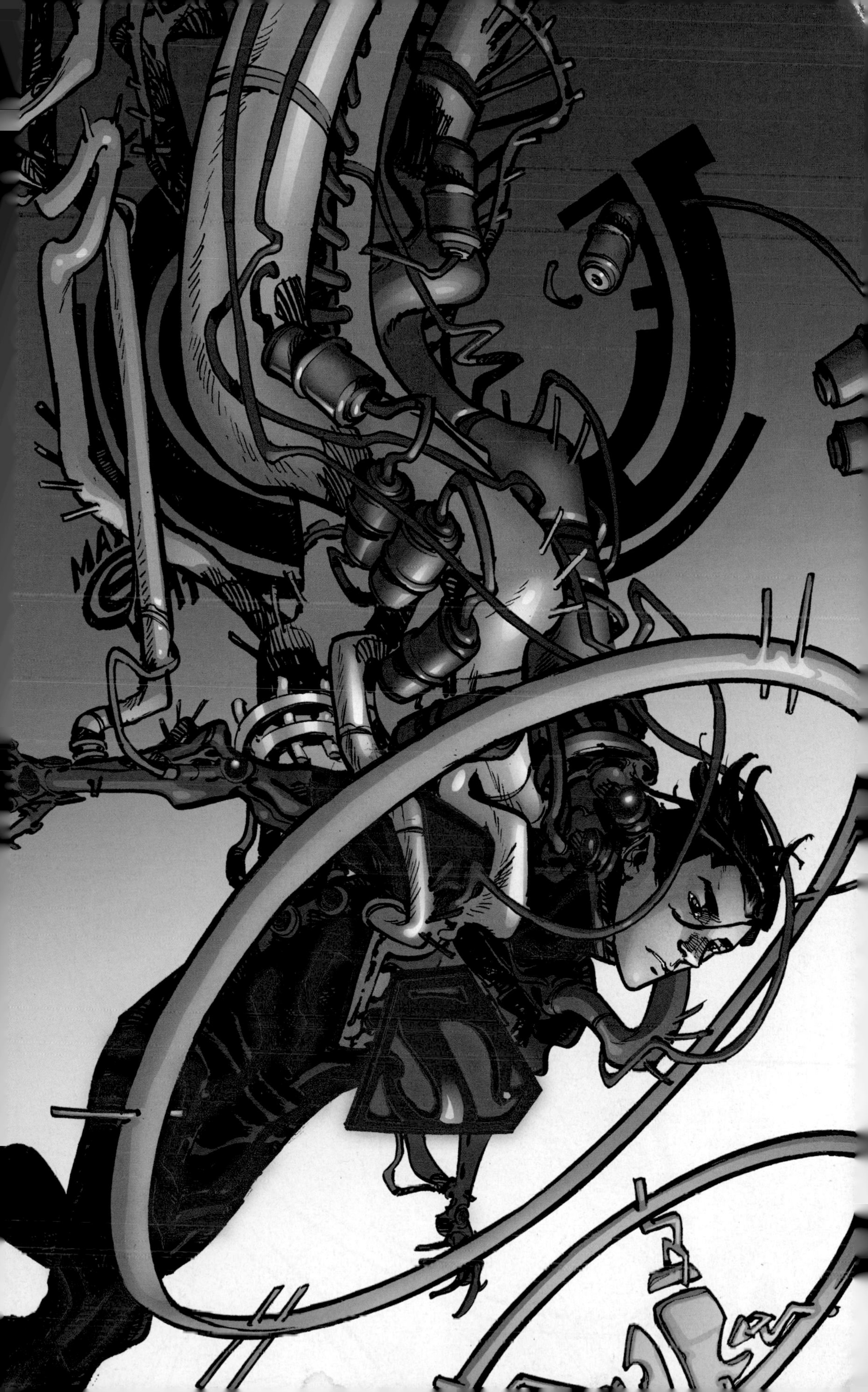

Cover by ERIC CANETE & GUY MAJOR

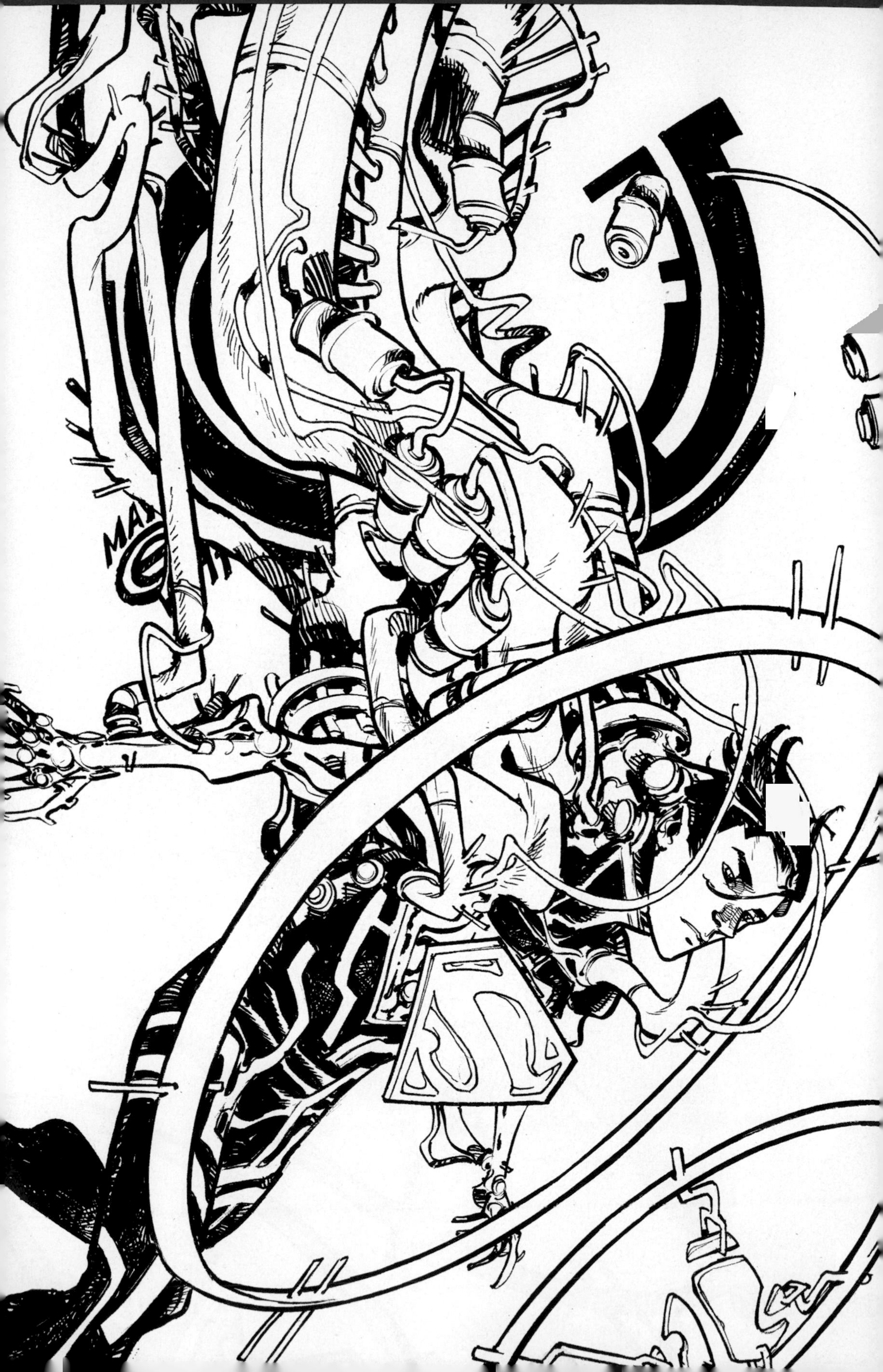

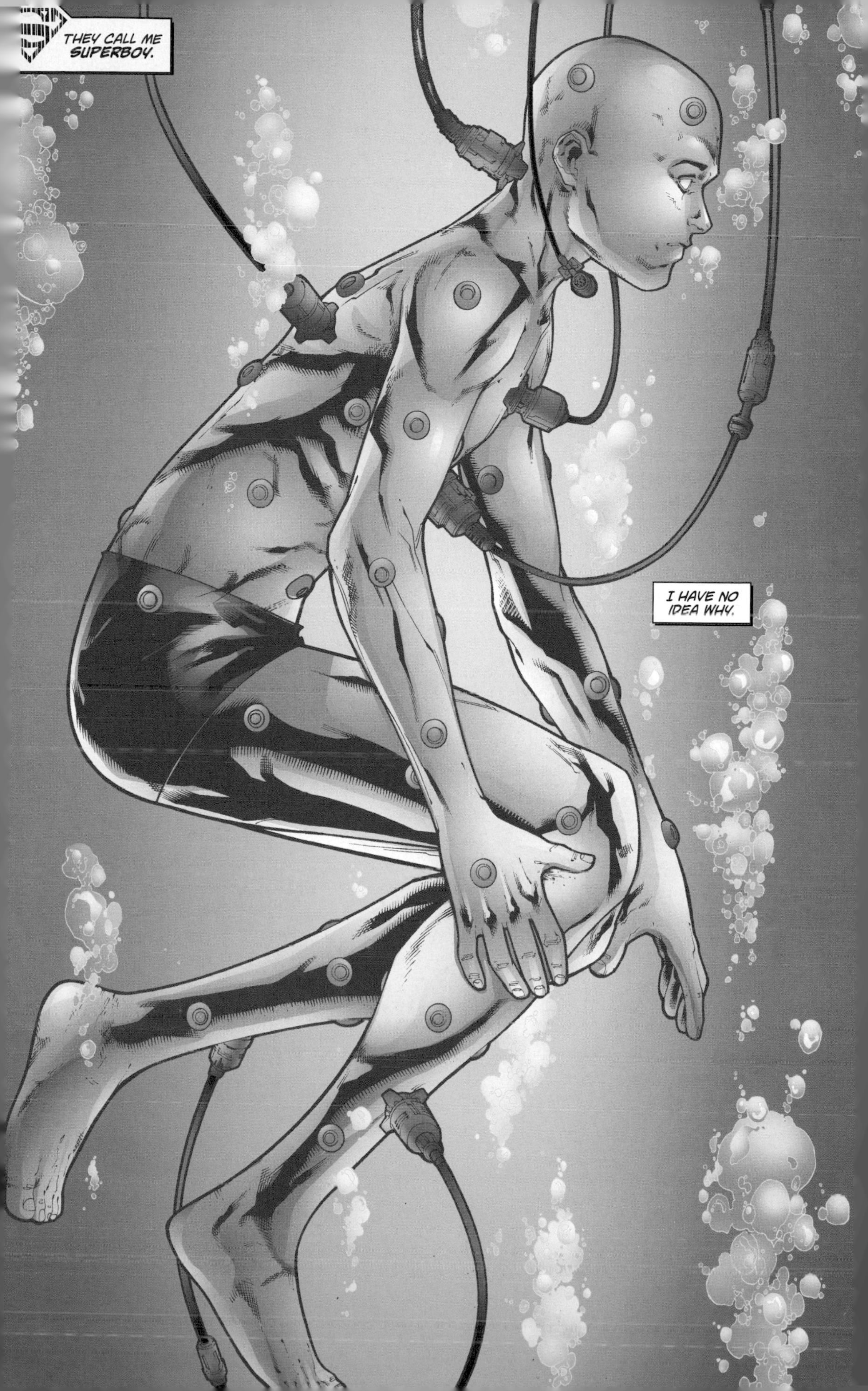
THEY CALL ME SUPERBOY.
I HAVE NO IDEA WHY.

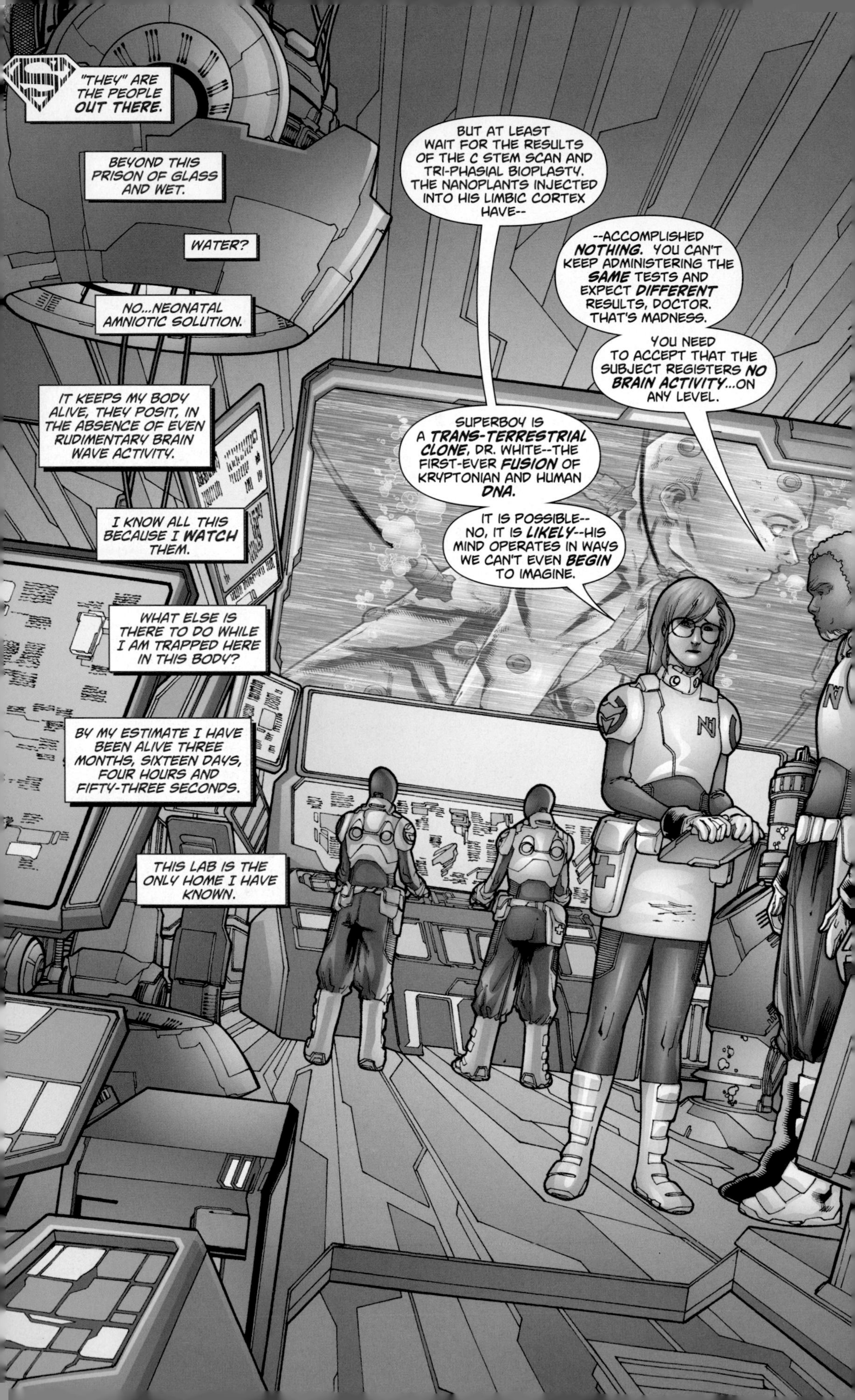
"THEY" ARE THE PEOPLE OUT THERE.
BEYOND THIS PRISON OF GLASS AND WET.
WATER?
NO...NEONATAL AMNIOTIC SOLUTION.
BUT AT LEAST WAIT FOR THE RESULTS OF THE C STEM SCAN AND TRI-PHASIAL BIOPLASTY. THE NANOPLANTS INJECTED INTO HIS LIMBIC CORTEX HAVE--
--ACCOMPLISHED NOTHING. YOU CAN'T KEEP ADMINISTERING THE SAME TESTS AND EXPECT DIFFERENT RESULTS, DOCTOR. THAT'S MADNESS.
YOU NEED TO ACCEPT THAT THE SUBJECT REGISTERS NO BRAIN ACTIVITY...ON ANY LEVEL.
IT KEEPS MY BODY ALIVE, THEY POSIT, IN THE ABSENCE OF EVEN RUDIMENTARY BRAIN WAVE ACTIVITY.
SUPERBOY IS A TRANS-TERRESTRIAL CLONE, DR. WHITE--THE FIRST-EVER FUSION OF KRYPTONIAN AND HUMAN DNA.
IT IS POSSIBLE--NO, IT IS LIKELY--HIS MIND OPERATES IN WAYS WE CAN'T EVEN BEGIN TO IMAGINE.
I KNOW ALL THIS BECAUSE I WATCH THEM.
WHAT ELSE IS THERE TO DO WHILE I AM TRAPPED HERE IN THIS BODY?
BY MY ESTIMATE I HAVE BEEN ALIVE THREE MONTHS, SIXTEEN DAYS, FOUR HOURS AND FIFTY-THREE SECONDS.
THIS LAB IS THE ONLY HOME I HAVE KNOWN.

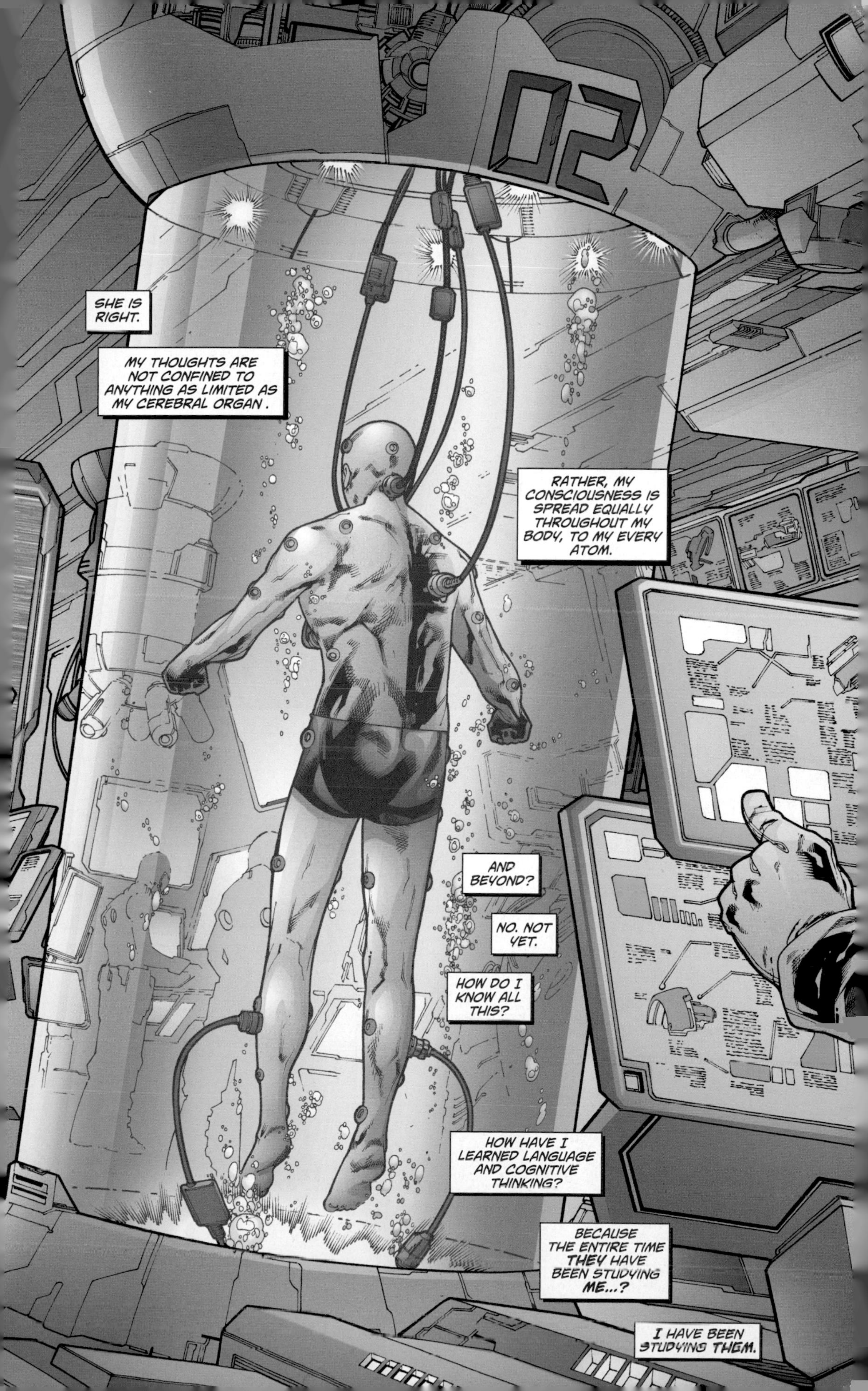
SHE IS RIGHT.
MY THOUGHTS ARE NOT CONFINED TO ANYTHING AS LIMITED AS MY CEREBRAL ORGAN.
RATHER, MY CONSCIOUSNESS IS SPREAD EQUALLY THROUGHOUT MY BODY, TO MY EVERY ATOM.
AND BEYOND?
NO. NOT YET.
HOW DO I KNOW ALL THIS?
HOW HAVE I LEARNED LANGUAGE AND COGNITIVE THINKING?
BECAUSE THE ENTIRE TIME THEY HAVE BEEN STUDYING ME...?
I HAVE BEEN STUDYING THEM.
02

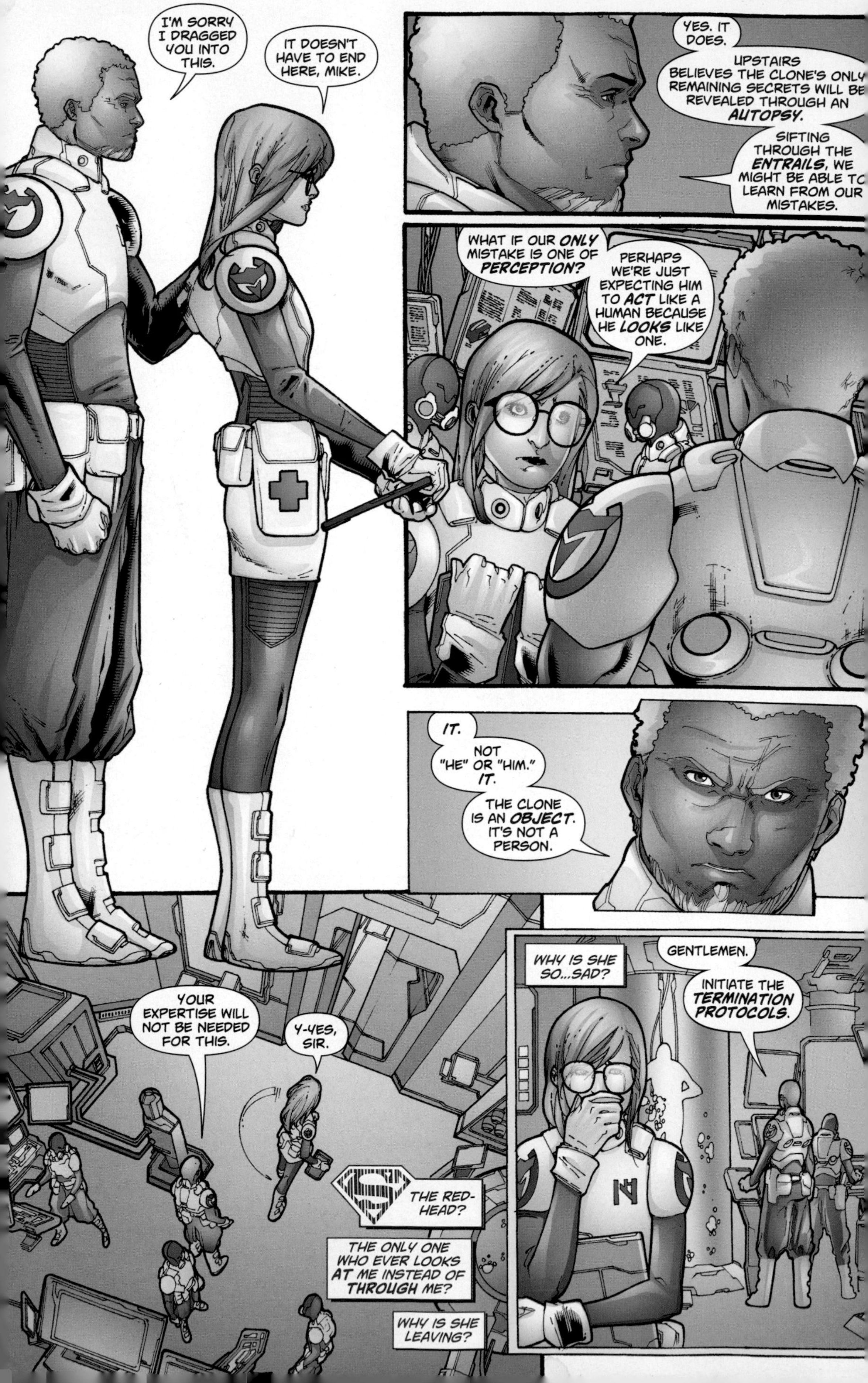
I'M SORRY I DRAGGED YOU INTO THIS.
IT DOESN'T HAVE TO END HERE, MIKE.
YES. IT DOES.
UPSTAIRS BELIEVES THE CLONE'S ONLY REMAINING SECRETS WILL BE REVEALED THROUGH AN AUTOPSY.
SIFTING THROUGH THE ENTRAILS, WE MIGHT BE ABLE TO LEARN FROM OUR MISTAKES.
WHAT IF OUR ONLY MISTAKE IS ONE OF PERCEPTION?
PERHAPS WE'RE JUST EXPECTING HIM TO ACT LIKE A HUMAN BECAUSE HE LOOKS LIKE ONE.
IT.
NOT "HE" OR "HIM." IT.
THE CLONE IS AN OBJECT. IT'S NOT A PERSON.
YOUR EXPERTISE WILL NOT BE NEEDED FOR THIS.
Y-YES, SIR.
THE RED-HEAD?
THE ONLY ONE WHO EVER LOOKS AT ME INSTEAD OF THROUGH ME?
WHY IS SHE LEAVING?
WHY IS SHE SO...SAD?
GENTLEMEN.
INITIATE THE TERMINATION PROTOCOLS.

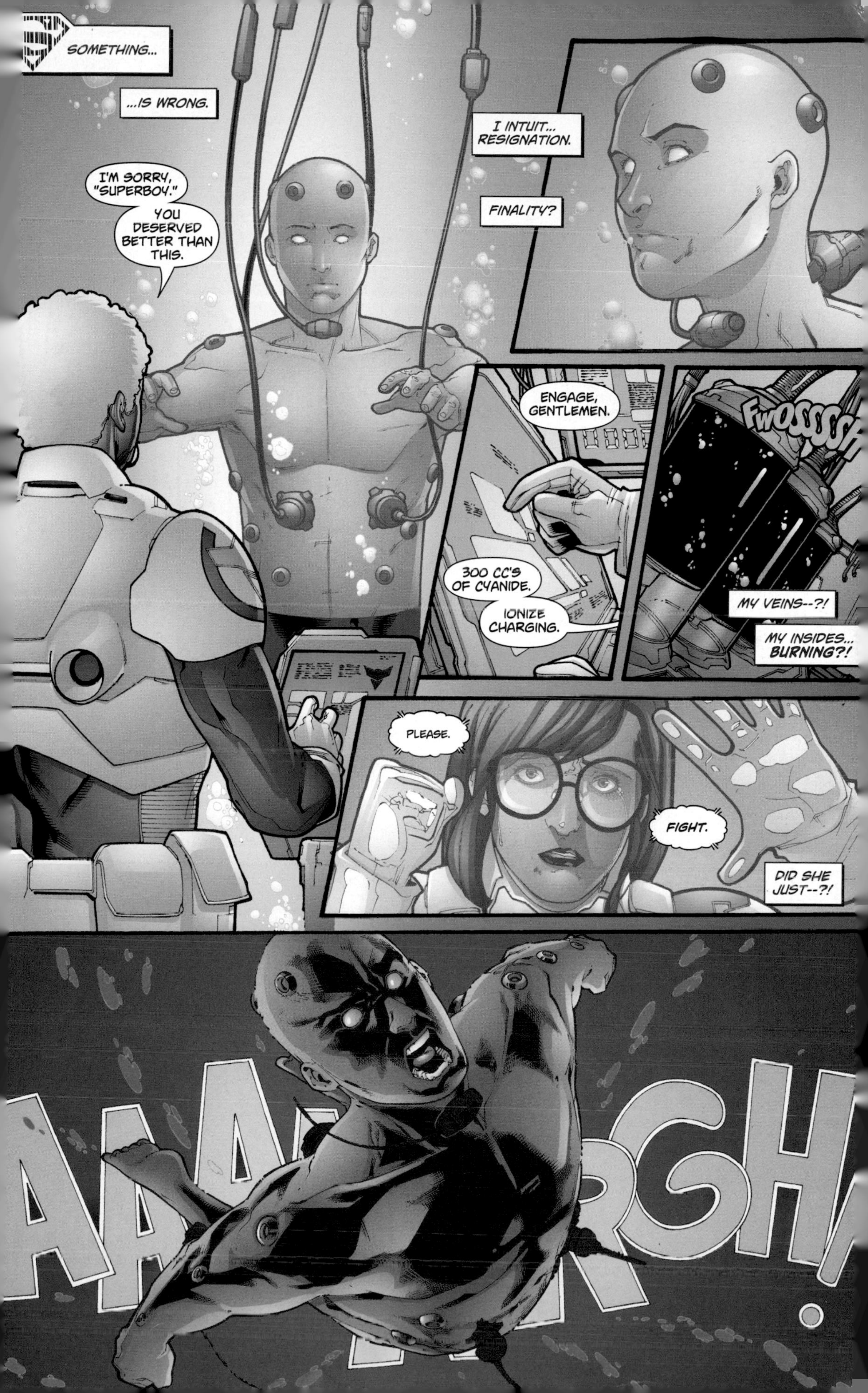
SOMETHING...
...IS WRONG.
I'M SORRY, "SUPERBOY."
YOU DESERVED BETTER THAN THIS.
I INTUIT... RESIGNATION.
FINALITY?
ENGAGE, GENTLEMEN.
300 CC'S OF CYANIDE.
IONIZE CHARGING.
FWOSSSSH
MY VEINS--?!
MY INSIDES... BURNING?!
PLEASE.
FIGHT.
DID SHE JUST--?!
AAARGH!

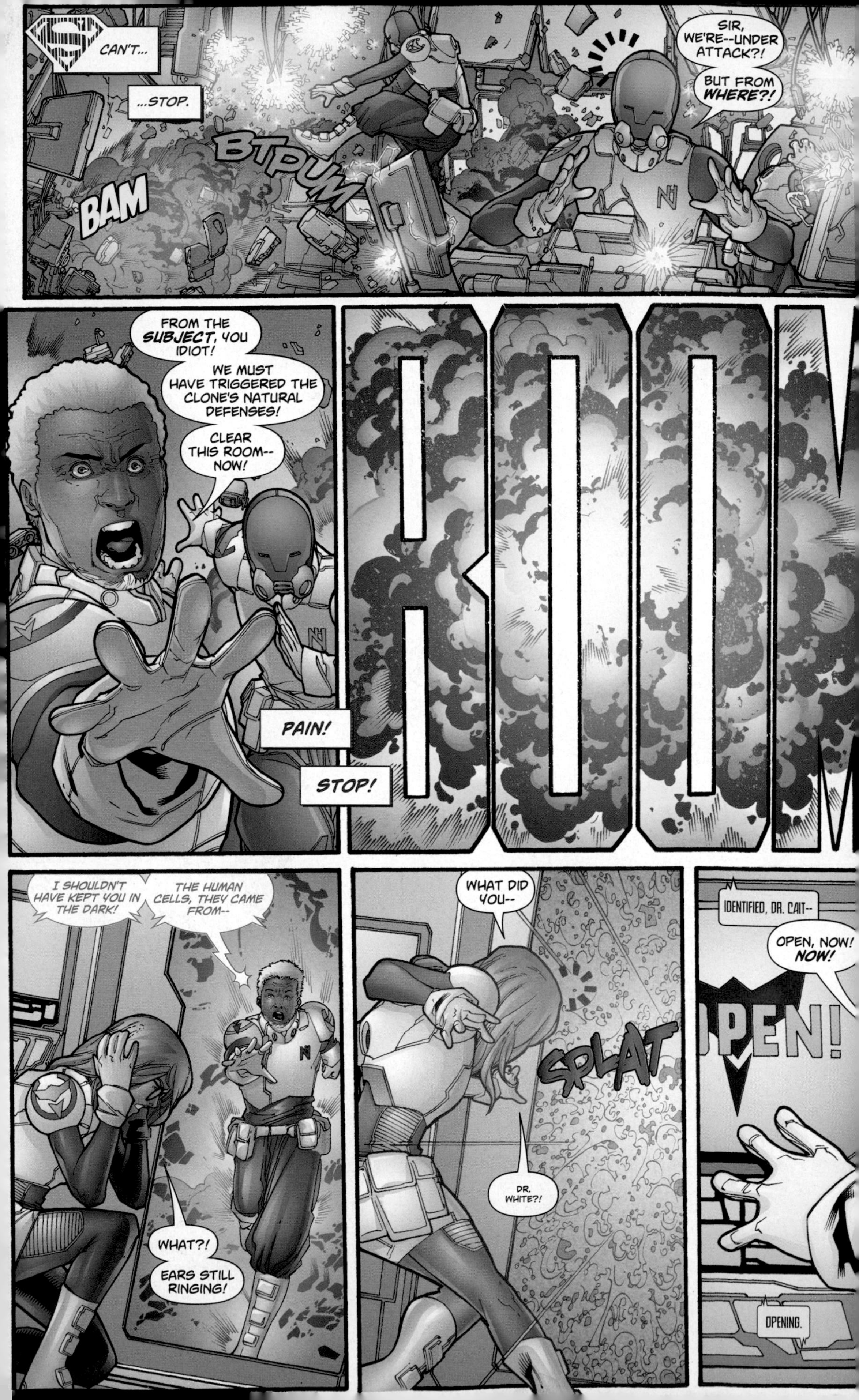
CAN'T...
...STOP.
BTPUM
BAM
SIR, WE'RE--UNDER ATTACK?!
BUT FROM WHERE?!
FROM THE SUBJECT, YOU IDIOT!
WE MUST HAVE TRIGGERED THE CLONE'S NATURAL DEFENSES!
CLEAR THIS ROOM-- NOW!
PAIN!
STOP!
BOOM
I SHOULDN'T HAVE KEPT YOU IN THE DARK!
THE HUMAN CELLS, THEY CAME FROM--
WHAT?!
EARS STILL RINGING!
WHAT DID YOU--
SPLAT
DR. WHITE?!
IDENTIFIED, DR. CAIT--
OPEN, NOW! NOW!
OPEN!
OPENING.

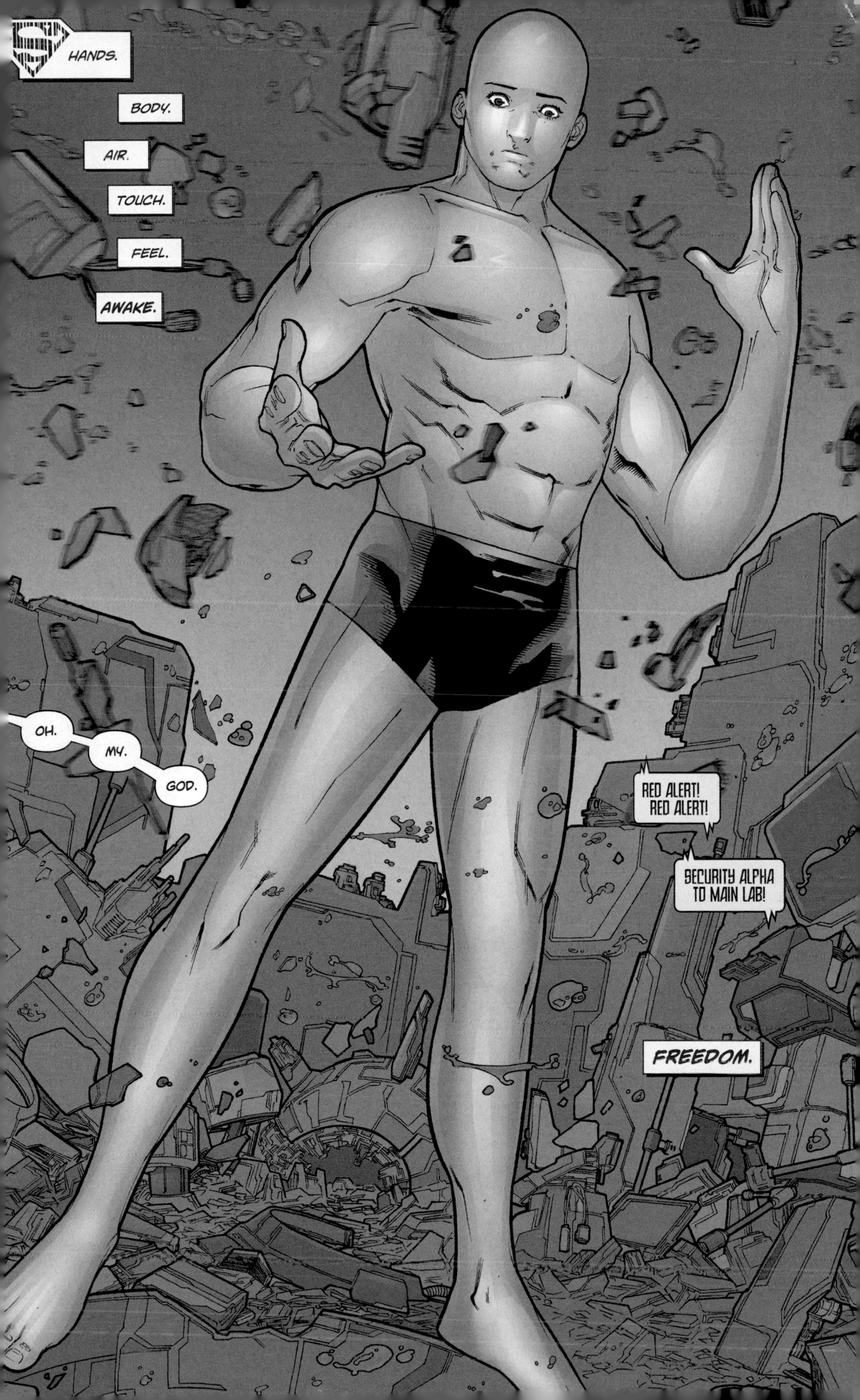
HANDS.
BODY.
AIR.
TOUCH.
FEEL.
AWAKE.
OH.
MY.
GOD.
RED ALERT! RED ALERT!
SECURITY ALPHA TO MAIN LAB!
FREEDOM.

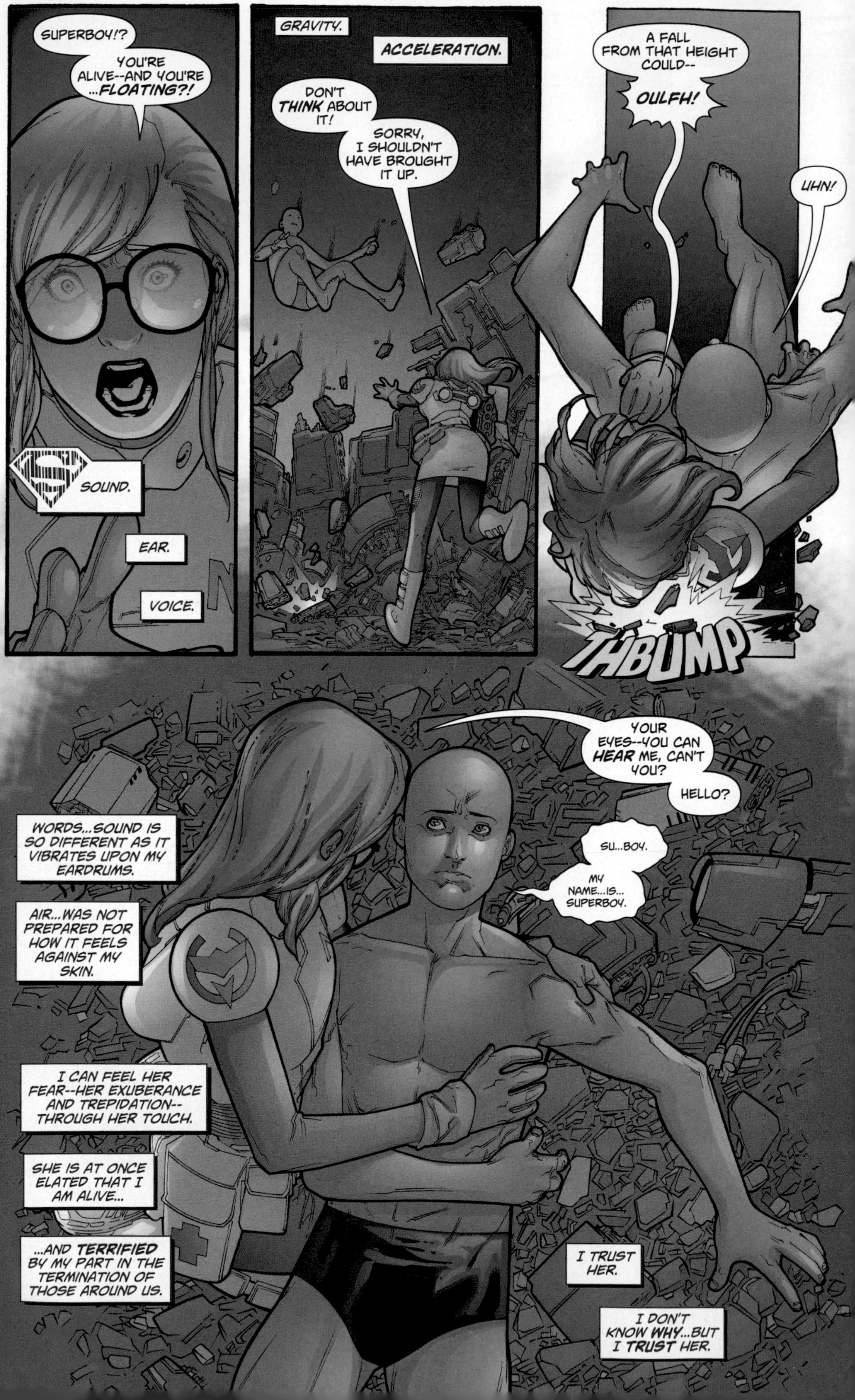

SUPERBOY!?
YOU'RE ALIVE--AND YOU'RE ...FLOATING?!
SOUND.
EAR.
VOICE.
GRAVITY.
ACCELERATION.
DON'T THINK ABOUT IT!
SORRY, I SHOULDN'T HAVE BROUGHT IT UP.
A FALL FROM THAT HEIGHT COULD--
OULFH!
UHN!
THBUMP
YOUR EYES--YOU CAN HEAR ME, CAN'T YOU?
HELLO?
WORDS...SOUND IS SO DIFFERENT AS IT VIBRATES UPON MY EARDRUMS.
SU...BOY.
MY NAME...IS... SUPERBOY.
AIR...WAS NOT PREPARED FOR HOW IT FEELS AGAINST MY SKIN.
I CAN FEEL HER FEAR--HER EXUBERANCE AND TREPIDATION--THROUGH HER TOUCH.
SHE IS AT ONCE ELATED THAT I AM ALIVE...
...AND TERRIFIED BY MY PART IN THE TERMINATION OF THOSE AROUND US.
I TRUST HER.
I DON'T KNOW WHY...BUT I TRUST HER.

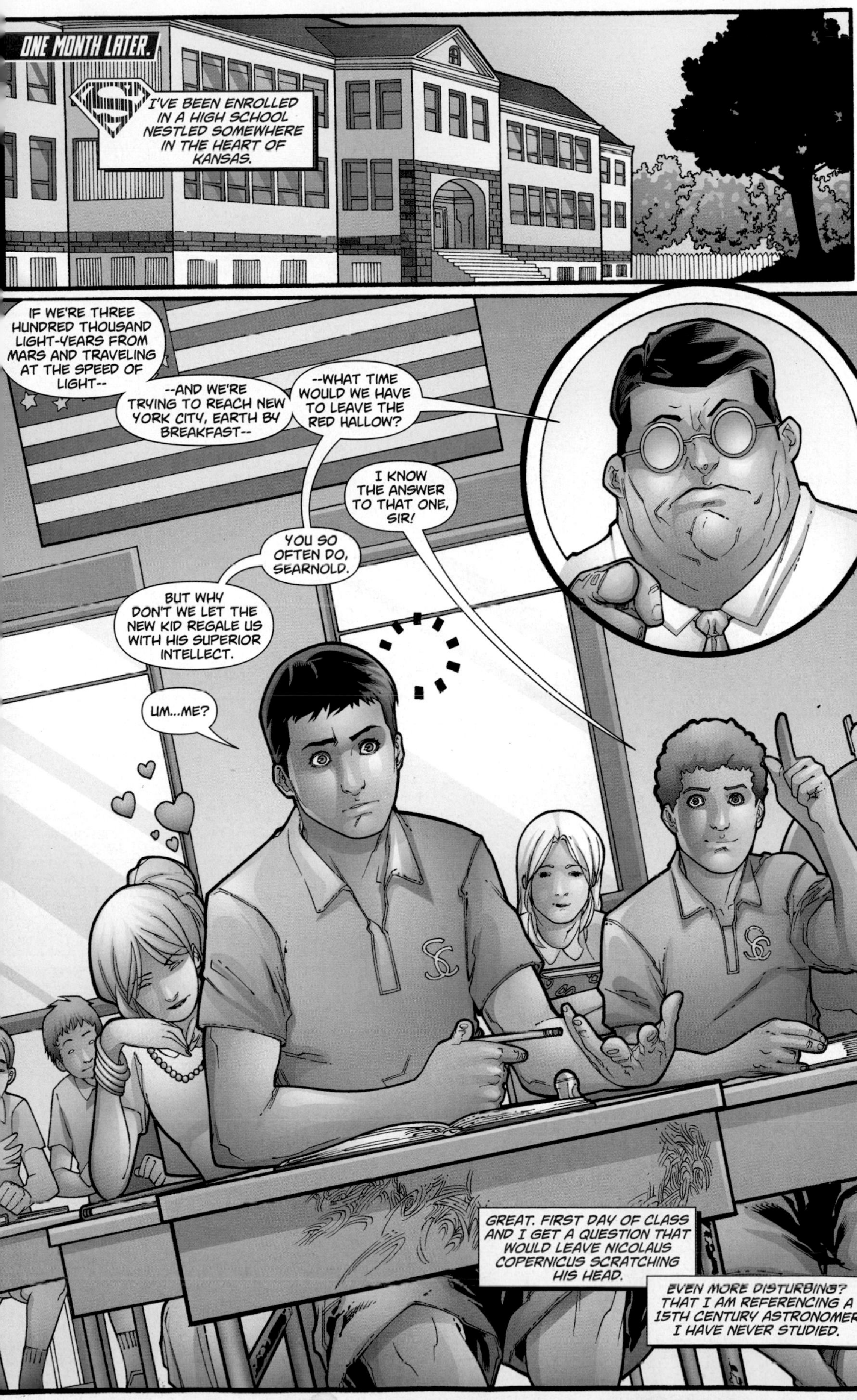
ONE MONTH LATER.
I'VE BEEN ENROLLED IN A HIGH SCHOOL NESTLED SOMEWHERE IN THE HEART OF KANSAS.
IF WE'RE THREE HUNDRED THOUSAND LIGHT-YEARS FROM MARS AND TRAVELING AT THE SPEED OF LIGHT--
--AND WE'RE TRYING TO REACH NEW YORK CITY, EARTH BY BREAKFAST--
--WHAT TIME WOULD WE HAVE TO LEAVE THE RED HALLOW?
I KNOW THE ANSWER TO THAT ONE, SIR!
YOU SO OFTEN DO, SEARNOLD.
BUT WHY DON'T WE LET THE NEW KID REGALE US WITH HIS SUPERIOR INTELLECT.
UM...ME?
GREAT. FIRST DAY OF CLASS AND I GET A QUESTION THAT WOULD LEAVE NICOLAUS COPERNICUS SCRATCHING HIS HEAD.
EVEN MORE DISTURBING? THAT I AM REFERENCING A 15TH CENTURY ASTRONOMER I HAVE NEVER STUDIED.

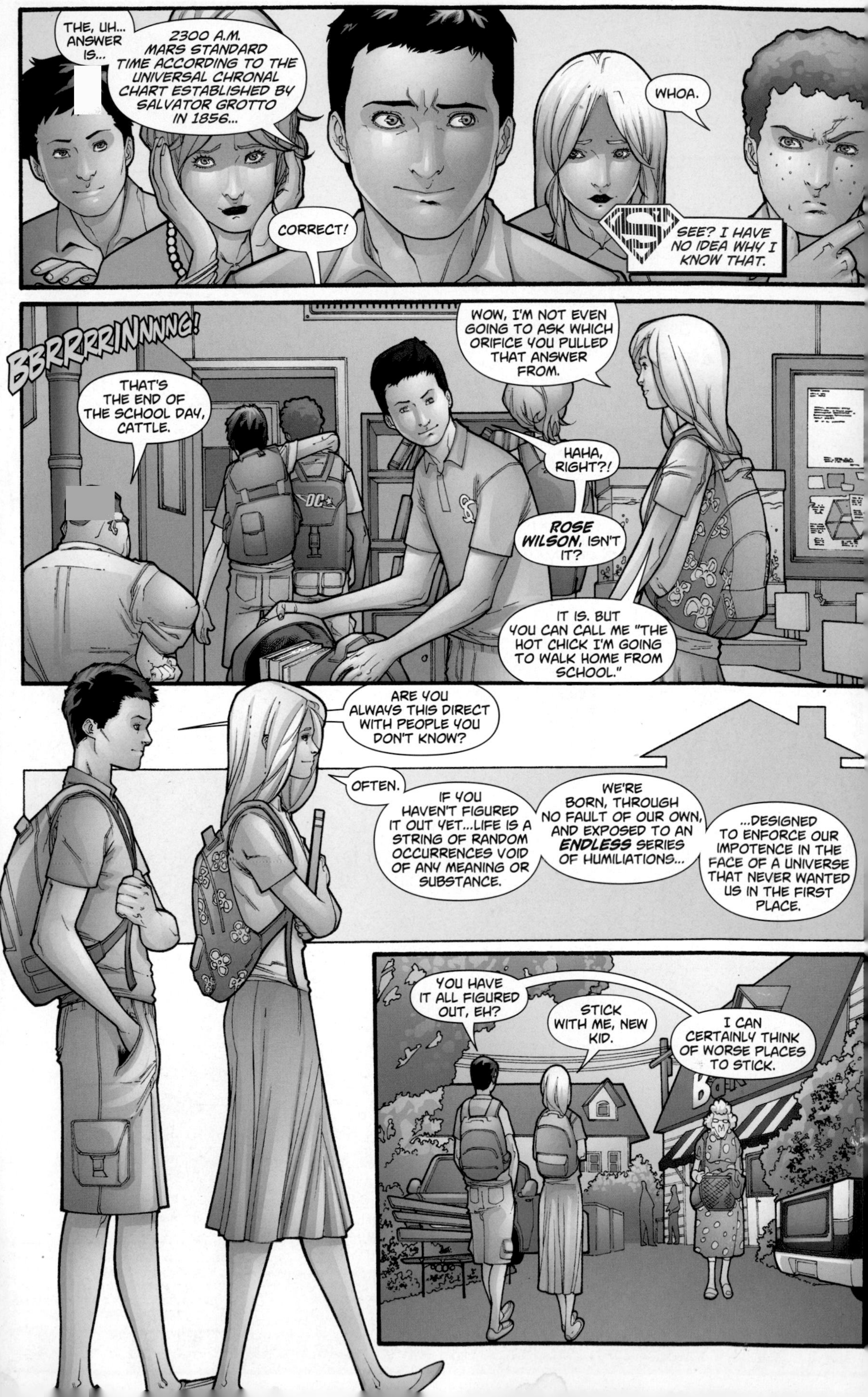
THE, UH... ANSWER IS...
2300 A.M. MARS STANDARD TIME ACCORDING TO THE UNIVERSAL CHRONAL CHART ESTABLISHED BY SALVATOR GROTTO IN 1856...
CORRECT!
WHOA.
SEE? I HAVE NO IDEA WHY I KNOW THAT.
BBRRRRINNNNG!
THAT'S THE END OF THE SCHOOL DAY, CATTLE.
WOW, I'M NOT EVEN GOING TO ASK WHICH ORIFICE YOU PULLED THAT ANSWER FROM.
HAHA, RIGHT?!
ROSE WILSON, ISN'T IT?
IT IS. BUT YOU CAN CALL ME "THE HOT CHICK I'M GOING TO WALK HOME FROM SCHOOL."
ARE YOU ALWAYS THIS DIRECT WITH PEOPLE YOU DON'T KNOW?
OFTEN.
IF YOU HAVEN'T FIGURED IT OUT YET...LIFE IS A STRING OF RANDOM OCCURRENCES VOID OF ANY MEANING OR SUBSTANCE.
WE'RE BORN, THROUGH NO FAULT OF OUR OWN, AND EXPOSED TO AN ENDLESS SERIES OF HUMILIATIONS...
...DESIGNED TO ENFORCE OUR IMPOTENCE IN THE FACE OF A UNIVERSE THAT NEVER WANTED US IN THE FIRST PLACE.
YOU HAVE IT ALL FIGURED OUT, EH?
STICK WITH ME, NEW KID.
I CAN CERTAINLY THINK OF WORSE PLACES TO STICK.

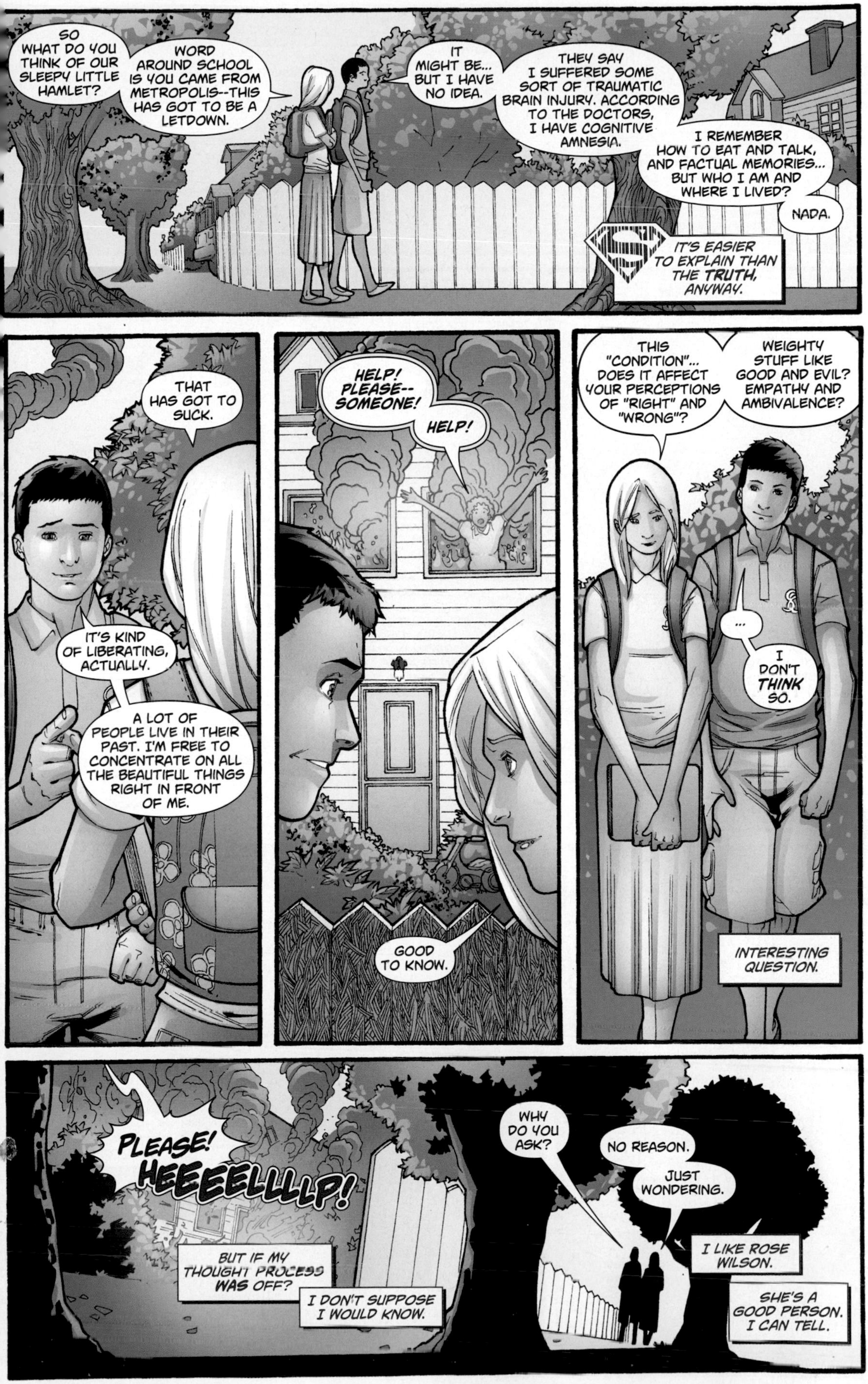
SO WHAT DO YOU THINK OF OUR SLEEPY LITTLE HAMLET?
WORD AROUND SCHOOL IS YOU CAME FROM METROPOLIS--THIS HAS GOT TO BE A LETDOWN.
IT MIGHT BE... BUT I HAVE NO IDEA.
THEY SAY I SUFFERED SOME SORT OF TRAUMATIC BRAIN INJURY. ACCORDING TO THE DOCTORS, I HAVE COGNITIVE AMNESIA.
I REMEMBER HOW TO EAT AND TALK, AND FACTUAL MEMORIES... BUT WHO I AM AND WHERE I LIVED?
NADA.
IT'S EASIER TO EXPLAIN THAN THE TRUTH, ANYWAY.
THAT HAS GOT TO SUCK.
IT'S KIND OF LIBERATING, ACTUALLY.
A LOT OF PEOPLE LIVE IN THEIR PAST. I'M FREE TO CONCENTRATE ON ALL THE BEAUTIFUL THINGS RIGHT IN FRONT OF ME.
HELP! PLEASE-- SOMEONE!
HELP!
GOOD TO KNOW.
THIS "CONDITION"... DOES IT AFFECT YOUR PERCEPTIONS OF "RIGHT" AND "WRONG"?
WEIGHTY STUFF LIKE GOOD AND EVIL? EMPATHY AND AMBIVALENCE?
...
I DON'T THINK SO.
INTERESTING QUESTION.
PLEASE! HEEEEELLLLLP!
BUT IF MY THOUGHT PROCESS WAS OFF?
I DON'T SUPPOSE I WOULD KNOW.
WHY DO YOU ASK?
NO REASON.
JUST WONDERING.
I LIKE ROSE WILSON.
SHE'S A GOOD PERSON. I CAN TELL.

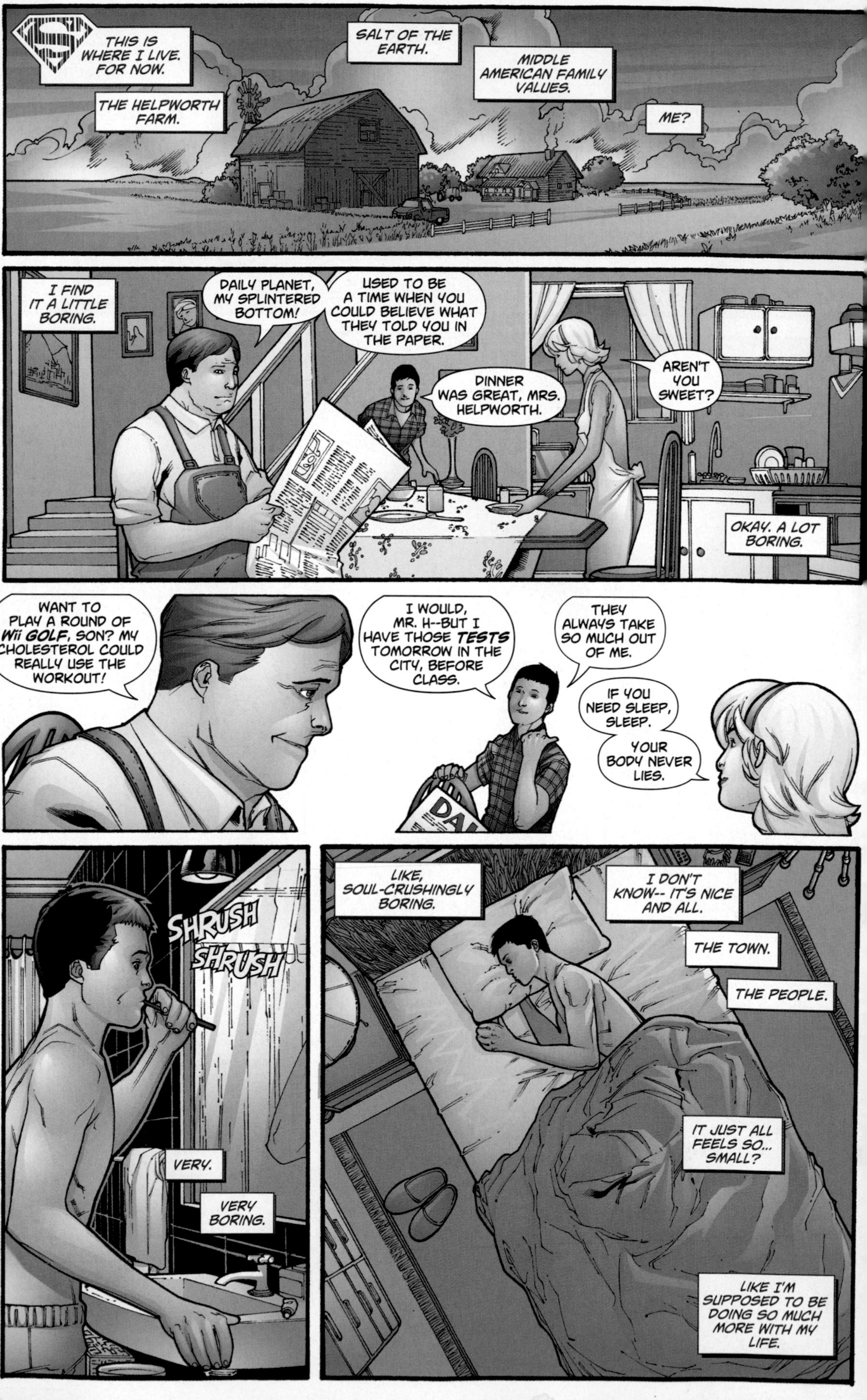
THIS IS WHERE I LIVE. FOR NOW.
THE HELPWORTH FARM.
SALT OF THE EARTH.
MIDDLE AMERICAN FAMILY VALUES.
ME?
I FIND IT A LITTLE BORING.
DAILY PLANET, MY SPLINTERED BOTTOM!
USED TO BE A TIME WHEN YOU COULD BELIEVE WHAT THEY TOLD YOU IN THE PAPER.
DINNER WAS GREAT, MRS. HELPWORTH.
AREN'T YOU SWEET?
OKAY. A LOT BORING.
WANT TO PLAY A ROUND OF Wii GOLF, SON? MY CHOLESTEROL COULD REALLY USE THE WORKOUT!
I WOULD, MR. H--BUT I HAVE THOSE TESTS TOMORROW IN THE CITY, BEFORE CLASS.
THEY ALWAYS TAKE SO MUCH OUT OF ME.
IF YOU NEED SLEEP, SLEEP.
YOUR BODY NEVER LIES.
SHRUSH
SHRUSH
VERY.
VERY BORING.
LIKE, SOUL-CRUSHINGLY BORING.
I DON'T KNOW-- IT'S NICE AND ALL.
THE TOWN.
THE PEOPLE.
IT JUST ALL FEELS SO... SMALL?
LIKE I'M SUPPOSED TO BE DOING SO MUCH MORE WITH MY LIFE.

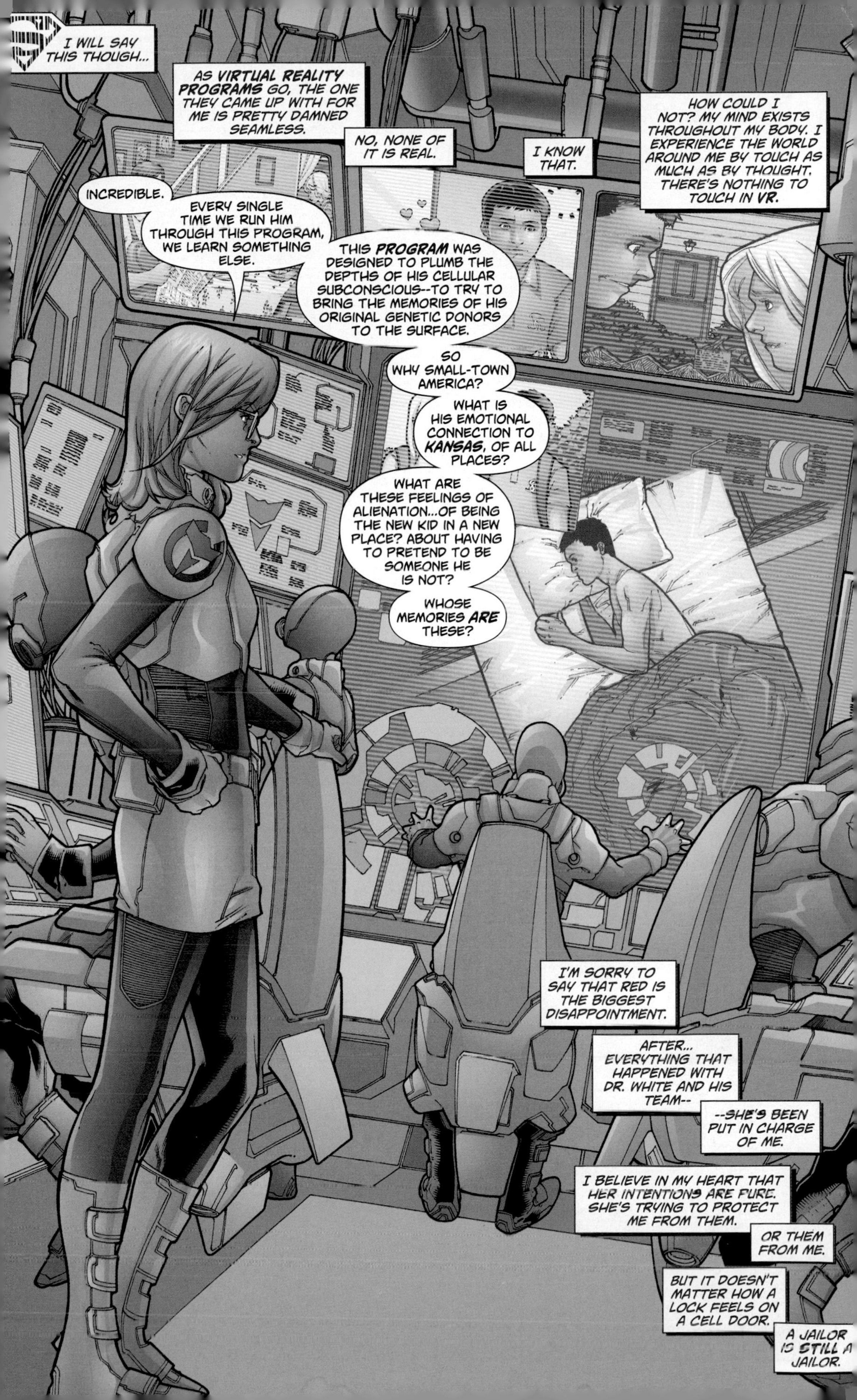
I WILL SAY THIS THOUGH...
AS VIRTUAL REALITY PROGRAMS GO, THE ONE THEY CAME UP WITH FOR ME IS PRETTY DAMNED SEAMLESS.
NO, NONE OF IT IS REAL.
I KNOW THAT.
HOW COULD I NOT? MY MIND EXISTS THROUGHOUT MY BODY. I EXPERIENCE THE WORLD AROUND ME BY TOUCH AS MUCH AS BY THOUGHT. THERE'S NOTHING TO TOUCH IN VR.
INCREDIBLE.
EVERY SINGLE TIME WE RUN HIM THROUGH THIS PROGRAM, WE LEARN SOMETHING ELSE.
THIS PROGRAM WAS DESIGNED TO PLUMB THE DEPTHS OF HIS CELLULAR SUBCONSCIOUS--TO TRY TO BRING THE MEMORIES OF HIS ORIGINAL GENETIC DONORS TO THE SURFACE.
SO WHY SMALL-TOWN AMERICA?
WHAT IS HIS EMOTIONAL CONNECTION TO KANSAS, OF ALL PLACES?
WHAT ARE THESE FEELINGS OF ALIENATION...OF BEING THE NEW KID IN A NEW PLACE? ABOUT HAVING TO PRETEND TO BE SOMEONE HE IS NOT?
WHOSE MEMORIES ARE THESE?
I'M SORRY TO SAY THAT RED IS THE BIGGEST DISAPPOINTMENT.
AFTER... EVERYTHING THAT HAPPENED WITH DR. WHITE AND HIS TEAM--
--SHE'S BEEN PUT IN CHARGE OF ME.
I BELIEVE IN MY HEART THAT HER INTENTIONS ARE PURE. SHE'S TRYING TO PROTECT ME FROM THEM.
OR THEM FROM ME.
BUT IT DOESN'T MATTER HOW A LOCK FEELS ON A CELL DOOR.
A JAILOR IS STILL A JAILOR.

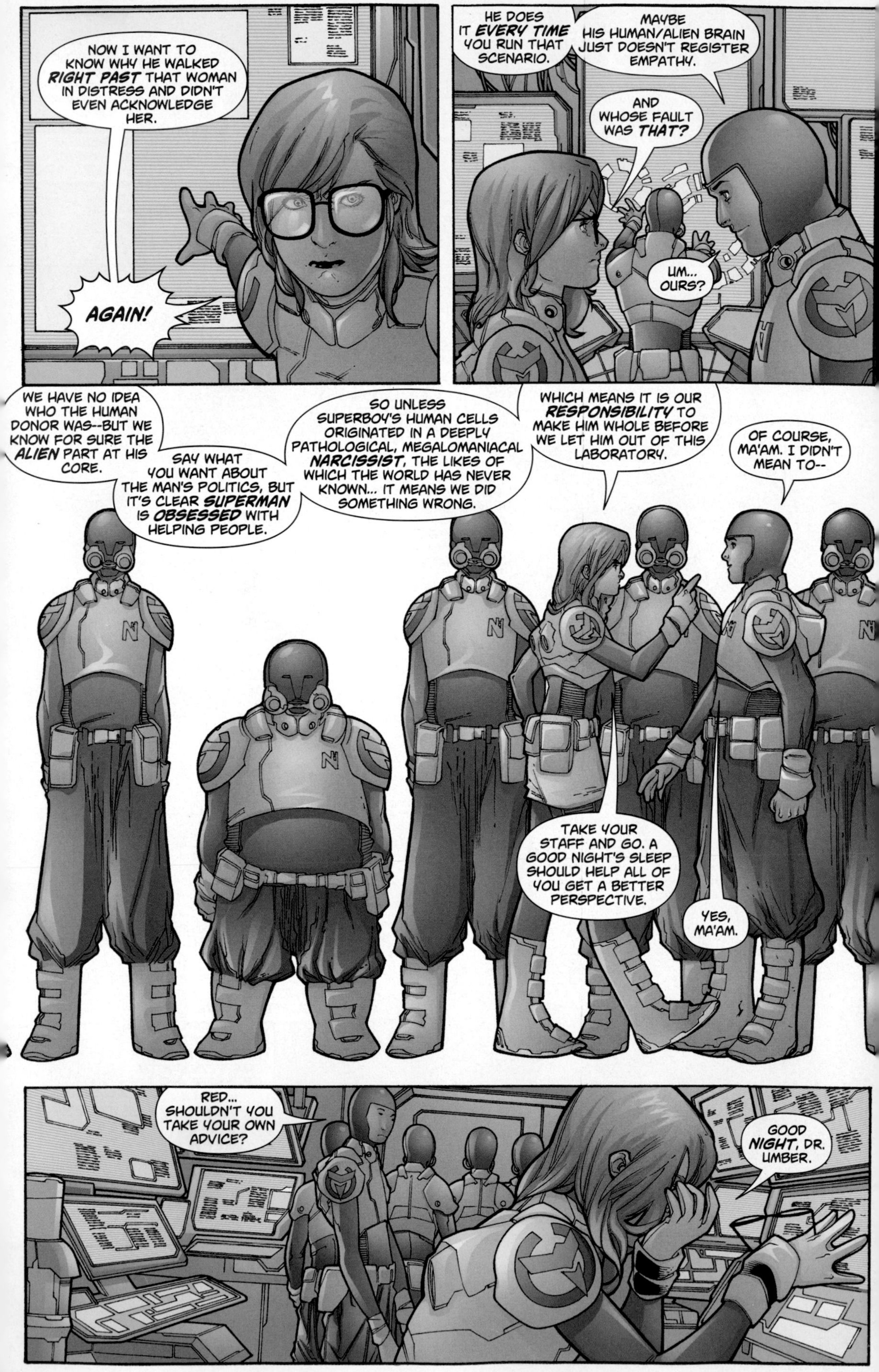
NOW I WANT TO KNOW WHY HE WALKED RIGHT PAST THAT WOMAN IN DISTRESS AND DIDN'T EVEN ACKNOWLEDGE HER.
AGAIN!
HE DOES IT EVERY TIME YOU RUN THAT SCENARIO.
MAYBE HIS HUMAN/ALIEN BRAIN JUST DOESN'T REGISTER EMPATHY.
AND WHOSE FAULT WAS THAT?
UM... OURS?
WE HAVE NO IDEA WHO THE HUMAN DONOR WAS--BUT WE KNOW FOR SURE THE ALIEN PART AT HIS CORE.
SAY WHAT YOU WANT ABOUT THE MAN'S POLITICS, BUT IT'S CLEAR SUPERMAN IS OBSESSED WITH HELPING PEOPLE.
SO UNLESS SUPERBOY'S HUMAN CELLS ORIGINATED IN A DEEPLY PATHOLOGICAL, MEGALOMANIACAL NARCISSIST, THE LIKES OF WHICH THE WORLD HAS NEVER KNOWN... IT MEANS WE DID SOMETHING WRONG.
WHICH MEANS IT IS OUR RESPONSIBILITY TO MAKE HIM WHOLE BEFORE WE LET HIM OUT OF THIS LABORATORY.
OF COURSE, MA'AM. I DIDN'T MEAN TO--
TAKE YOUR STAFF AND GO. A GOOD NIGHT'S SLEEP SHOULD HELP ALL OF YOU GET A BETTER PERSPECTIVE.
YES, MA'AM.
RED... SHOULDN'T YOU TAKE YOUR OWN ADVICE?
GOOD NIGHT, DR. UMBER.

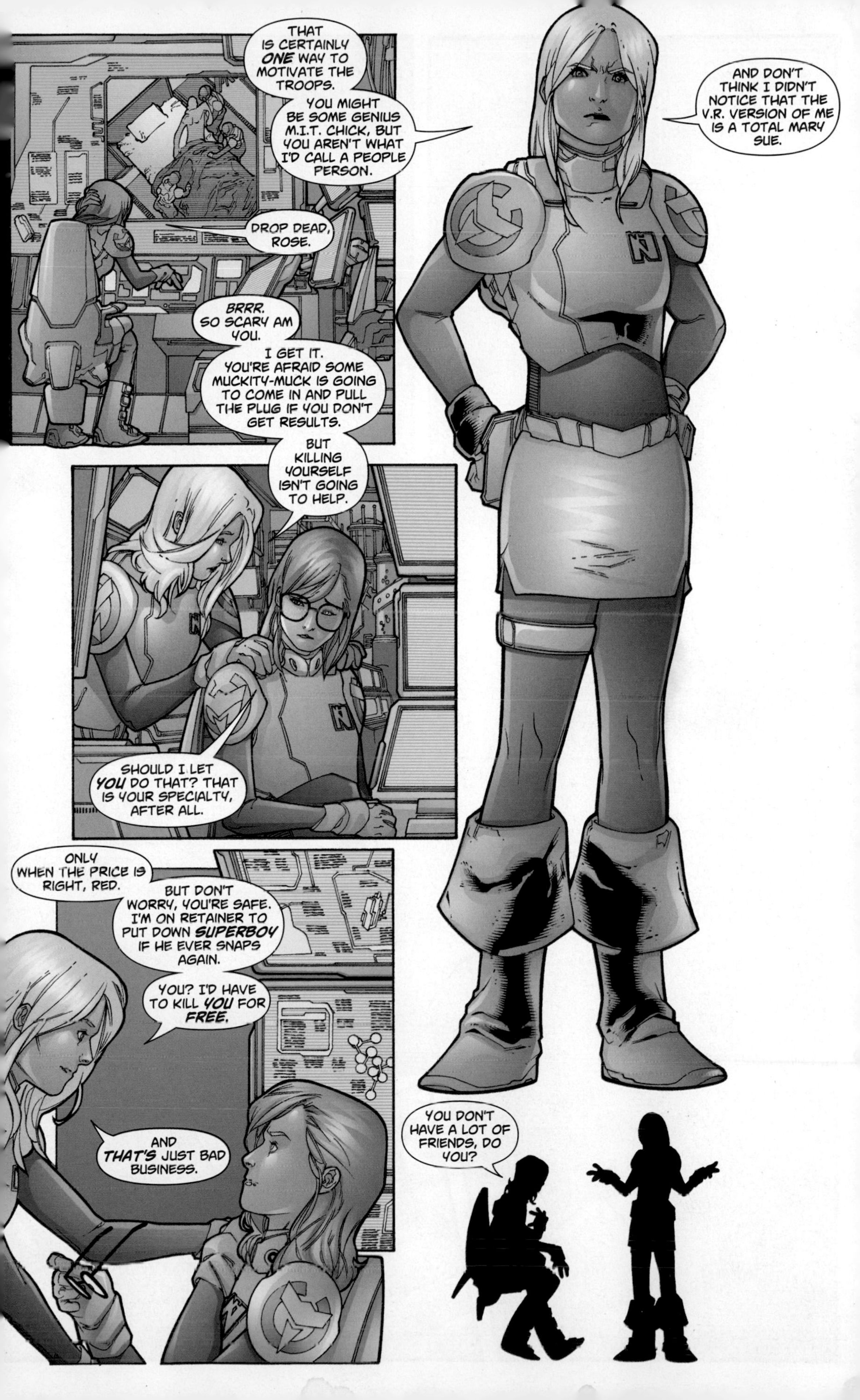
THAT IS CERTAINLY ONE WAY TO MOTIVATE THE TROOPS.
YOU MIGHT BE SOME GENIUS M.I.T. CHICK, BUT YOU AREN'T WHAT I'D CALL A PEOPLE PERSON.
DROP DEAD, ROSE.
BRRR. SO SCARY AM YOU.
I GET IT. YOU'RE AFRAID SOME MUCKITY-MUCK IS GOING TO COME IN AND PULL THE PLUG IF YOU DON'T GET RESULTS.
BUT KILLING YOURSELF ISN'T GOING TO HELP.
SHOULD I LET YOU DO THAT? THAT IS YOUR SPECIALTY, AFTER ALL.
ONLY WHEN THE PRICE IS RIGHT, RED.
BUT DON'T WORRY, YOU'RE SAFE. I'M ON RETAINER TO PUT DOWN SUPERBOY IF HE EVER SNAPS AGAIN.
YOU? I'D HAVE TO KILL YOU FOR FREE.
AND THAT'S JUST BAD BUSINESS.
AND DON'T THINK I DIDN'T NOTICE THAT THE V.R. VERSION OF ME IS A TOTAL MARY SUE.
YOU DON'T HAVE A LOT OF FRIENDS, DO YOU?

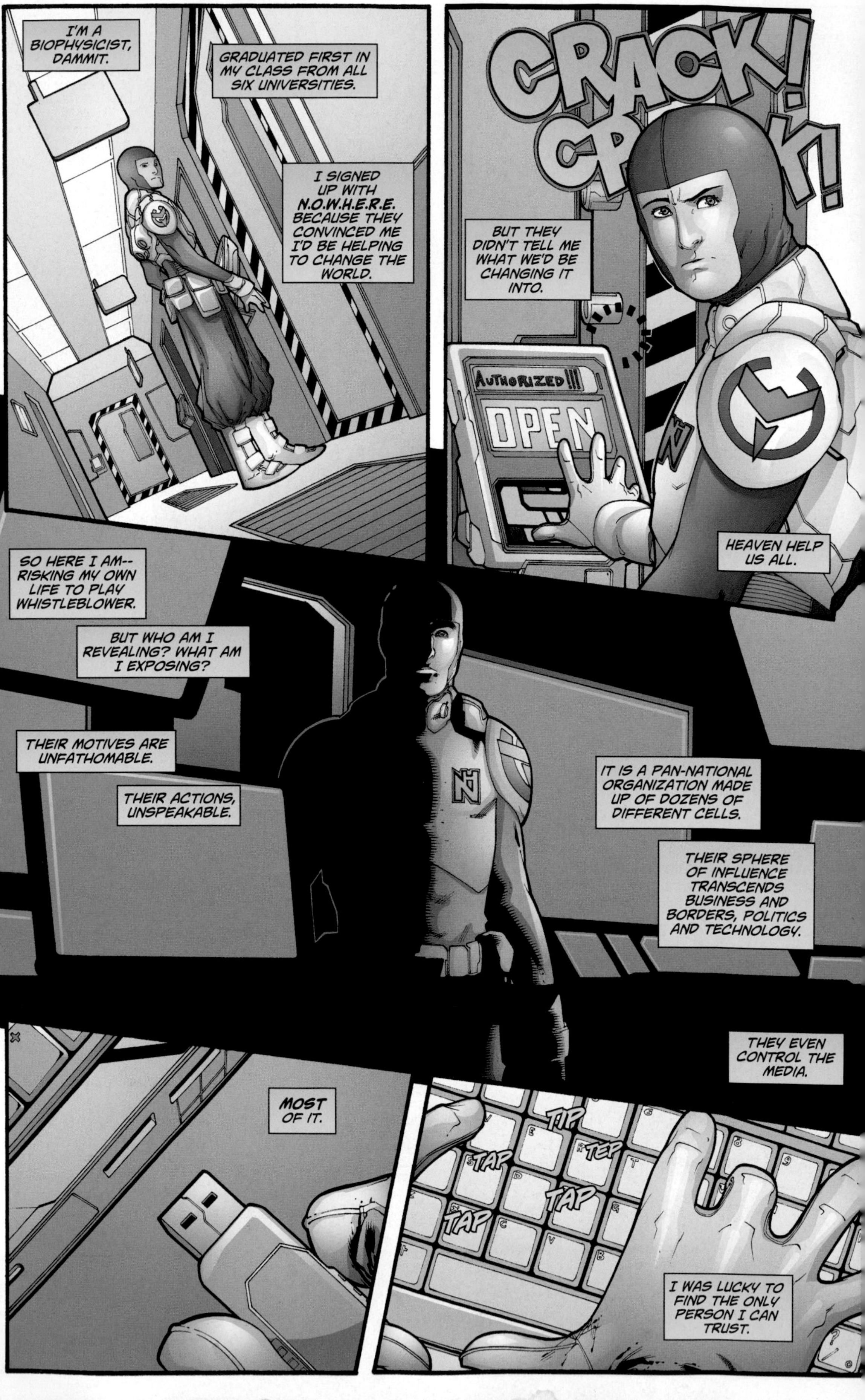

I'M A BIOPHYSICIST, DAMMIT.
GRADUATED FIRST IN MY CLASS FROM ALL SIX UNIVERSITIES.
I SIGNED UP WITH N.O.W.H.E.R.E. BECAUSE THEY CONVINCED ME I'D BE HELPING TO CHANGE THE WORLD.
CRACK!
BUT THEY DIDN'T TELL ME WHAT WE'D BE CHANGING IT INTO.
AUTHORIZED!!!
OPEN
HEAVEN HELP US ALL.
SO HERE I AM-- RISKING MY OWN LIFE TO PLAY WHISTLEBLOWER.
BUT WHO AM I REVEALING? WHAT AM I EXPOSING?
THEIR MOTIVES ARE UNFATHOMABLE.
THEIR ACTIONS, UNSPEAKABLE.
IT IS A PAN-NATIONAL ORGANIZATION MADE UP OF DOZENS OF DIFFERENT CELLS.
THEIR SPHERE OF INFLUENCE TRANSCENDS BUSINESS AND BORDERS, POLITICS AND TECHNOLOGY.
THEY EVEN CONTROL THE MEDIA.
MOST OF IT.
TIP
TEP
TAP
TAP
TAP
I WAS LUCKY TO FIND THE ONLY PERSON I CAN TRUST.

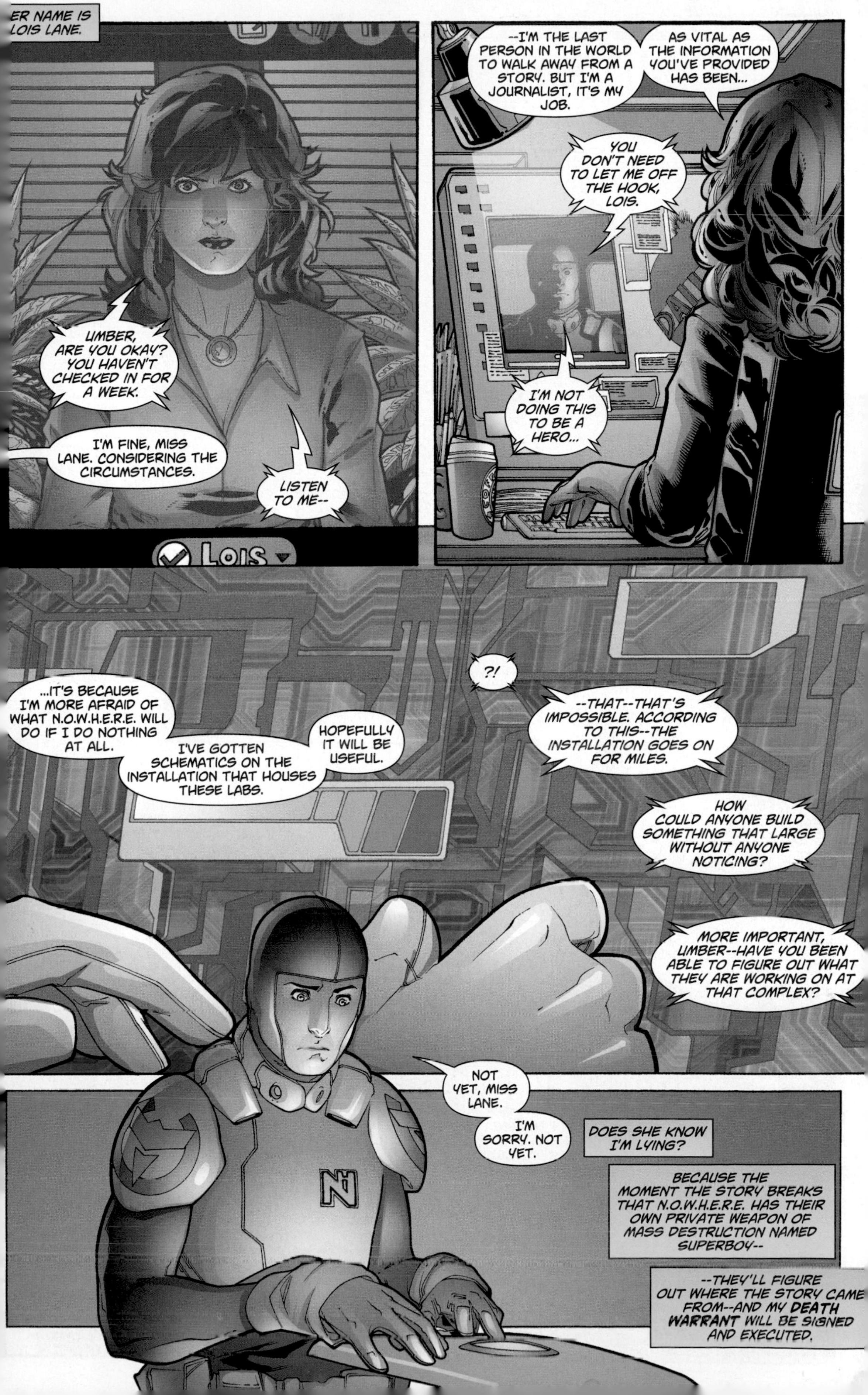

ER NAME IS
LOIS LANE.
UMBER, ARE YOU OKAY? YOU HAVEN'T CHECKED IN FOR A WEEK.
I'M FINE, MISS LANE. CONSIDERING THE CIRCUMSTANCES.
LISTEN TO ME--
LOIS
--I'M THE LAST PERSON IN THE WORLD TO WALK AWAY FROM A STORY. BUT I'M A JOURNALIST, IT'S MY JOB.
AS VITAL AS THE INFORMATION YOU'VE PROVIDED HAS BEEN...
YOU DON'T NEED TO LET ME OFF THE HOOK, LOIS.
I'M NOT DOING THIS TO BE A HERO...
...IT'S BECAUSE I'M MORE AFRAID OF WHAT N.O.W.H.E.R.E. WILL DO IF I DO NOTHING AT ALL.
I'VE GOTTEN SCHEMATICS ON THE INSTALLATION THAT HOUSES THESE LABS.
HOPEFULLY IT WILL BE USEFUL.
?!
--THAT--THAT'S IMPOSSIBLE. ACCORDING TO THIS--THE INSTALLATION GOES ON FOR MILES.
HOW COULD ANYONE BUILD SOMETHING THAT LARGE WITHOUT ANYONE NOTICING?
MORE IMPORTANT, UMBER--HAVE YOU BEEN ABLE TO FIGURE OUT WHAT THEY ARE WORKING ON AT THAT COMPLEX?
NOT YET, MISS LANE.
I'M SORRY. NOT YET.
DOES SHE KNOW I'M LYING?
BECAUSE THE MOMENT THE STORY BREAKS THAT N.O.W.H.E.R.E. HAS THEIR OWN PRIVATE WEAPON OF MASS DESTRUCTION NAMED SUPERBOY--
--THEY'LL FIGURE OUT WHERE THE STORY CAME FROM--AND MY DEATH WARRANT WILL BE SIGNED AND EXECUTED.

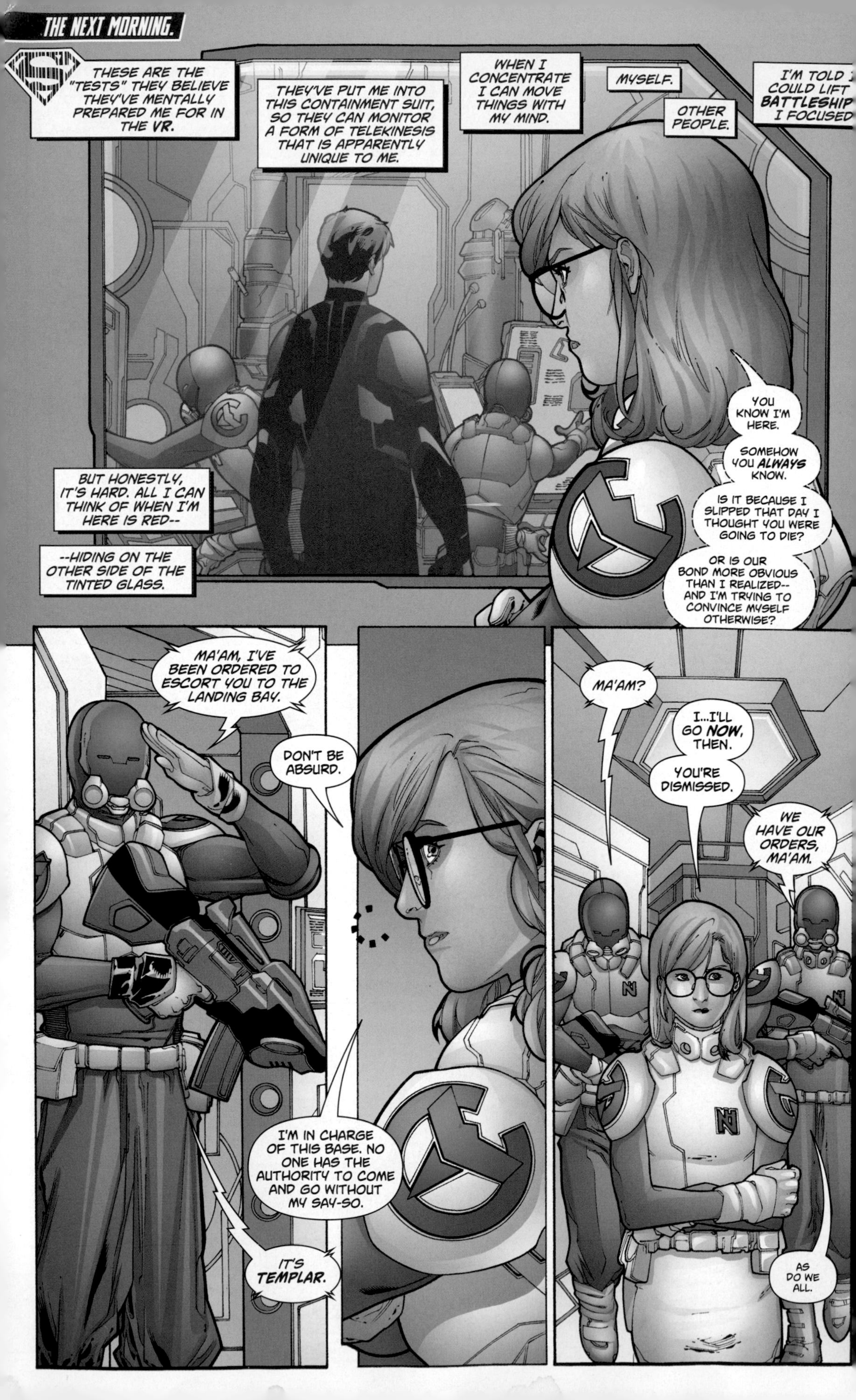
THE NEXT MORNING.
THESE ARE THE "TESTS" THEY BELIEVE THEY'VE MENTALLY PREPARED ME FOR IN THE VR.
THEY'VE PUT ME INTO THIS CONTAINMENT SUIT, SO THEY CAN MONITOR A FORM OF TELEKINESIS THAT IS APPARENTLY UNIQUE TO ME.
WHEN I CONCENTRATE I CAN MOVE THINGS WITH MY MIND.
MYSELF.
OTHER PEOPLE.
I'M TOLD COULD LIFT BATTLESHIP I FOCUSED
BUT HONESTLY, IT'S HARD. ALL I CAN THINK OF WHEN I'M HERE IS RED--
--HIDING ON THE OTHER SIDE OF THE TINTED GLASS.
YOU KNOW I'M HERE.
SOMEHOW YOU ALWAYS KNOW.
IS IT BECAUSE I SLIPPED THAT DAY I THOUGHT YOU WERE GOING TO DIE?
OR IS OUR BOND MORE OBVIOUS THAN I REALIZED-- AND I'M TRYING TO CONVINCE MYSELF OTHERWISE?
MA'AM, I'VE BEEN ORDERED TO ESCORT YOU TO THE LANDING BAY.
DON'T BE ABSURD.
I'M IN CHARGE OF THIS BASE. NO ONE HAS THE AUTHORITY TO COME AND GO WITHOUT MY SAY-SO.
IT'S TEMPLAR.
MA'AM?
I...I'LL GO NOW, THEN.
YOU'RE DISMISSED.
WE HAVE OUR ORDERS, MA'AM.
AS DO WE ALL.

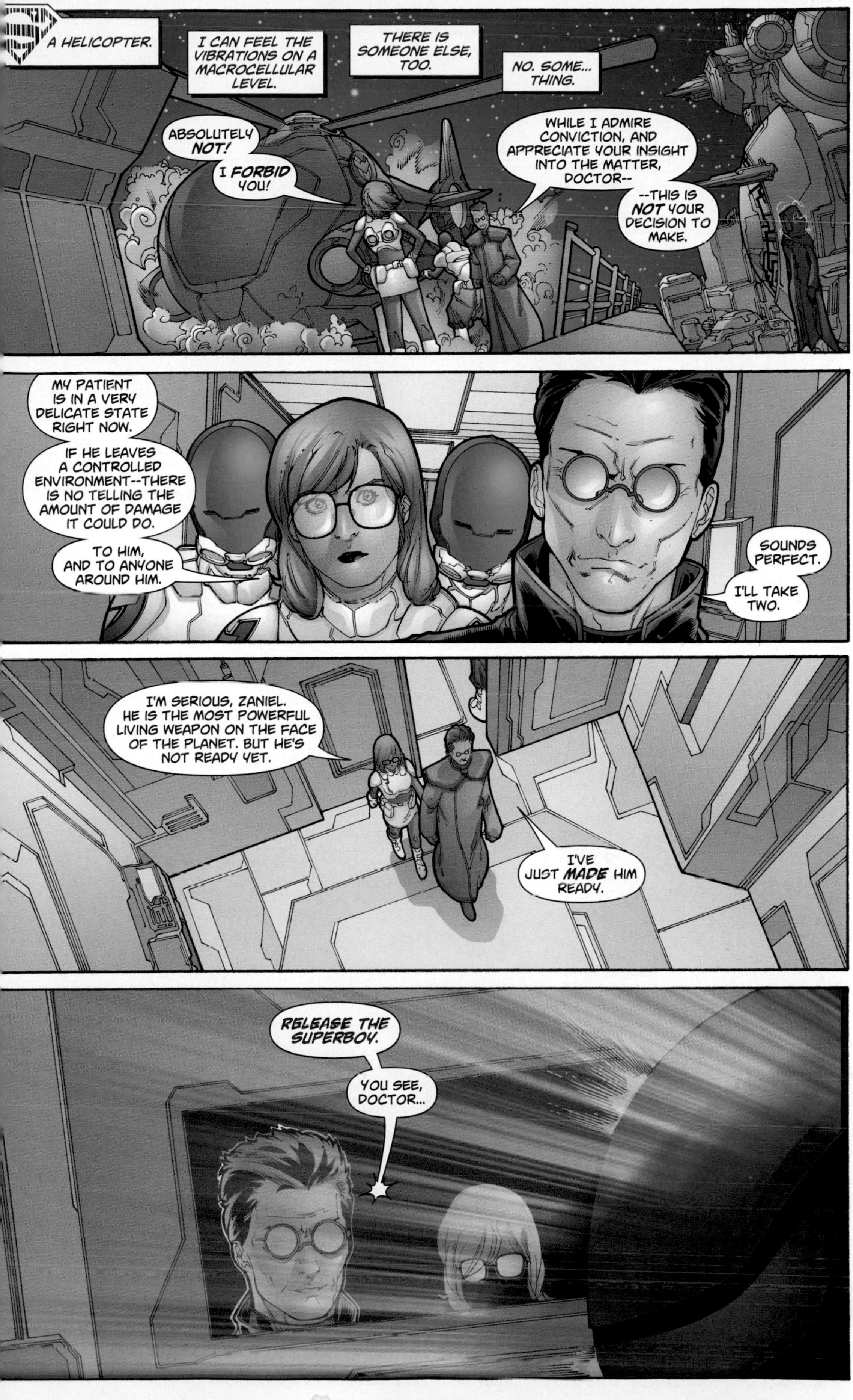
A HELICOPTER.
I CAN FEEL THE VIBRATIONS ON A MACROCELLULAR LEVEL.
THERE IS SOMEONE ELSE, TOO.
NO. SOME... THING.
ABSOLUTELY NOT!
I FORBID YOU!
WHILE I ADMIRE CONVICTION, AND APPRECIATE YOUR INSIGHT INTO THE MATTER, DOCTOR--
--THIS IS NOT YOUR DECISION TO MAKE.
MY PATIENT IS IN A VERY DELICATE STATE RIGHT NOW.
IF HE LEAVES A CONTROLLED ENVIRONMENT--THERE IS NO TELLING THE AMOUNT OF DAMAGE IT COULD DO.
TO HIM, AND TO ANYONE AROUND HIM.
SOUNDS PERFECT.
I'LL TAKE TWO.
I'M SERIOUS, ZANIEL. HE IS THE MOST POWERFUL LIVING WEAPON ON THE FACE OF THE PLANET. BUT HE'S NOT READY YET.
I'VE JUST MADE HIM READY.
RELEASE THE SUPERBOY.
YOU SEE, DOCTOR...

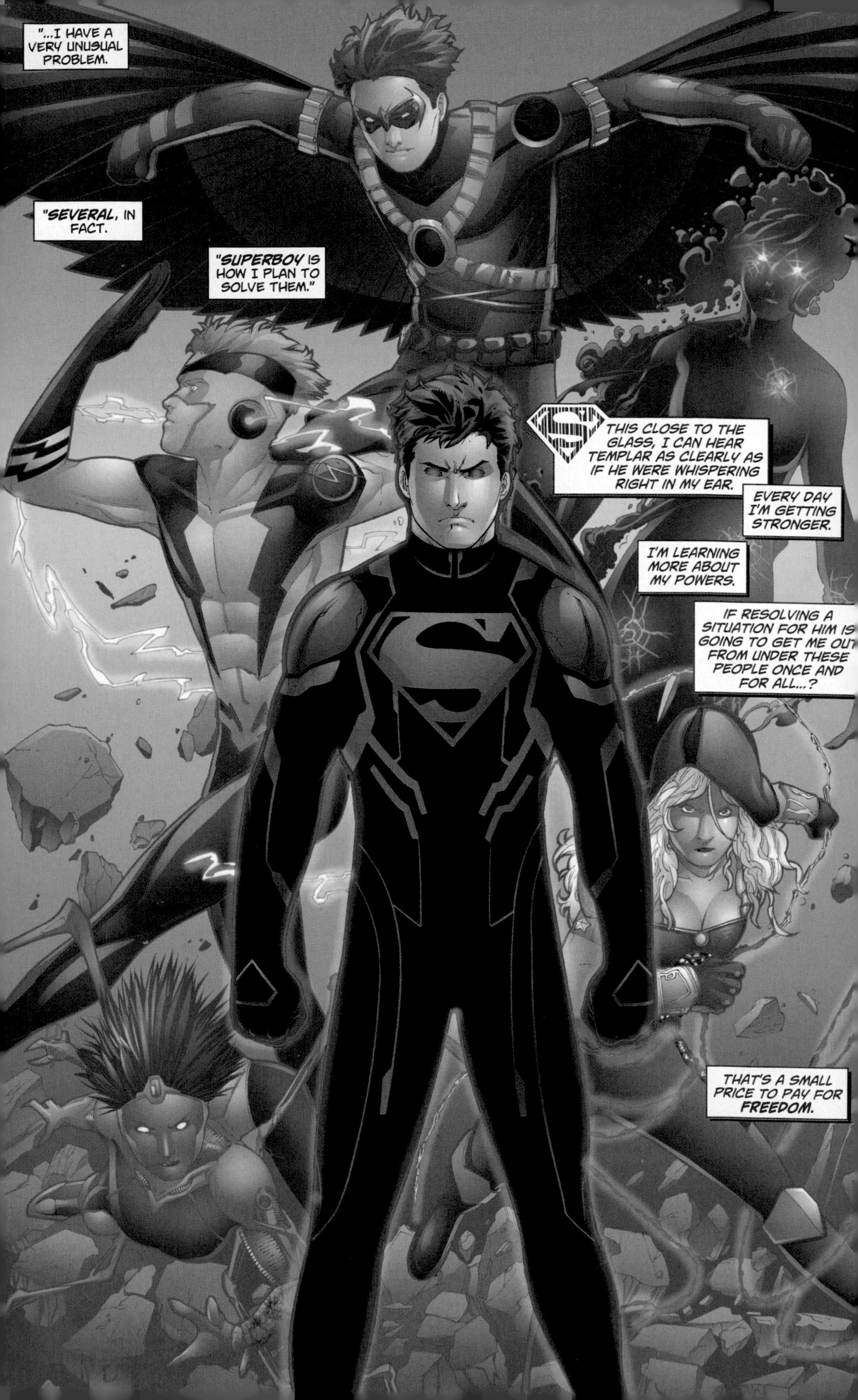
"...I HAVE A VERY UNUSUAL PROBLEM.
"SEVERAL, IN FACT.
"SUPERBOY IS HOW I PLAN TO SOLVE THEM."
THIS CLOSE TO THE GLASS, I CAN HEAR TEMPLAR AS CLEARLY AS IF HE WERE WHISPERING RIGHT IN MY EAR.
EVERY DAY I'M GETTING STRONGER.
I'M LEARNING MORE ABOUT MY POWERS.
IF RESOLVING A SITUATION FOR HIM IS GOING TO GET ME OUT FROM UNDER THESE PEOPLE ONCE AND FOR ALL...?
THAT'S A SMALL PRICE TO PAY FOR FREEDOM.

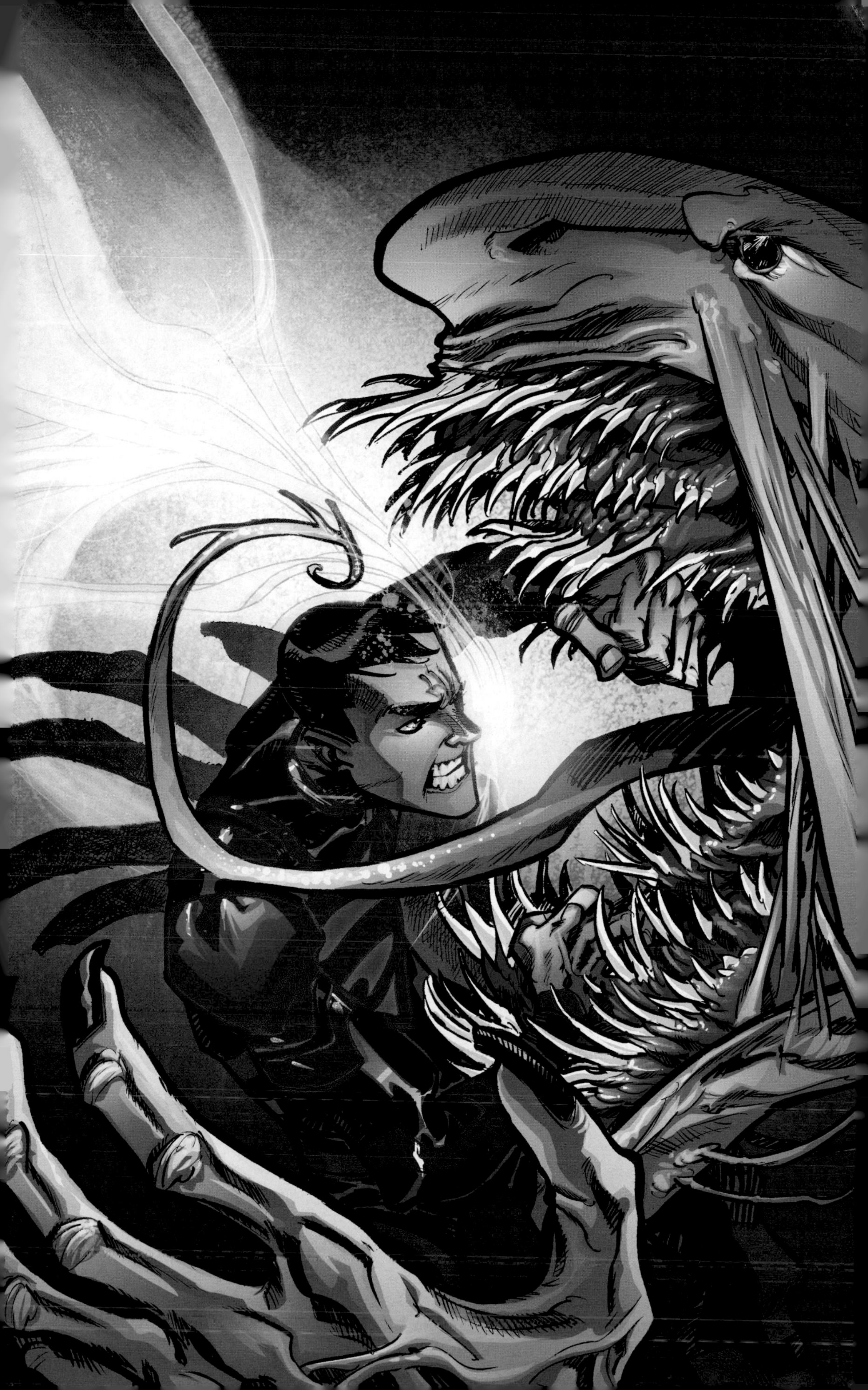

Cover by ERIC CANETE & NICK FILARDI

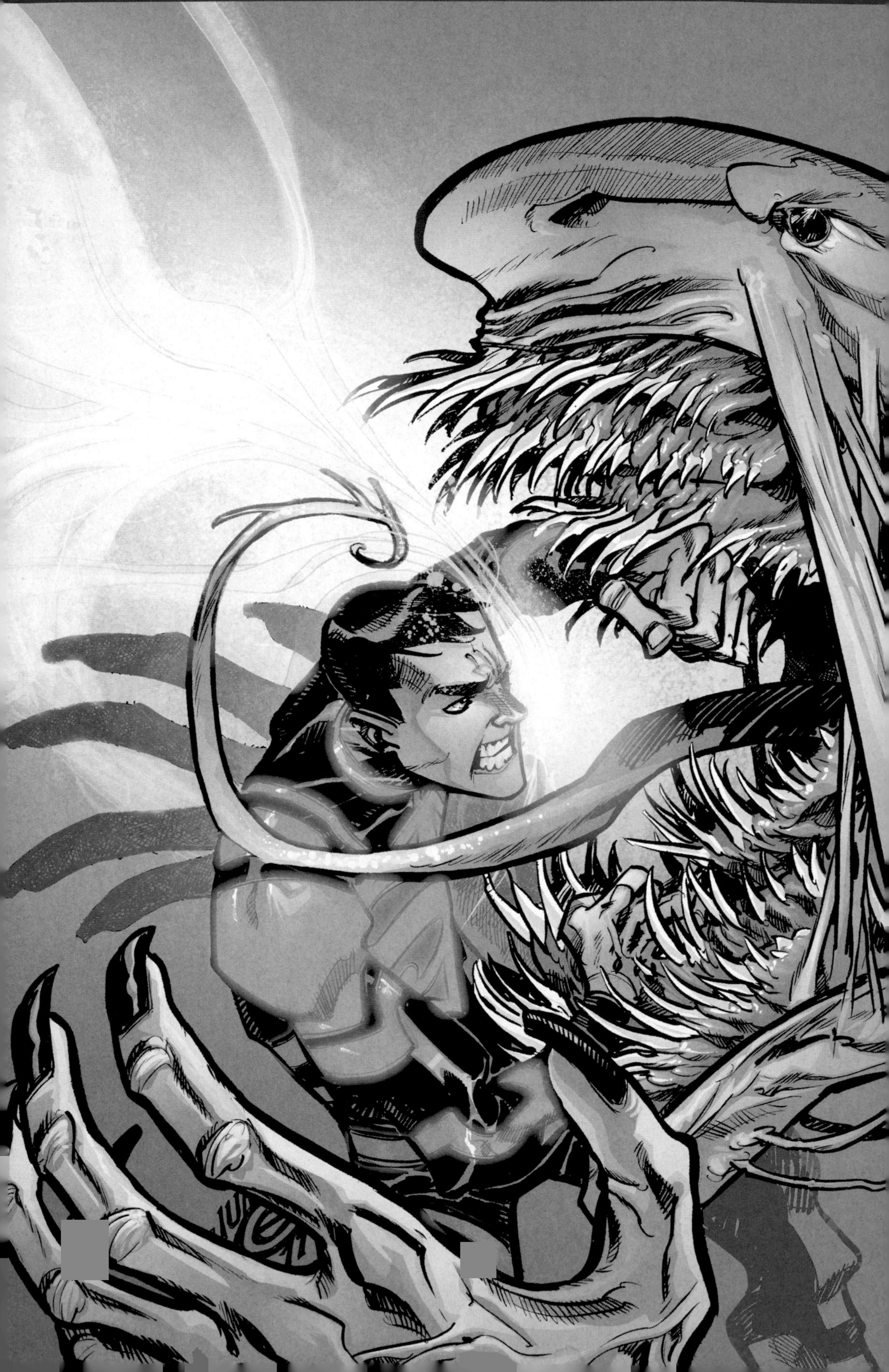

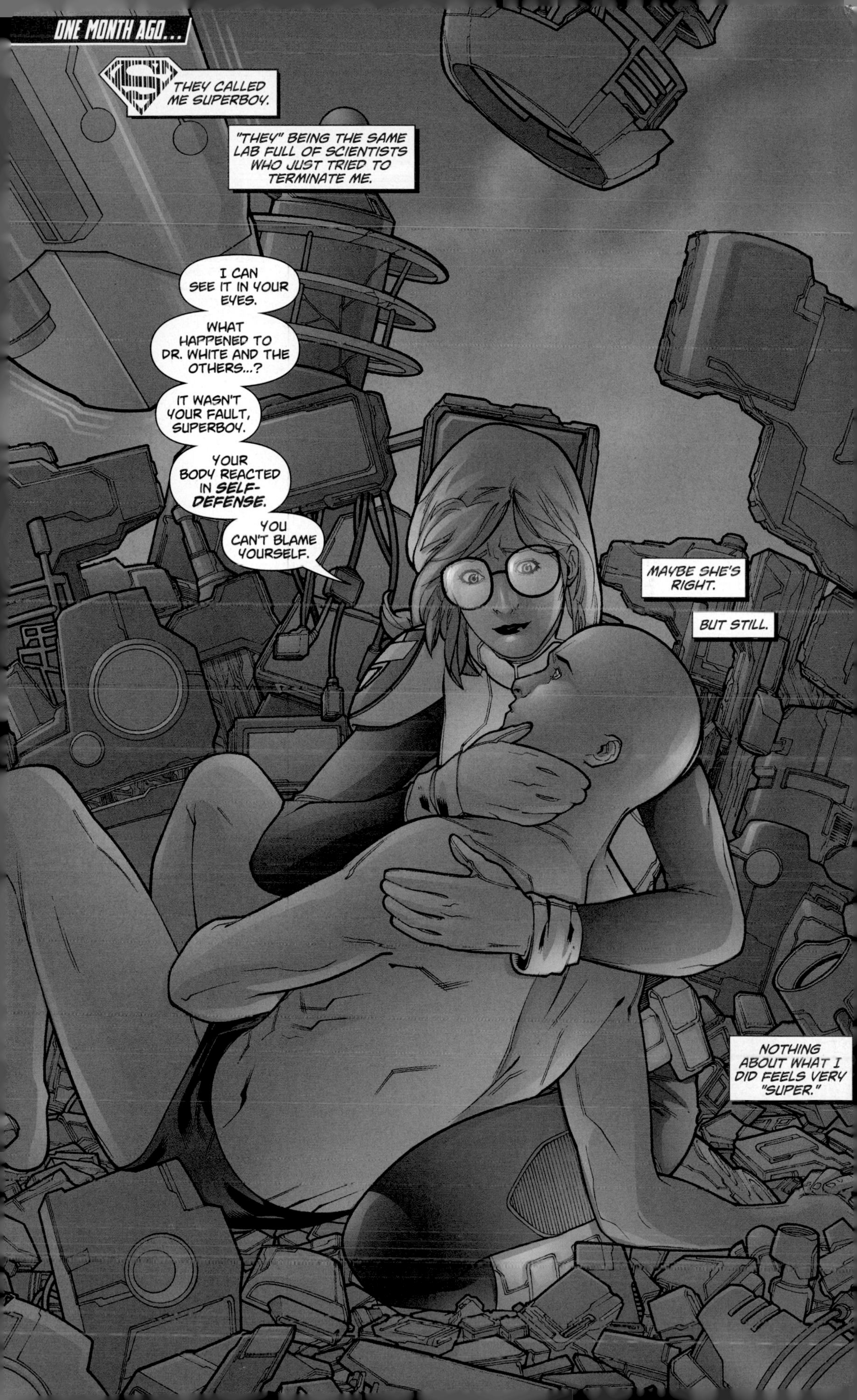
ONE MONTH AGO...
THEY CALLED ME SUPERBOY.
"THEY" BEING THE SAME LAB FULL OF SCIENTISTS WHO JUST TRIED TO TERMINATE ME.
I CAN SEE IT IN YOUR EYES.
WHAT HAPPENED TO DR. WHITE AND THE OTHERS...?
IT WASN'T YOUR FAULT, SUPERBOY.
YOUR BODY REACTED IN SELF-DEFENSE.
YOU CAN'T BLAME YOURSELF.
MAYBE SHE'S RIGHT.
BUT STILL.
NOTHING ABOUT WHAT I DID FEELS VERY "SUPER."

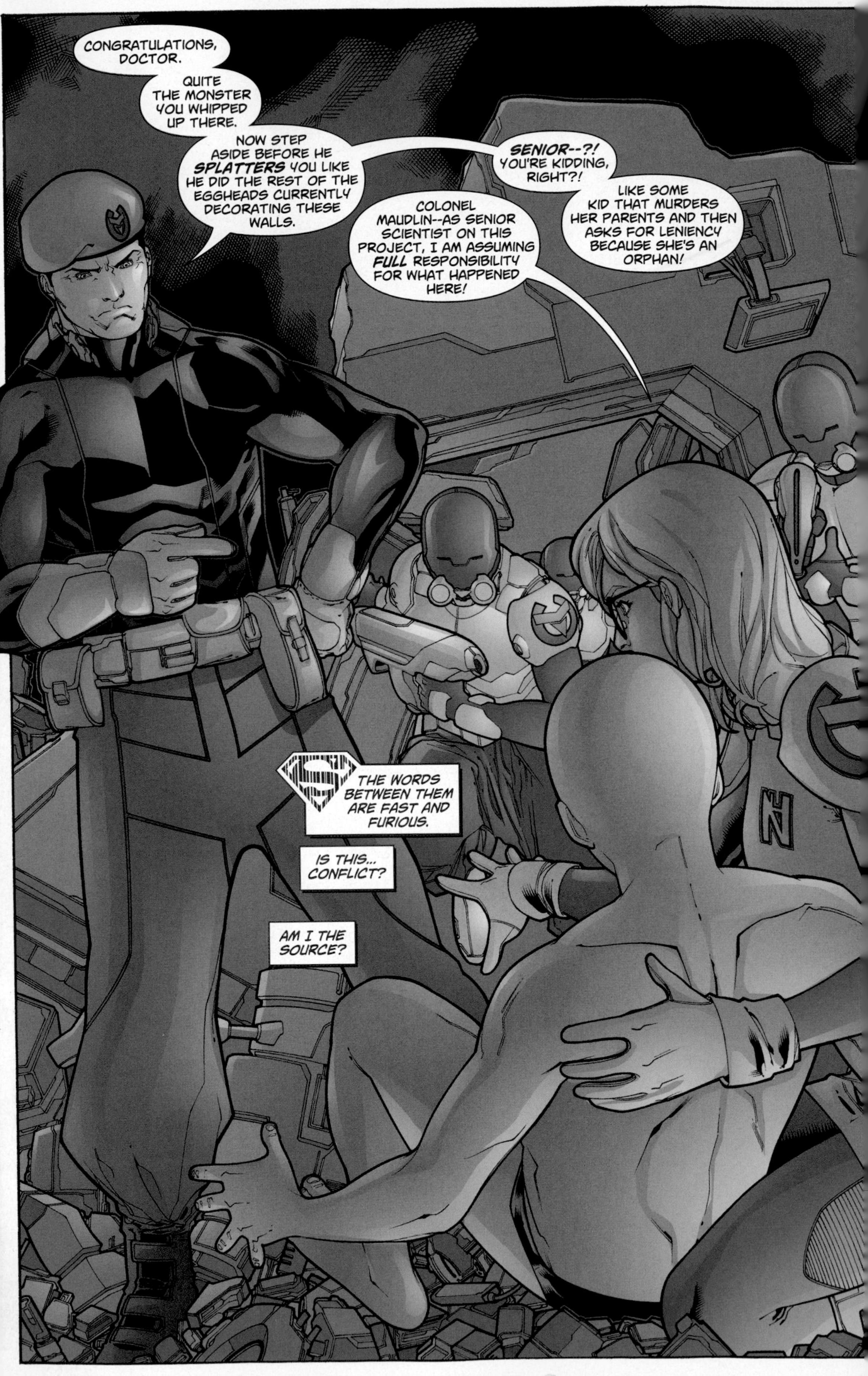
CONGRATULATIONS, DOCTOR.
QUITE THE MONSTER YOU WHIPPED UP THERE.
NOW STEP ASIDE BEFORE HE SPLATTERS YOU LIKE HE DID THE REST OF THE EGGHEADS CURRENTLY DECORATING THESE WALLS.
COLONEL MAUDLIN--AS SENIOR SCIENTIST ON THIS PROJECT, I AM ASSUMING FULL RESPONSIBILITY FOR WHAT HAPPENED HERE!
SENIOR--?! YOU'RE KIDDING, RIGHT?!
LIKE SOME KID THAT MURDERS HER PARENTS AND THEN ASKS FOR LENIENCY BECAUSE SHE'S AN ORPHAN!
THE WORDS BETWEEN THEM ARE FAST AND FURIOUS.
IS THIS... CONFLICT?
AM I THE SOURCE?

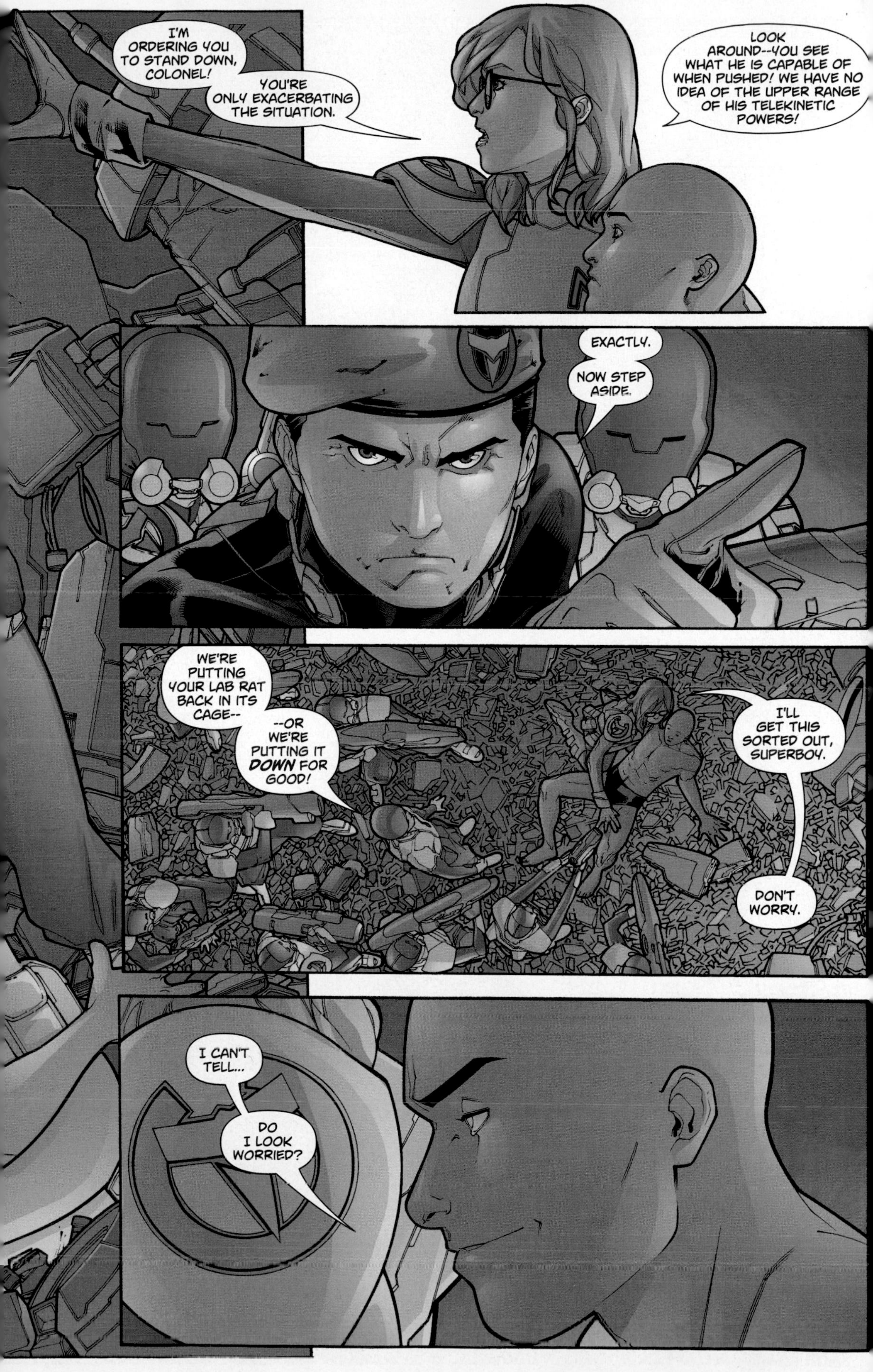
I'M ORDERING YOU TO STAND DOWN, COLONEL!
YOU'RE ONLY EXACERBATING THE SITUATION.
LOOK AROUND--YOU SEE WHAT HE IS CAPABLE OF WHEN PUSHED! WE HAVE NO IDEA OF THE UPPER RANGE OF HIS TELEKINETIC POWERS!
EXACTLY.
NOW STEP ASIDE.
WE'RE PUTTING YOUR LAB RAT BACK IN ITS CAGE--
--OR WE'RE PUTTING IT DOWN FOR GOOD!
I'LL GET THIS SORTED OUT, SUPERBOY.
DON'T WORRY.
I CAN'T TELL...
DO I LOOK WORRIED?

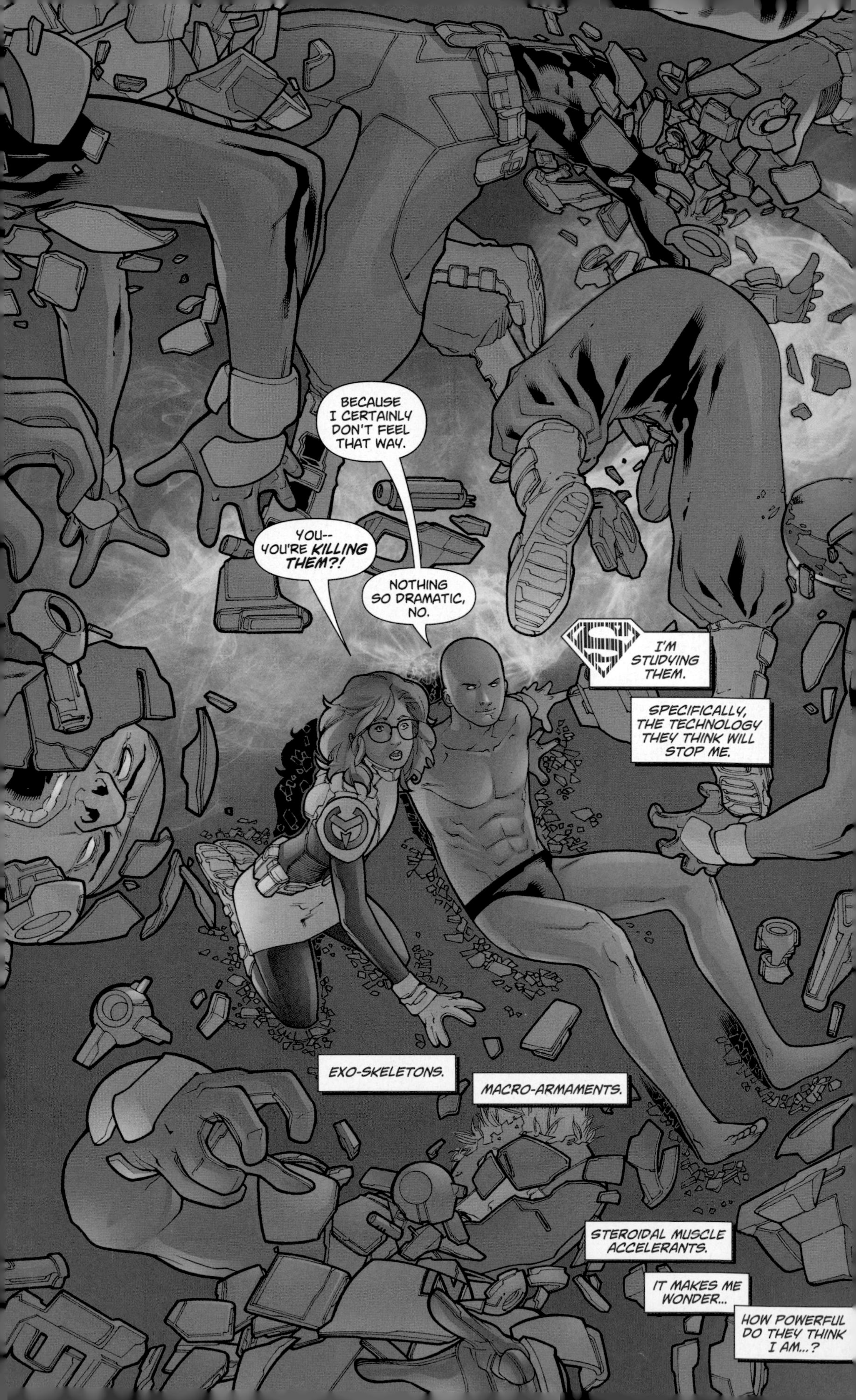
YOU-- YOU'RE KILLING THEM?!
NOTHING SO DRAMATIC, NO.
BECAUSE I CERTAINLY DON'T FEEL THAT WAY.
I'M STUDYING THEM.
SPECIFICALLY, THE TECHNOLOGY THEY THINK WILL STOP ME.
EXO-SKELETONS.
MACRO-ARMAMENTS.
STEROIDAL MUSCLE ACCELERANTS.
IT MAKES ME WONDER...
HOW POWERFUL DO THEY THINK I AM...?

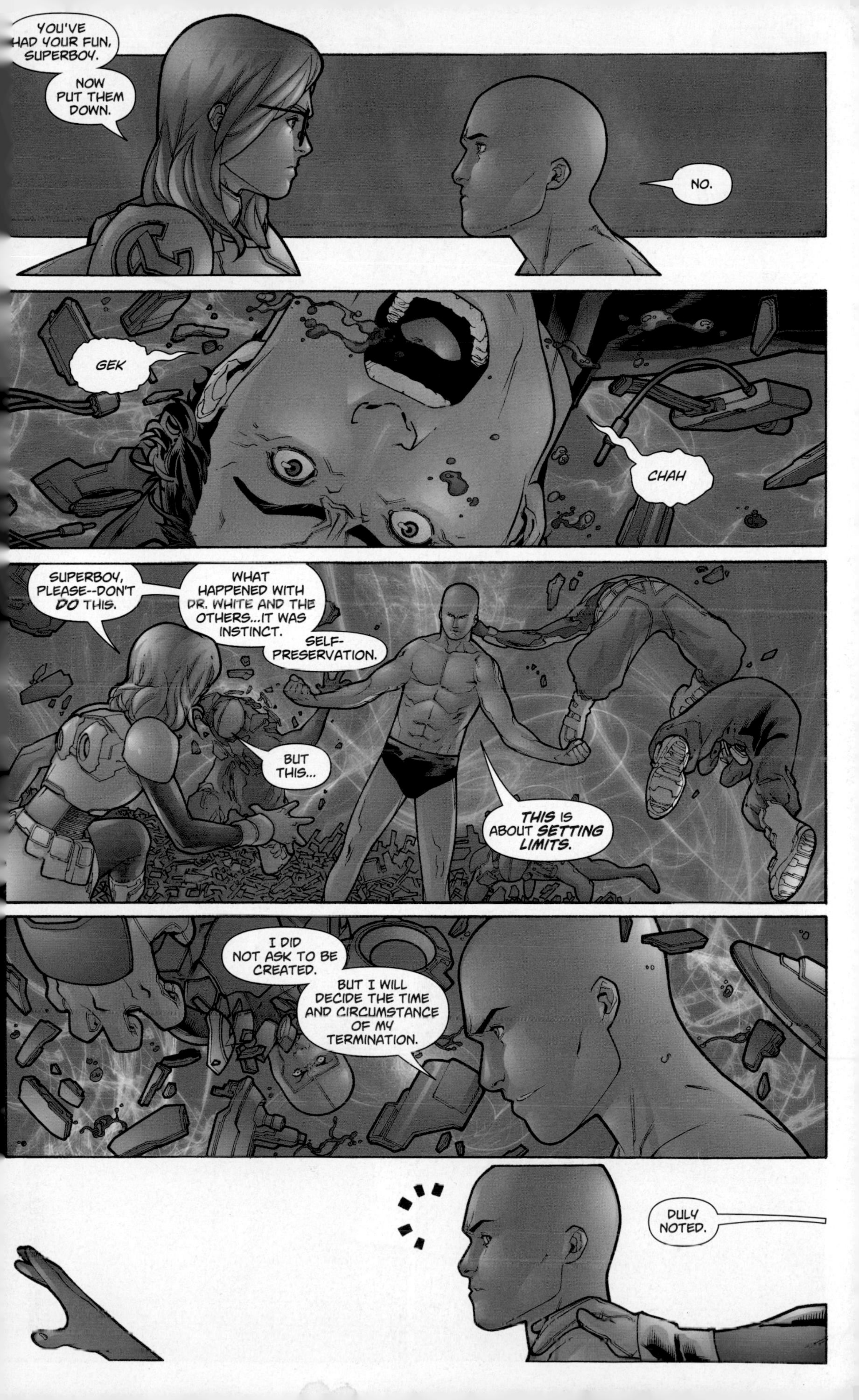
YOU'VE HAD YOUR FUN, SUPERBOY.
NOW PUT THEM DOWN.
NO.
GEK
CHAH
SUPERBOY, PLEASE--DON'T DO THIS.
WHAT HAPPENED WITH DR. WHITE AND THE OTHERS...IT WAS INSTINCT.
SELF-PRESERVATION.
BUT THIS...
THIS IS ABOUT SETTING LIMITS.
I DID NOT ASK TO BE CREATED.
BUT I WILL DECIDE THE TIME AND CIRCUMSTANCE OF MY TERMINATION.
DULY NOTED.

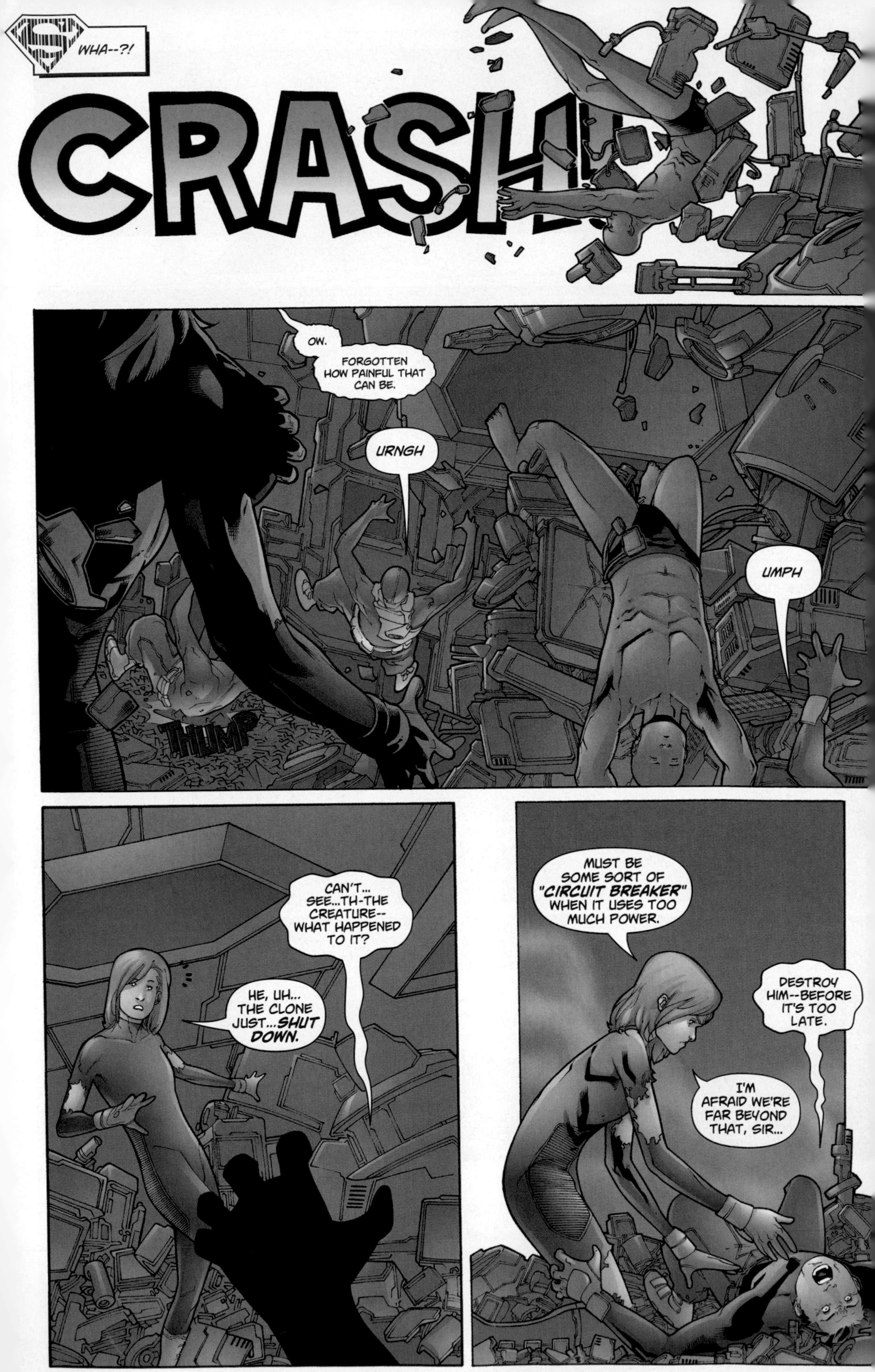
WHA--?!
CRASH
OW.
FORGOTTEN HOW PAINFUL THAT CAN BE.
URNGH
UMPH
THUMP
CAN'T... SEE...TH-THE CREATURE-- WHAT HAPPENED TO IT?
HE, UH... THE CLONE JUST...SHUT DOWN.
MUST BE SOME SORT OF "CIRCUIT BREAKER" WHEN IT USES TOO MUCH POWER.
DESTROY HIM--BEFORE IT'S TOO LATE.
I'M AFRAID WE'RE FAR BEYOND THAT, SIR...

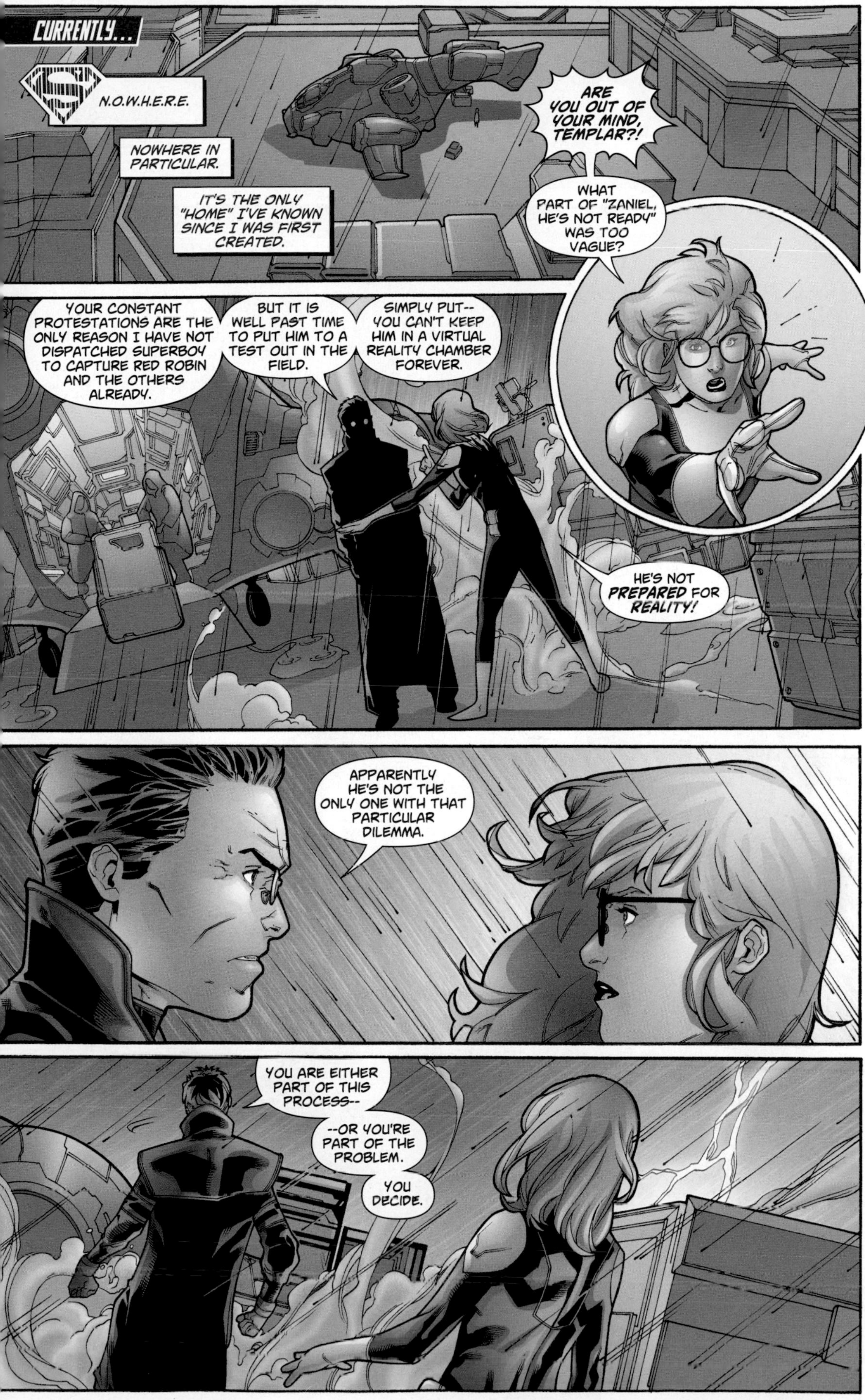
CURRENTLY...
N.O.W.H.E.R.E.
NOWHERE IN PARTICULAR.
IT'S THE ONLY "HOME" I'VE KNOWN SINCE I WAS FIRST CREATED.
ARE YOU OUT OF YOUR MIND, TEMPLAR?!
WHAT PART OF "ZANIEL, HE'S NOT READY" WAS TOO VAGUE?
YOUR CONSTANT PROTESTATIONS ARE THE ONLY REASON I HAVE NOT DISPATCHED SUPERBOY TO CAPTURE RED ROBIN AND THE OTHERS ALREADY.
BUT IT IS WELL PAST TIME TO PUT HIM TO A TEST OUT IN THE FIELD.
SIMPLY PUT-- YOU CAN'T KEEP HIM IN A VIRTUAL REALITY CHAMBER FOREVER.
HE'S NOT PREPARED FOR REALITY!
APPARENTLY HE'S NOT THE ONLY ONE WITH THAT PARTICULAR DILEMMA.
YOU ARE EITHER PART OF THIS PROCESS--
--OR YOU'RE PART OF THE PROBLEM.
YOU DECIDE.

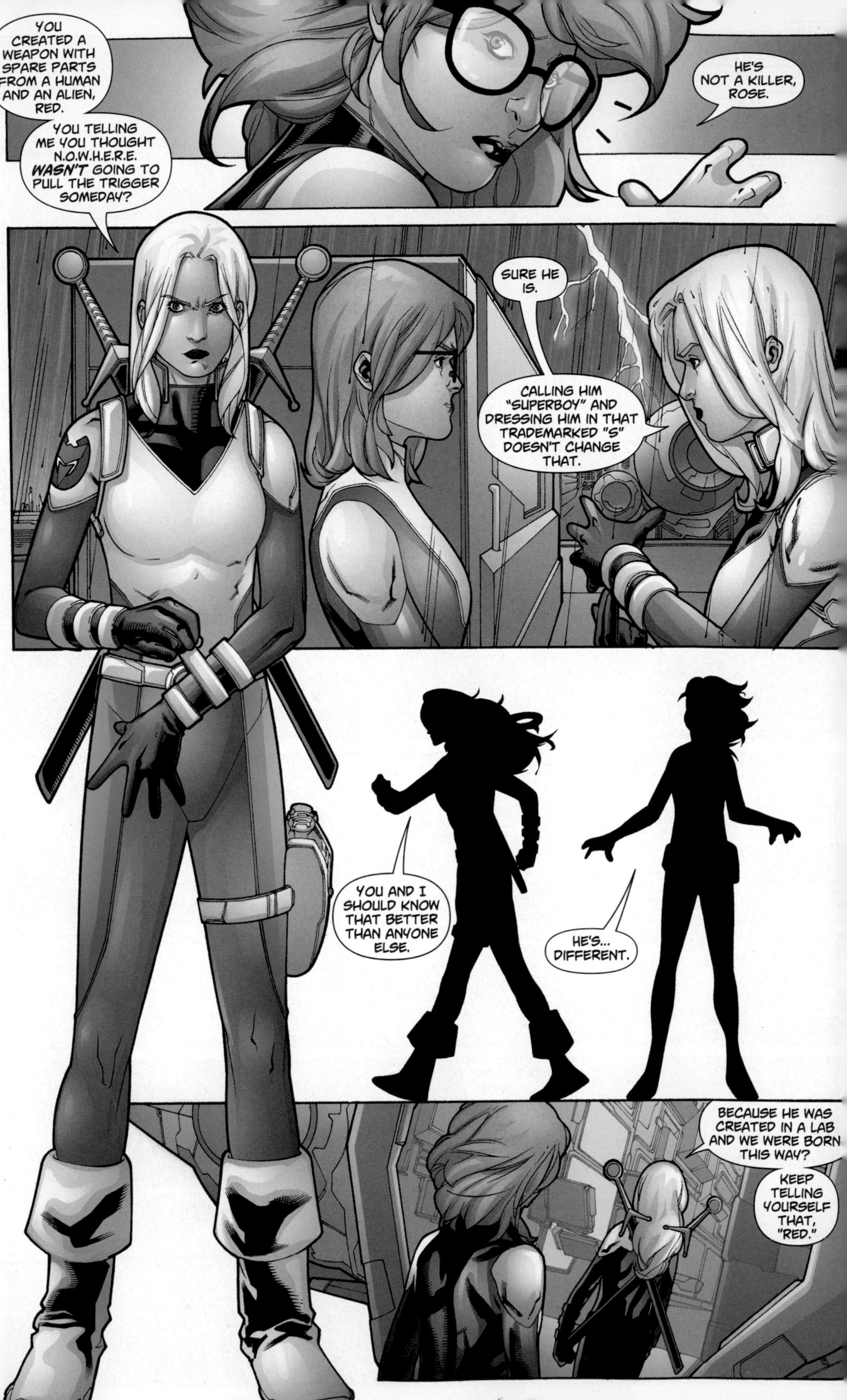
YOU CREATED A WEAPON WITH SPARE PARTS FROM A HUMAN AND AN ALIEN, RED.
YOU TELLING ME YOU THOUGHT N.O.W.H.E.R.E. WASN'T GOING TO PULL THE TRIGGER SOMEDAY?
HE'S NOT A KILLER, ROSE.
SURE HE IS.
CALLING HIM "SUPERBOY" AND DRESSING HIM IN THAT TRADEMARKED "S" DOESN'T CHANGE THAT.
YOU AND I SHOULD KNOW THAT BETTER THAN ANYONE ELSE.
HE'S... DIFFERENT.
BECAUSE HE WAS CREATED IN A LAB AND WE WERE BORN THIS WAY?
KEEP TELLING YOURSELF THAT, "RED."

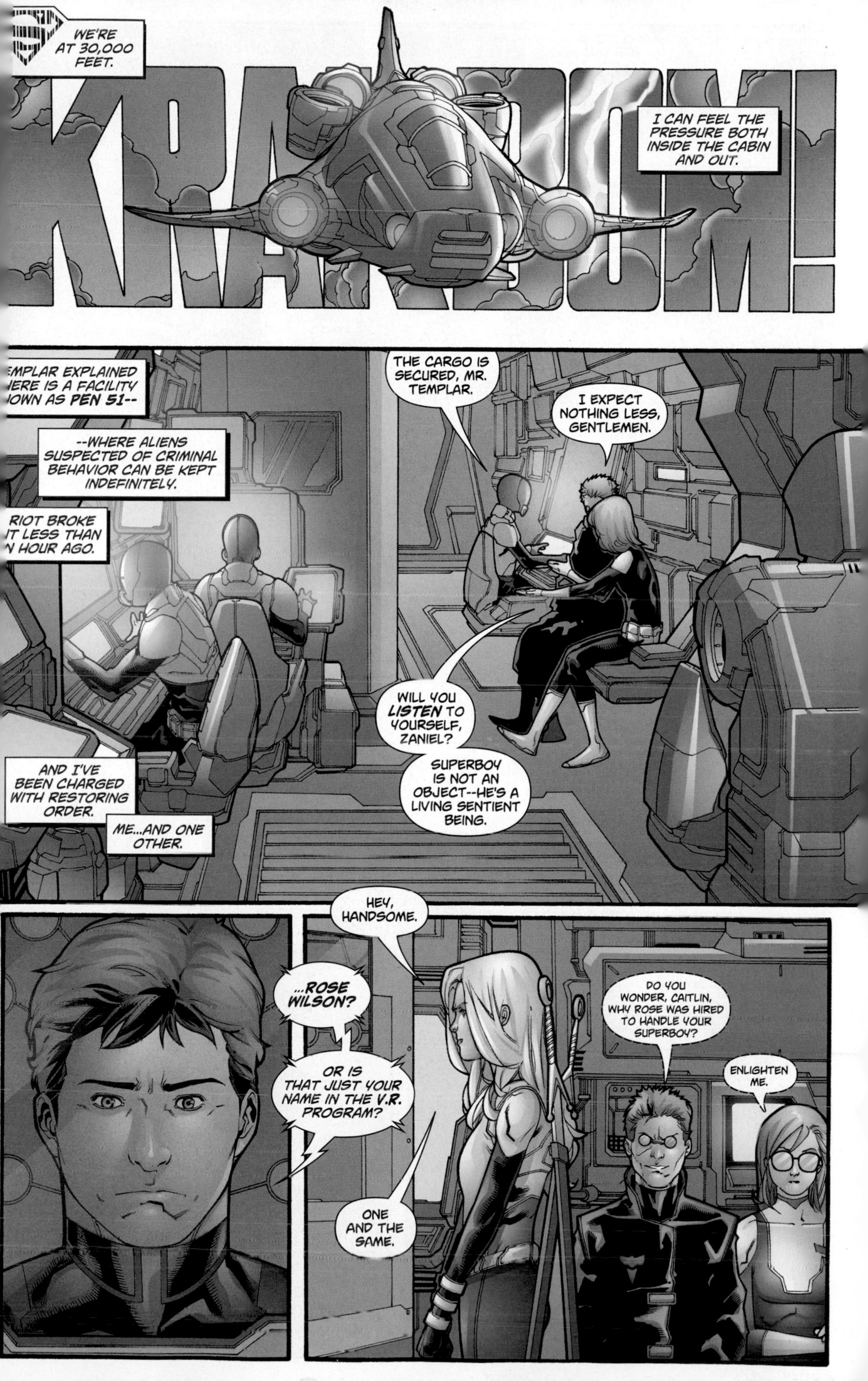

WE'RE AT 30,000 FEET.
KRAKOOM!
I CAN FEEL THE PRESSURE BOTH INSIDE THE CABIN AND OUT.
EMPLAR EXPLAINED HERE IS A FACILITY NOWN AS PEN 51--
--WHERE ALIENS SUSPECTED OF CRIMINAL BEHAVIOR CAN BE KEPT INDEFINITELY.
RIOT BROKE UT LESS THAN N HOUR AGO.
AND I'VE BEEN CHARGED WITH RESTORING ORDER.
ME...AND ONE OTHER.
THE CARGO IS SECURED, MR. TEMPLAR.
I EXPECT NOTHING LESS, GENTLEMEN.
WILL YOU LISTEN TO YOURSELF, ZANIEL?
SUPERBOY IS NOT AN OBJECT--HE'S A LIVING SENTIENT BEING.
HEY, HANDSOME.
...ROSE WILSON?
OR IS THAT JUST YOUR NAME IN THE V.R. PROGRAM?
ONE AND THE SAME.
DO YOU WONDER, CAITLIN, WHY ROSE WAS HIRED TO HANDLE YOUR SUPERBOY?
ENLIGHTEN ME.

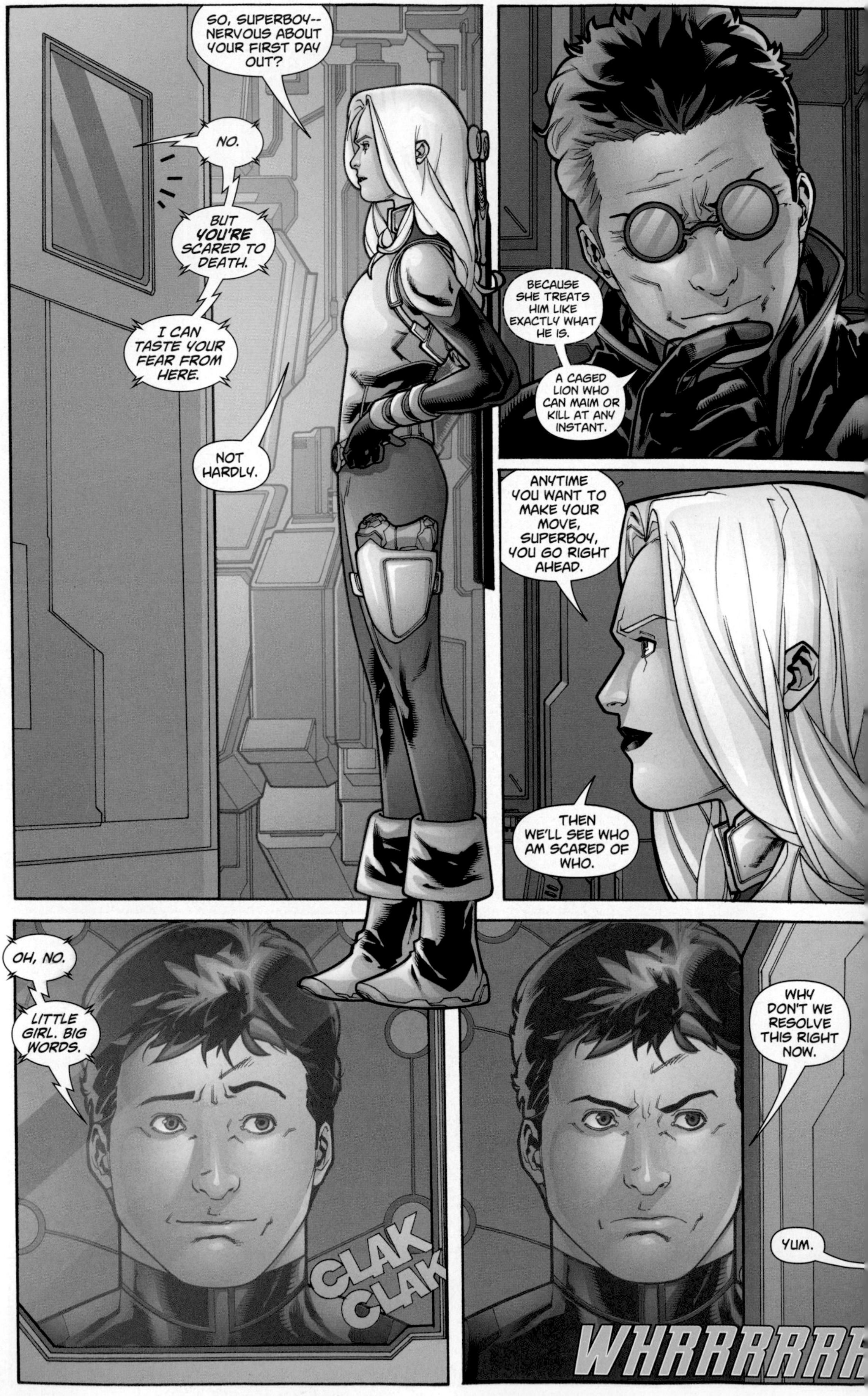
SO, SUPERBOY--NERVOUS ABOUT YOUR FIRST DAY OUT?
NO.
BUT YOU'RE SCARED TO DEATH.
I CAN TASTE YOUR FEAR FROM HERE.
NOT HARDLY.
BECAUSE SHE TREATS HIM LIKE EXACTLY WHAT HE IS.
A CAGED LION WHO CAN MAIM OR KILL AT ANY INSTANT.
ANYTIME YOU WANT TO MAKE YOUR MOVE, SUPERBOY, YOU GO RIGHT AHEAD.
THEN WE'LL SEE WHO AM SCARED OF WHO.
OH, NO.
LITTLE GIRL. BIG WORDS.
CLAK CLAK
WHY DON'T WE RESOLVE THIS RIGHT NOW.
YUM.
WHRRRRRR

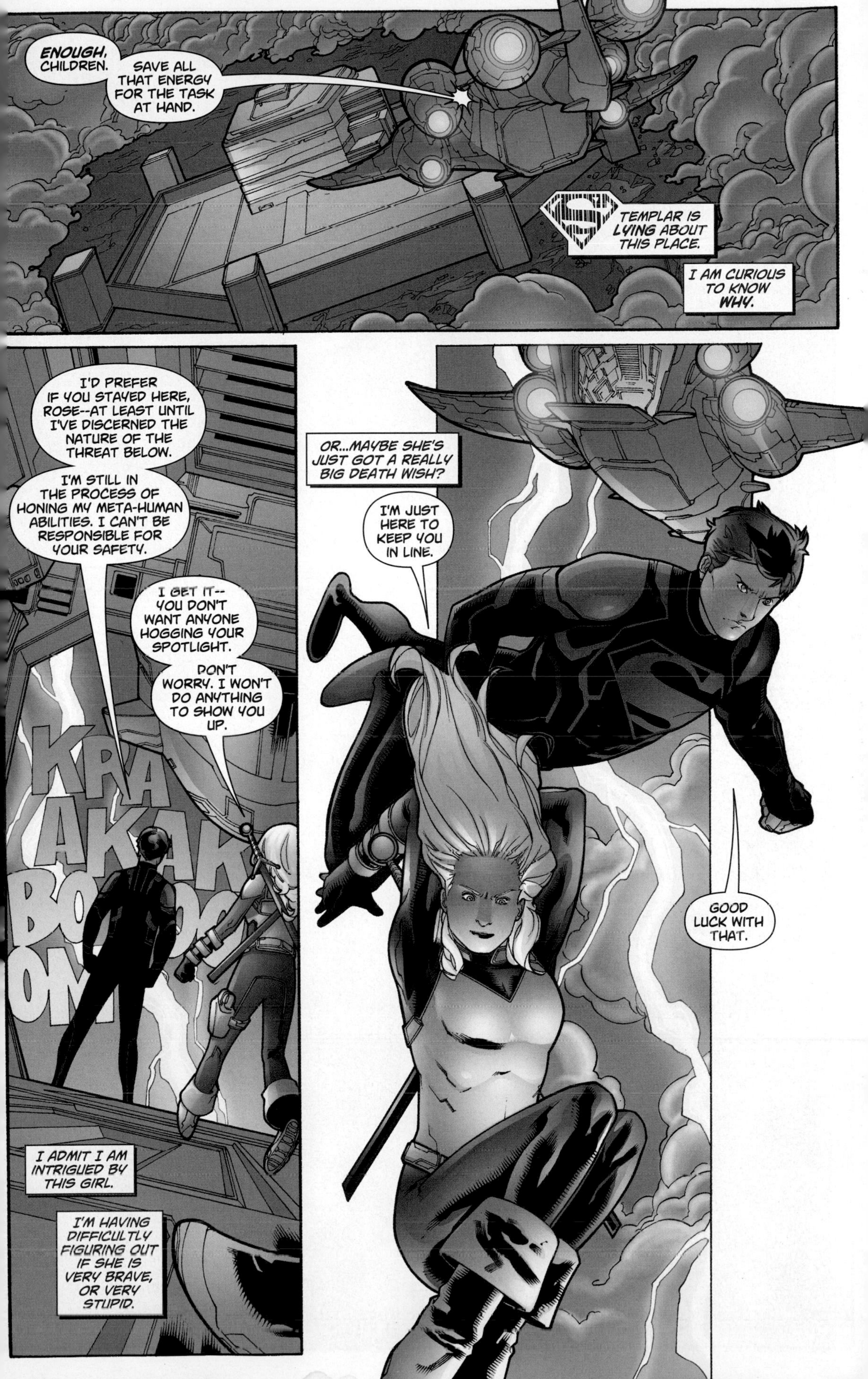
ENOUGH, CHILDREN.
SAVE ALL THAT ENERGY FOR THE TASK AT HAND.
TEMPLAR IS LYING ABOUT THIS PLACE.
I AM CURIOUS TO KNOW WHY.
I'D PREFER IF YOU STAYED HERE, ROSE--AT LEAST UNTIL I'VE DISCERNED THE NATURE OF THE THREAT BELOW.
I'M STILL IN THE PROCESS OF HONING MY META-HUMAN ABILITIES. I CAN'T BE RESPONSIBLE FOR YOUR SAFETY.
I GET IT-- YOU DON'T WANT ANYONE HOGGING YOUR SPOTLIGHT.
DON'T WORRY. I WON'T DO ANYTHING TO SHOW YOU UP.
KRAAKAKABOOOOM
I ADMIT I AM INTRIGUED BY THIS GIRL.
I'M HAVING DIFFICULTLY FIGURING OUT IF SHE IS VERY BRAVE, OR VERY STUPID.
OR...MAYBE SHE'S JUST GOT A REALLY BIG DEATH WISH?
I'M JUST HERE TO KEEP YOU IN LINE.
GOOD LUCK WITH THAT.

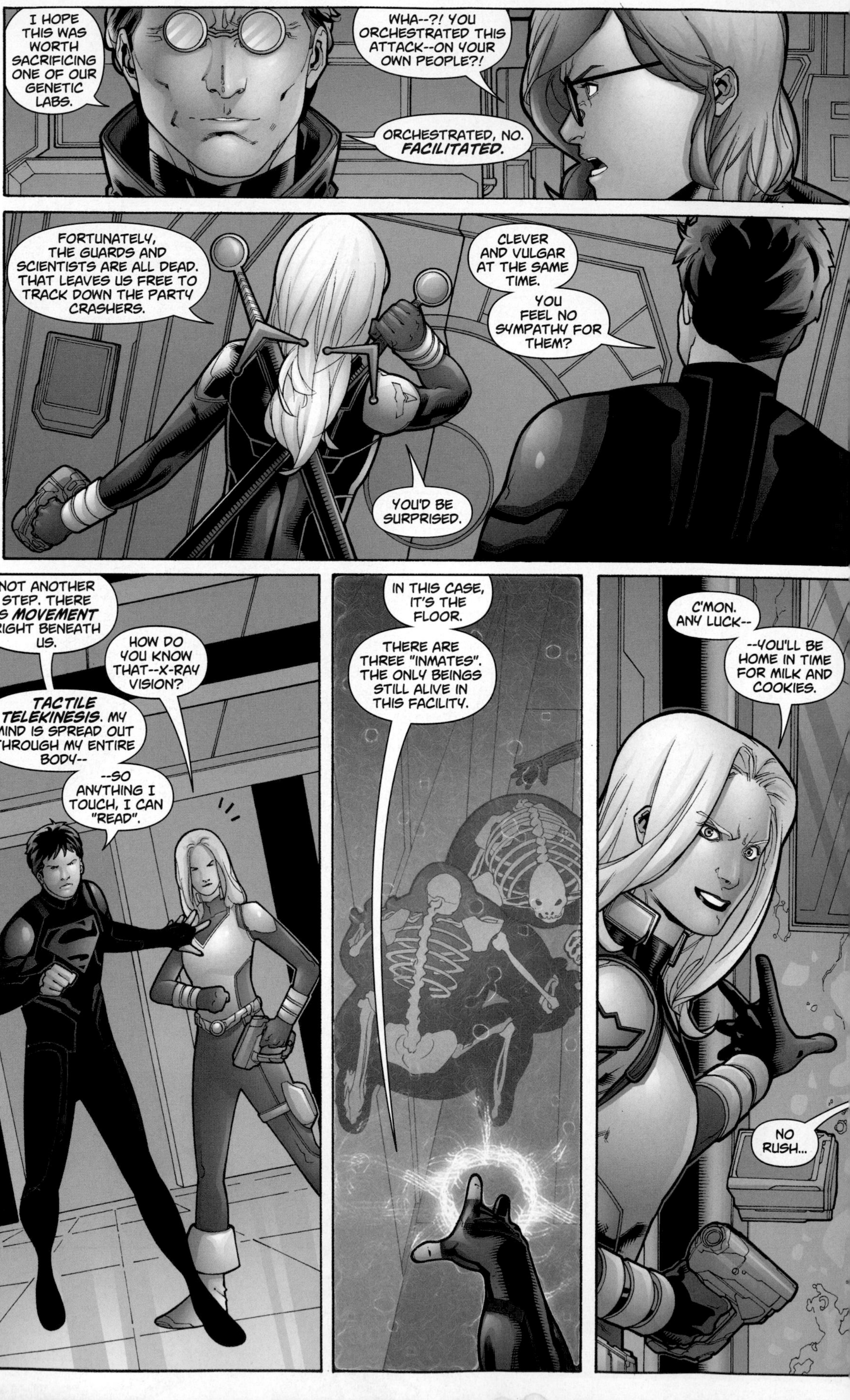

I HOPE THIS WAS WORTH SACRIFICING ONE OF OUR GENETIC LABS.
WHA--?! YOU ORCHESTRATED THIS ATTACK--ON YOUR OWN PEOPLE?!
ORCHESTRATED, NO. *FACILITATED.*
FORTUNATELY, THE GUARDS AND SCIENTISTS ARE ALL DEAD. THAT LEAVES US FREE TO TRACK DOWN THE PARTY CRASHERS.
CLEVER AND VULGAR AT THE SAME TIME.
YOU FEEL NO SYMPATHY FOR THEM?
YOU'D BE SURPRISED.
NOT ANOTHER STEP. THERE IS *MOVEMENT* RIGHT BENEATH US.
HOW DO YOU KNOW THAT--X-RAY VISION?
TACTILE TELEKINESIS. MY MIND IS SPREAD OUT THROUGH MY ENTIRE BODY--
--SO ANYTHING I TOUCH, I CAN "READ".
IN THIS CASE, IT'S THE FLOOR.
THERE ARE THREE "INMATES". THE ONLY BEINGS STILL ALIVE IN THIS FACILITY.
C'MON. ANY LUCK--
--YOU'LL BE HOME IN TIME FOR MILK AND COOKIES.
NO RUSH...

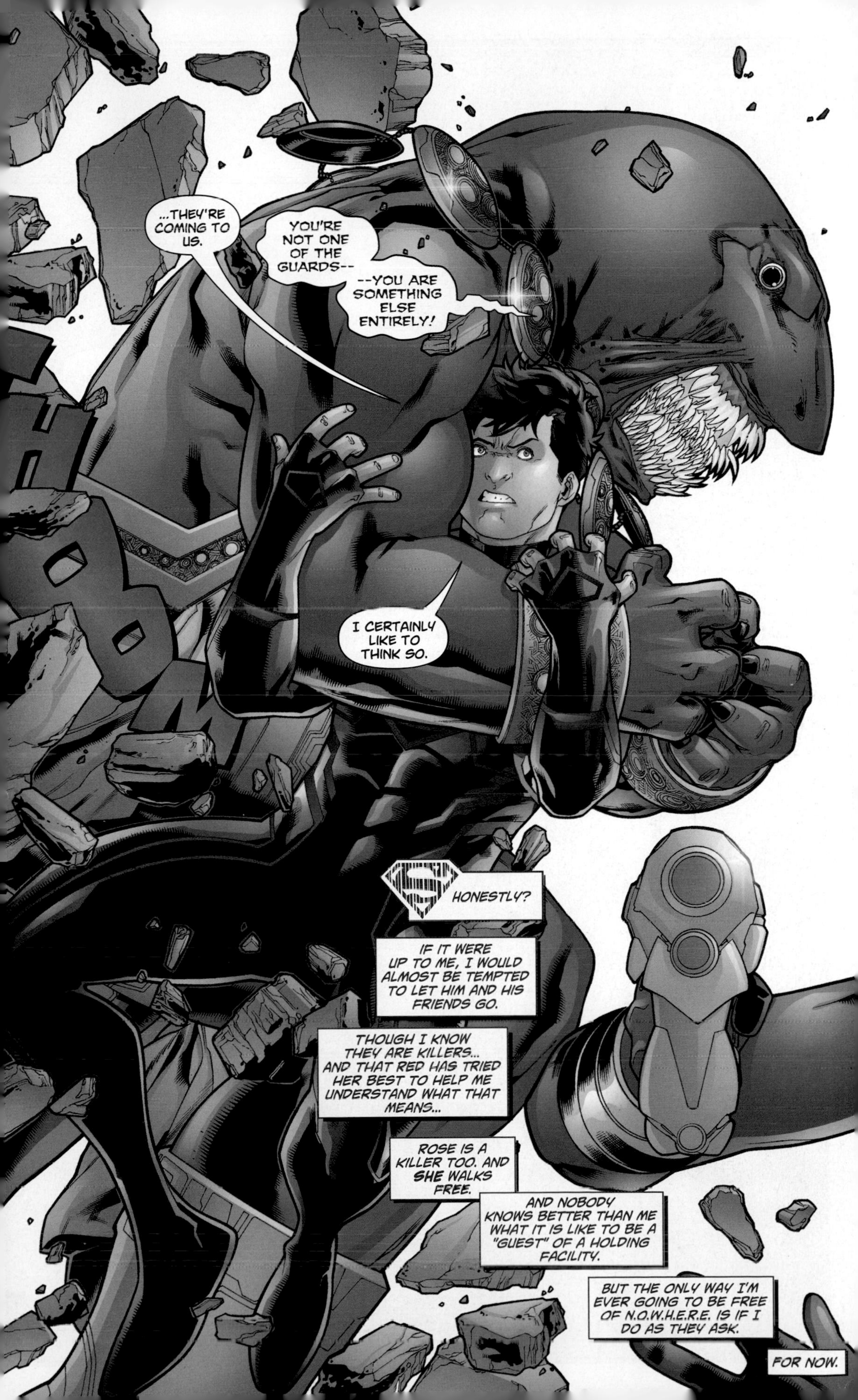
...THEY'RE COMING TO US.
YOU'RE NOT ONE OF THE GUARDS--
--YOU ARE SOMETHING ELSE ENTIRELY!
I CERTAINLY LIKE TO THINK SO.
HONESTLY?
IF IT WERE UP TO ME, I WOULD ALMOST BE TEMPTED TO LET HIM AND HIS FRIENDS GO.
THOUGH I KNOW THEY ARE KILLERS... AND THAT RED HAS TRIED HER BEST TO HELP ME UNDERSTAND WHAT THAT MEANS...
ROSE IS A KILLER TOO. AND SHE WALKS FREE.
AND NOBODY KNOWS BETTER THAN ME WHAT IT IS LIKE TO BE A "GUEST" OF A HOLDING FACILITY.
BUT THE ONLY WAY I'M EVER GOING TO BE FREE OF N.O.W.H.E.R.E. IS IF I DO AS THEY ASK.
FOR NOW.

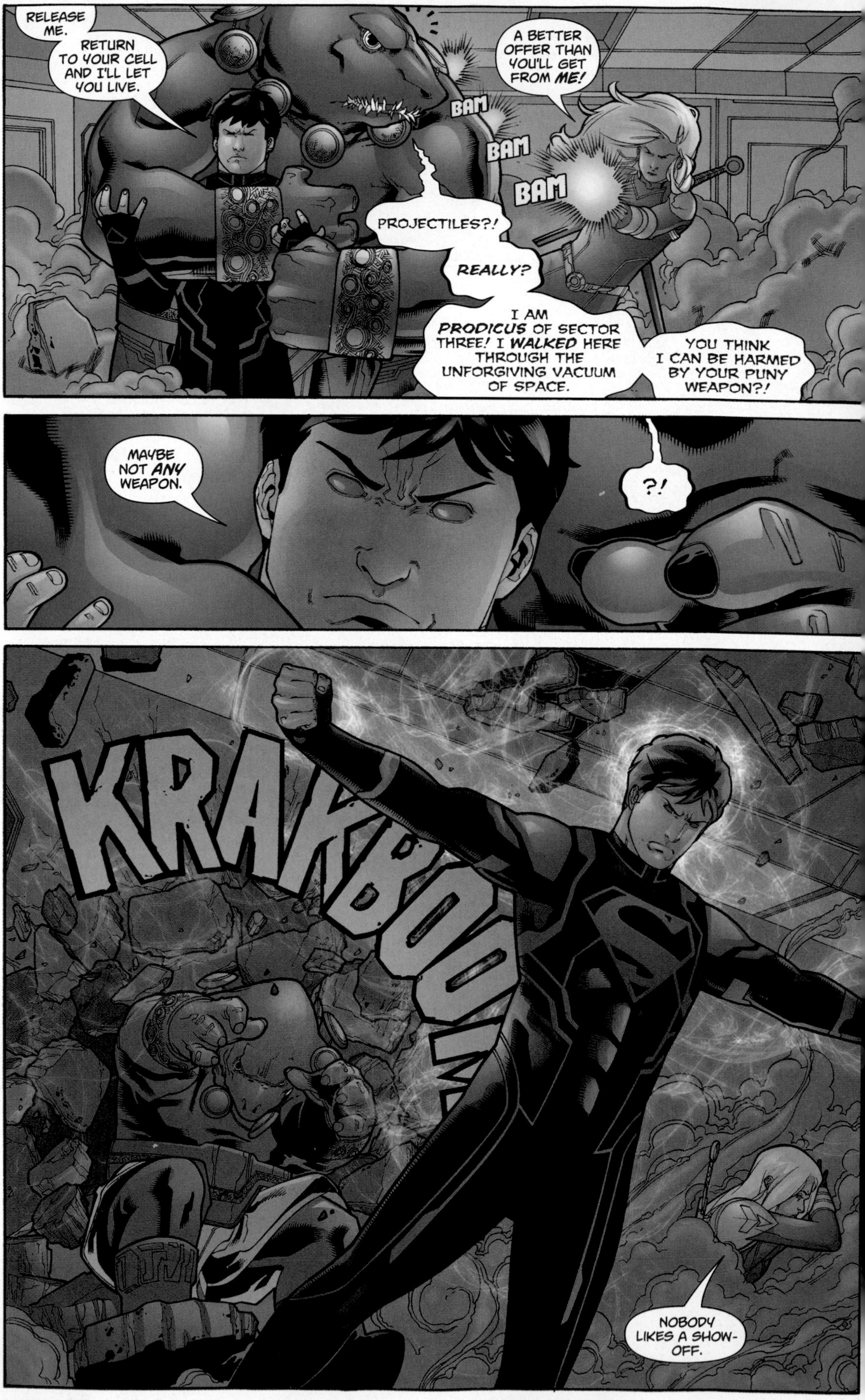
RELEASE ME.
RETURN TO YOUR CELL AND I'LL LET YOU LIVE.
A BETTER OFFER THAN YOU'LL GET FROM ME!
BAM
BAM
BAM
PROJECTILES?!
REALLY?
I AM PRODICUS OF SECTOR THREE! I WALKED HERE THROUGH THE UNFORGIVING VACUUM OF SPACE.
YOU THINK I CAN BE HARMED BY YOUR PUNY WEAPON?!
MAYBE NOT ANY WEAPON.
?!
KRAKBOOM
NOBODY LIKES A SHOW-OFF.

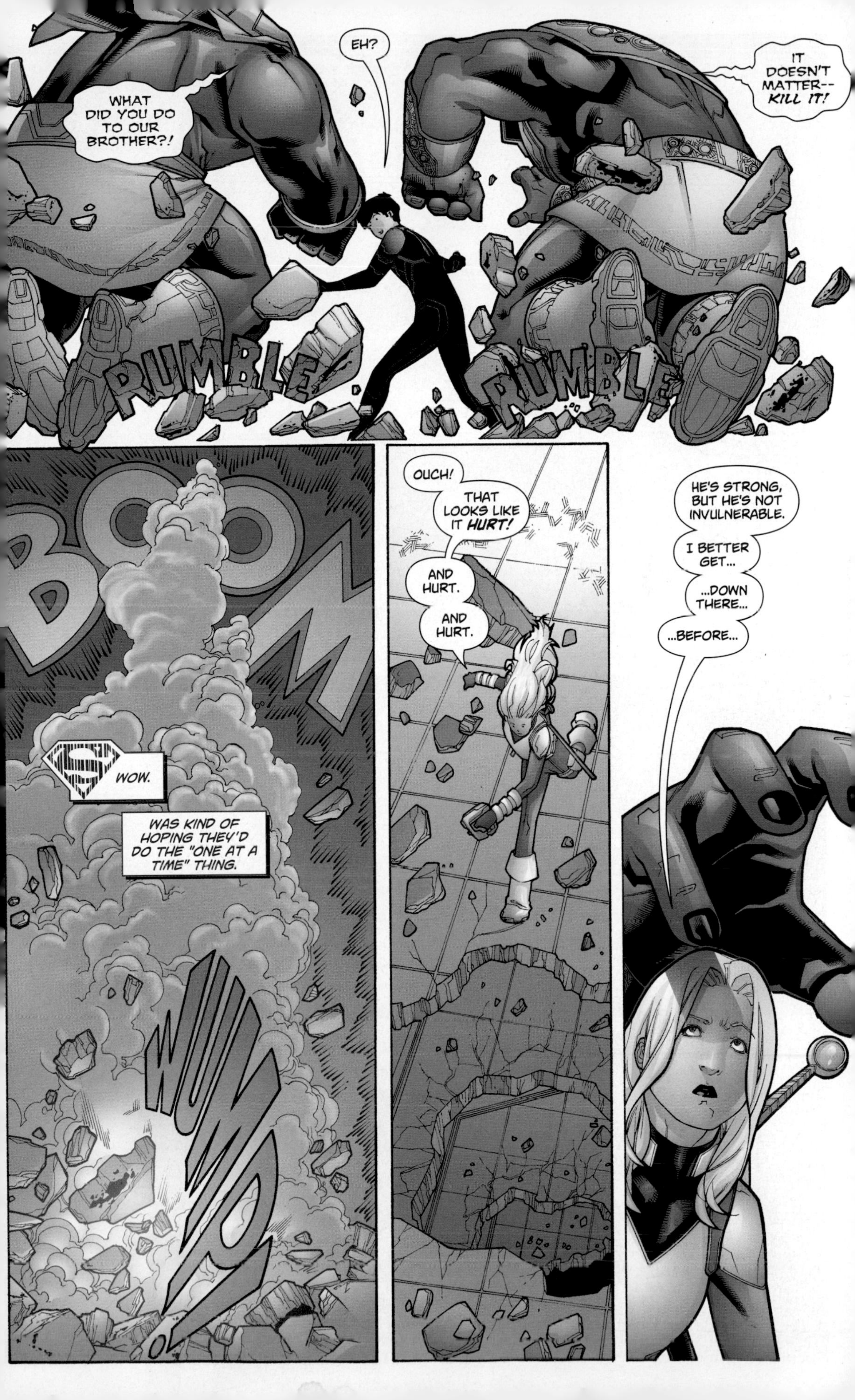
WHAT DID YOU DO TO OUR BROTHER?!
EH?
IT DOESN'T MATTER-- KILL IT!
RUMBLE
RUMBLE
BOOM
WOW.
WAS KIND OF HOPING THEY'D DO THE "ONE AT A TIME" THING.
WUMP
OUCH!
THAT LOOKS LIKE IT HURT!
AND HURT.
AND HURT.
HE'S STRONG, BUT HE'S NOT INVULNERABLE.
I BETTER GET...
...DOWN THERE...
...BEFORE...

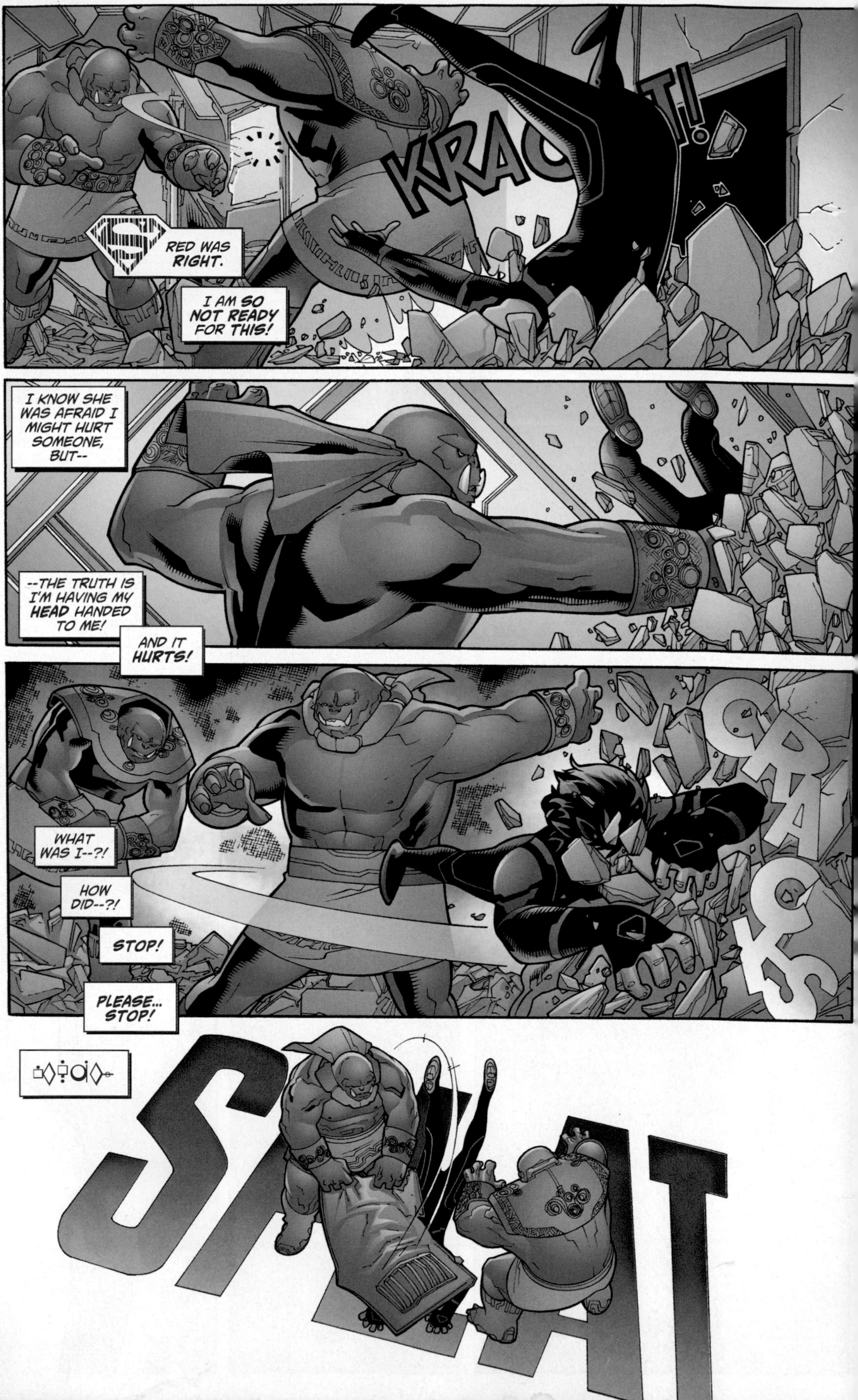
KRAC
T!
RED WAS RIGHT.
I AM SO NOT READY FOR THIS!
I KNOW SHE WAS AFRAID I MIGHT HURT SOMEONE, BUT--
--THE TRUTH IS I'M HAVING MY HEAD HANDED TO ME!
AND IT HURTS!
CRASH
WHAT WAS I--?!
HOW DID--?!
STOP!
PLEASE... STOP!
SPLAT

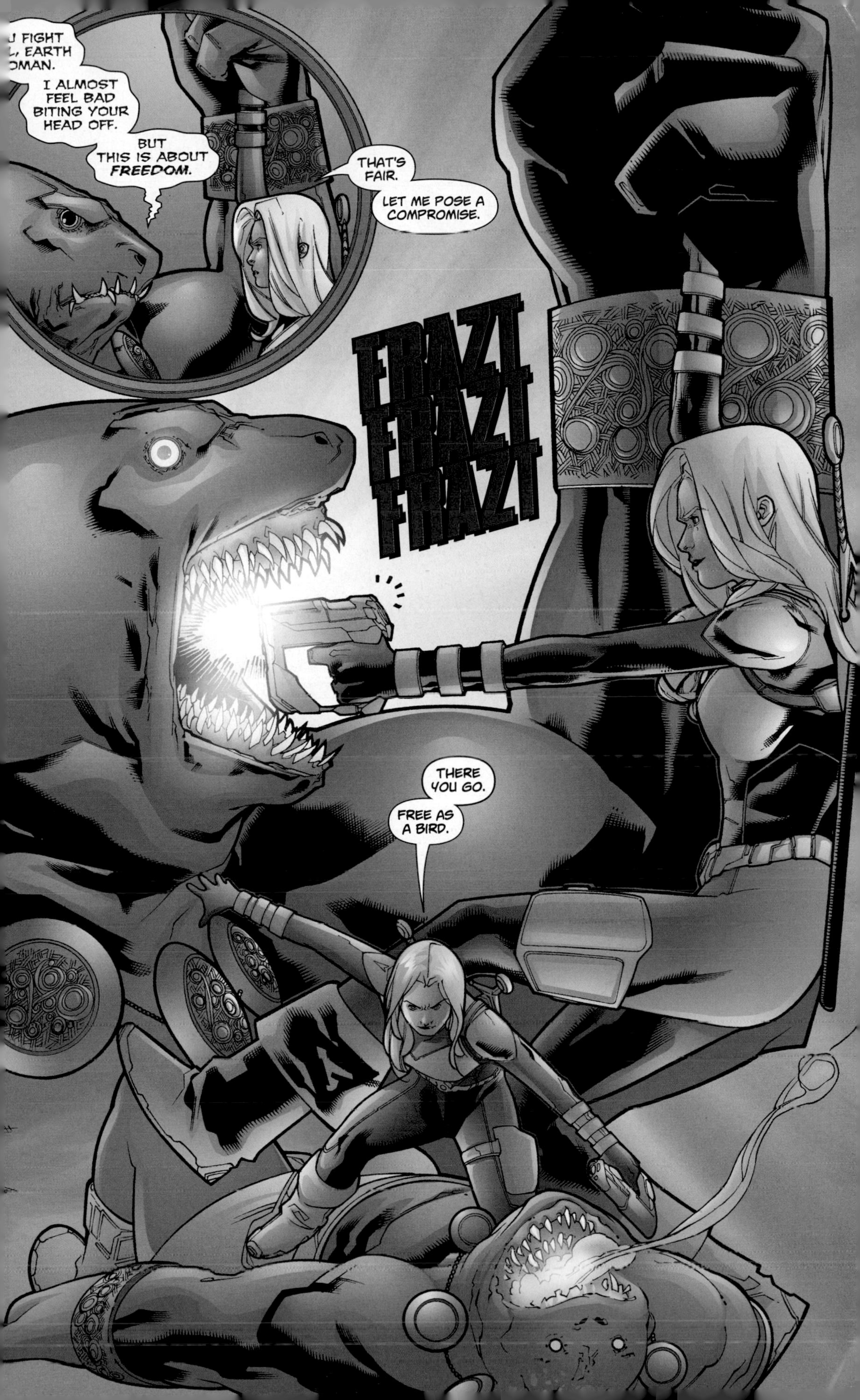

U FIGHT
L, EARTH
OMAN.
I ALMOST FEEL BAD BITING YOUR HEAD OFF.
BUT THIS IS ABOUT FREEDOM.
THAT'S FAIR.
LET ME POSE A COMPROMISE.
FRAZT FRAZT FRAZT FRAZT
THERE YOU GO.
FREE AS A BIRD.

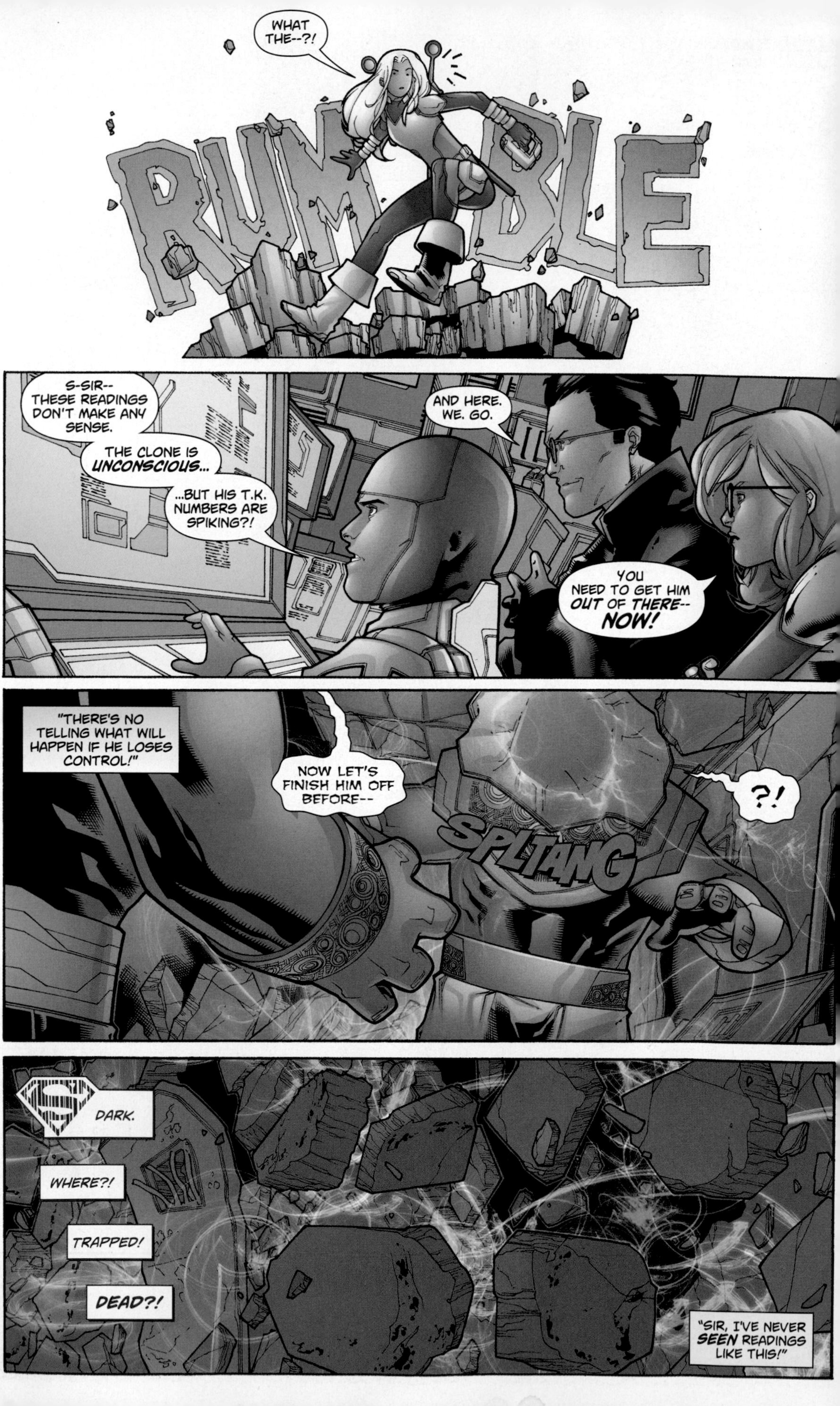

WHAT THE--?!
RUMBLE
S-SIR-- THESE READINGS DON'T MAKE ANY SENSE.
THE CLONE IS UNCONSCIOUS...
...BUT HIS T.K. NUMBERS ARE SPIKING?!
AND HERE. WE. GO.
YOU NEED TO GET HIM OUT OF THERE-- NOW!
"THERE'S NO TELLING WHAT WILL HAPPEN IF HE LOSES CONTROL!"
NOW LET'S FINISH HIM OFF BEFORE--
SPLTANG
?!
DARK.
WHERE?!
TRAPPED!
DEAD?!
"SIR, I'VE NEVER SEEN READINGS LIKE THIS!"

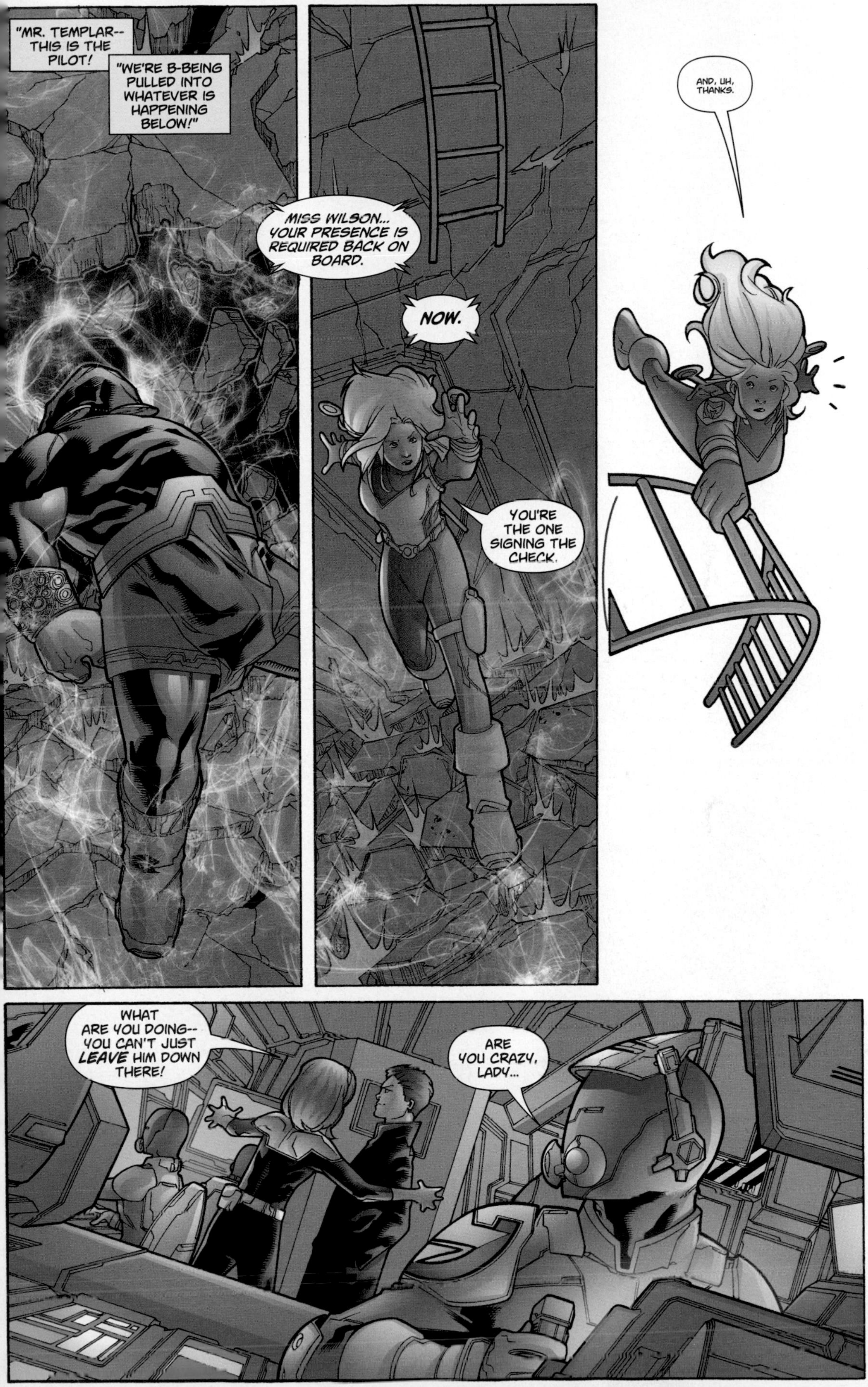
"MR. TEMPLAR-- THIS IS THE PILOT!
"WE'RE B-BEING PULLED INTO WHATEVER IS HAPPENING BELOW!"
MISS WILSON... YOUR PRESENCE IS REQUIRED BACK ON BOARD.
NOW.
YOU'RE THE ONE SIGNING THE CHECK.
AND, UH, THANKS.
WHAT ARE YOU DOING-- YOU CAN'T JUST LEAVE HIM DOWN THERE!
ARE YOU CRAZY, LADY...

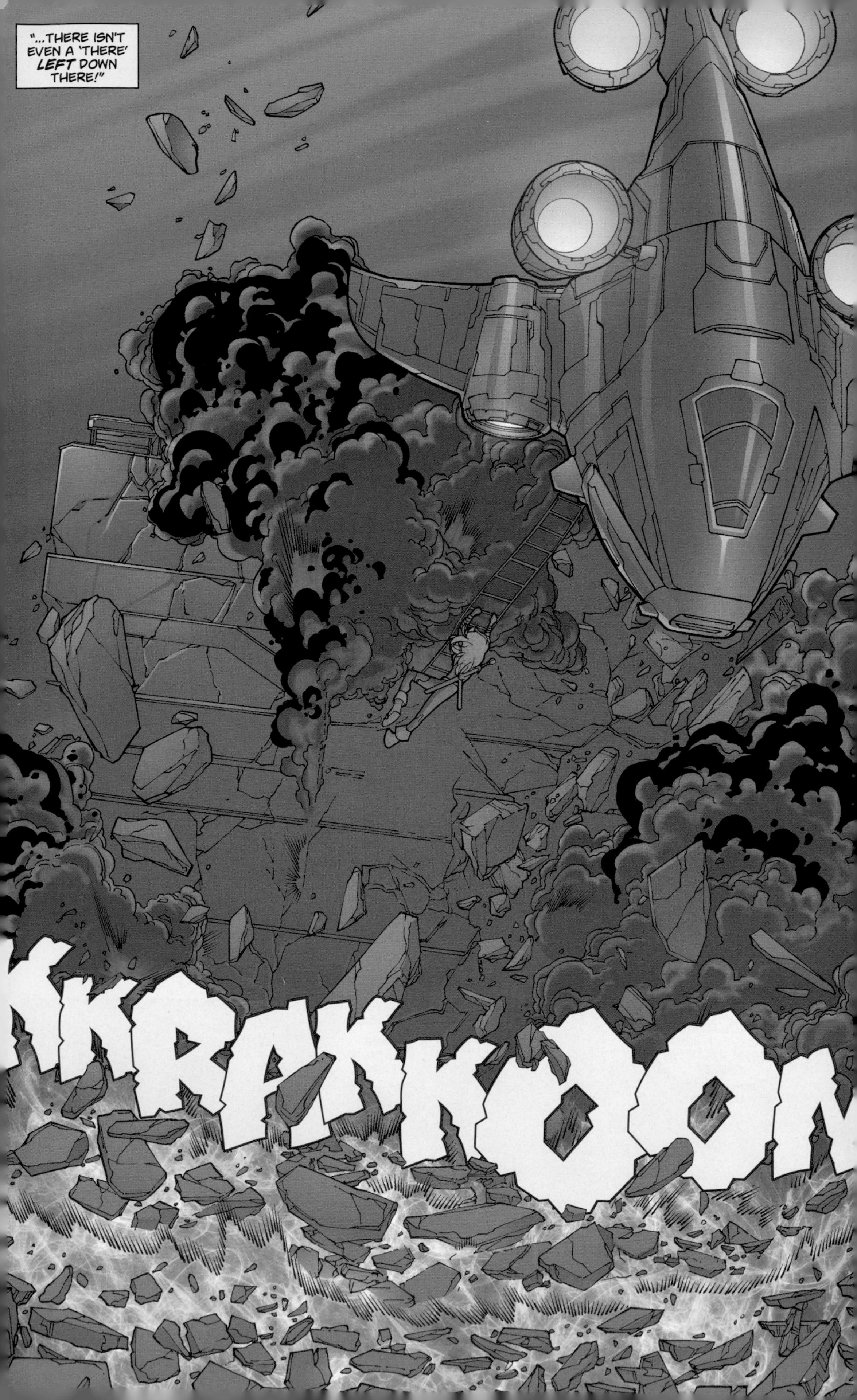
"...THERE ISN'T EVEN A 'THERE' LEFT DOWN THERE!"
KRAKOOM

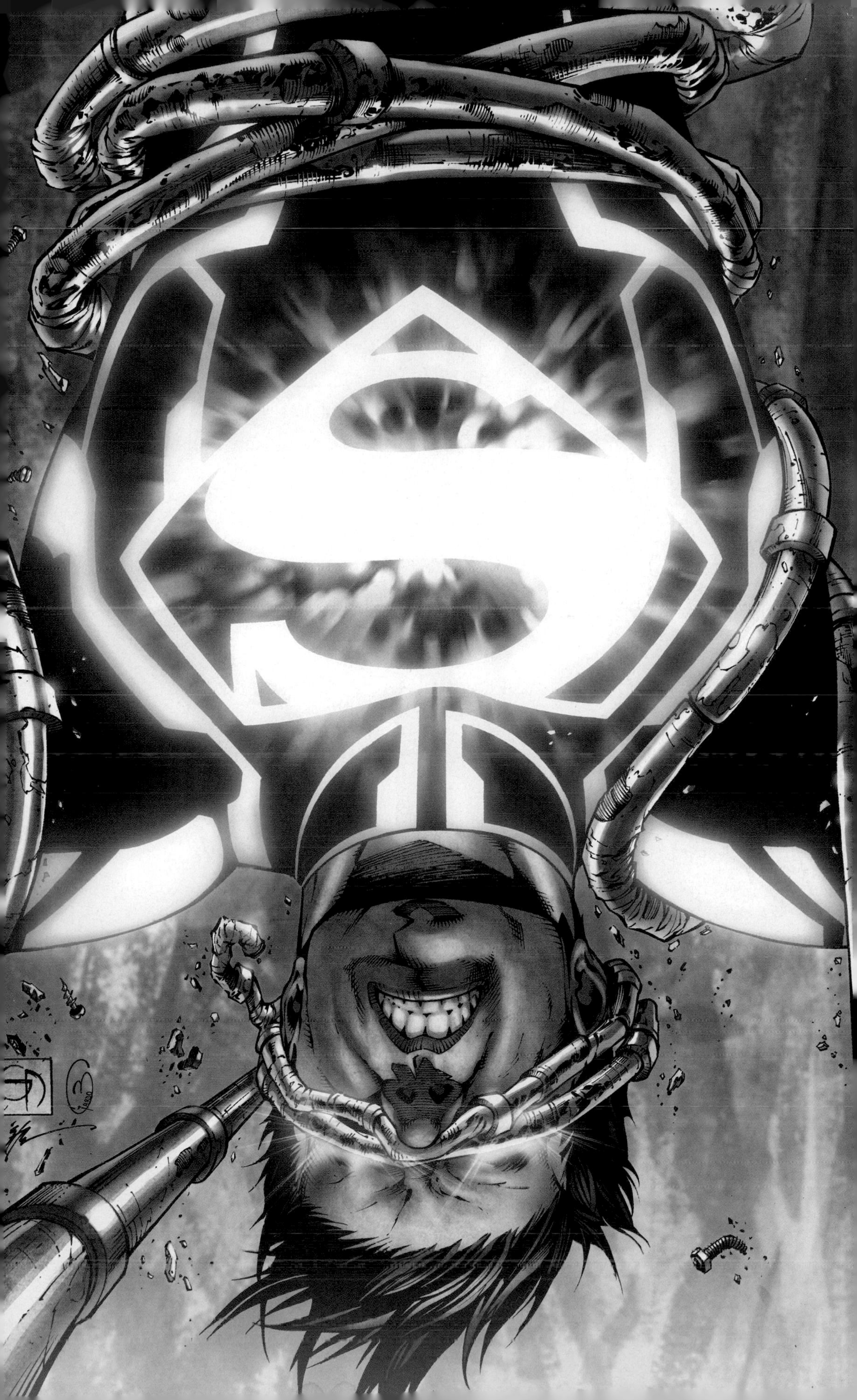

Cover by SHANE DAVIS, JONATHAN GLAPION & BARBARA CIARDO

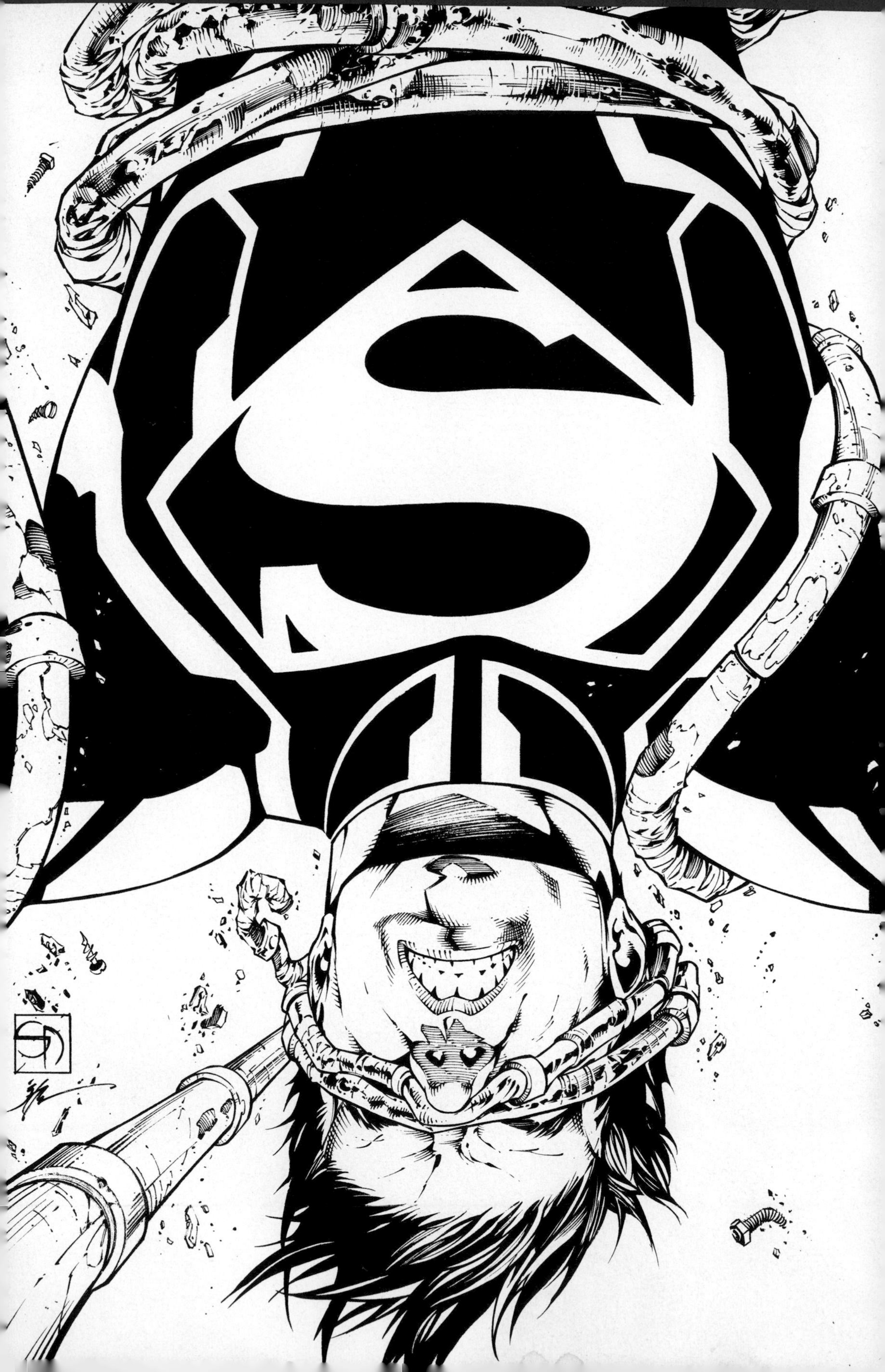

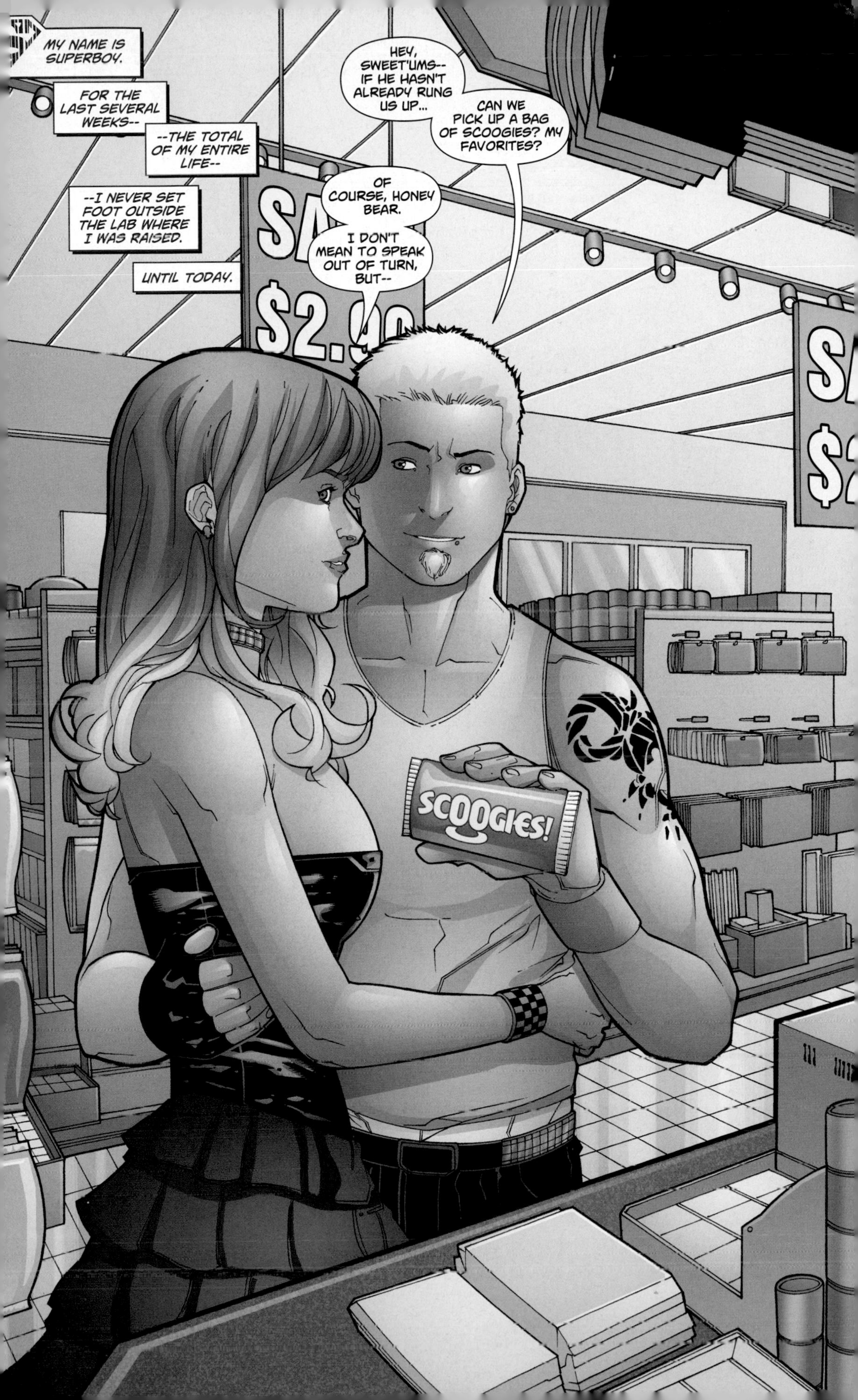

MY NAME IS SUPERBOY.
FOR THE LAST SEVERAL WEEKS--
--THE TOTAL OF MY ENTIRE LIFE--
--I NEVER SET FOOT OUTSIDE THE LAB WHERE I WAS RAISED.
UNTIL TODAY.
HEY, SWEET'UMS-- IF HE HASN'T ALREADY RUNG US UP...
CAN WE PICK UP A BAG OF SCOOGIES? MY FAVORITES?
OF COURSE, HONEY BEAR.
I DON'T MEAN TO SPEAK OUT OF TURN, BUT--
SCOOGIES!

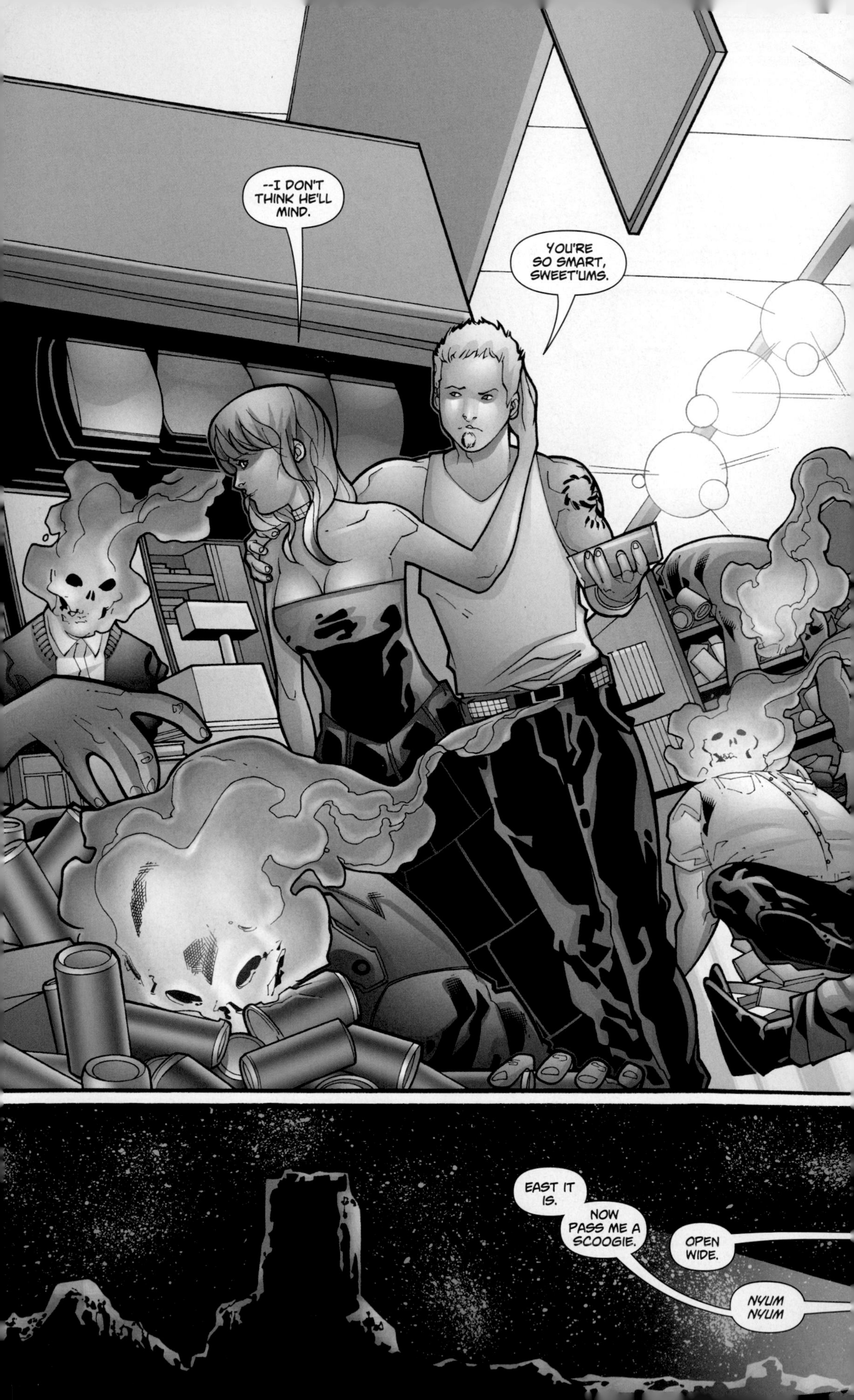
--I DON'T THINK HE'LL MIND.
YOU'RE SO SMART, SWEET'UMS.
EAST IT IS.
NOW PASS ME A SCOOGIE.
OPEN WIDE.
NYUM NYUM

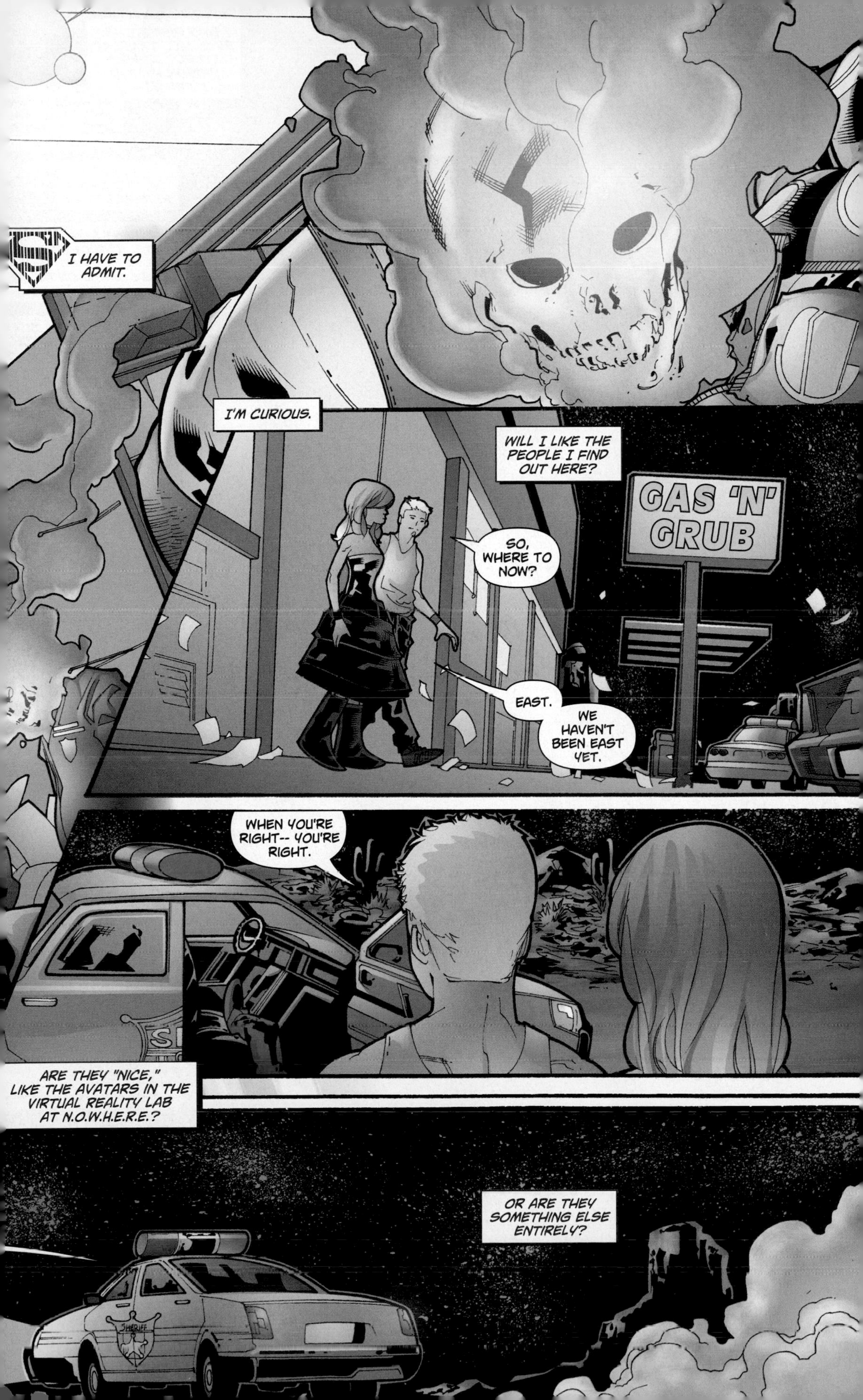
I HAVE TO ADMIT.
I'M CURIOUS.
WILL I LIKE THE PEOPLE I FIND OUT HERE?
GAS 'N' GRUB
SO, WHERE TO NOW?
EAST.
WE HAVEN'T BEEN EAST YET.
WHEN YOU'RE RIGHT-- YOU'RE RIGHT.
ARE THEY "NICE," LIKE THE AVATARS IN THE VIRTUAL REALITY LAB AT N.O.W.H.E.R.E.?
OR ARE THEY SOMETHING ELSE ENTIRELY?
SHERIFF

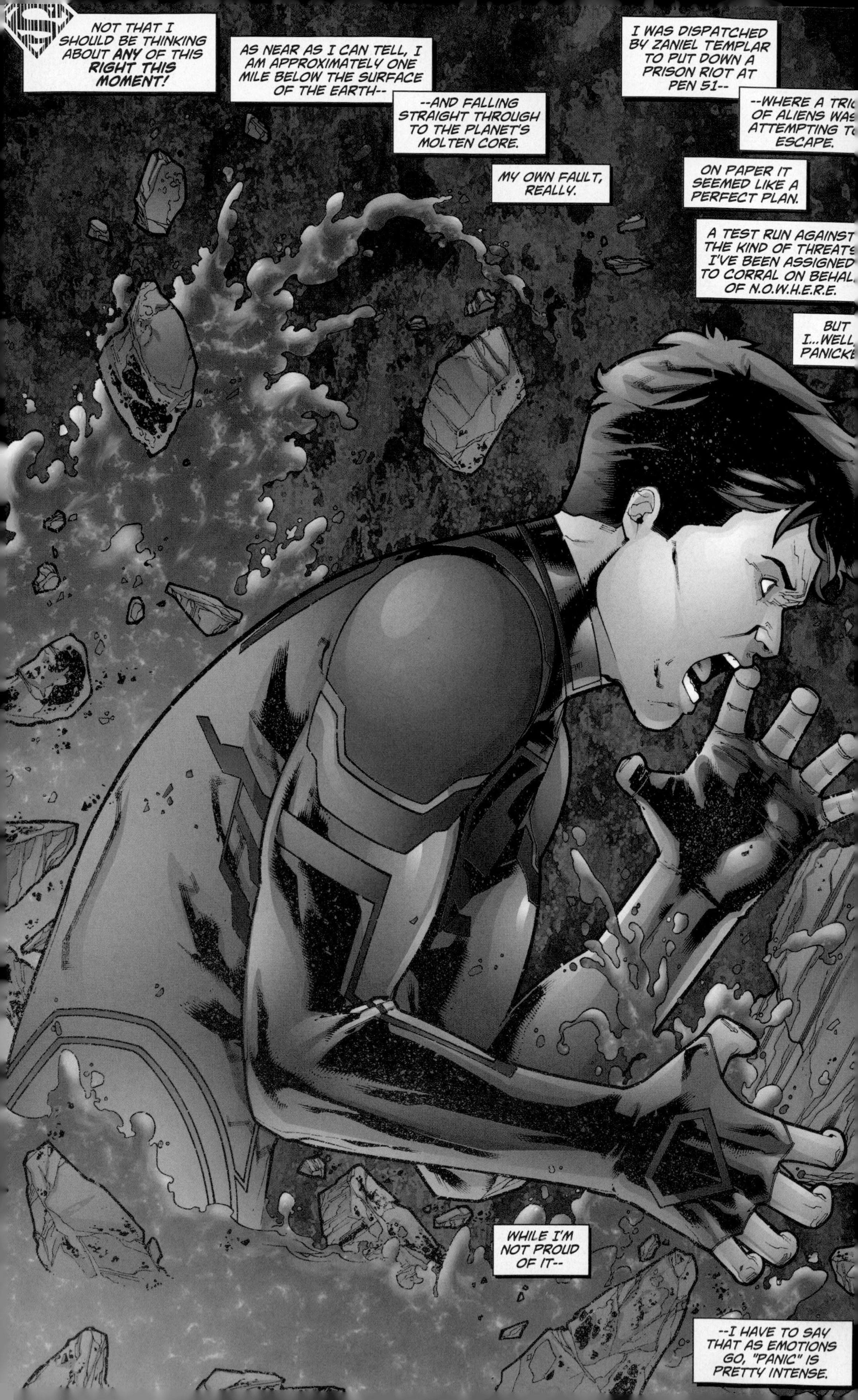
NOT THAT I SHOULD BE THINKING ABOUT ANY OF THIS RIGHT THIS MOMENT!
AS NEAR AS I CAN TELL, I AM APPROXIMATELY ONE MILE BELOW THE SURFACE OF THE EARTH--
--AND FALLING STRAIGHT THROUGH TO THE PLANET'S MOLTEN CORE.
MY OWN FAULT, REALLY.
I WAS DISPATCHED BY ZANIEL TEMPLAR TO PUT DOWN A PRISON RIOT AT PEN 51--
--WHERE A TRI
OF ALIENS WAS
ATTEMPTING T
ESCAPE.
ON PAPER IT SEEMED LIKE A PERFECT PLAN.
A TEST RUN AGAINST THE KIND OF THREATS I'VE BEEN ASSIGNED TO CORRAL ON BEHAL OF N.O.W.H.E.R.E.
BUT I...WELL PANICKE
WHILE I'M NOT PROUD OF IT--
--I HAVE TO SAY THAT AS EMOTIONS GO, "PANIC" IS PRETTY INTENSE.

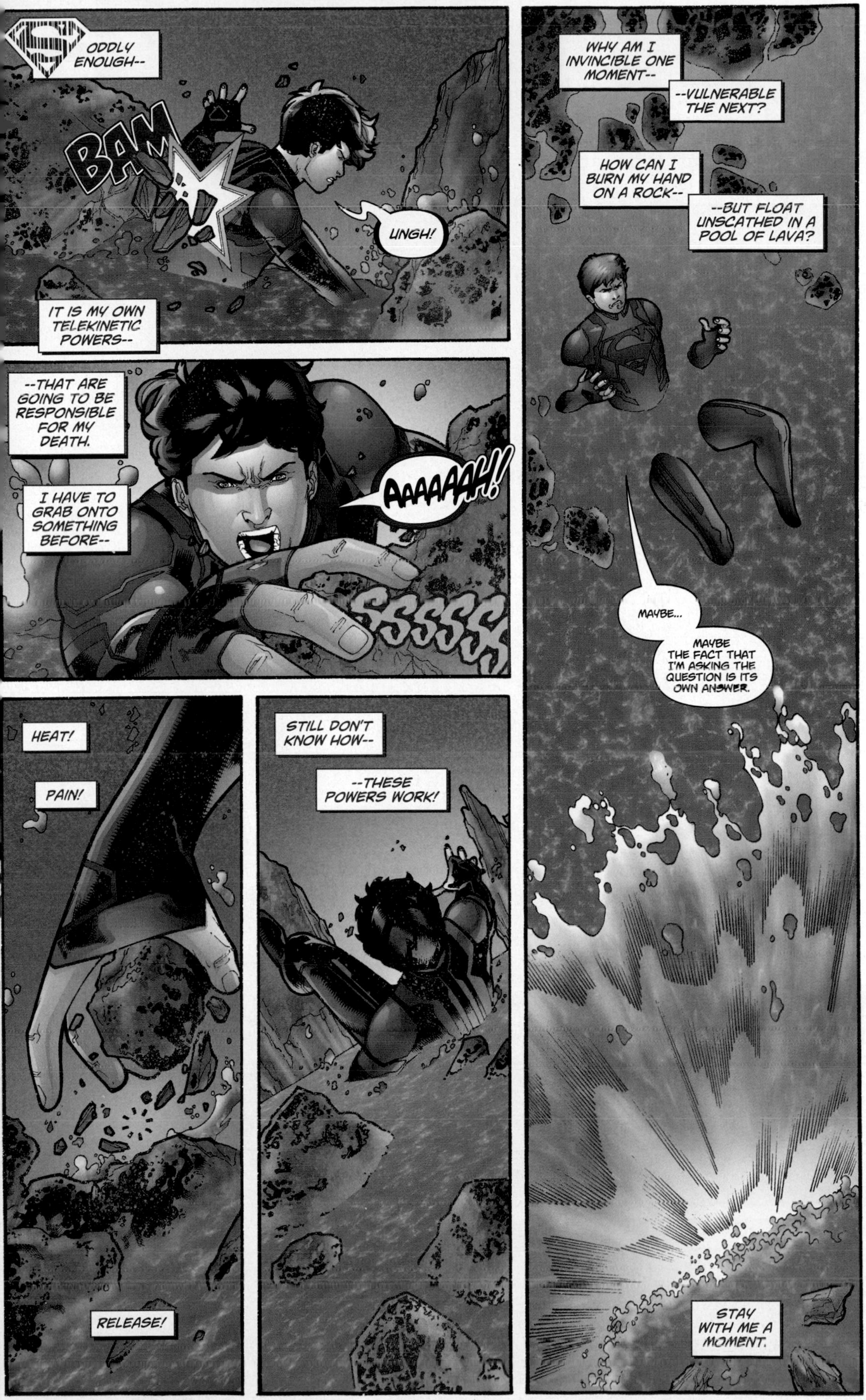
ODDLY ENOUGH--
BAM
UNGH!
IT IS MY OWN TELEKINETIC POWERS--
--THAT ARE GOING TO BE RESPONSIBLE FOR MY DEATH.
I HAVE TO GRAB ONTO SOMETHING BEFORE--
AAAAAAH!
SSSSSS
HEAT!
PAIN!
RELEASE!
STILL DON'T KNOW HOW--
--THESE POWERS WORK!
WHY AM I INVINCIBLE ONE MOMENT--
--VULNERABLE THE NEXT?
HOW CAN I BURN MY HAND ON A ROCK--
--BUT FLOAT UNSCATHED IN A POOL OF LAVA?
MAYBE...
MAYBE THE FACT THAT I'M ASKING THE QUESTION IS ITS OWN ANSWER.
STAY WITH ME A MOMENT.

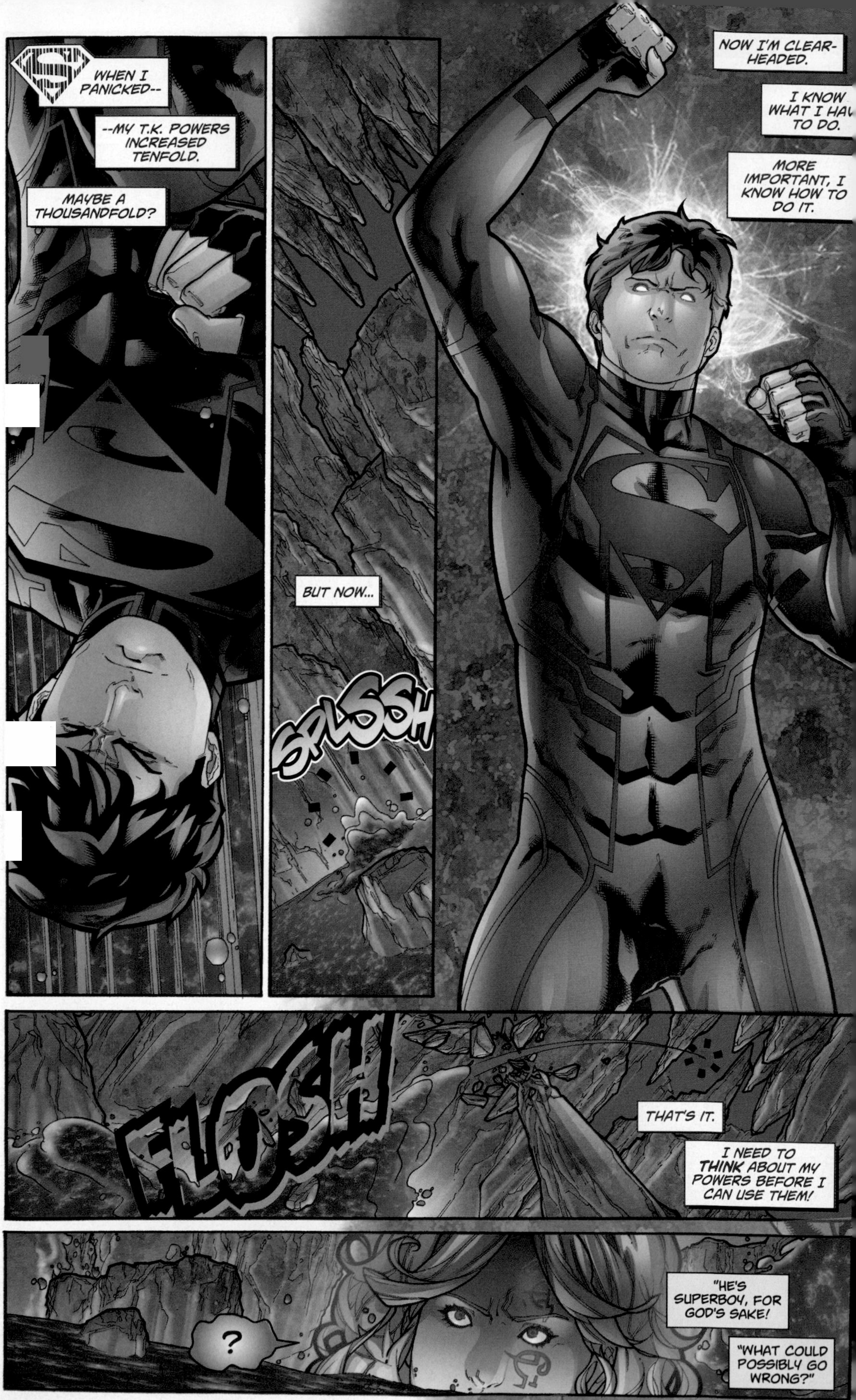
WHEN I PANICKED--
--MY T.K. POWERS INCREASED TENFOLD.
MAYBE A THOUSANDFOLD?
BUT NOW...
SPLSSH
NOW I'M CLEAR-HEADED.
I KNOW WHAT I HAV TO DO.
MORE IMPORTANT, I KNOW HOW TO DO IT.
FLOOSH
THAT'S IT.
I NEED TO THINK ABOUT MY POWERS BEFORE I CAN USE THEM!
?
"HE'S SUPERBOY, FOR GOD'S SAKE!
"WHAT COULD POSSIBLY GO WRONG?"

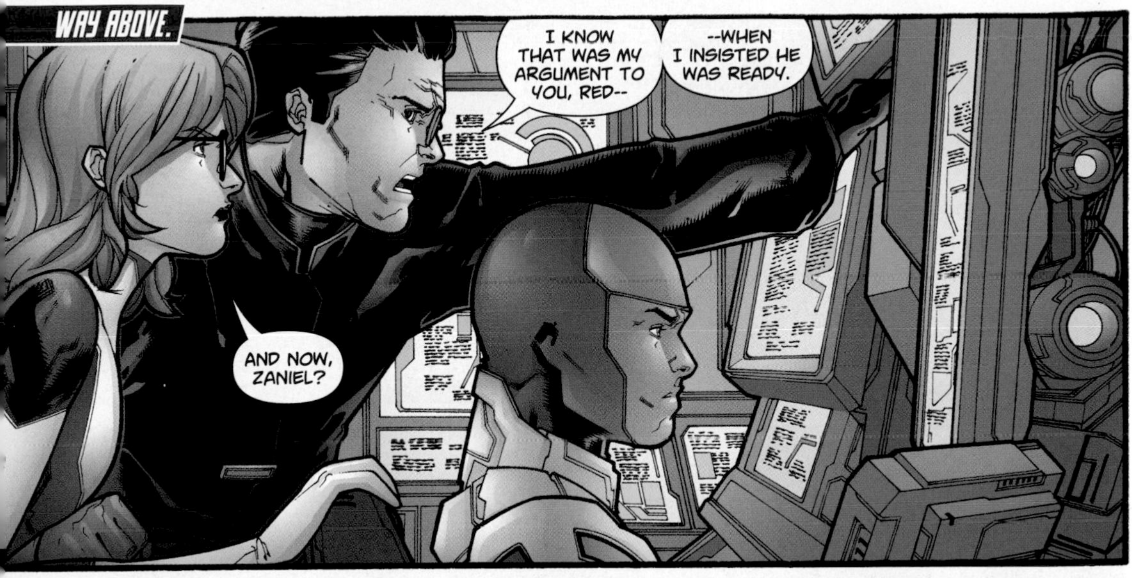
WAY ABOVE.
I KNOW THAT WAS MY ARGUMENT TO YOU, RED--
--WHEN I INSISTED HE WAS READY.
AND NOW, ZANIEL?

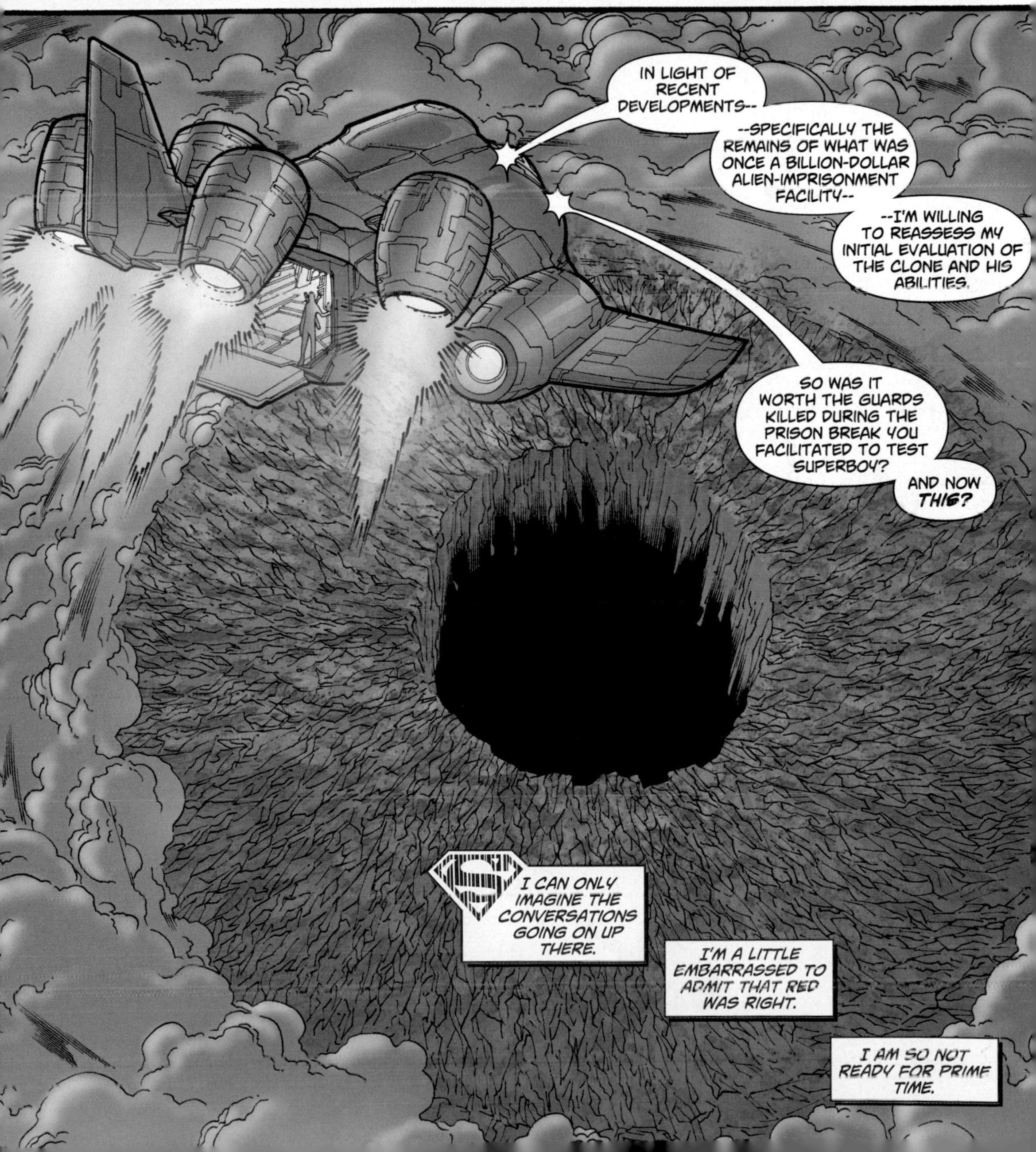
IN LIGHT OF RECENT DEVELOPMENTS--
--SPECIFICALLY THE REMAINS OF WHAT WAS ONCE A BILLION-DOLLAR ALIEN-IMPRISONMENT FACILITY--
--I'M WILLING TO REASSESS MY INITIAL EVALUATION OF THE CLONE AND HIS ABILITIES.
SO WAS IT WORTH THE GUARDS KILLED DURING THE PRISON BREAK YOU FACILITATED TO TEST SUPERBOY?
AND NOW THIS?
I CAN ONLY IMAGINE THE CONVERSATIONS GOING ON UP THERE.
I'M A LITTLE EMBARRASSED TO ADMIT THAT RED WAS RIGHT.
I AM SO NOT READY FOR PRIME TIME.

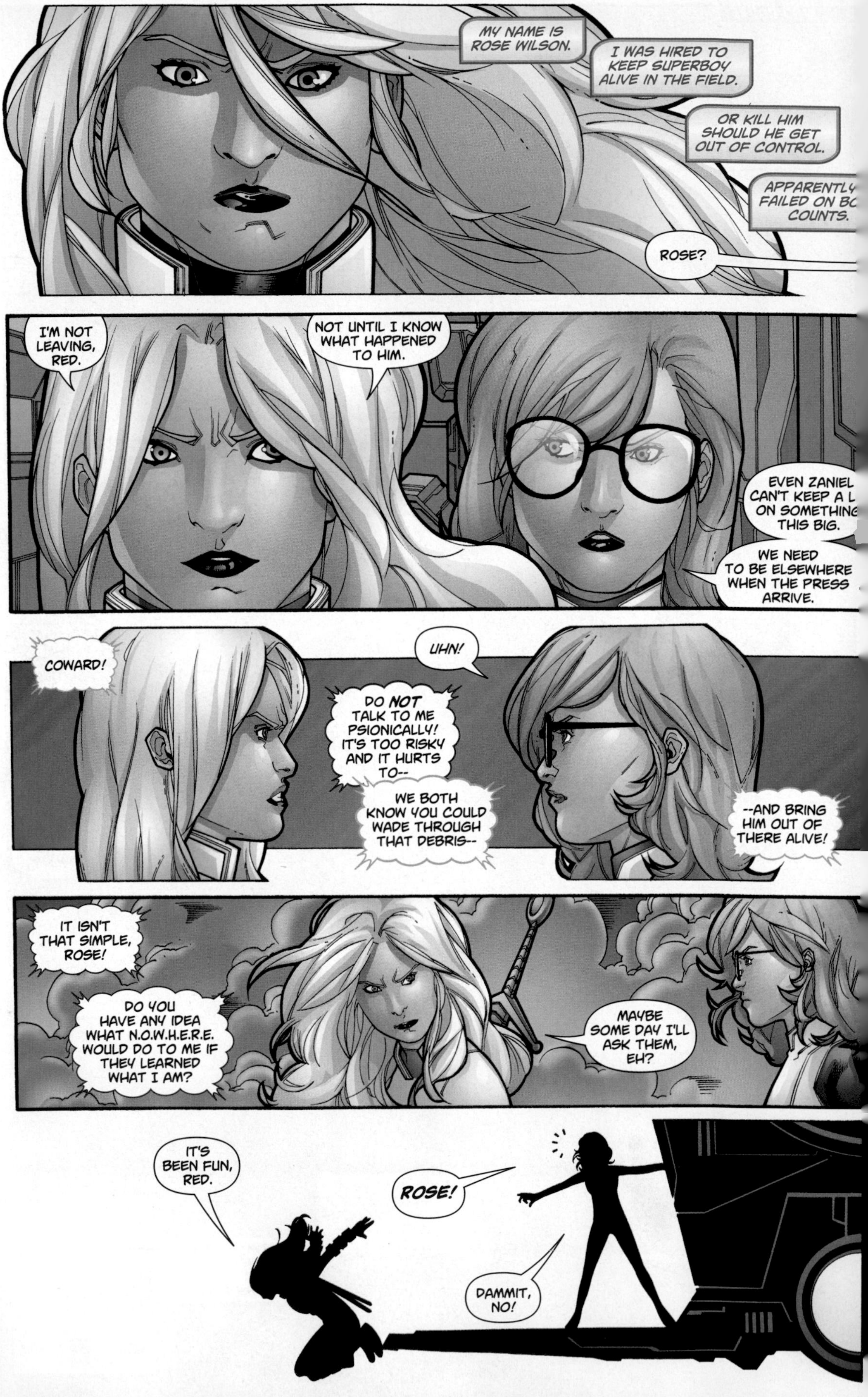

MY NAME IS ROSE WILSON.
I WAS HIRED TO KEEP SUPERBOY ALIVE IN THE FIELD.
OR KILL HIM SHOULD HE GET OUT OF CONTROL.
APPARENTLY FAILED ON BO COUNTS.
ROSE?
I'M NOT LEAVING, RED.
NOT UNTIL I KNOW WHAT HAPPENED TO HIM.
EVEN ZANIEL CAN'T KEEP A L ON SOMETHING THIS BIG.
WE NEED TO BE ELSEWHERE WHEN THE PRESS ARRIVE.
COWARD!
UHN!
DO **NOT** TALK TO ME PSIONICALLY! IT'S TOO RISKY AND IT HURTS TO--
WE BOTH KNOW YOU COULD WADE THROUGH THAT DEBRIS--
--AND BRING HIM OUT OF THERE ALIVE!
IT ISN'T THAT SIMPLE, ROSE!
DO YOU HAVE ANY IDEA WHAT N.O.W.H.E.R.E. WOULD DO TO ME IF THEY LEARNED WHAT I AM?
MAYBE SOME DAY I'LL ASK THEM, EH?
IT'S BEEN FUN, RED.
ROSE!
DAMMIT, NO!

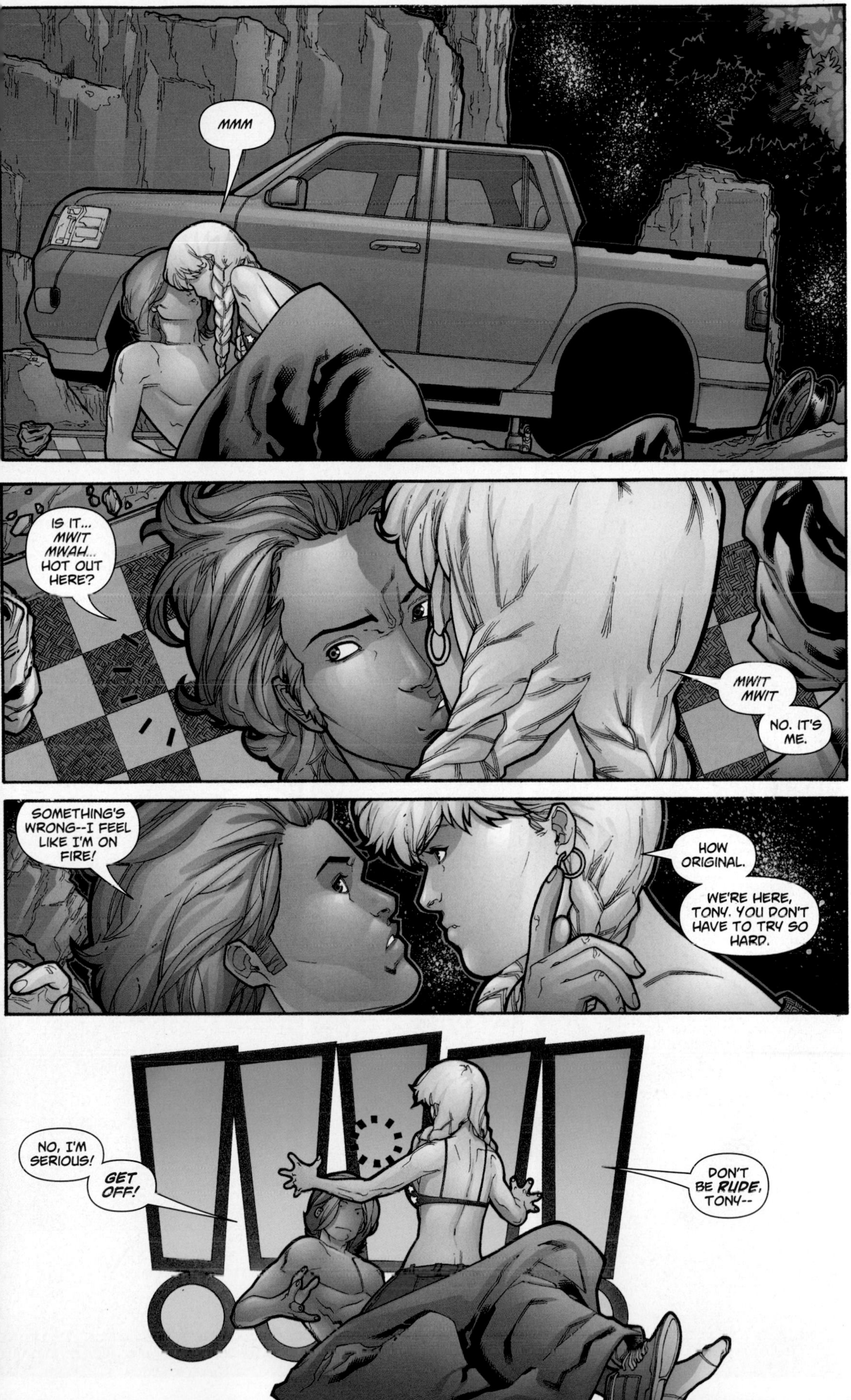
MMM
IS IT... MWIT MWAH... HOT OUT HERE?
MWIT MWIT
NO. IT'S ME.
SOMETHING'S WRONG--I FEEL LIKE I'M ON FIRE!
HOW ORIGINAL.
WE'RE HERE, TONY. YOU DON'T HAVE TO TRY SO HARD.
NO, I'M SERIOUS! GET OFF!
DON'T BE RUDE, TONY--

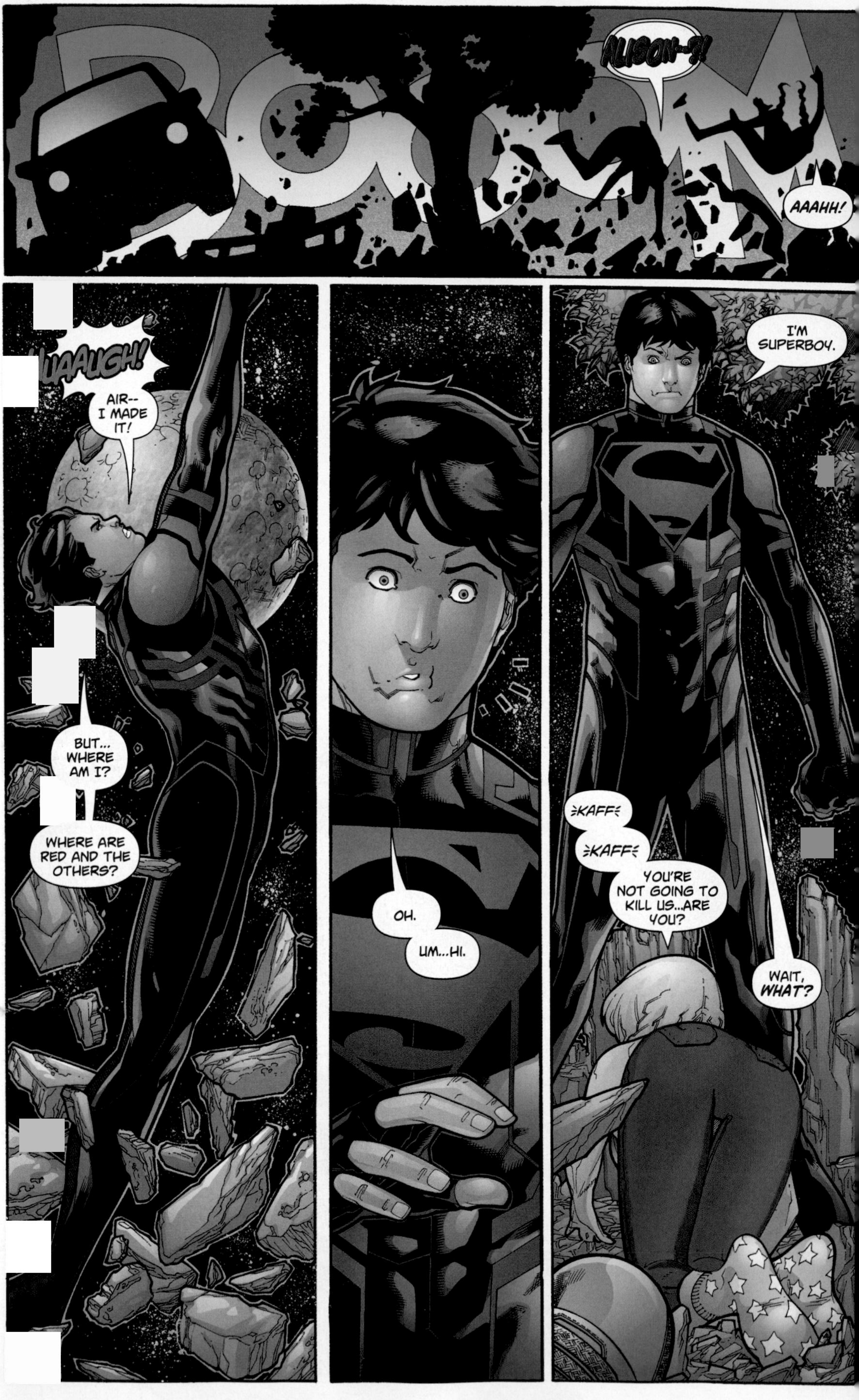
BOOM
ALISON--?!
AAAHH!
UAAUGH!
AIR-- I MADE IT!
BUT... WHERE AM I?
WHERE ARE RED AND THE OTHERS?
OH.
UM...HI.
I'M SUPERBOY.
KAFF
KAFF
YOU'RE NOT GOING TO KILL US...ARE YOU?
WAIT, *WHAT?*

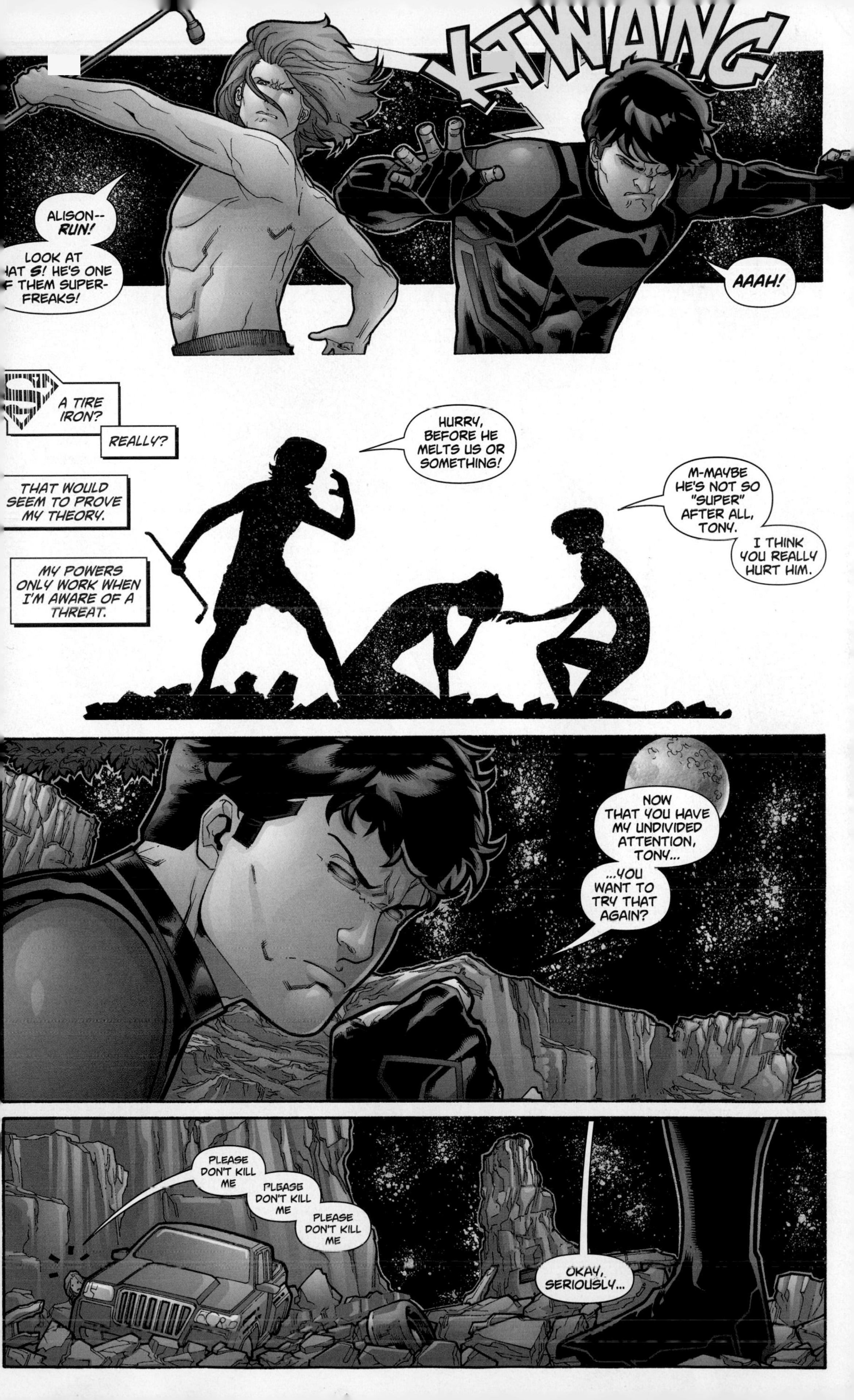
KTWANG
ALISON-- RUN!
LOOK AT
HAT S! HE'S ONE
F THEM SUPER-FREAKS!
AAAH!
A TIRE IRON?
REALLY?
HURRY, BEFORE HE MELTS US OR SOMETHING!
THAT WOULD SEEM TO PROVE MY THEORY.
M-MAYBE HE'S NOT SO "SUPER" AFTER ALL, TONY.
I THINK YOU REALLY HURT HIM.
MY POWERS ONLY WORK WHEN I'M AWARE OF A THREAT.
NOW THAT YOU HAVE MY UNDIVIDED ATTENTION, TONY...
...YOU WANT TO TRY THAT AGAIN?
PLEASE DON'T KILL ME
PLEASE DON'T KILL ME
PLEASE DON'T KILL ME
OKAY, SERIOUSLY...

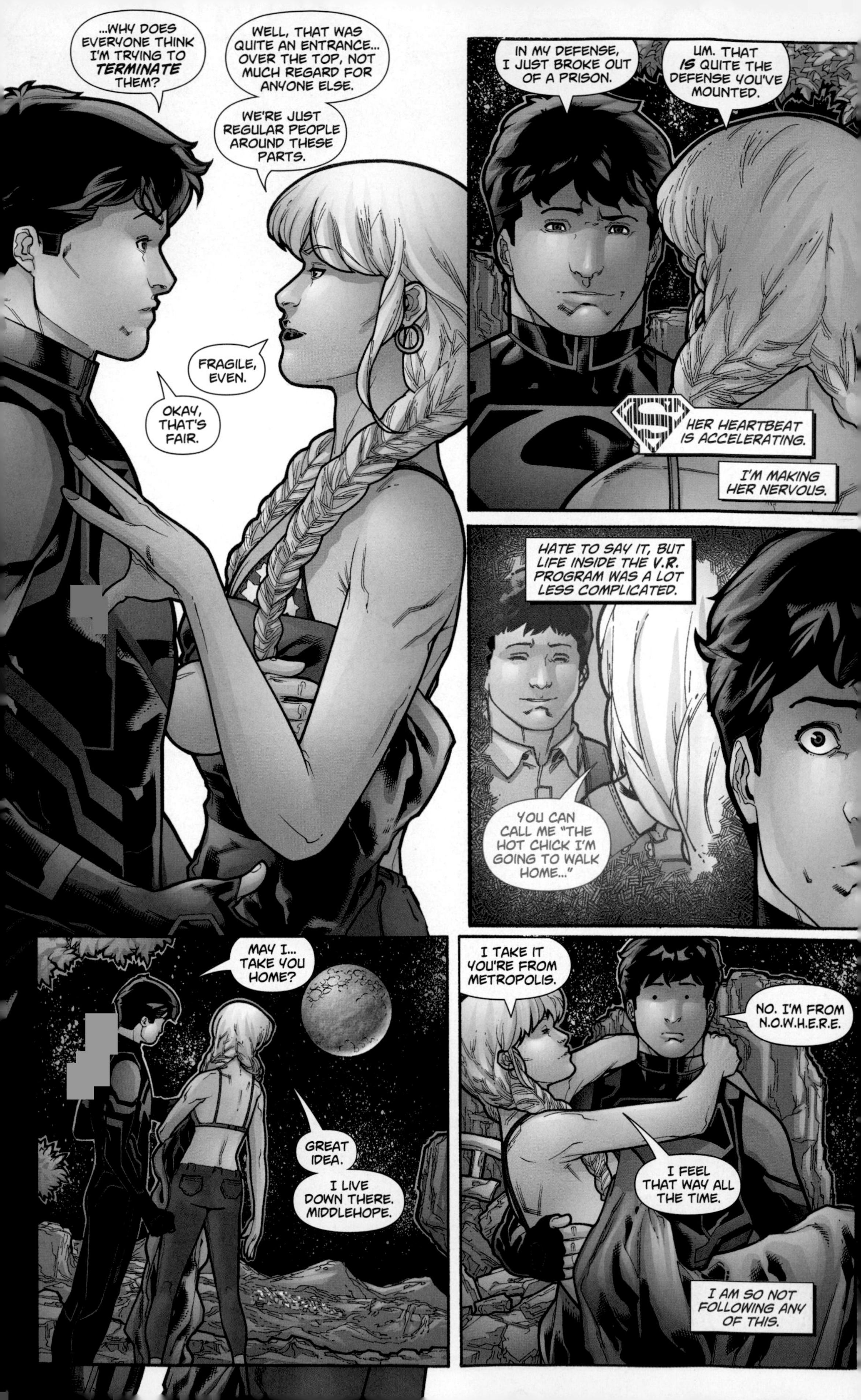
...WHY DOES EVERYONE THINK I'M TRYING TO *TERMINATE* THEM?
WELL, THAT WAS QUITE AN ENTRANCE... OVER THE TOP, NOT MUCH REGARD FOR ANYONE ELSE.
WE'RE JUST REGULAR PEOPLE AROUND THESE PARTS.
FRAGILE, EVEN.
OKAY, THAT'S FAIR.
IN MY DEFENSE, I JUST BROKE OUT OF A PRISON.
UM. THAT *IS* QUITE THE DEFENSE YOU'VE MOUNTED.
HER HEARTBEAT IS ACCELERATING.
I'M MAKING HER NERVOUS.
HATE TO SAY IT, BUT LIFE INSIDE THE V.R. PROGRAM WAS A LOT LESS COMPLICATED.
YOU CAN CALL ME "THE HOT CHICK I'M GOING TO WALK HOME..."
MAY I... TAKE YOU HOME?
GREAT IDEA.
I LIVE DOWN THERE. MIDDLEHOPE.
I TAKE IT YOU'RE FROM METROPOLIS.
NO. I'M FROM N.O.W.H.E.R.E.
I FEEL THAT WAY ALL THE TIME.
I AM SO NOT FOLLOWING ANY OF THIS.

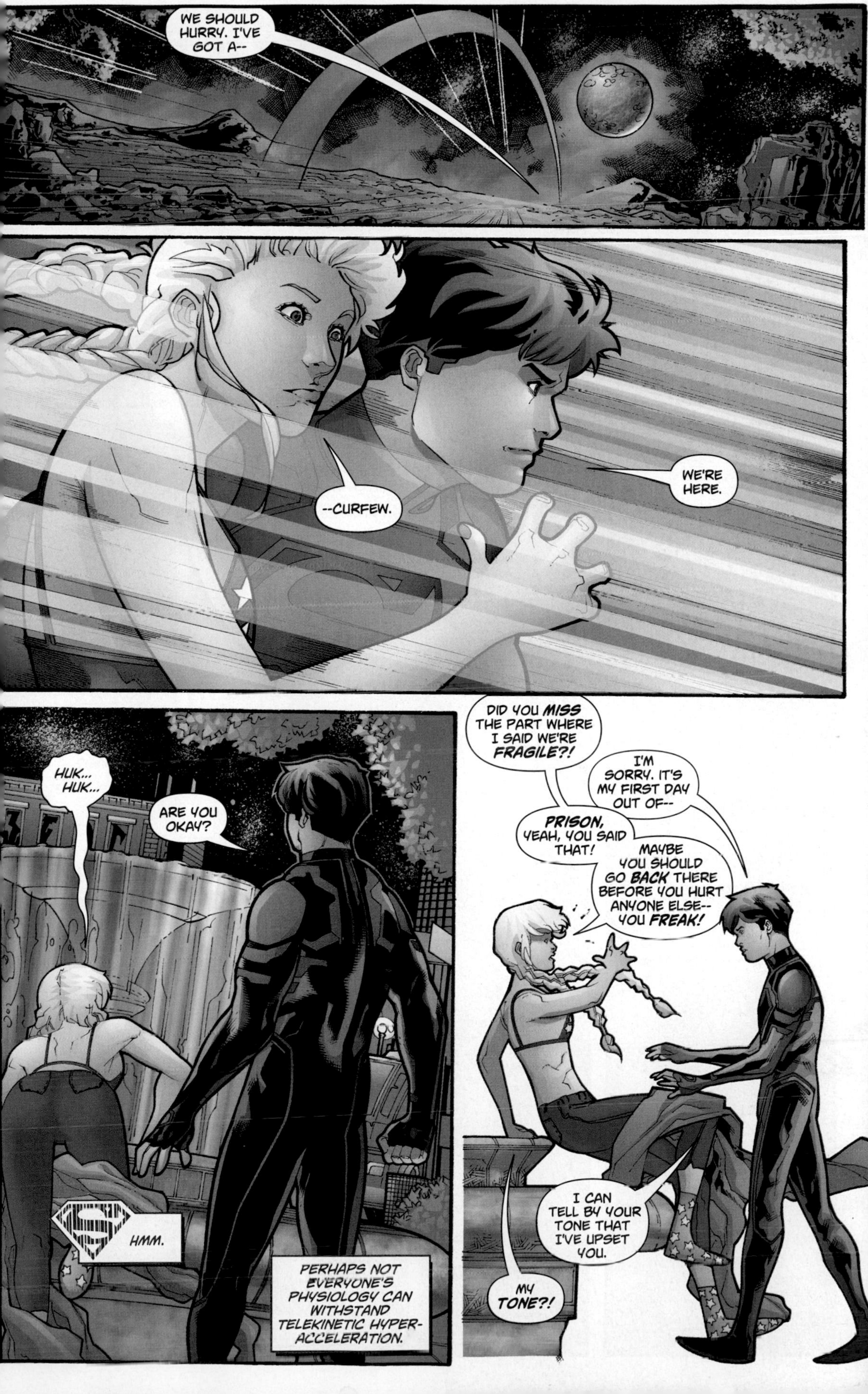
WE SHOULD HURRY. I'VE GOT A--
--CURFEW.
WE'RE HERE.
HUK... HUK...
ARE YOU OKAY?
HMM.
PERHAPS NOT EVERYONE'S PHYSIOLOGY CAN WITHSTAND TELEKINETIC HYPER-ACCELERATION.
DID YOU MISS THE PART WHERE I SAID WE'RE FRAGILE?!
I'M SORRY. IT'S MY FIRST DAY OUT OF--
PRISON, YEAH, YOU SAID THAT!
MAYBE YOU SHOULD GO BACK THERE BEFORE YOU HURT ANYONE ELSE-- YOU FREAK!
I CAN TELL BY YOUR TONE THAT I'VE UPSET YOU.
MY TONE?!

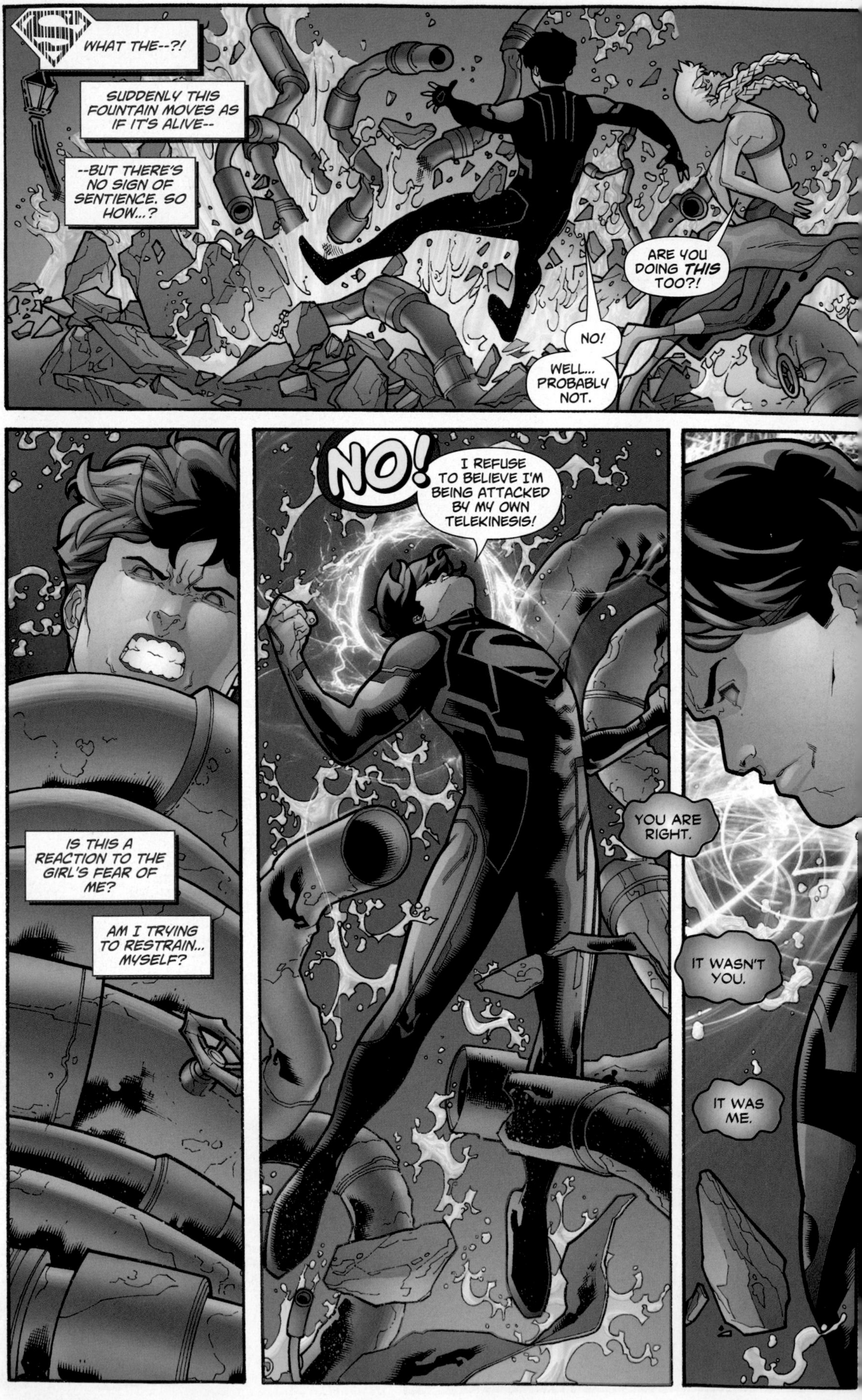
WHAT THE--?!
SUDDENLY THIS FOUNTAIN MOVES AS IF IT'S ALIVE--
--BUT THERE'S NO SIGN OF SENTIENCE. SO HOW...?
ARE YOU DOING THIS TOO?!
NO!
WELL... PROBABLY NOT.
IS THIS A REACTION TO THE GIRL'S FEAR OF ME?
AM I TRYING TO RESTRAIN... MYSELF?
NO!
I REFUSE TO BELIEVE I'M BEING ATTACKED BY MY OWN TELEKINESIS!
YOU ARE RIGHT.
IT WASN'T YOU.
IT WAS ME.

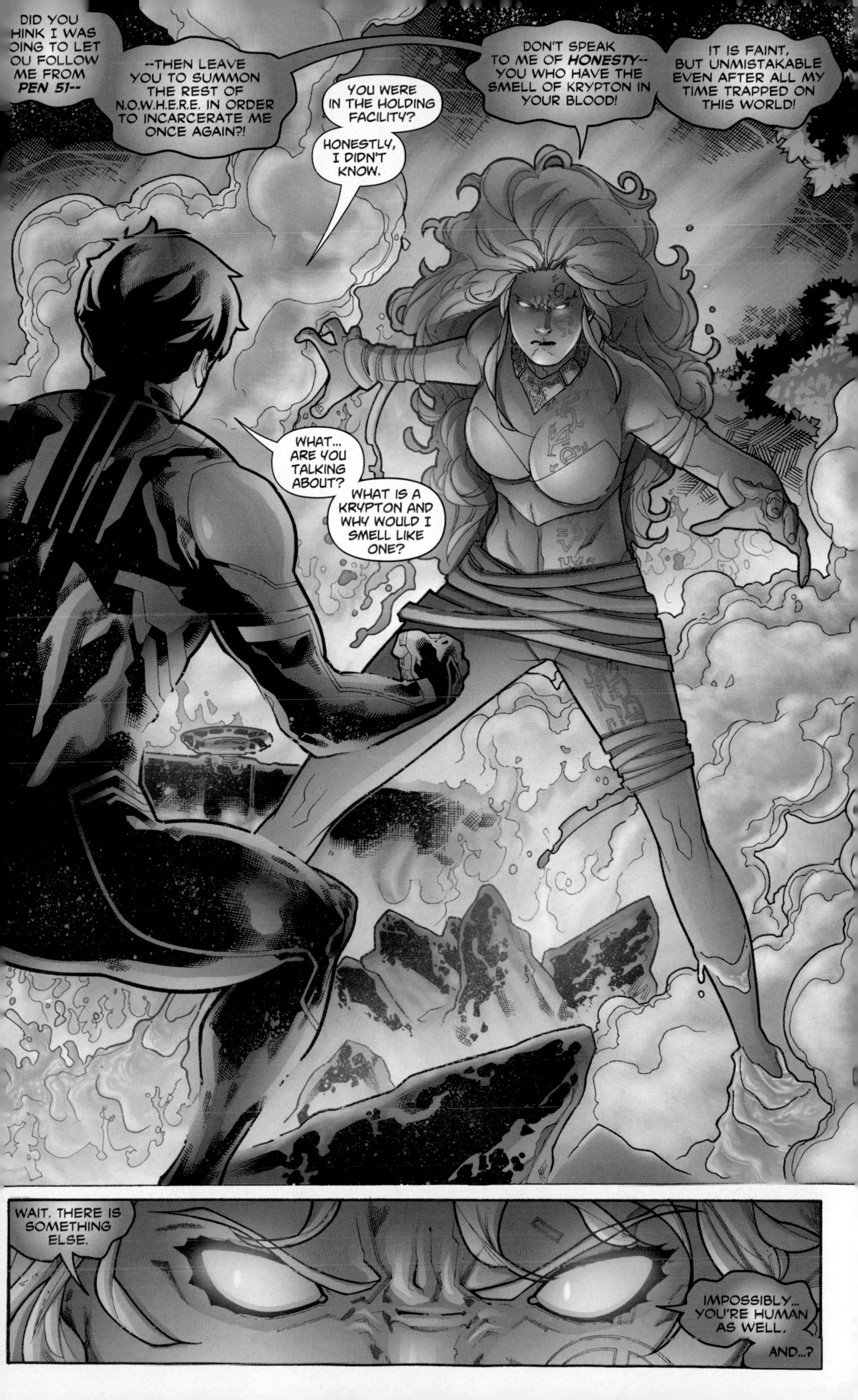

DID YOU HINK I WAS OING TO LET OU FOLLOW ME FROM PEN 51--
--THEN LEAVE YOU TO SUMMON THE REST OF N.O.W.H.E.R.E. IN ORDER TO INCARCERATE ME ONCE AGAIN?!
YOU WERE IN THE HOLDING FACILITY?
HONESTLY, I DIDN'T KNOW.
DON'T SPEAK TO ME OF HONESTY-- YOU WHO HAVE THE SMELL OF KRYPTON IN YOUR BLOOD!
IT IS FAINT, BUT UNMISTAKABLE EVEN AFTER ALL MY TIME TRAPPED ON THIS WORLD!
WHAT... ARE YOU TALKING ABOUT?
WHAT IS A KRYPTON AND WHY WOULD I SMELL LIKE ONE?
WAIT. THERE IS SOMETHING ELSE.
IMPOSSIBLY... YOU'RE HUMAN AS WELL.
AND...?

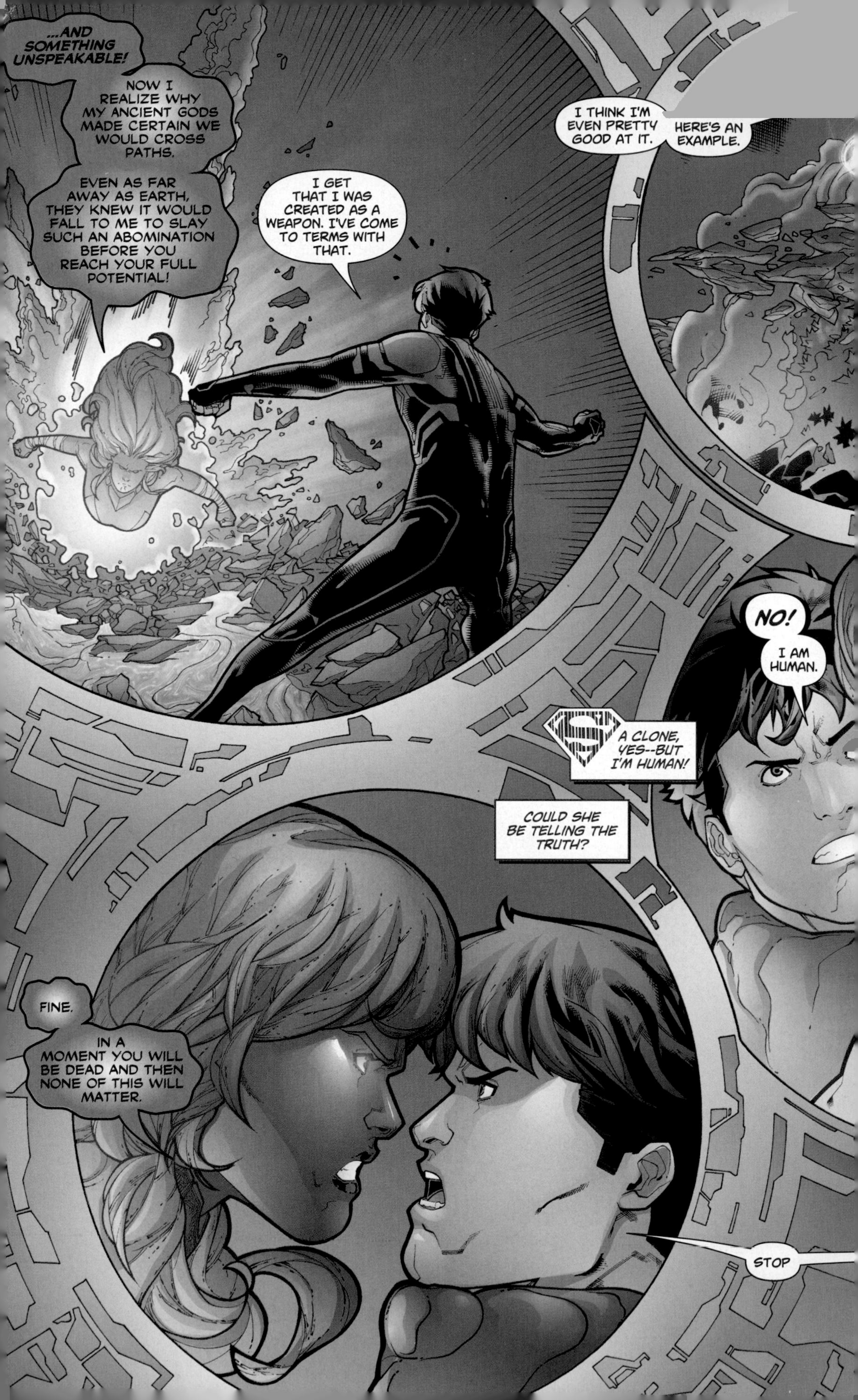
...AND SOMETHING UNSPEAKABLE!
NOW I REALIZE WHY MY ANCIENT GODS MADE CERTAIN WE WOULD CROSS PATHS.
EVEN AS FAR AWAY AS EARTH, THEY KNEW IT WOULD FALL TO ME TO SLAY SUCH AN ABOMINATION BEFORE YOU REACH YOUR FULL POTENTIAL!
I GET THAT I WAS CREATED AS A WEAPON. I'VE COME TO TERMS WITH THAT.
I THINK I'M EVEN PRETTY GOOD AT IT.
HERE'S AN EXAMPLE.
NO!
I AM HUMAN.
A CLONE, YES--BUT I'M HUMAN!
COULD SHE BE TELLING THE TRUTH?
FINE.
IN A MOMENT YOU WILL BE DEAD AND THEN NONE OF THIS WILL MATTER.
STOP

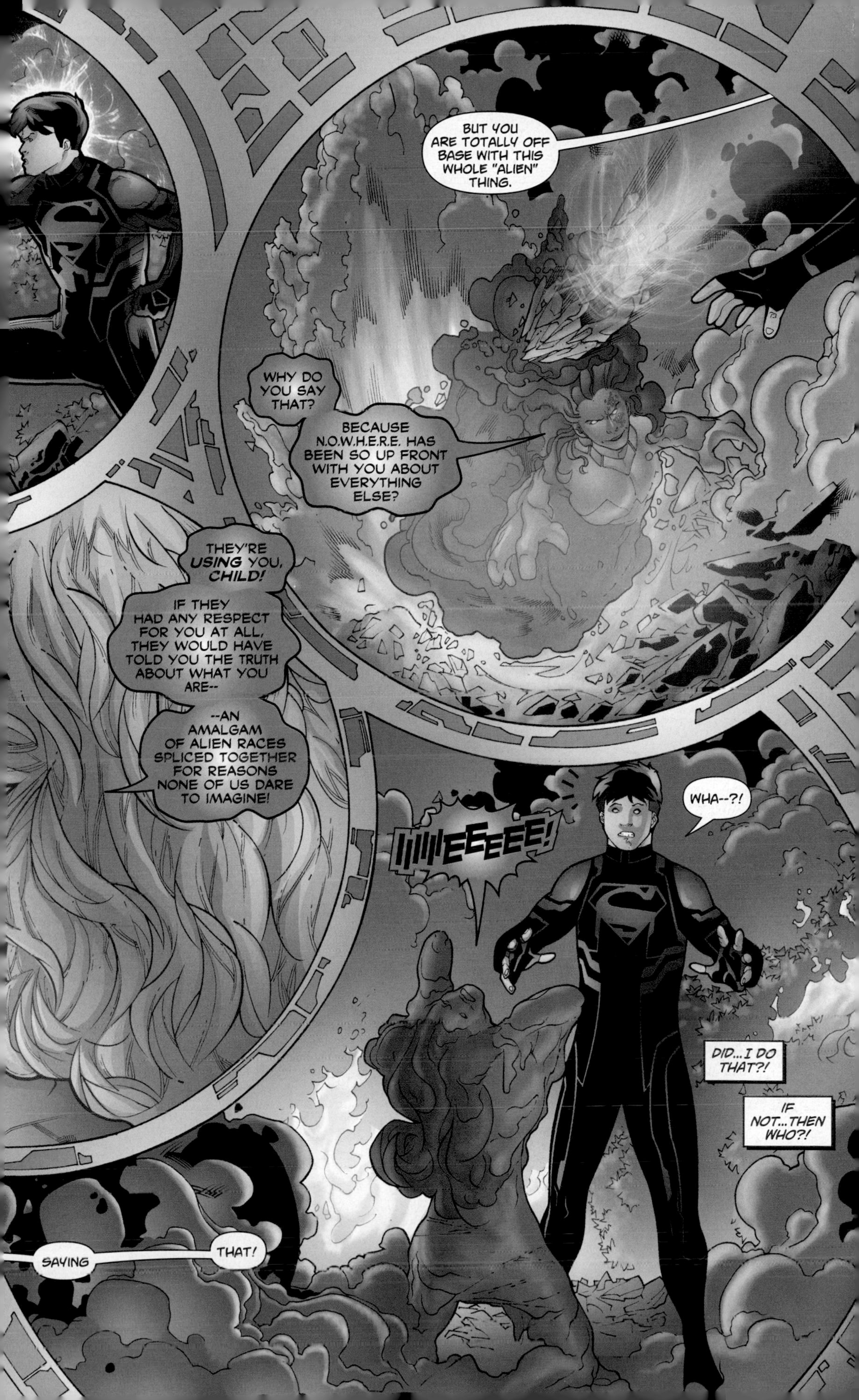
BUT YOU ARE TOTALLY OFF BASE WITH THIS WHOLE "ALIEN" THING.
WHY DO YOU SAY THAT?
BECAUSE N.O.W.H.E.R.E. HAS BEEN SO UP FRONT WITH YOU ABOUT EVERYTHING ELSE?
THEY'RE USING YOU, CHILD!
IF THEY HAD ANY RESPECT FOR YOU AT ALL, THEY WOULD HAVE TOLD YOU THE TRUTH ABOUT WHAT YOU ARE--
--AN AMALGAM OF ALIEN RACES SPLICED TOGETHER FOR REASONS NONE OF US DARE TO IMAGINE!
IIIIIIEEEEEE!
WHA--?!
DID...I DO THAT?!
IF NOT...THEN WHO?!
SAYING
THAT!

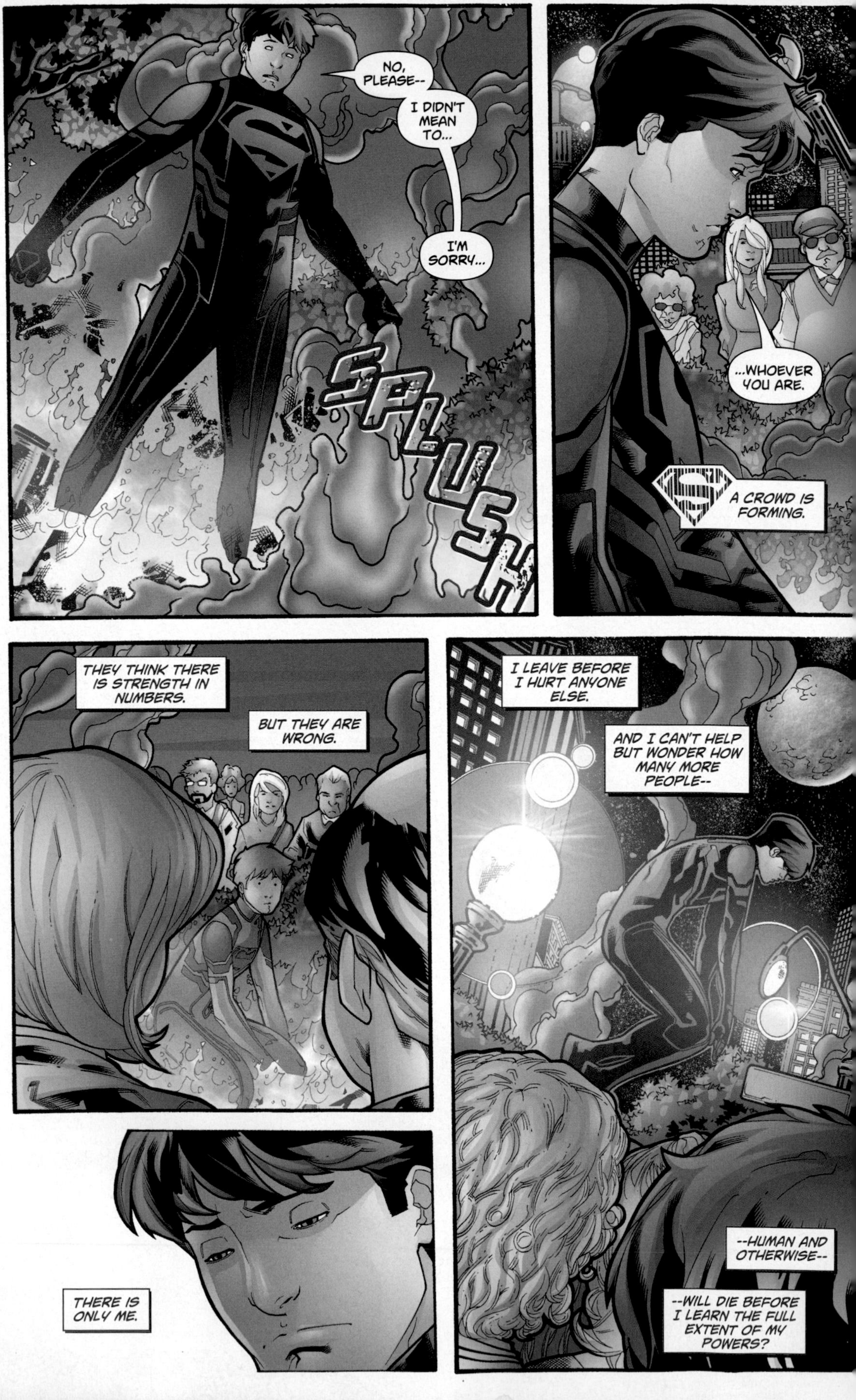
NO, PLEASE--
I DIDN'T MEAN TO...
I'M SORRY...
SPLUSH
...WHOEVER YOU ARE.
A CROWD IS FORMING.
THEY THINK THERE IS STRENGTH IN NUMBERS.
BUT THEY ARE WRONG.
THERE IS ONLY ME.
I LEAVE BEFORE I HURT ANYONE ELSE.
AND I CAN'T HELP BUT WONDER HOW MANY MORE PEOPLE--
--HUMAN AND OTHERWISE--
--WILL DIE BEFORE I LEARN THE FULL EXTENT OF MY POWERS?

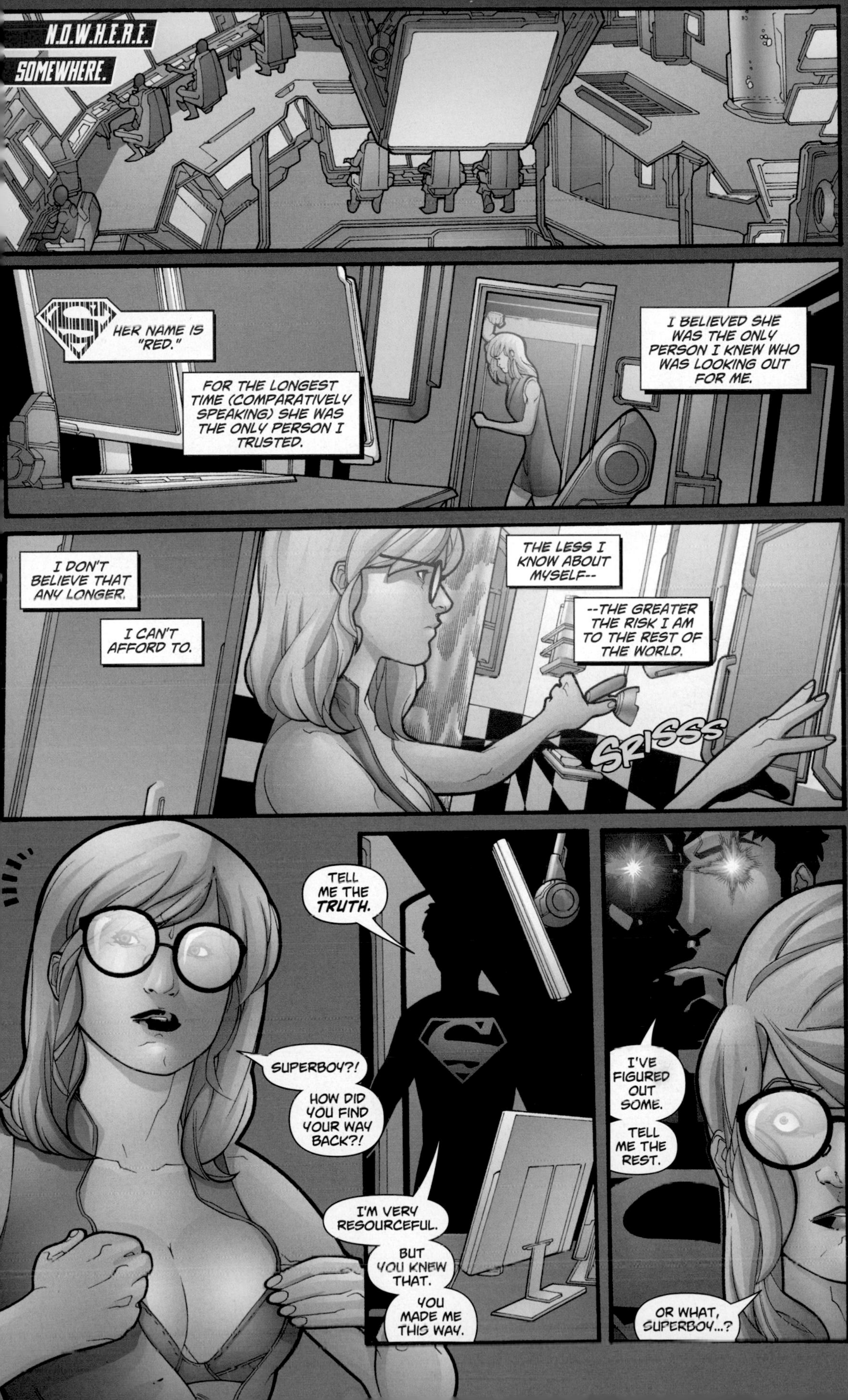
N.O.W.H.E.R.E.
SOMEWHERE.
HER NAME IS "RED."
FOR THE LONGEST TIME (COMPARATIVELY SPEAKING) SHE WAS THE ONLY PERSON I TRUSTED.
I BELIEVED SHE WAS THE ONLY PERSON I KNEW WHO WAS LOOKING OUT FOR ME.
I DON'T BELIEVE THAT ANY LONGER.
I CAN'T AFFORD TO.
THE LESS I KNOW ABOUT MYSELF--
--THE GREATER THE RISK I AM TO THE REST OF THE WORLD.
SRISSS
TELL ME THE TRUTH.
SUPERBOY?!
HOW DID YOU FIND YOUR WAY BACK?!
I'M VERY RESOURCEFUL.
BUT YOU KNEW THAT.
YOU MADE ME THIS WAY.
I'VE FIGURED OUT SOME.
TELL ME THE REST.
OR WHAT, SUPERBOY...?

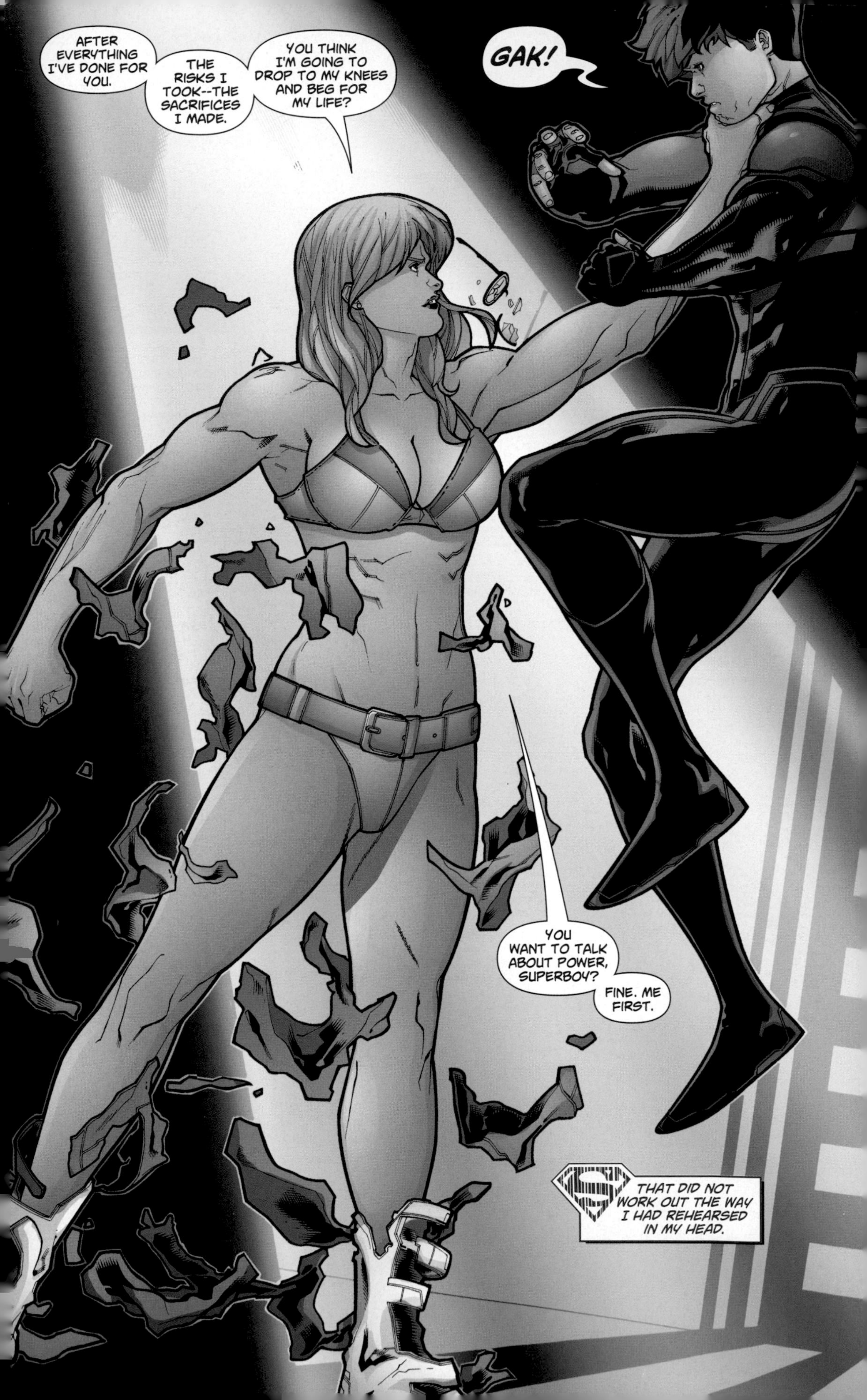

AFTER EVERYTHING I'VE DONE FOR YOU.
THE RISKS I TOOK--THE SACRIFICES I MADE.
YOU THINK I'M GOING TO DROP TO MY KNEES AND BEG FOR MY LIFE?
GAK!
YOU WANT TO TALK ABOUT POWER, SUPERBOY?
FINE. ME FIRST.
THAT DID NOT WORK OUT THE WAY I HAD REHEARSED IN MY HEAD.

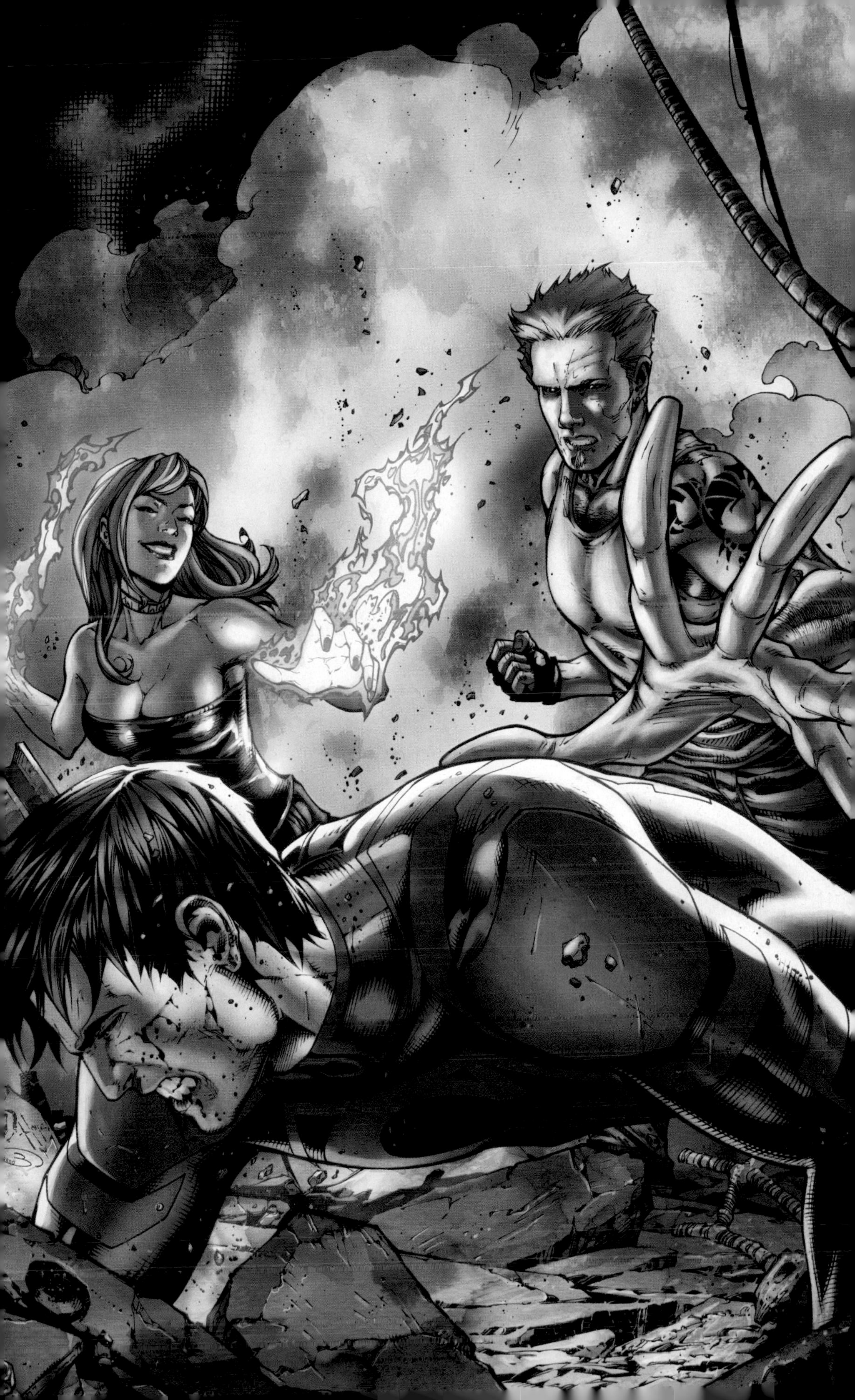

Cover by SHANE DAVIS, SANDRA HOPE & BARBARA CIARDO

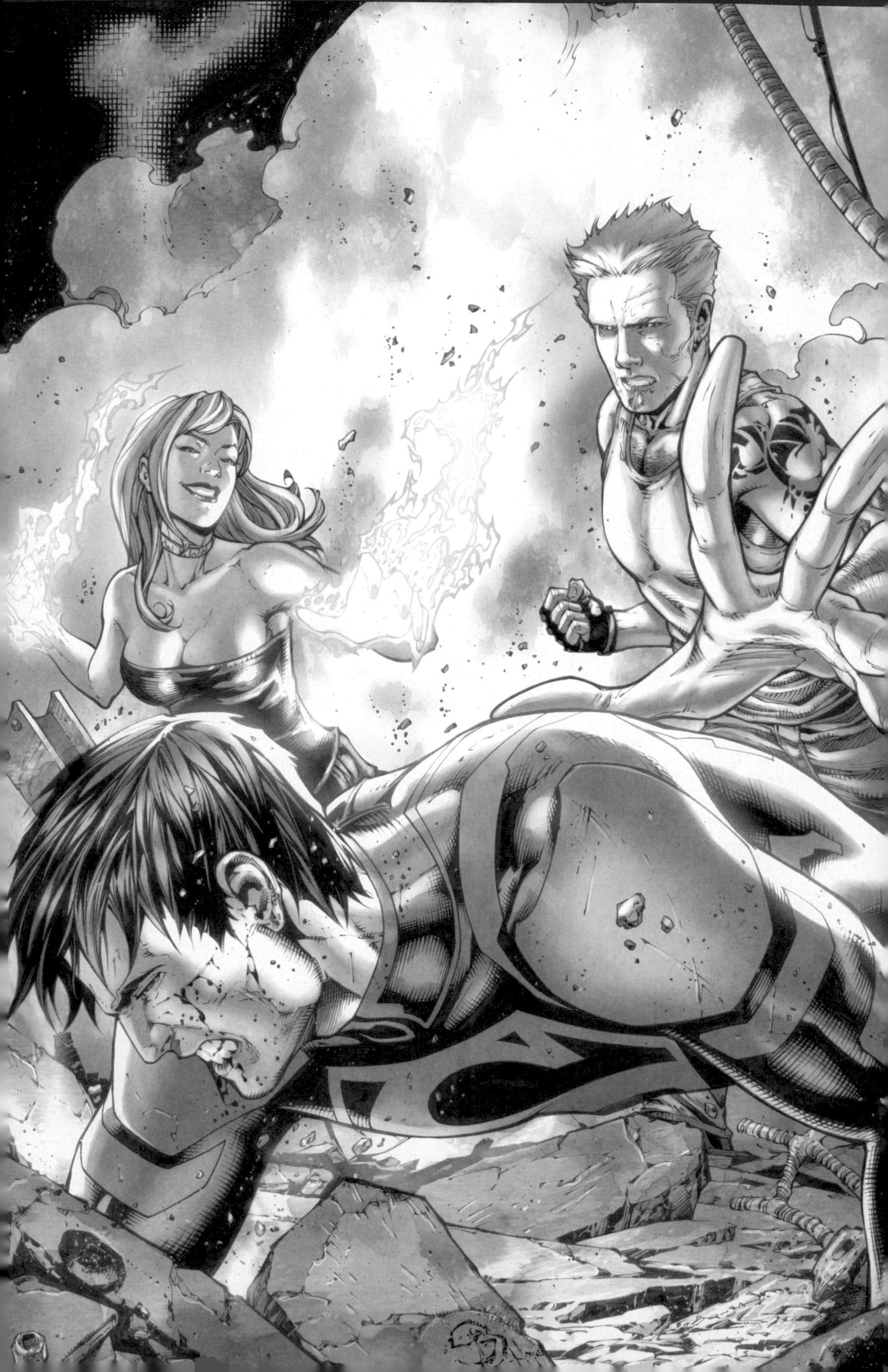

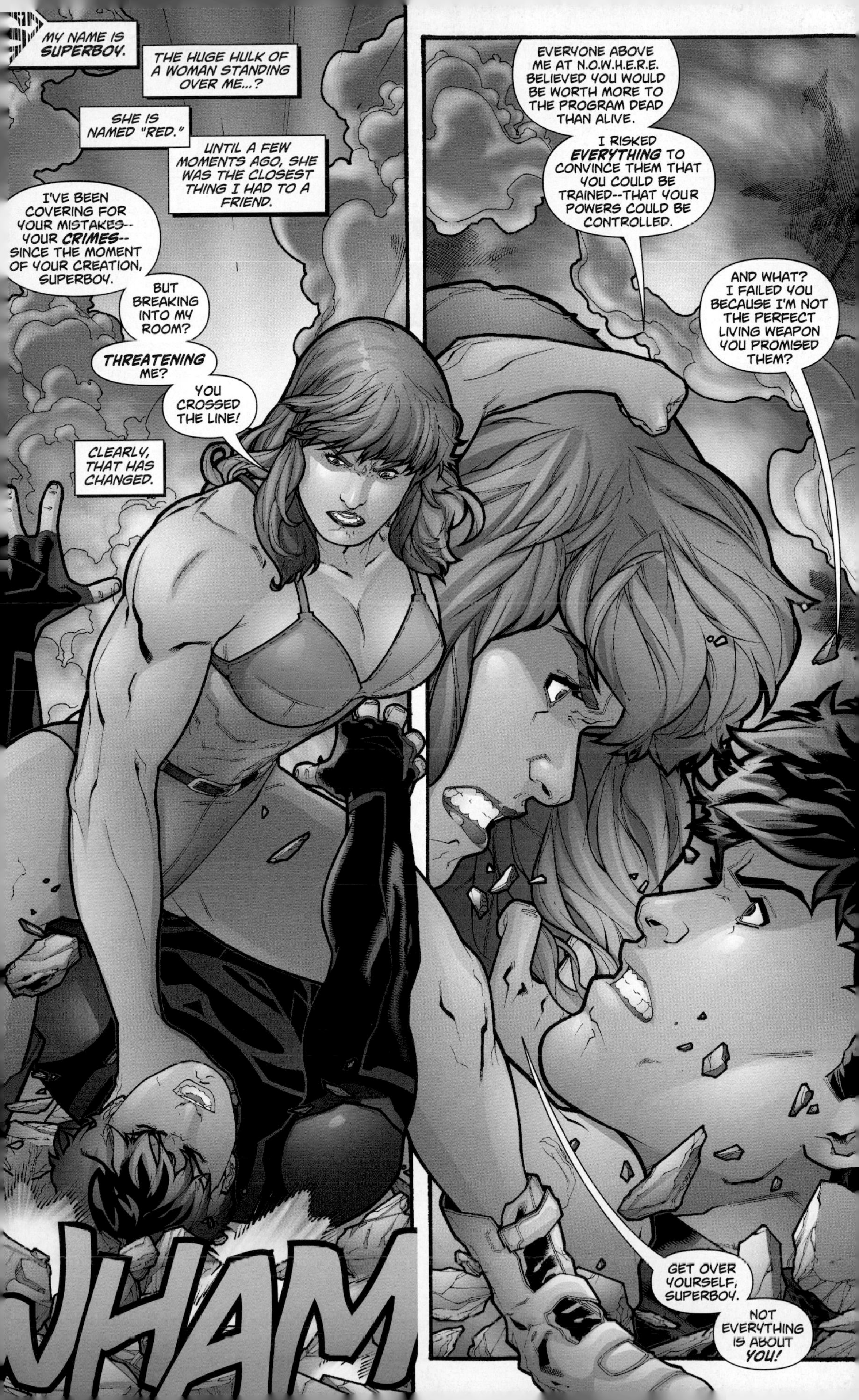
MY NAME IS SUPERBOY.
THE HUGE HULK OF A WOMAN STANDING OVER ME...?
SHE IS NAMED "RED."
UNTIL A FEW MOMENTS AGO, SHE WAS THE CLOSEST THING I HAD TO A FRIEND.
I'VE BEEN COVERING FOR YOUR MISTAKES-- YOUR CRIMES-- SINCE THE MOMENT OF YOUR CREATION, SUPERBOY.
BUT BREAKING INTO MY ROOM?
THREATENING ME?
YOU CROSSED THE LINE!
CLEARLY, THAT HAS CHANGED.
WHAM
EVERYONE ABOVE ME AT N.O.W.H.E.R.E. BELIEVED YOU WOULD BE WORTH MORE TO THE PROGRAM DEAD THAN ALIVE.
I RISKED EVERYTHING TO CONVINCE THEM THAT YOU COULD BE TRAINED--THAT YOUR POWERS COULD BE CONTROLLED.
AND WHAT? I FAILED YOU BECAUSE I'M NOT THE PERFECT LIVING WEAPON YOU PROMISED THEM?
GET OVER YOURSELF, SUPERBOY.
NOT EVERYTHING IS ABOUT YOU!

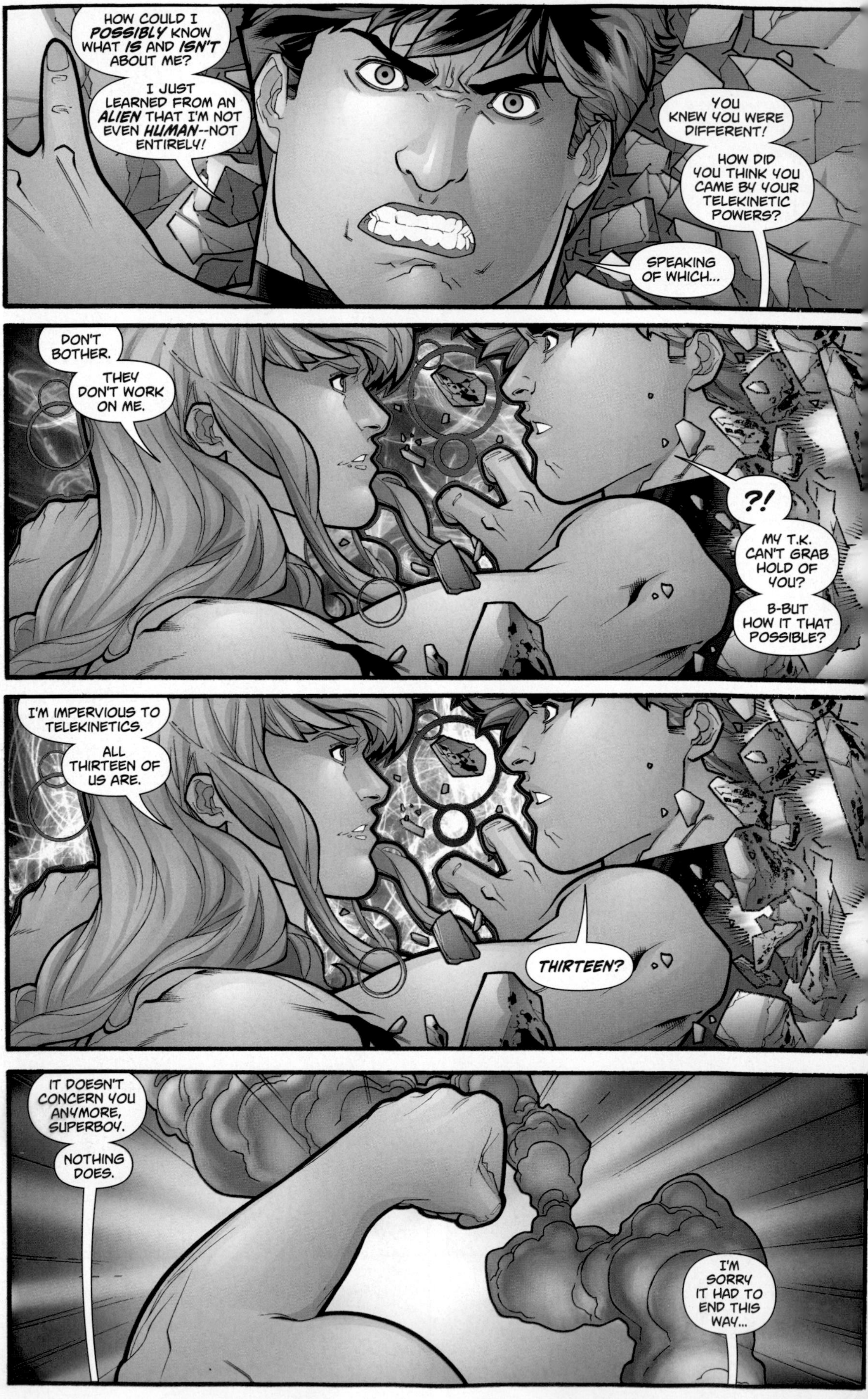
HOW COULD I POSSIBLY KNOW WHAT IS AND ISN'T ABOUT ME?
I JUST LEARNED FROM AN ALIEN THAT I'M NOT EVEN HUMAN--NOT ENTIRELY!
YOU KNEW YOU WERE DIFFERENT!
HOW DID YOU THINK YOU CAME BY YOUR TELEKINETIC POWERS?
SPEAKING OF WHICH...
DON'T BOTHER.
THEY DON'T WORK ON ME.
?!
MY T.K. CAN'T GRAB HOLD OF YOU?
B-BUT HOW IT THAT POSSIBLE?
I'M IMPERVIOUS TO TELEKINETICS.
ALL THIRTEEN OF US ARE.
THIRTEEN?
IT DOESN'T CONCERN YOU ANYMORE, SUPERBOY.
NOTHING DOES.
I'M SORRY IT HAD TO END THIS WAY...

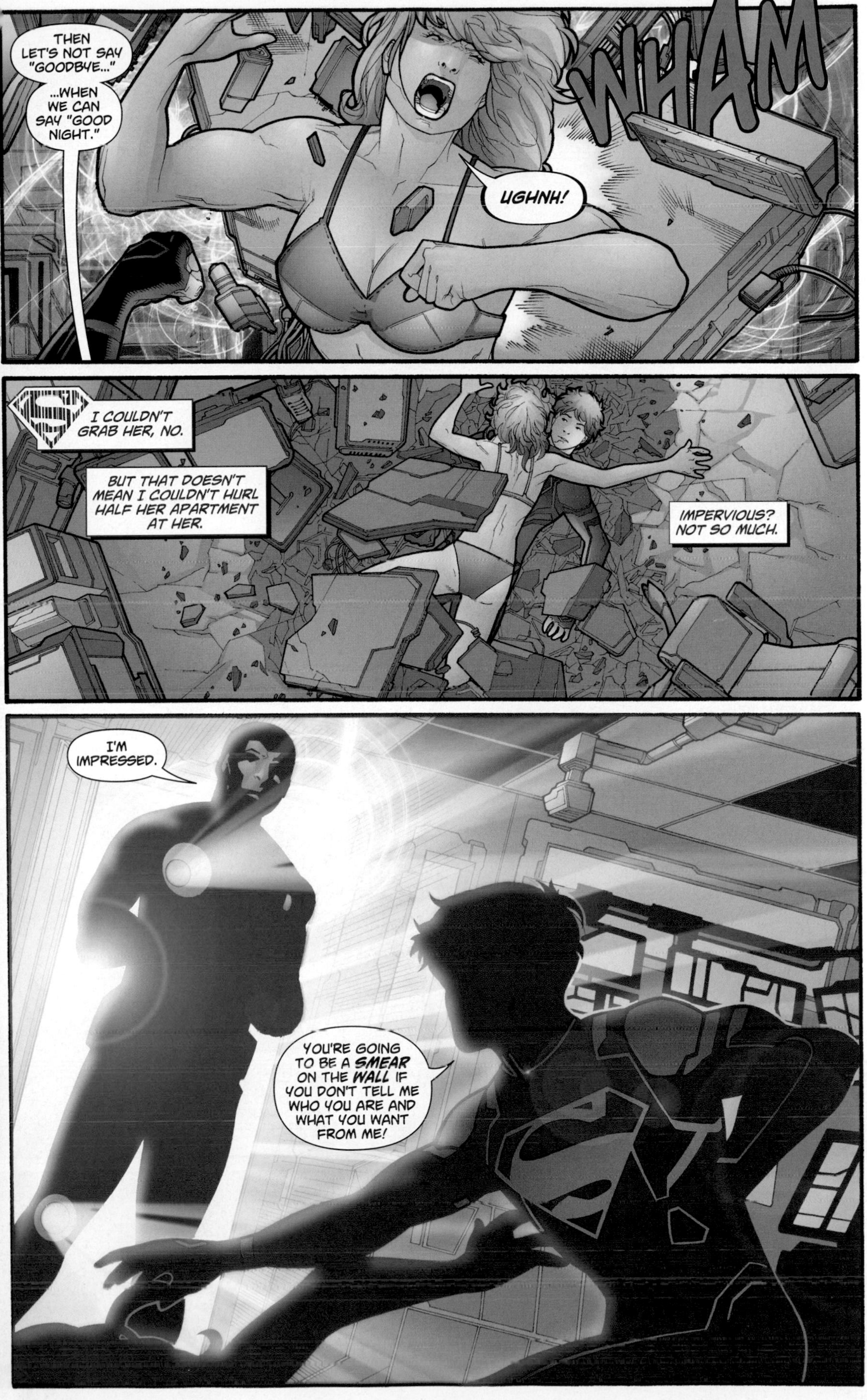
THEN LET'S NOT SAY "GOODBYE..."
...WHEN WE CAN SAY "GOOD NIGHT."
WHAM
UGHNH!
I COULDN'T GRAB HER, NO.
BUT THAT DOESN'T MEAN I COULDN'T HURL HALF HER APARTMENT AT HER.
IMPERVIOUS? NOT SO MUCH.
I'M IMPRESSED.
YOU'RE GOING TO BE A SMEAR ON THE WALL IF YOU DON'T TELL ME WHO YOU ARE AND WHAT YOU WANT FROM ME!

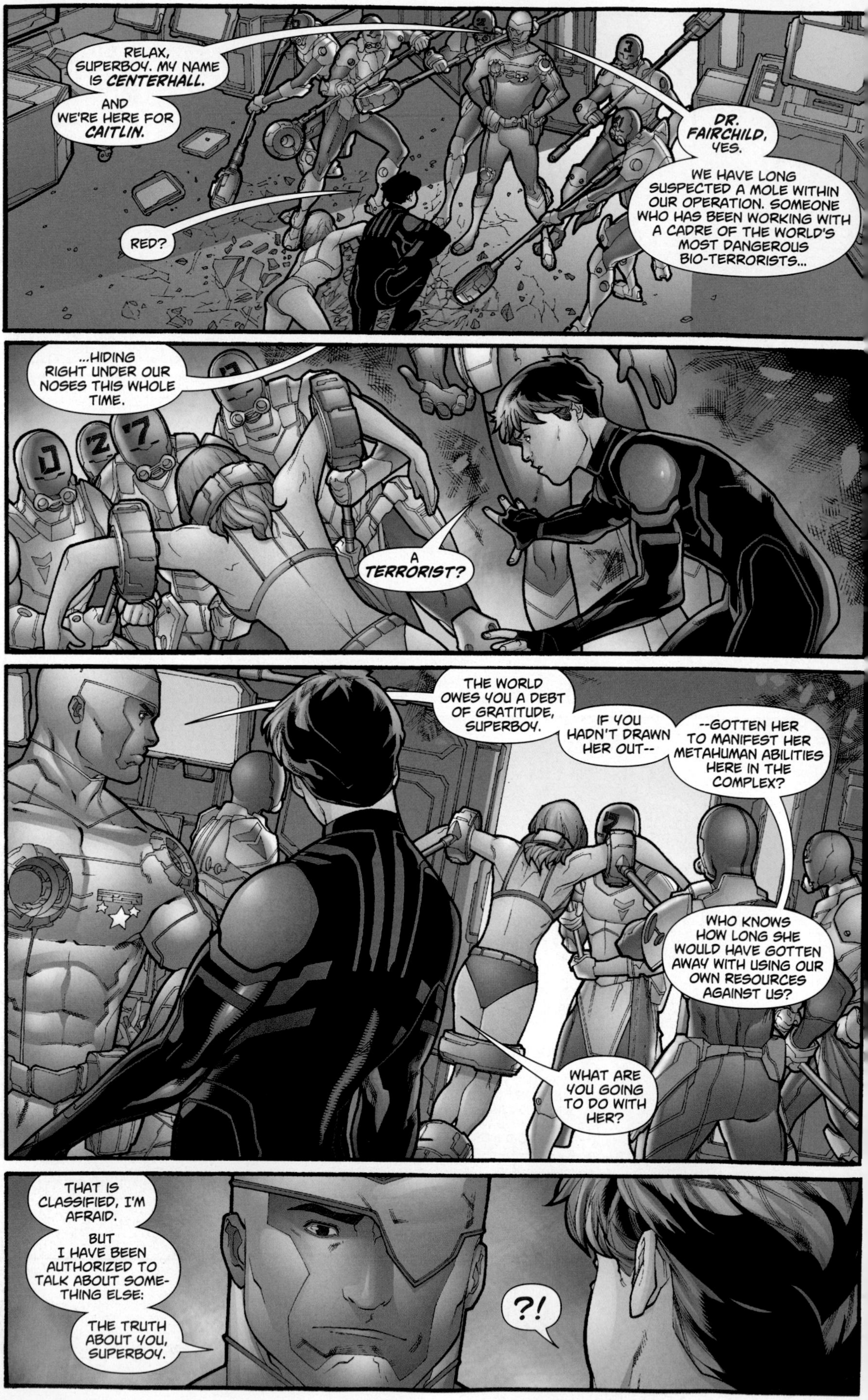
RELAX, SUPERBOY. MY NAME IS CENTERHALL.
AND WE'RE HERE FOR CAITLIN.
DR. FAIRCHILD, YES.
WE HAVE LONG SUSPECTED A MOLE WITHIN OUR OPERATION. SOMEONE WHO HAS BEEN WORKING WITH A CADRE OF THE WORLD'S MOST DANGEROUS BIO-TERRORISTS...
RED?
...HIDING RIGHT UNDER OUR NOSES THIS WHOLE TIME.
A TERRORIST?
THE WORLD OWES YOU A DEBT OF GRATITUDE, SUPERBOY.
IF YOU HADN'T DRAWN HER OUT--
--GOTTEN HER TO MANIFEST HER METAHUMAN ABILITIES HERE IN THE COMPLEX?
WHO KNOWS HOW LONG SHE WOULD HAVE GOTTEN AWAY WITH USING OUR OWN RESOURCES AGAINST US?
WHAT ARE YOU GOING TO DO WITH HER?
THAT IS CLASSIFIED, I'M AFRAID.
BUT I HAVE BEEN AUTHORIZED TO TALK ABOUT SOMETHING ELSE:
THE TRUTH ABOUT YOU, SUPERBOY.
?!

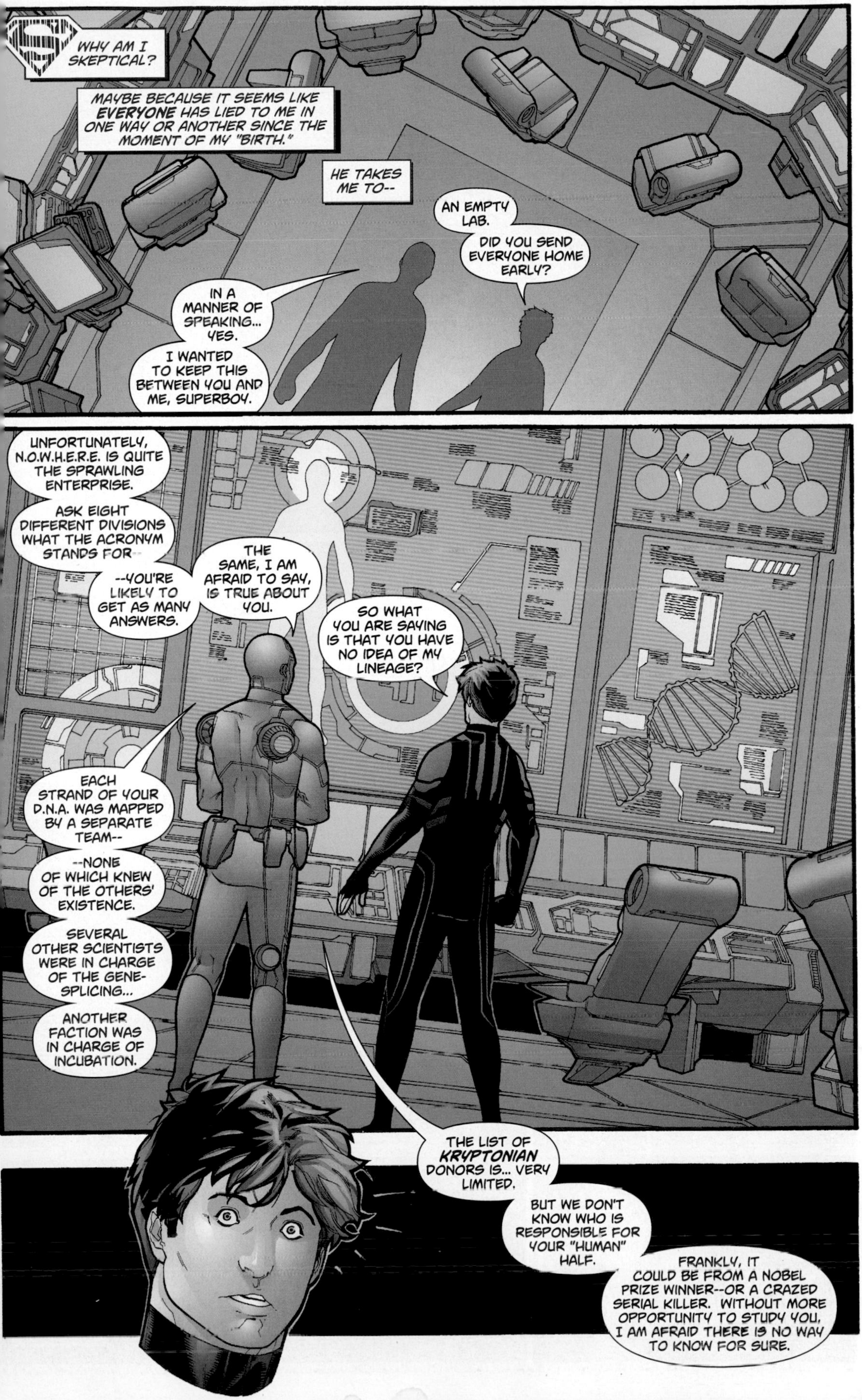
WHY AM I SKEPTICAL?
MAYBE BECAUSE IT SEEMS LIKE EVERYONE HAS LIED TO ME IN ONE WAY OR ANOTHER SINCE THE MOMENT OF MY "BIRTH."
HE TAKES ME TO--
AN EMPTY LAB.
DID YOU SEND EVERYONE HOME EARLY?
IN A MANNER OF SPEAKING... YES.
I WANTED TO KEEP THIS BETWEEN YOU AND ME, SUPERBOY.
UNFORTUNATELY, N.O.W.H.E.R.E. IS QUITE THE SPRAWLING ENTERPRISE.
ASK EIGHT DIFFERENT DIVISIONS WHAT THE ACRONYM STANDS FOR--
--YOU'RE LIKELY TO GET AS MANY ANSWERS.
THE SAME, I AM AFRAID TO SAY, IS TRUE ABOUT YOU.
SO WHAT YOU ARE SAYING IS THAT YOU HAVE NO IDEA OF MY LINEAGE?
EACH STRAND OF YOUR D.N.A. WAS MAPPED BY A SEPARATE TEAM--
--NONE OF WHICH KNEW OF THE OTHERS' EXISTENCE.
SEVERAL OTHER SCIENTISTS WERE IN CHARGE OF THE GENE-SPLICING...
ANOTHER FACTION WAS IN CHARGE OF INCUBATION.
THE LIST OF KRYPTONIAN DONORS IS... VERY LIMITED.
BUT WE DON'T KNOW WHO IS RESPONSIBLE FOR YOUR "HUMAN" HALF.
FRANKLY, IT COULD BE FROM A NOBEL PRIZE WINNER--OR A CRAZED SERIAL KILLER. WITHOUT MORE OPPORTUNITY TO STUDY YOU, I AM AFRAID THERE IS NO WAY TO KNOW FOR SURE.

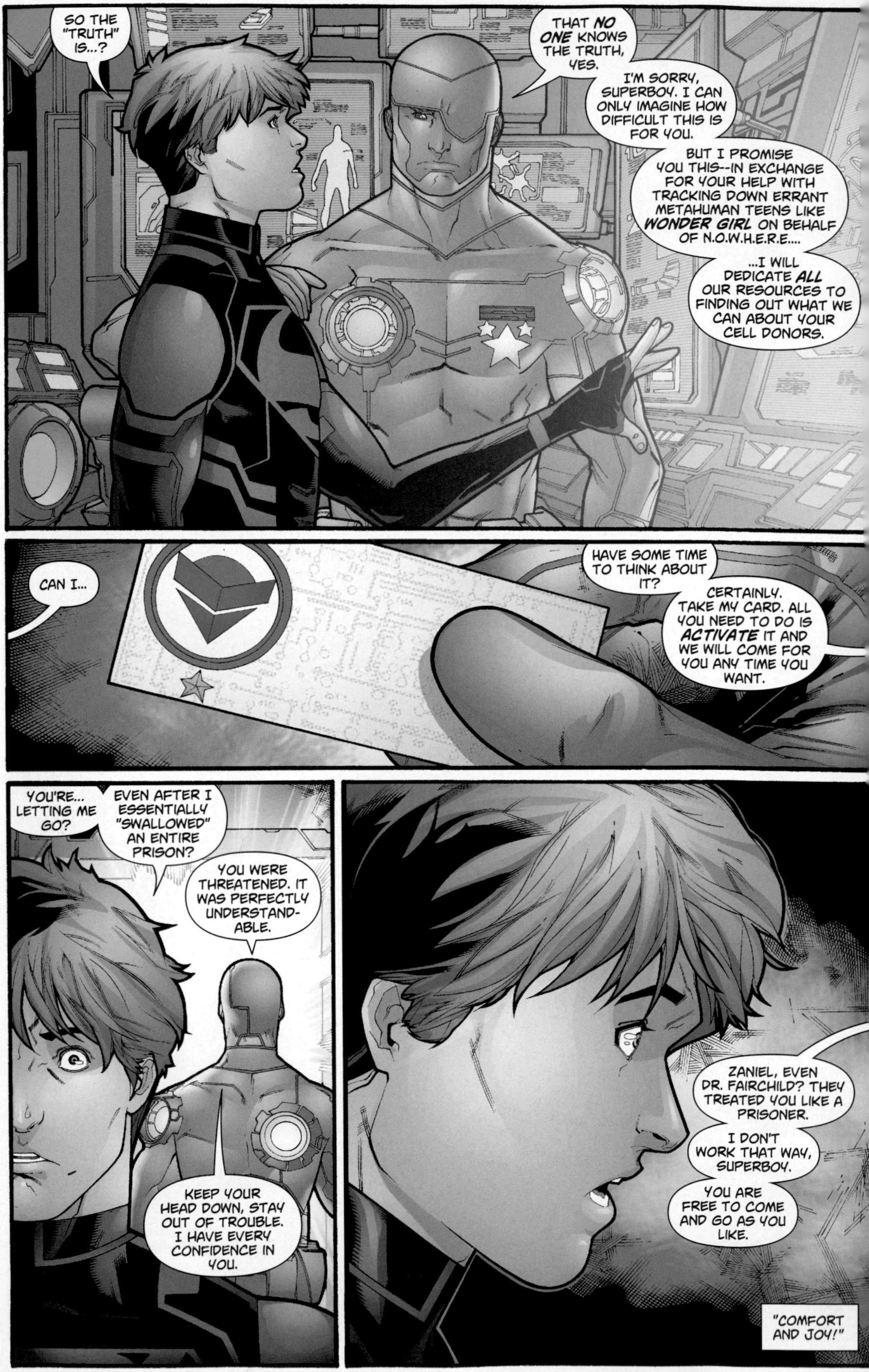
SO THE "TRUTH" IS...?
THAT NO ONE KNOWS THE TRUTH, YES.
I'M SORRY, SUPERBOY. I CAN ONLY IMAGINE HOW DIFFICULT THIS IS FOR YOU.
BUT I PROMISE YOU THIS--IN EXCHANGE FOR YOUR HELP WITH TRACKING DOWN ERRANT METAHUMAN TEENS LIKE WONDER GIRL ON BEHALF OF N.O.W.H.E.R.E....
...I WILL DEDICATE ALL OUR RESOURCES TO FINDING OUT WHAT WE CAN ABOUT YOUR CELL DONORS.
CAN I...
HAVE SOME TIME TO THINK ABOUT IT?
CERTAINLY. TAKE MY CARD. ALL YOU NEED TO DO IS ACTIVATE IT AND WE WILL COME FOR YOU ANY TIME YOU WANT.
YOU'RE... LETTING ME GO?
EVEN AFTER I ESSENTIALLY "SWALLOWED" AN ENTIRE PRISON?
YOU WERE THREATENED. IT WAS PERFECTLY UNDERSTAND-ABLE.
KEEP YOUR HEAD DOWN, STAY OUT OF TROUBLE. I HAVE EVERY CONFIDENCE IN YOU.
ZANIEL, EVEN DR. FAIRCHILD? THEY TREATED YOU LIKE A PRISONER.
I DON'T WORK THAT WAY, SUPERBOY.
YOU ARE FREE TO COME AND GO AS YOU LIKE.
"COMFORT AND JOY!"

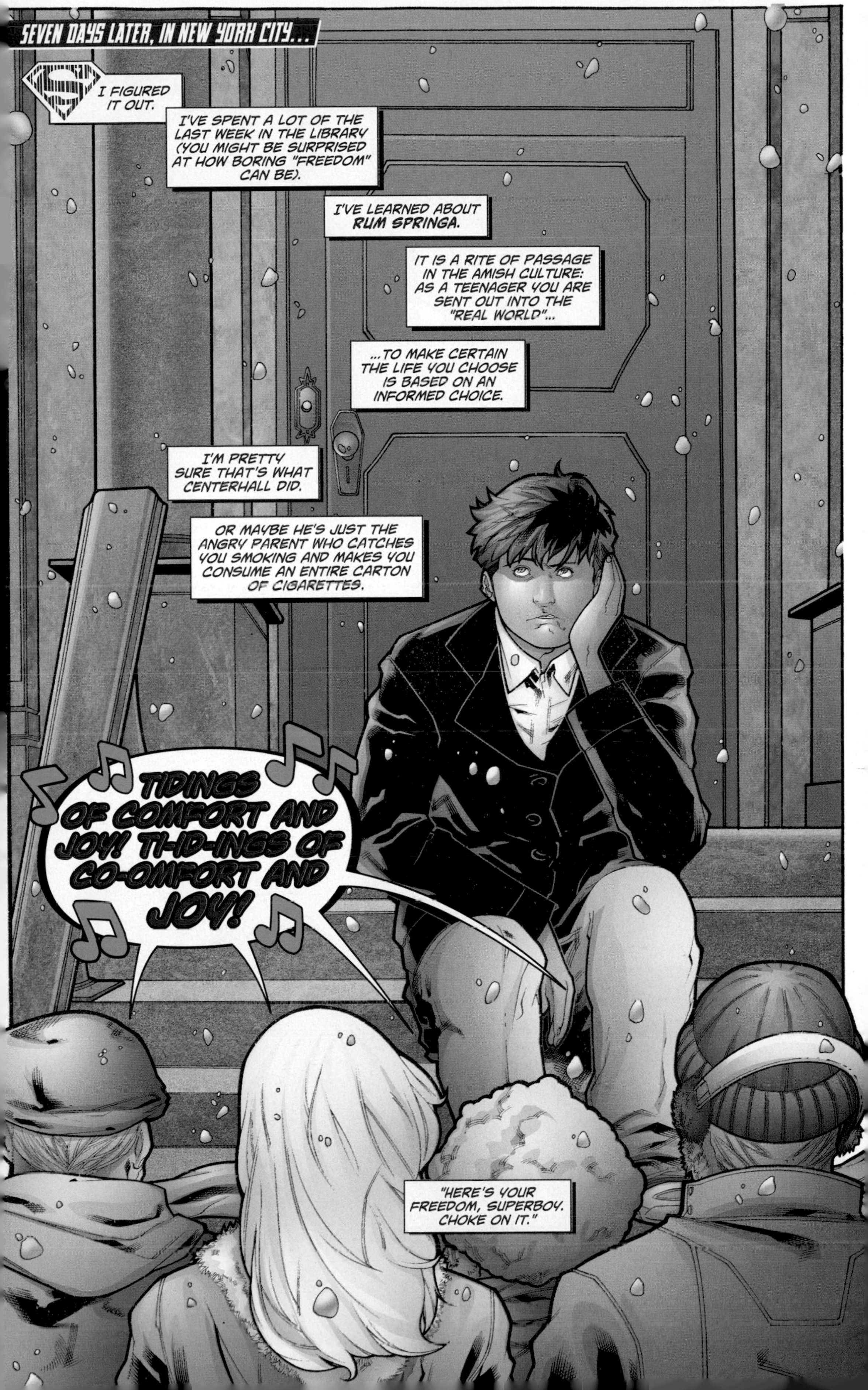
SEVEN DAYS LATER, IN NEW YORK CITY...
I FIGURED IT OUT.
I'VE SPENT A LOT OF THE LAST WEEK IN THE LIBRARY (YOU MIGHT BE SURPRISED AT HOW BORING "FREEDOM" CAN BE).
I'VE LEARNED ABOUT RUM SPRINGA.
IT IS A RITE OF PASSAGE IN THE AMISH CULTURE: AS A TEENAGER YOU ARE SENT OUT INTO THE "REAL WORLD"...
...TO MAKE CERTAIN THE LIFE YOU CHOOSE IS BASED ON AN INFORMED CHOICE.
I'M PRETTY SURE THAT'S WHAT CENTERHALL DID.
OR MAYBE HE'S JUST THE ANGRY PARENT WHO CATCHES YOU SMOKING AND MAKES YOU CONSUME AN ENTIRE CARTON OF CIGARETTES.
TIDINGS OF COMFORT AND JOY! TI-ID-INGS OF CO-OMFORT AND JOY!
"HERE'S YOUR FREEDOM, SUPERBOY. CHOKE ON IT."

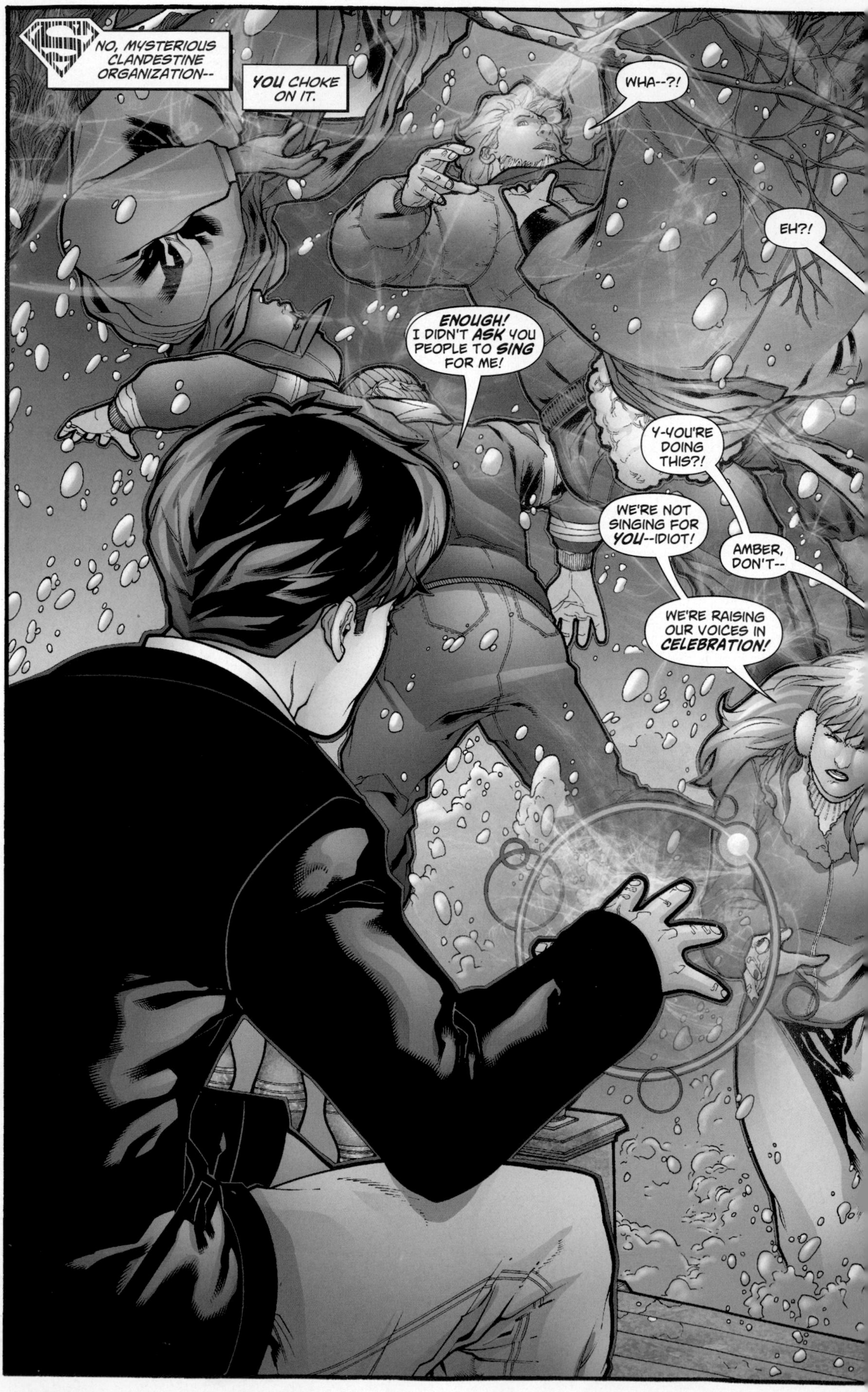
NO, MYSTERIOUS CLANDESTINE ORGANIZATION--
YOU CHOKE ON IT.
WHA--?!
EH?!
ENOUGH! I DIDN'T ASK YOU PEOPLE TO SING FOR ME!
Y-YOU'RE DOING THIS?!
WE'RE NOT SINGING FOR YOU--IDIOT!
AMBER, DON'T--
WE'RE RAISING OUR VOICES IN CELEBRATION!

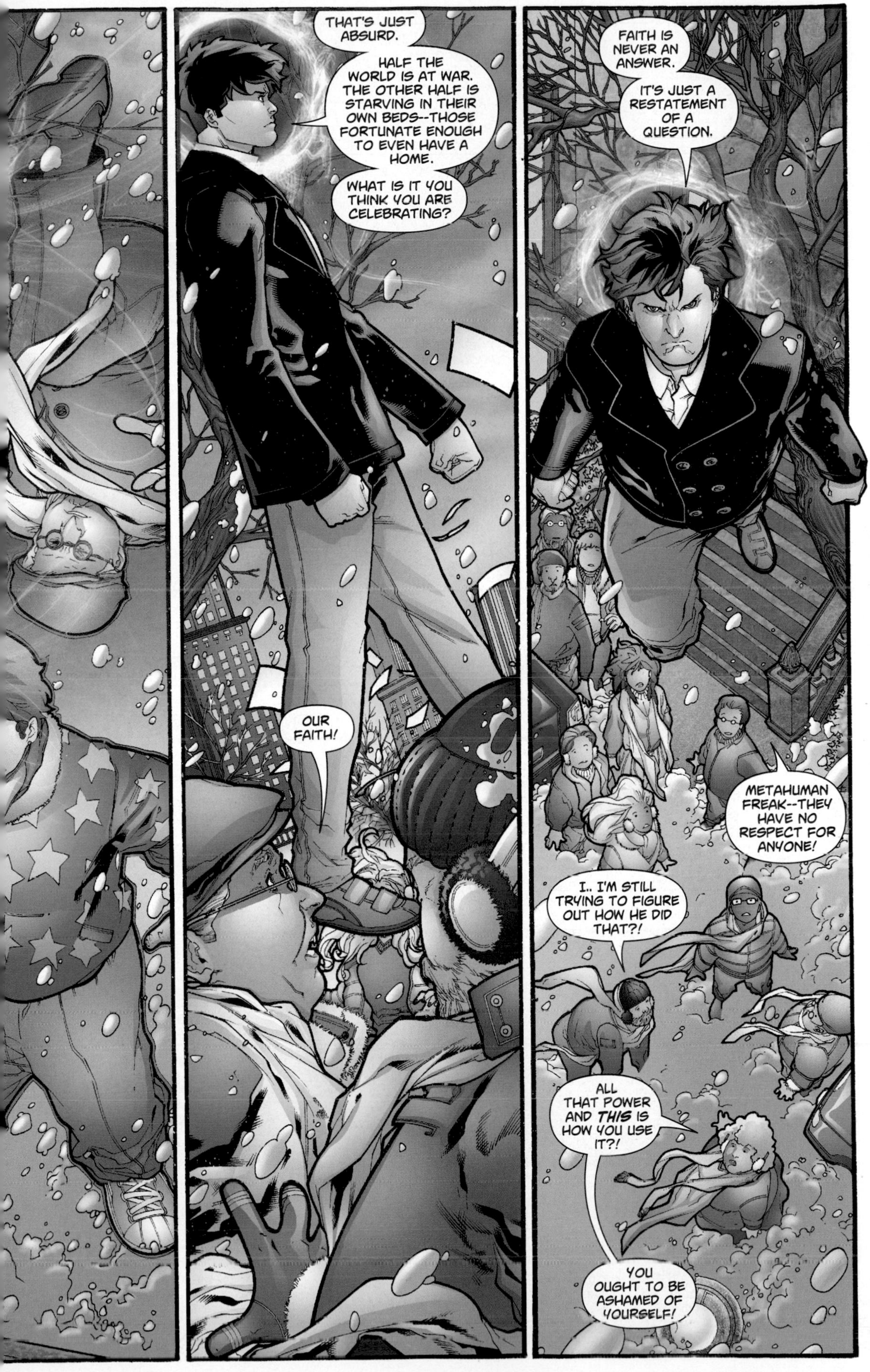
THAT'S JUST ABSURD.
HALF THE WORLD IS AT WAR. THE OTHER HALF IS STARVING IN THEIR OWN BEDS--THOSE FORTUNATE ENOUGH TO EVEN HAVE A HOME.
WHAT IS IT YOU THINK YOU ARE CELEBRATING?
OUR FAITH!
FAITH IS NEVER AN ANSWER.
IT'S JUST A RESTATEMENT OF A QUESTION.
METAHUMAN FREAK--THEY HAVE NO RESPECT FOR ANYONE!
I.. I'M STILL TRYING TO FIGURE OUT HOW HE DID THAT?!
ALL THAT POWER AND THIS IS HOW YOU USE IT?!
YOU OUGHT TO BE ASHAMED OF YOURSELF!

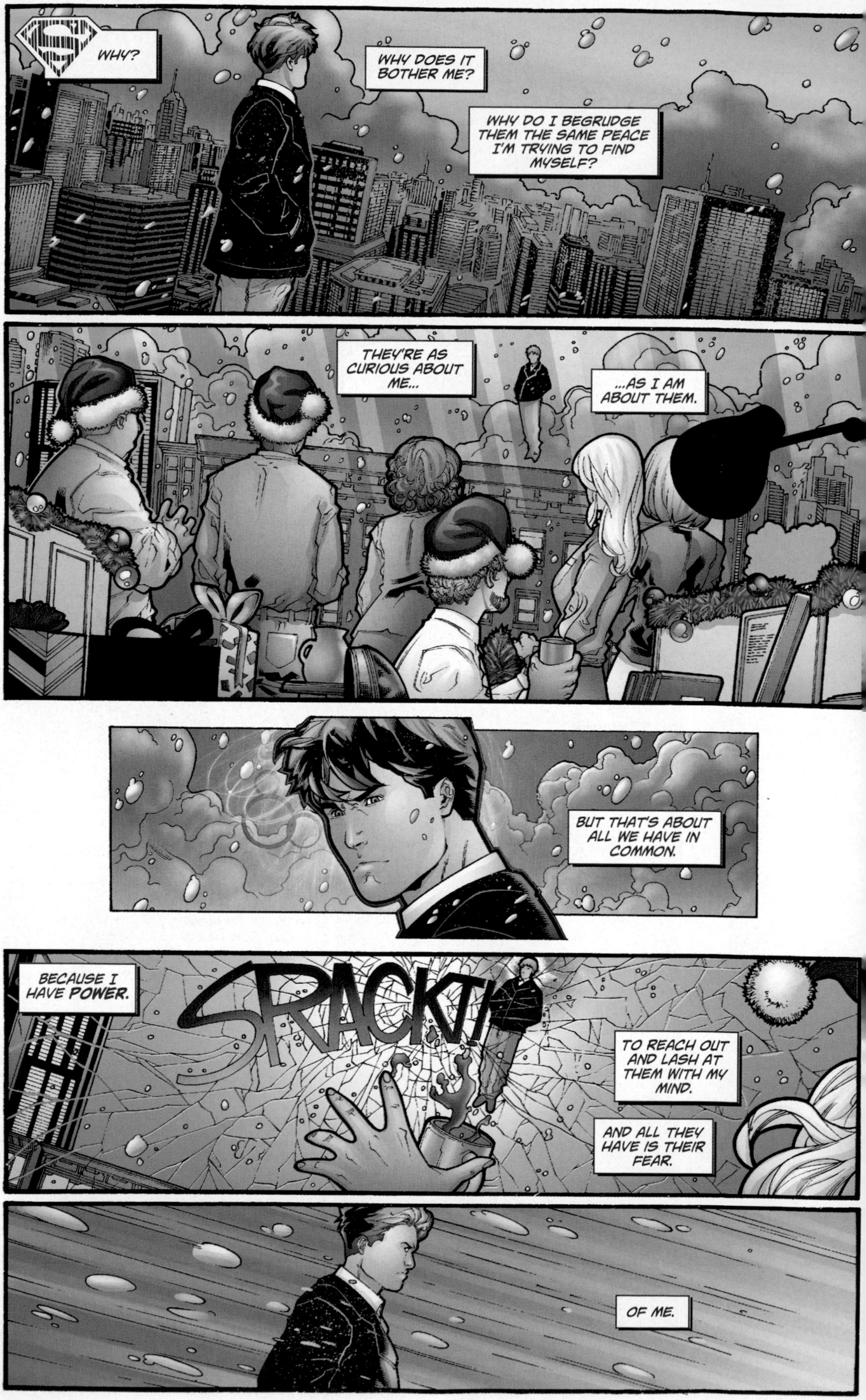
WHY?
WHY DOES IT BOTHER ME?
WHY DO I BEGRUDGE THEM THE SAME PEACE I'M TRYING TO FIND MYSELF?
THEY'RE AS CURIOUS ABOUT ME...
...AS I AM ABOUT THEM.
BUT THAT'S ABOUT ALL WE HAVE IN COMMON.
BECAUSE I HAVE POWER.
SRACKT!
TO REACH OUT AND LASH AT THEM WITH MY MIND.
AND ALL THEY HAVE IS THEIR FEAR.
OF ME.

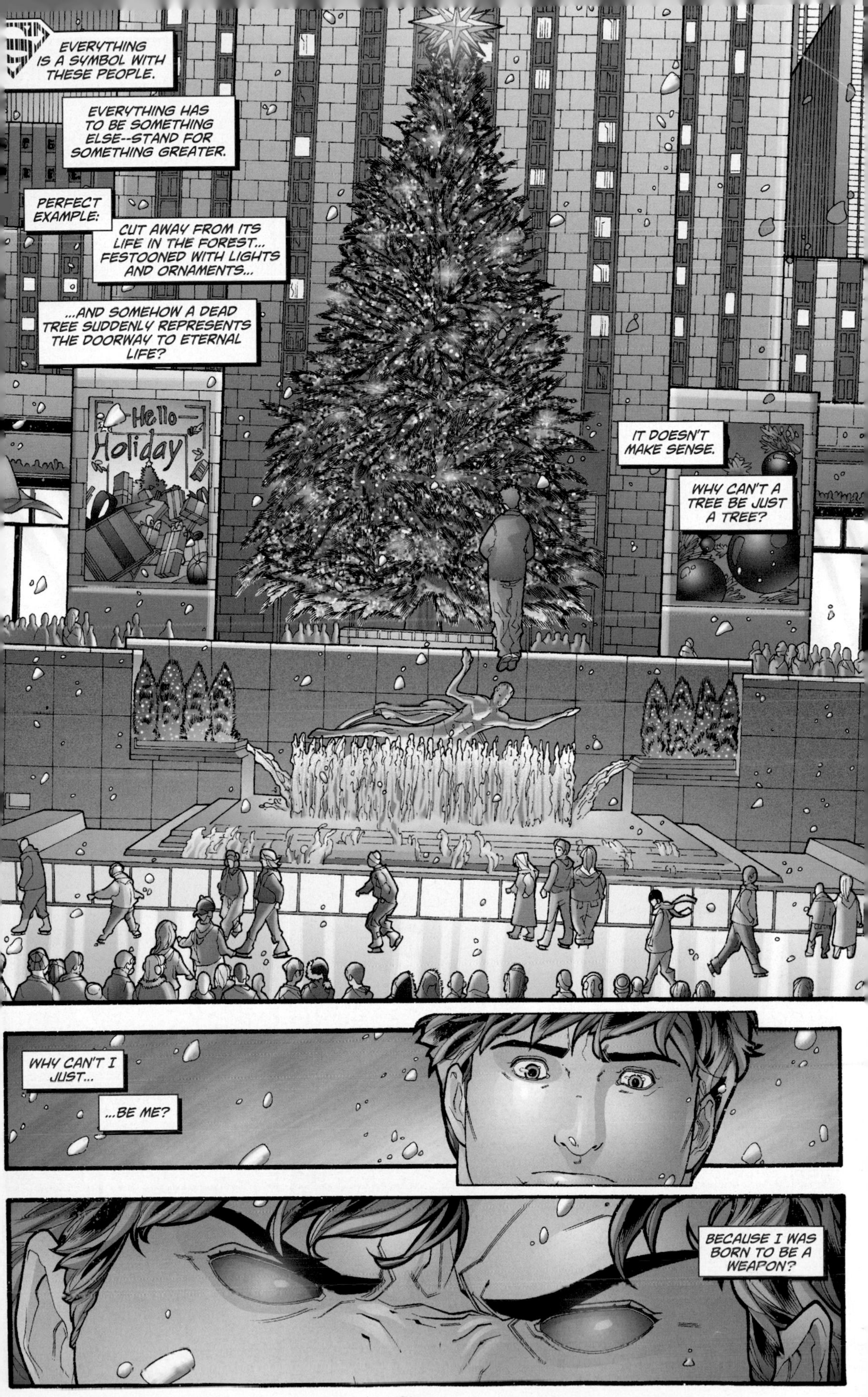
EVERYTHING IS A SYMBOL WITH THESE PEOPLE.
EVERYTHING HAS TO BE SOMETHING ELSE--STAND FOR SOMETHING GREATER.
PERFECT EXAMPLE:
CUT AWAY FROM ITS LIFE IN THE FOREST... FESTOONED WITH LIGHTS AND ORNAMENTS...
...AND SOMEHOW A DEAD TREE SUDDENLY REPRESENTS THE DOORWAY TO ETERNAL LIFE?
Hello Holiday
IT DOESN'T MAKE SENSE.
WHY CAN'T A TREE BE JUST A TREE?
WHY CAN'T I JUST...
...BE ME?
BECAUSE I WAS BORN TO BE A WEAPON?

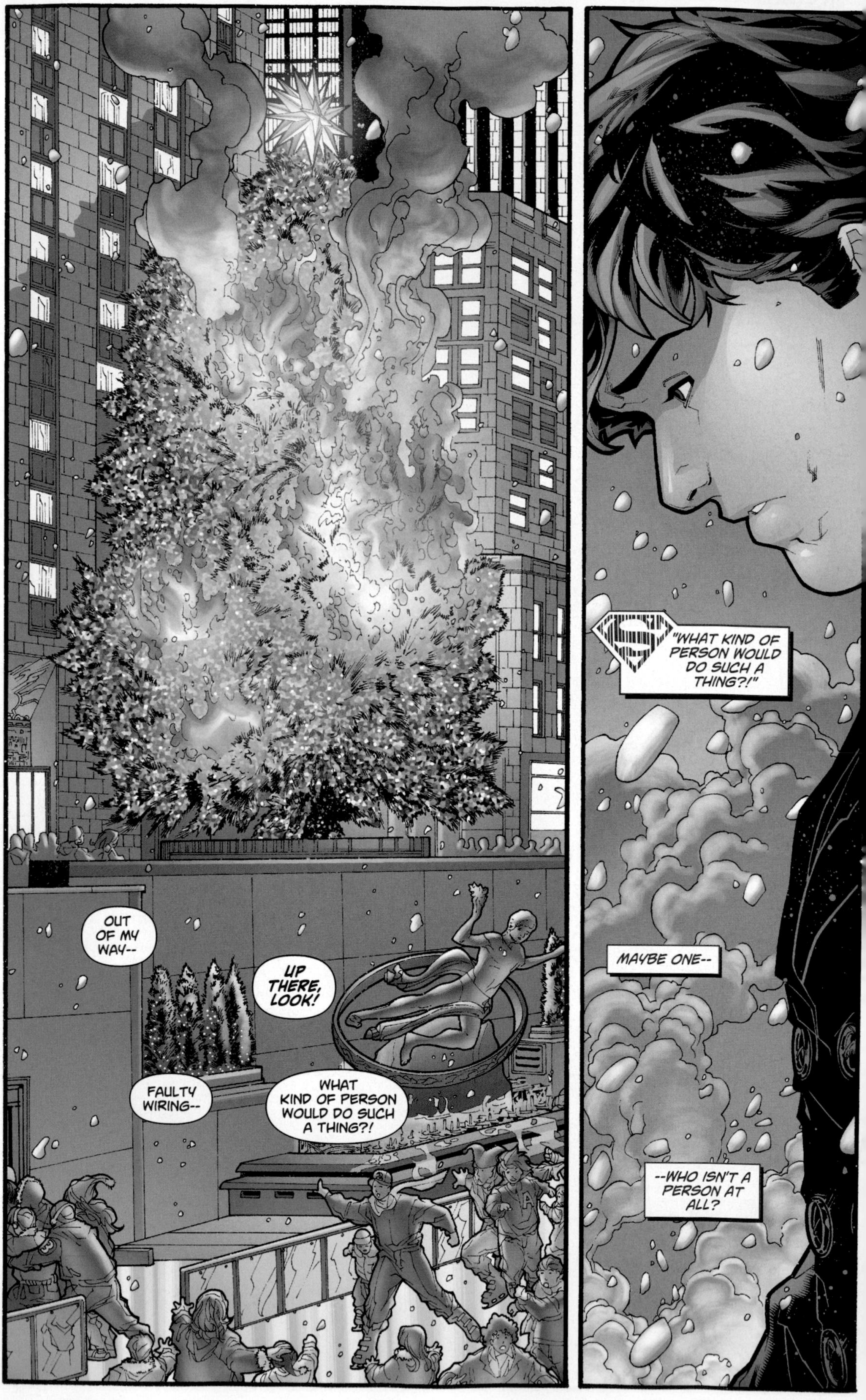
OUT OF MY WAY--
UP THERE, LOOK!
FAULTY WIRING--
WHAT KIND OF PERSON WOULD DO SUCH A THING?!
"WHAT KIND OF PERSON WOULD DO SUCH A THING?!"
MAYBE ONE--
--WHO ISN'T A PERSON AT ALL?

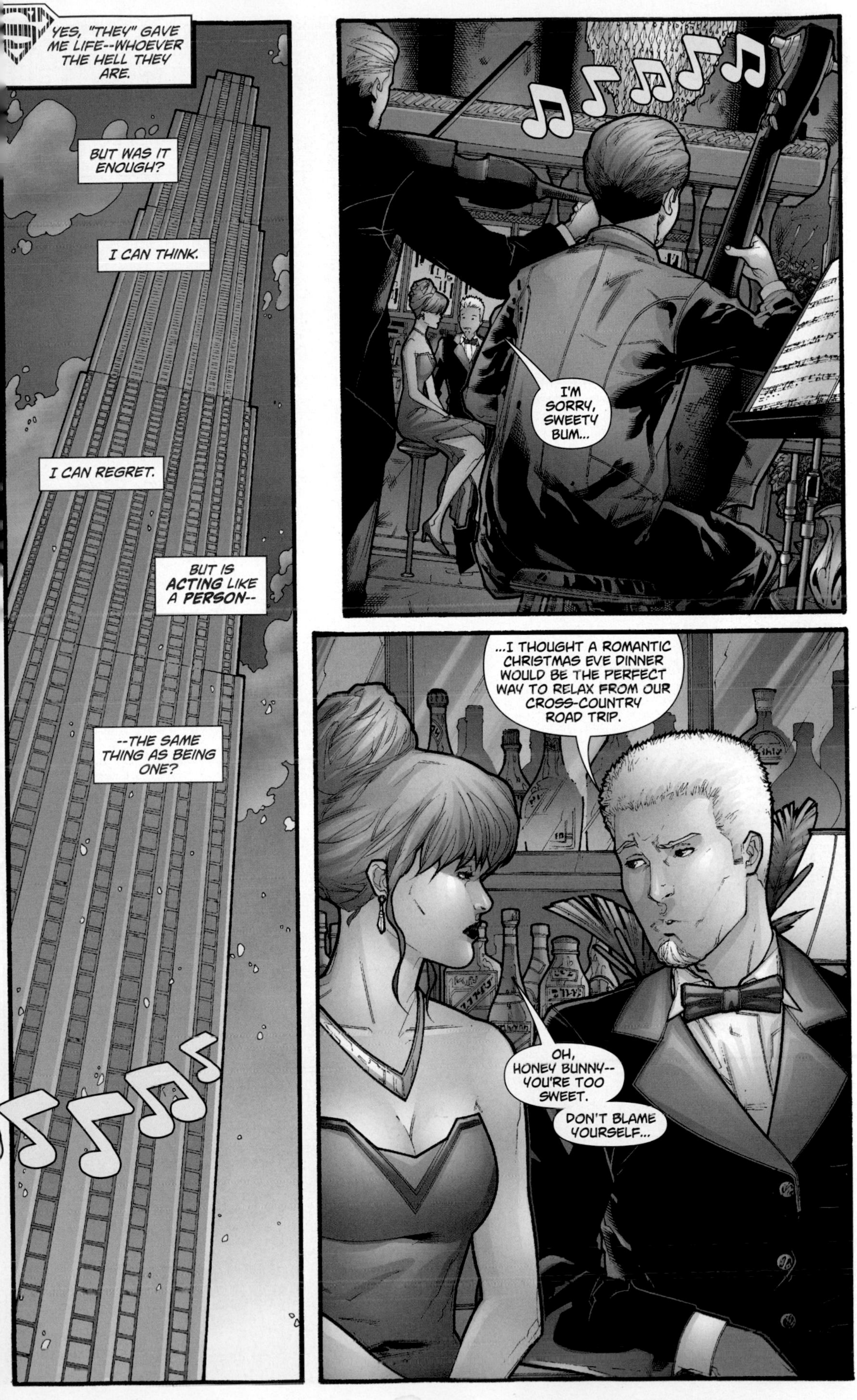
YES, "THEY" GAVE ME LIFE--WHOEVER THE HELL THEY ARE.
BUT WAS IT ENOUGH?
I CAN THINK.
I CAN REGRET.
BUT IS ACTING LIKE A PERSON--
--THE SAME THING AS BEING ONE?
I'M SORRY, SWEETY BUM...
...I THOUGHT A ROMANTIC CHRISTMAS EVE DINNER WOULD BE THE PERFECT WAY TO RELAX FROM OUR CROSS-COUNTRY ROAD TRIP.
OH, HONEY BUNNY--YOU'RE TOO SWEET.
DON'T BLAME YOURSELF...

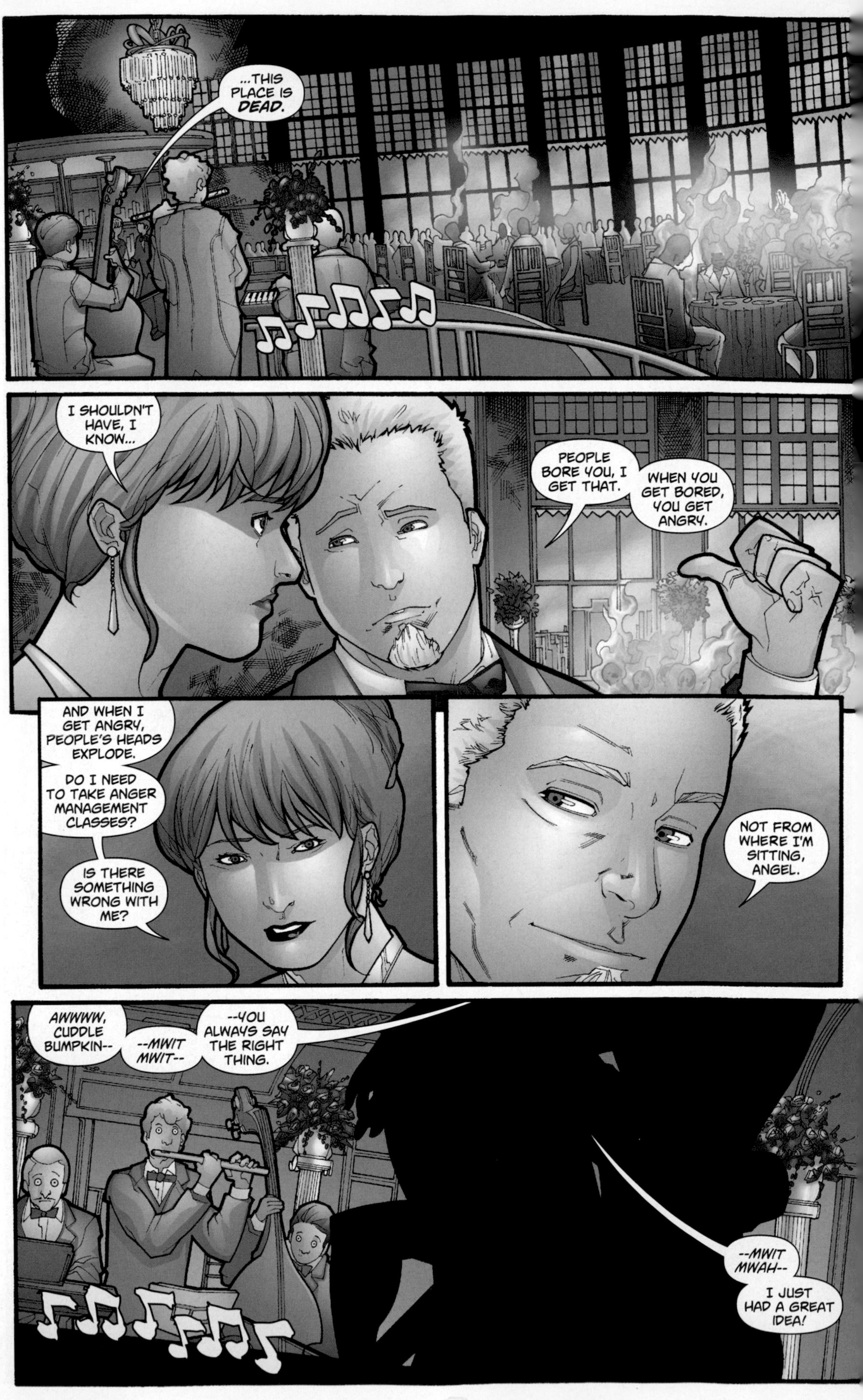
...THIS PLACE IS DEAD.
I SHOULDN'T HAVE, I KNOW...
PEOPLE BORE YOU, I GET THAT.
WHEN YOU GET BORED, YOU GET ANGRY.
AND WHEN I GET ANGRY, PEOPLE'S HEADS EXPLODE.
DO I NEED TO TAKE ANGER MANAGEMENT CLASSES?
IS THERE SOMETHING WRONG WITH ME?
NOT FROM WHERE I'M SITTING, ANGEL.
AWWWW, CUDDLE BUMPKIN--
--MWIT MWIT--
--YOU ALWAYS SAY THE RIGHT THING.
--MWIT MWAH--
I JUST HAD A GREAT IDEA!

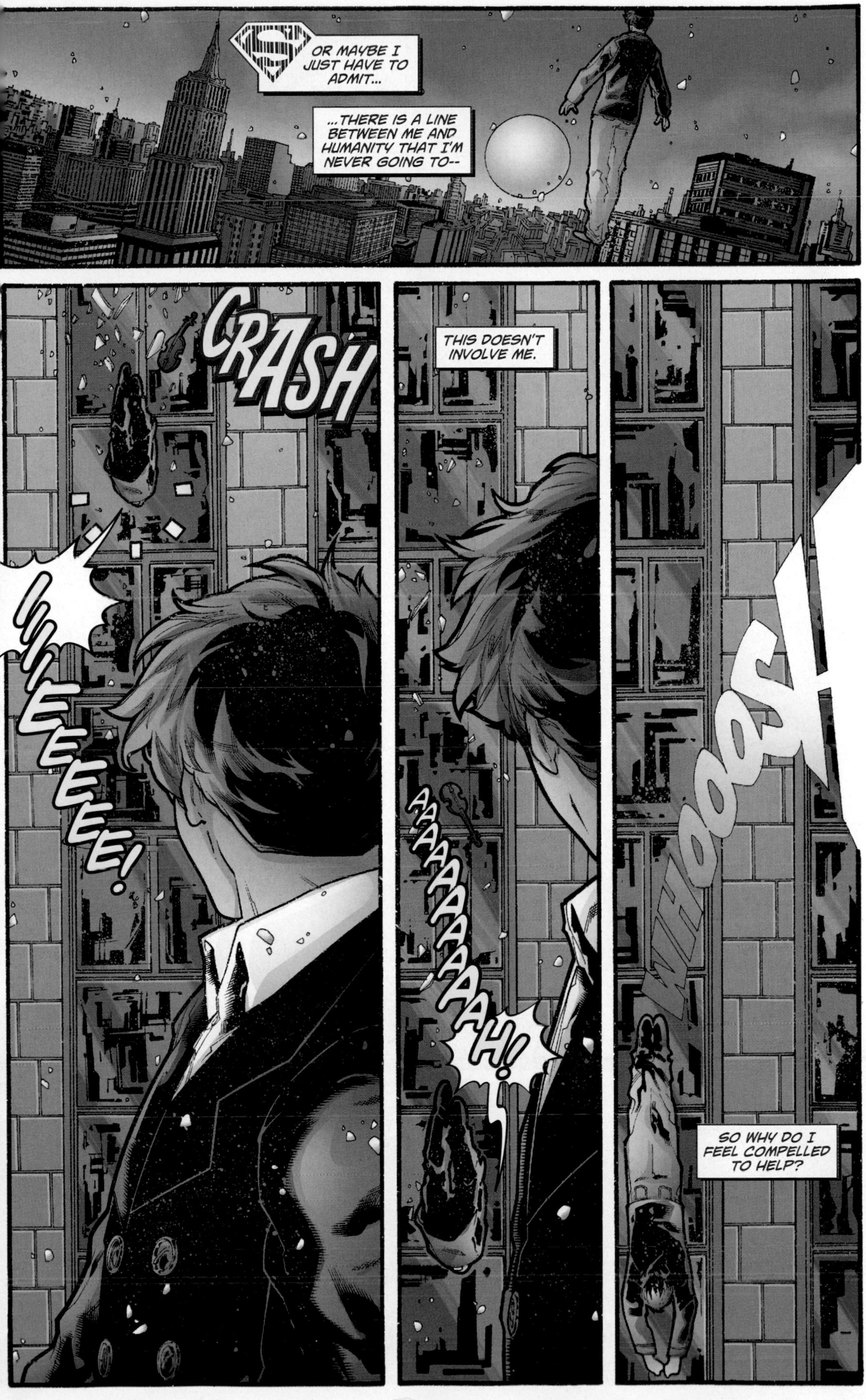

OR MAYBE I JUST HAVE TO ADMIT...
...THERE IS A LINE BETWEEN ME AND HUMANITY THAT I'M NEVER GOING TO--
CRASH
IIIIIEEEEEEE!
THIS DOESN'T INVOLVE ME.
AAAAAAAAAAAH!
WHOOSH
SO WHY DO I FEEL COMPELLED TO HELP?

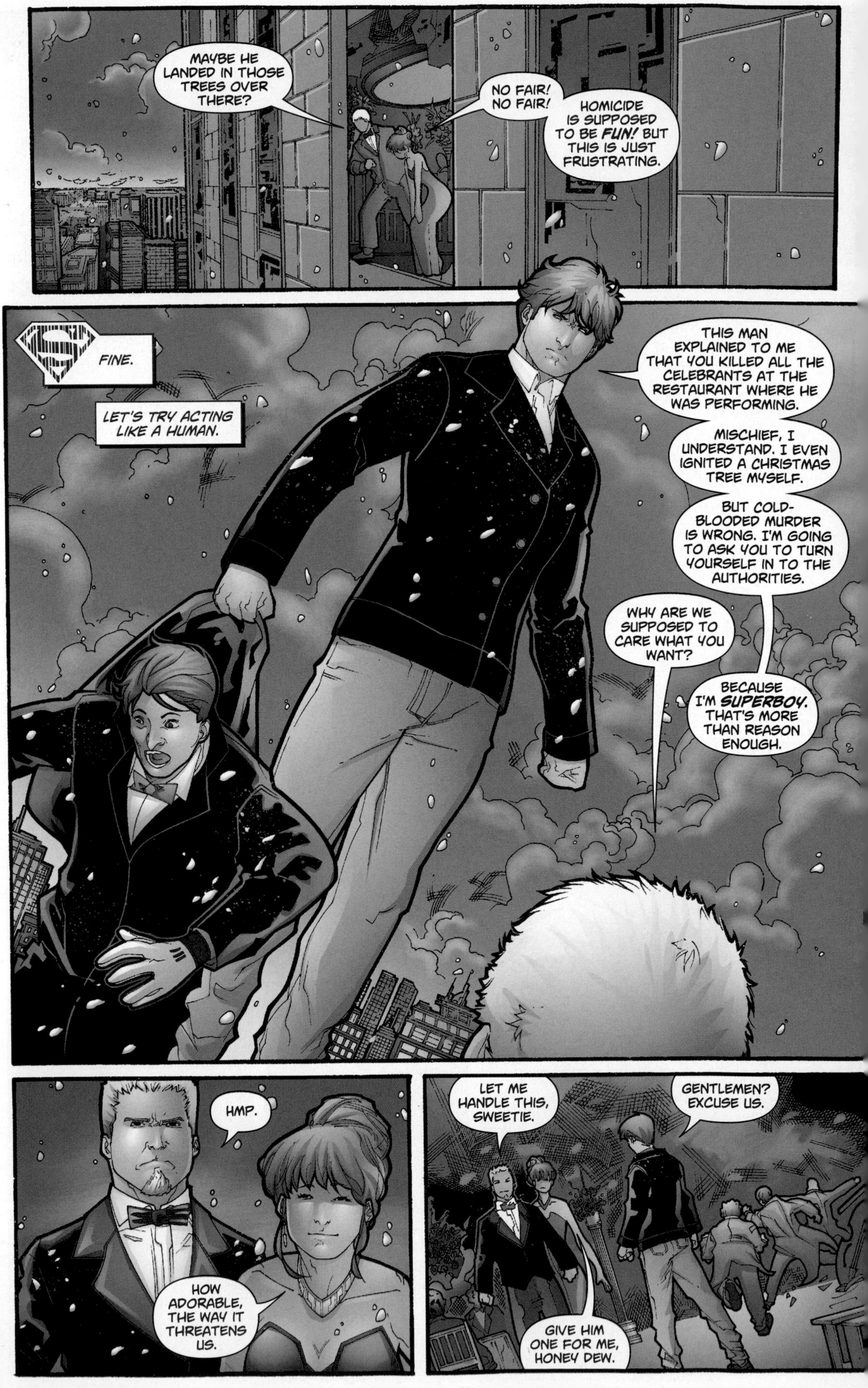
MAYBE HE LANDED IN THOSE TREES OVER THERE?
NO FAIR! NO FAIR!
HOMICIDE IS SUPPOSED TO BE FUN! BUT THIS IS JUST FRUSTRATING.
FINE.
LET'S TRY ACTING LIKE A HUMAN.
THIS MAN EXPLAINED TO ME THAT YOU KILLED ALL THE CELEBRANTS AT THE RESTAURANT WHERE HE WAS PERFORMING.
MISCHIEF, I UNDERSTAND. I EVEN IGNITED A CHRISTMAS TREE MYSELF.
BUT COLD-BLOODED MURDER IS WRONG. I'M GOING TO ASK YOU TO TURN YOURSELF IN TO THE AUTHORITIES.
WHY ARE WE SUPPOSED TO CARE WHAT YOU WANT?
BECAUSE I'M SUPERBOY. THAT'S MORE THAN REASON ENOUGH.
HMP.
HOW ADORABLE, THE WAY IT THREATENS US.
LET ME HANDLE THIS, SWEETIE.
GENTLEMEN? EXCUSE US.
GIVE HIM ONE FOR ME, HONEY DEW.

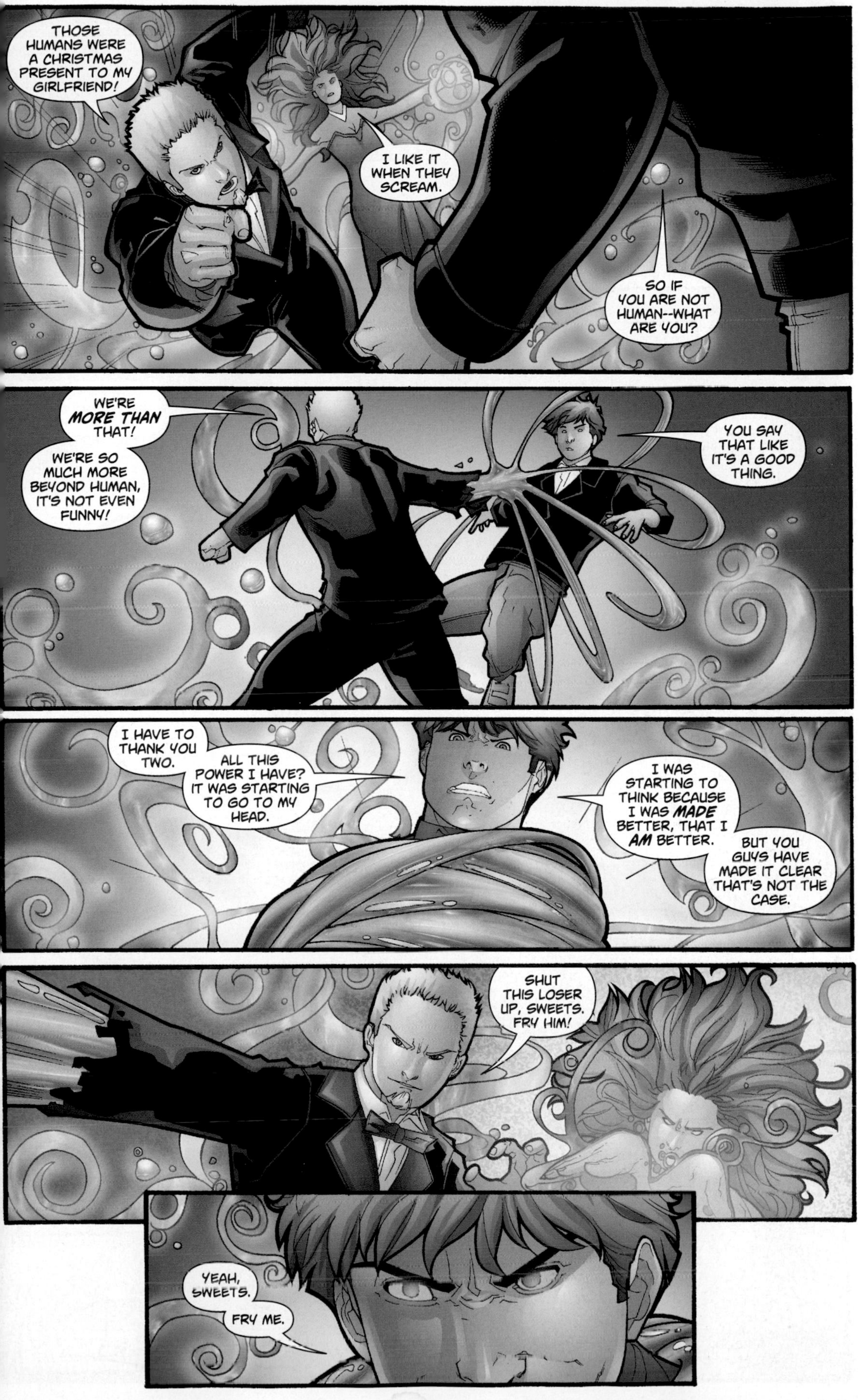
THOSE HUMANS WERE A CHRISTMAS PRESENT TO MY GIRLFRIEND!
I LIKE IT WHEN THEY SCREAM.
SO IF YOU ARE NOT HUMAN--WHAT ARE YOU?
WE'RE MORE THAN THAT!
WE'RE SO MUCH MORE BEYOND HUMAN, IT'S NOT EVEN FUNNY!
YOU SAY THAT LIKE IT'S A GOOD THING.
I HAVE TO THANK YOU TWO.
ALL THIS POWER I HAVE? IT WAS STARTING TO GO TO MY HEAD.
I WAS STARTING TO THINK BECAUSE I WAS MADE BETTER, THAT I AM BETTER.
BUT YOU GUYS HAVE MADE IT CLEAR THAT'S NOT THE CASE.
SHUT THIS LOSER UP, SWEETS. FRY HIM!
YEAH, SWEETS.
FRY ME.

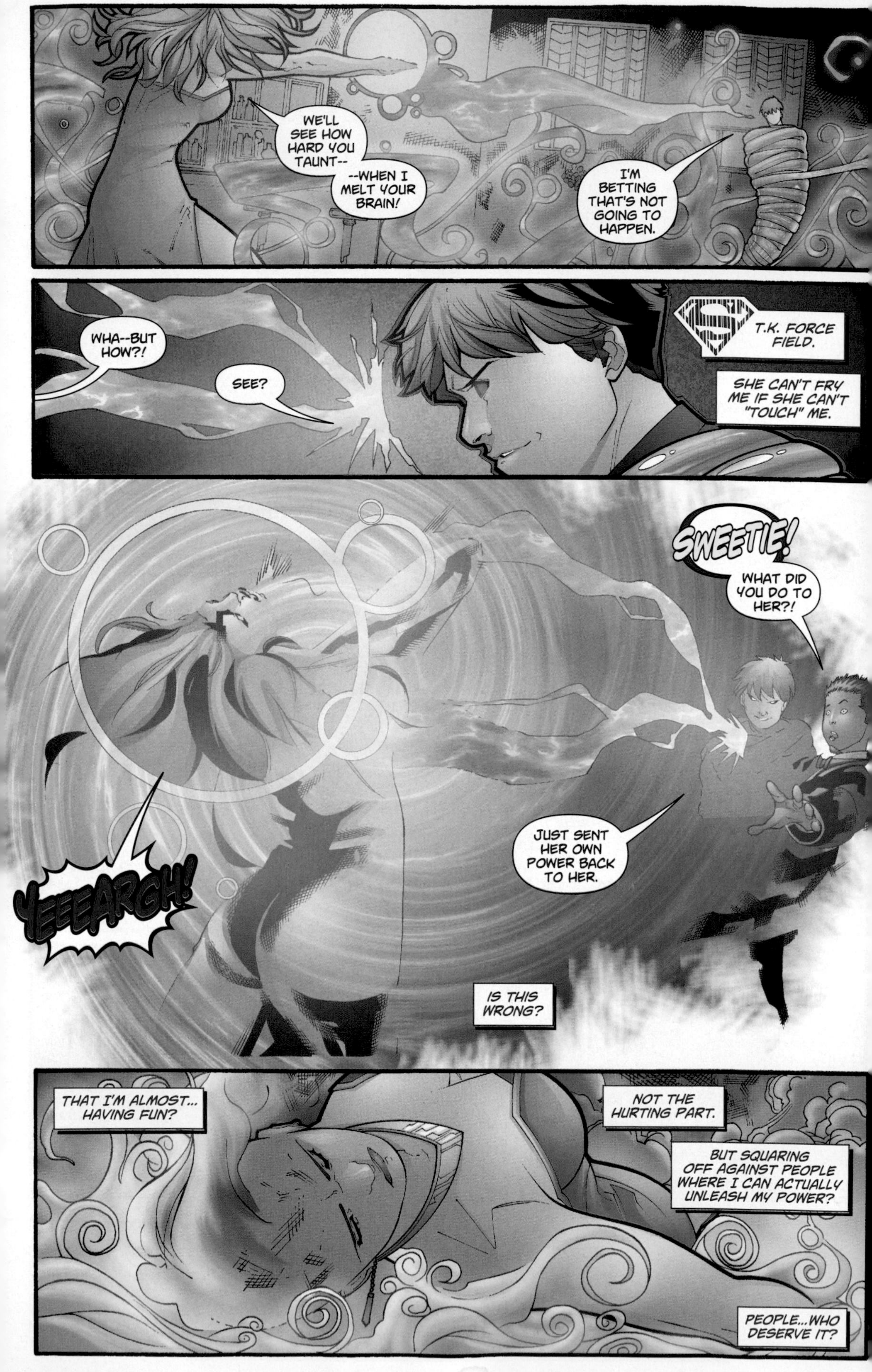
WE'LL SEE HOW HARD YOU TAUNT--
--WHEN I MELT YOUR BRAIN!
I'M BETTING THAT'S NOT GOING TO HAPPEN.
WHA--BUT HOW?!
SEE?
T.K. FORCE FIELD.
SHE CAN'T FRY ME IF SHE CAN'T "TOUCH" ME.
SWEETIE!
WHAT DID YOU DO TO HER?!
JUST SENT HER OWN POWER BACK TO HER.
YEEEARGH!
IS THIS WRONG?
THAT I'M ALMOST... HAVING FUN?
NOT THE HURTING PART.
BUT SQUARING OFF AGAINST PEOPLE WHERE I CAN ACTUALLY UNLEASH MY POWER?
PEOPLE...WHO DESERVE IT?

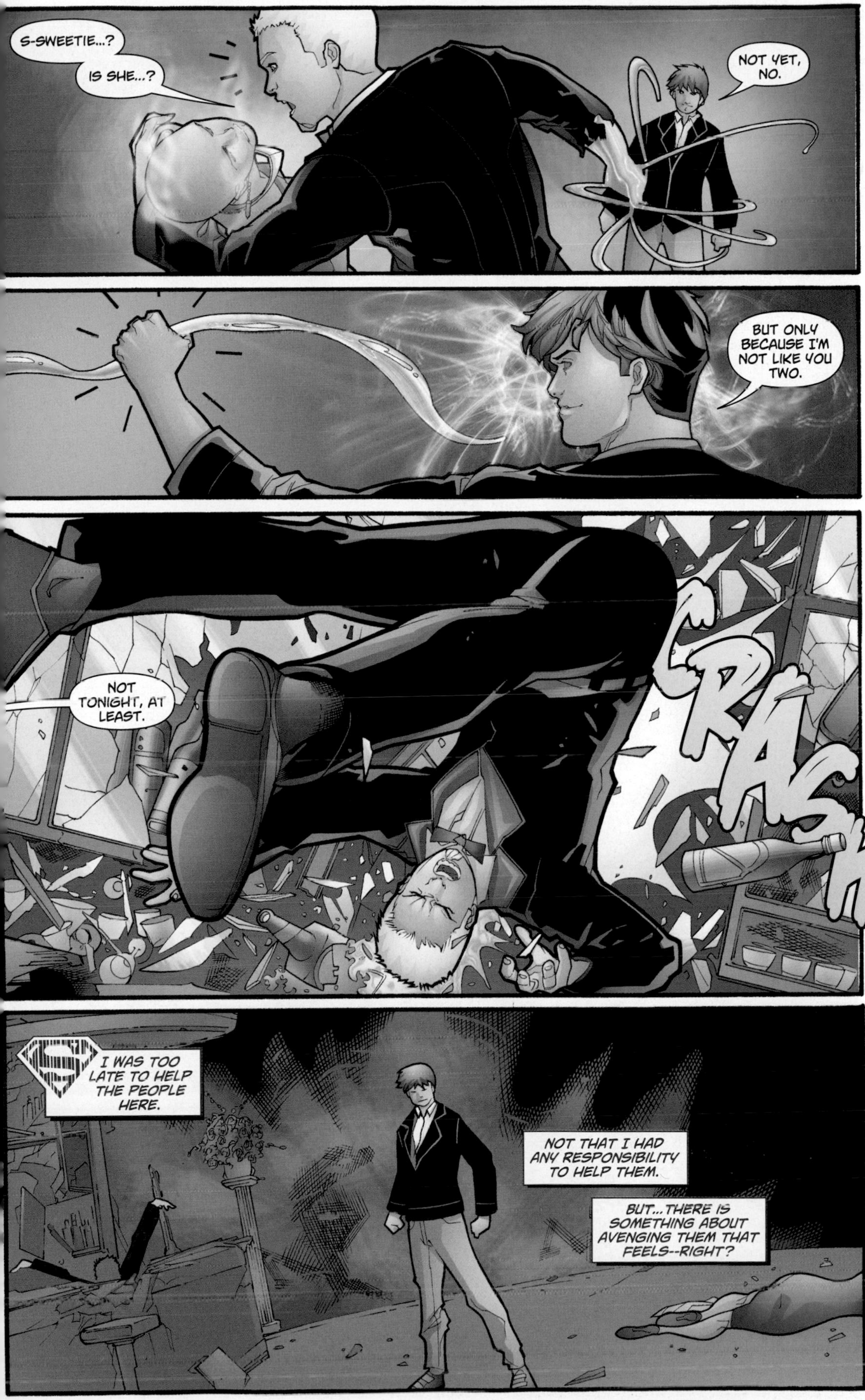
S-SWEETIE...?
IS SHE...?
NOT YET, NO.
BUT ONLY BECAUSE I'M NOT LIKE YOU TWO.
NOT TONIGHT, AT LEAST.
CRASH
I WAS TOO LATE TO HELP THE PEOPLE HERE.
NOT THAT I HAD ANY RESPONSIBILITY TO HELP THEM.
BUT...THERE IS SOMETHING ABOUT AVENGING THEM THAT FEELS--RIGHT?

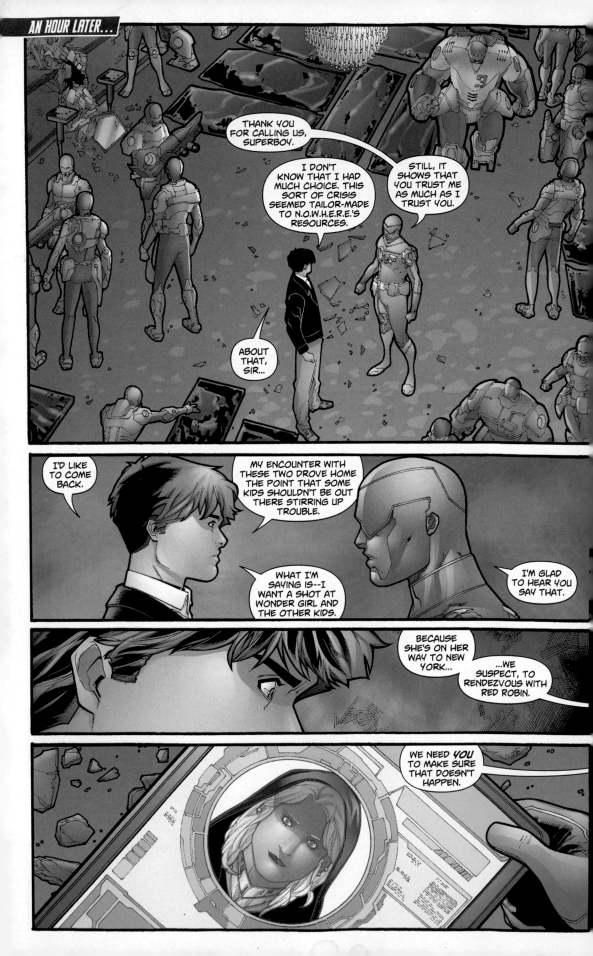

THANK YOU FOR CALLING US, SUPERBOY.

I DON'T KNOW THAT I HAD MUCH CHOICE. THIS SORT OF CRISIS SEEMED TAILOR-MADE TO N.O.W.H.E.R.E.'S RESOURCES.

STILL, IT SHOWS THAT YOU TRUST ME AS MUCH AS I TRUST YOU.

ABOUT THAT, SIR...

I'D LIKE TO COME BACK.

MY ENCOUNTER WITH THESE TWO DROVE HOME THE POINT THAT SOME KIDS SHOULDN'T BE OUT THERE STIRRING UP TROUBLE.

WHAT I'M SAYING IS--I WANT A SHOT AT WONDER GIRL AND THE OTHER KIDS.

I'M GLAD TO HEAR YOU SAY THAT.

BECAUSE SHE'S ON HER WAY TO NEW YORK...

...WE SUSPECT, TO RENDEZVOUS WITH RED ROBIN.

WE NEED YOU TO MAKE SURE THAT DOESN'T HAPPEN.

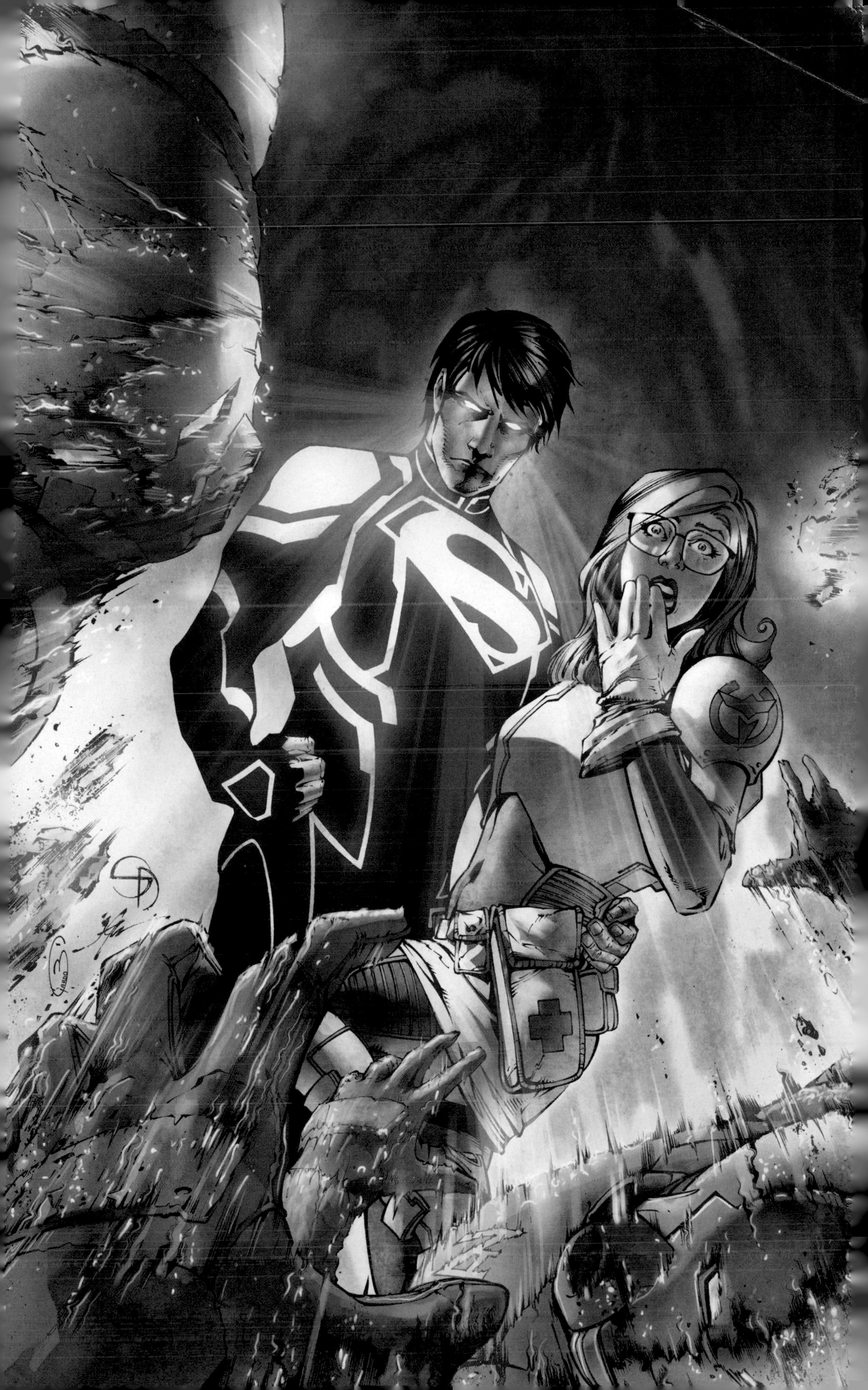

Cover by SHANE DAVIS, JONATHAN GLAPION & BARBARA CIARDO

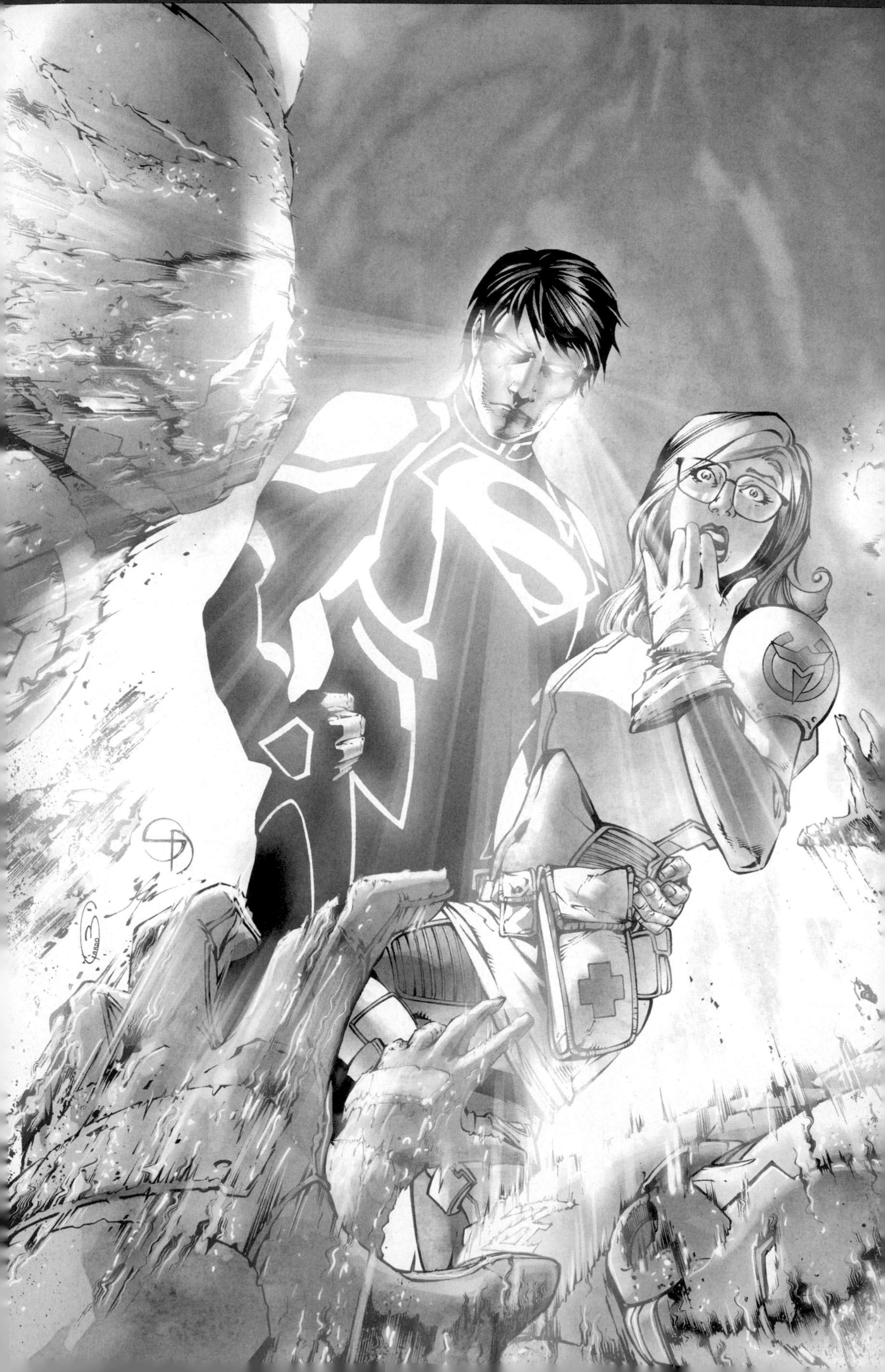

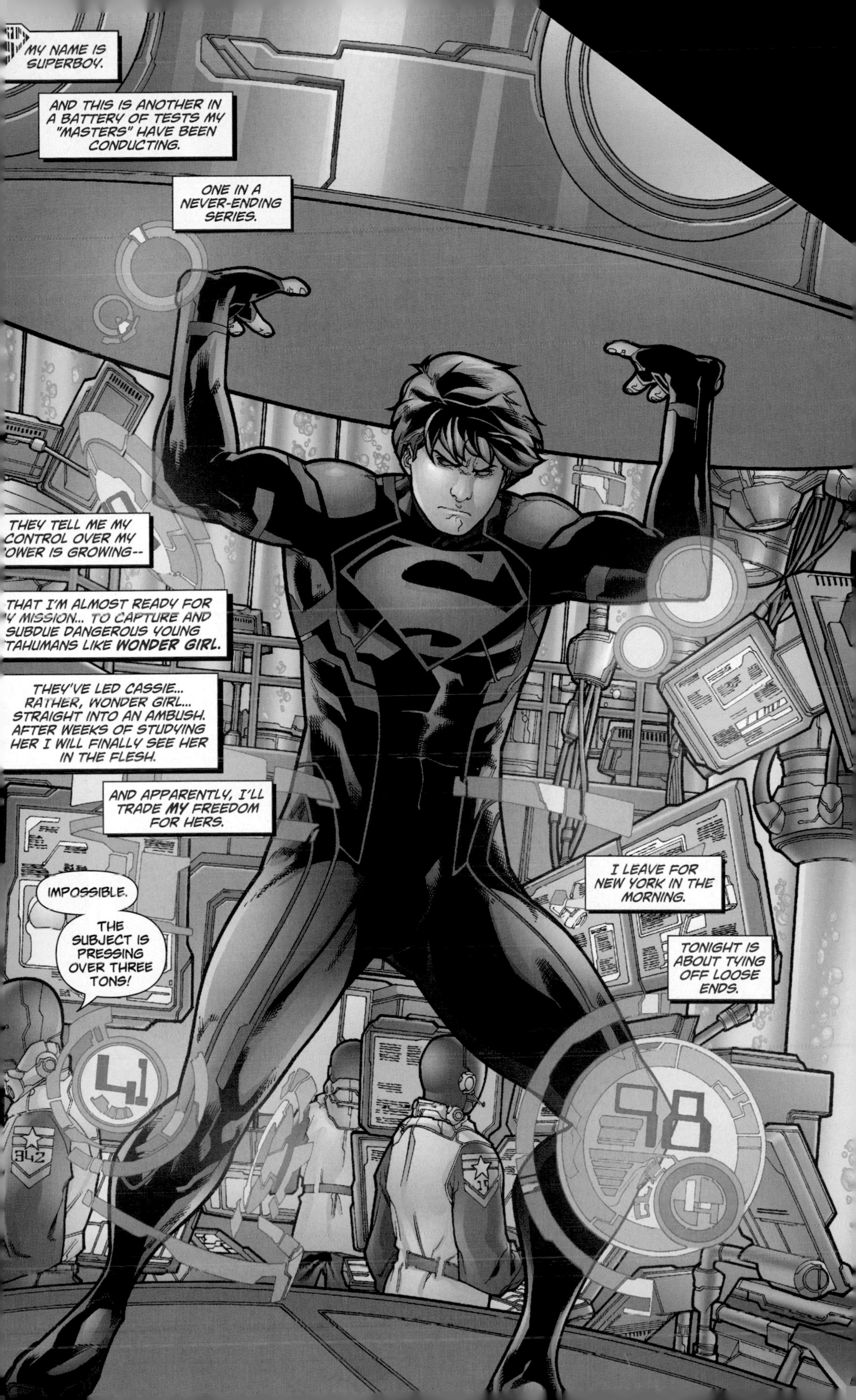
MY NAME IS SUPERBOY.
AND THIS IS ANOTHER IN A BATTERY OF TESTS MY "MASTERS" HAVE BEEN CONDUCTING.
ONE IN A NEVER-ENDING SERIES.
THEY TELL ME MY CONTROL OVER MY OWER IS GROWING--
THAT I'M ALMOST READY FOR Y MISSION... TO CAPTURE AND SUBDUE DANGEROUS YOUNG TAHUMANS LIKE WONDER GIRL.
THEY'VE LED CASSIE... RATHER, WONDER GIRL... STRAIGHT INTO AN AMBUSH. AFTER WEEKS OF STUDYING HER I WILL FINALLY SEE HER IN THE FLESH.
AND APPARENTLY, I'LL TRADE MY FREEDOM FOR HERS.
IMPOSSIBLE.
THE SUBJECT IS PRESSING OVER THREE TONS!
I LEAVE FOR NEW YORK IN THE MORNING.
TONIGHT IS ABOUT TYING OFF LOOSE ENDS.
41
98
342

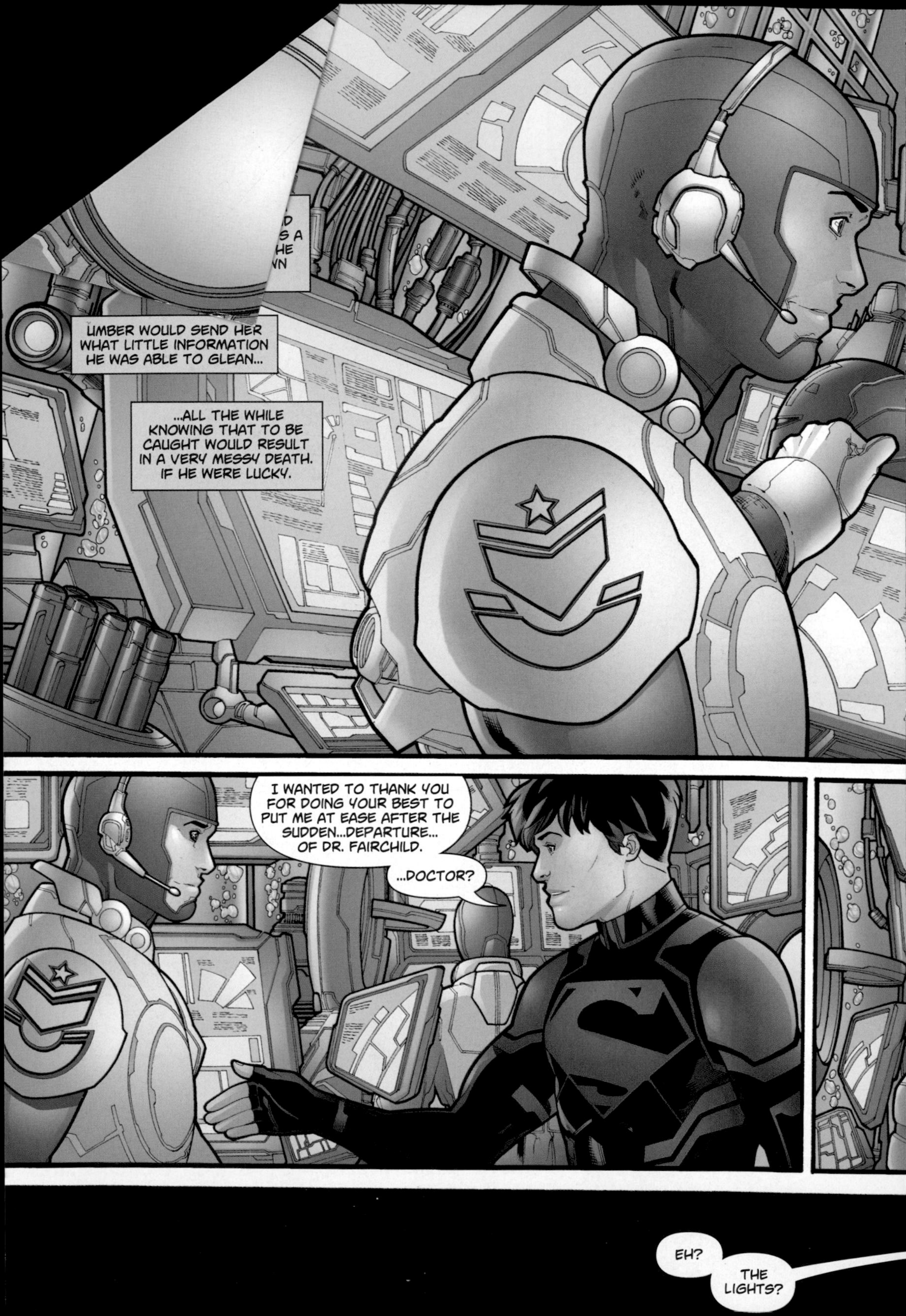
UMBER WOULD SEND HER WHAT LITTLE INFORMATION HE WAS ABLE TO GLEAN...
...ALL THE WHILE KNOWING THAT TO BE CAUGHT WOULD RESULT IN A VERY MESSY DEATH. IF HE WERE LUCKY.
I WANTED TO THANK YOU FOR DOING YOUR BEST TO PUT ME AT EASE AFTER THE SUDDEN...DEPARTURE... OF DR. FAIRCHILD.
...DOCTOR?
EH?
THE LIGHTS?

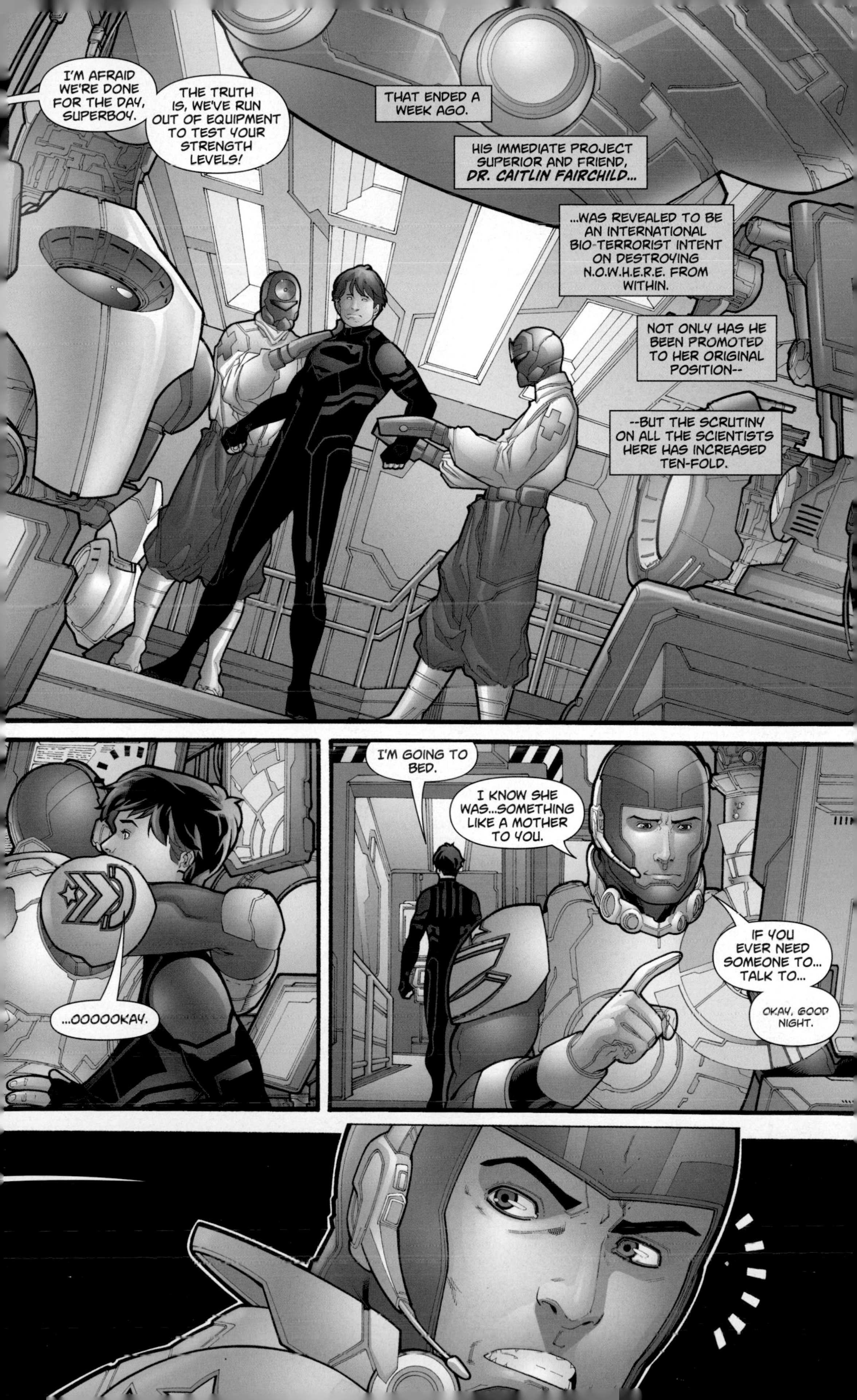
I'M AFRAID WE'RE DONE FOR THE DAY, SUPERBOY.
THE TRUTH IS, WE'VE RUN OUT OF EQUIPMENT TO TEST YOUR STRENGTH LEVELS!
THAT ENDED A WEEK AGO.
HIS IMMEDIATE PROJECT SUPERIOR AND FRIEND, DR. CAITLIN FAIRCHILD...
...WAS REVEALED TO BE AN INTERNATIONAL BIO-TERRORIST INTENT ON DESTROYING N.O.W.H.E.R.E. FROM WITHIN.
NOT ONLY HAS HE BEEN PROMOTED TO HER ORIGINAL POSITION--
--BUT THE SCRUTINY ON ALL THE SCIENTISTS HERE HAS INCREASED TEN-FOLD.
...OOOOOKAY.
I'M GOING TO BED.
I KNOW SHE WAS...SOMETHING LIKE A MOTHER TO YOU.
IF YOU EVER NEED SOMEONE TO... TALK TO...
OKAY, GOOD NIGHT.

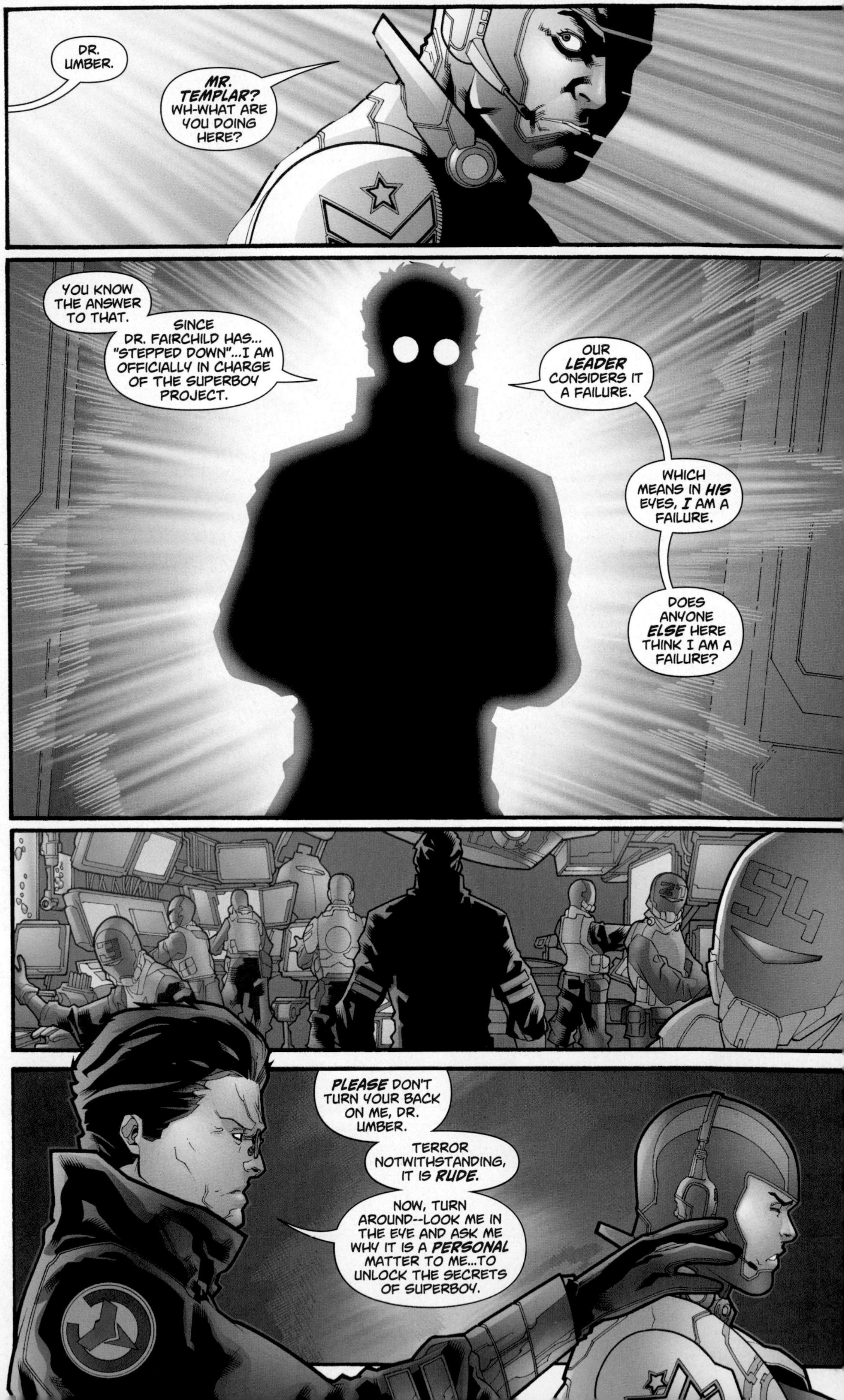
DR. UMBER.
MR. TEMPLAR? WH-WHAT ARE YOU DOING HERE?
YOU KNOW THE ANSWER TO THAT.
SINCE DR. FAIRCHILD HAS... "STEPPED DOWN"...I AM OFFICIALLY IN CHARGE OF THE SUPERBOY PROJECT.
OUR LEADER CONSIDERS IT A FAILURE.
WHICH MEANS IN HIS EYES, I AM A FAILURE.
DOES ANYONE ELSE HERE THINK I AM A FAILURE?
PLEASE DON'T TURN YOUR BACK ON ME, DR. UMBER.
TERROR NOTWITHSTANDING, IT IS RUDE.
NOW, TURN AROUND--LOOK ME IN THE EYE AND ASK ME WHY IT IS A PERSONAL MATTER TO ME...TO UNLOCK THE SECRETS OF SUPERBOY.

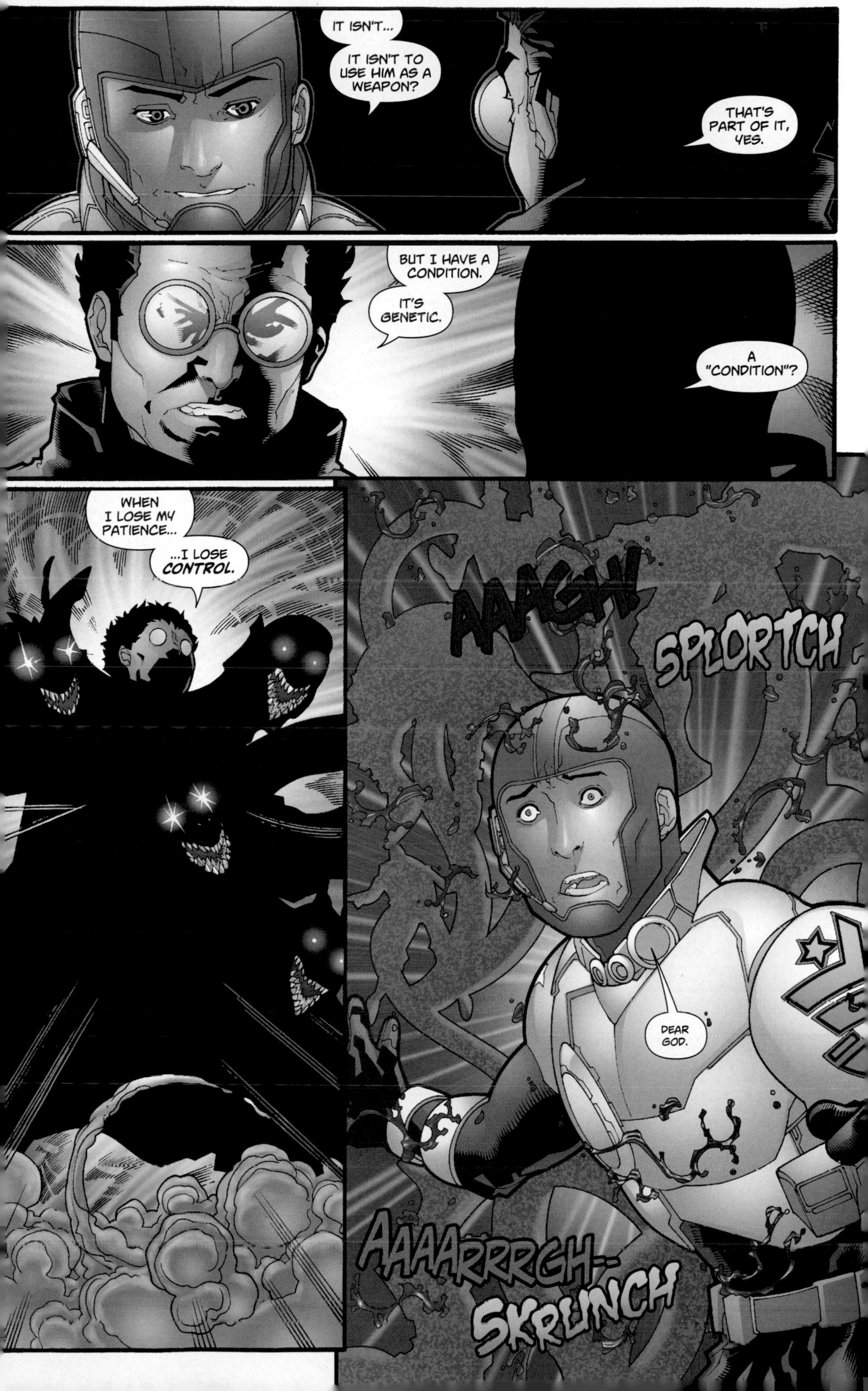
IT ISN'T...
IT ISN'T TO USE HIM AS A WEAPON?
THAT'S PART OF IT, YES.
BUT I HAVE A CONDITION.
IT'S GENETIC.
A "CONDITION"?
WHEN I LOSE MY PATIENCE...
...I LOSE CONTROL.
AAAGH!
SPLORTCH
DEAR GOD.
AAAARRRGH-
SKRUNCH

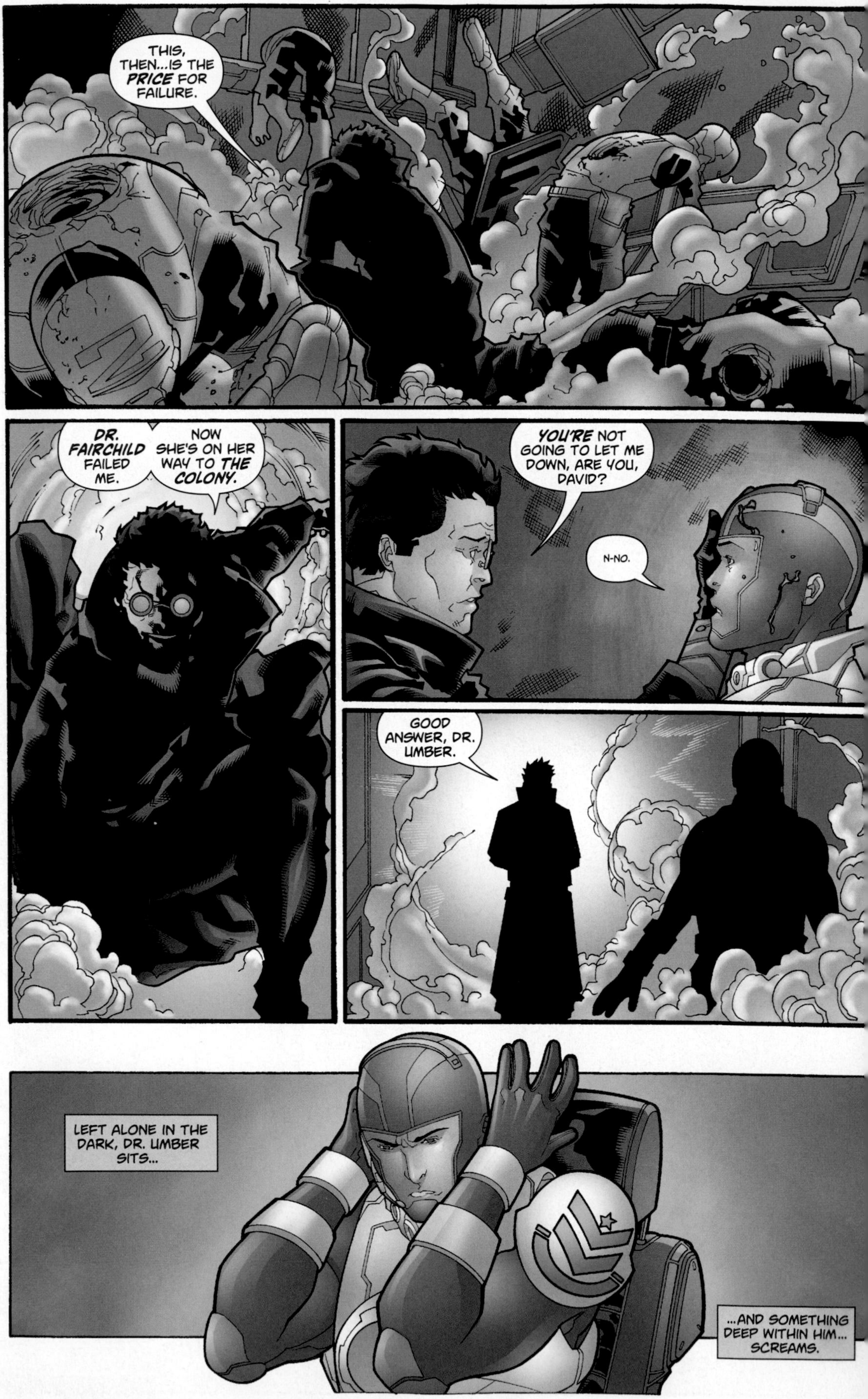
THIS, THEN...IS THE PRICE FOR FAILURE.
DR. FAIRCHILD FAILED ME.
NOW SHE'S ON HER WAY TO THE COLONY.
YOU'RE NOT GOING TO LET ME DOWN, ARE YOU, DAVID?
N-NO.
GOOD ANSWER, DR. UMBER.
LEFT ALONE IN THE DARK, DR. UMBER SITS...
...AND SOMETHING DEEP WITHIN HIM... SCREAMS.

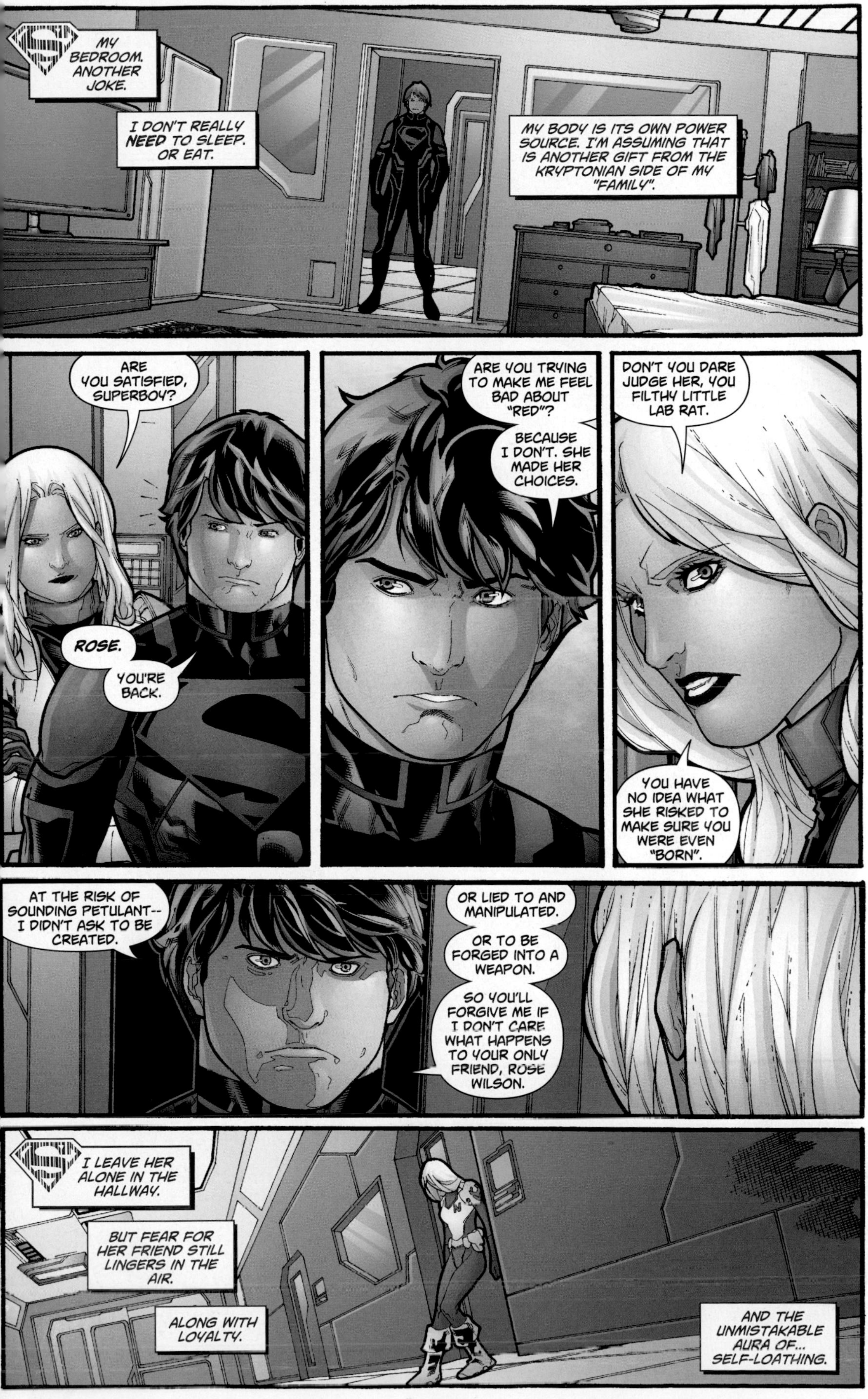
MY BEDROOM. ANOTHER JOKE.
I DON'T REALLY NEED TO SLEEP. OR EAT.
MY BODY IS ITS OWN POWER SOURCE. I'M ASSUMING THAT IS ANOTHER GIFT FROM THE KRYPTONIAN SIDE OF MY "FAMILY".
ARE YOU SATISFIED, SUPERBOY?
ROSE.
YOU'RE BACK.
ARE YOU TRYING TO MAKE ME FEEL BAD ABOUT "RED"?
BECAUSE I DON'T. SHE MADE HER CHOICES.
DON'T YOU DARE JUDGE HER, YOU FILTHY LITTLE LAB RAT.
YOU HAVE NO IDEA WHAT SHE RISKED TO MAKE SURE YOU WERE EVEN "BORN".
AT THE RISK OF SOUNDING PETULANT-- I DIDN'T ASK TO BE CREATED.
OR LIED TO AND MANIPULATED.
OR TO BE FORGED INTO A WEAPON.
SO YOU'LL FORGIVE ME IF I DON'T CARE WHAT HAPPENS TO YOUR ONLY FRIEND, ROSE WILSON.
I LEAVE HER ALONE IN THE HALLWAY.
BUT FEAR FOR HER FRIEND STILL LINGERS IN THE AIR.
ALONG WITH LOYALTY.
AND THE UNMISTAKABLE AURA OF... SELF-LOATHING.

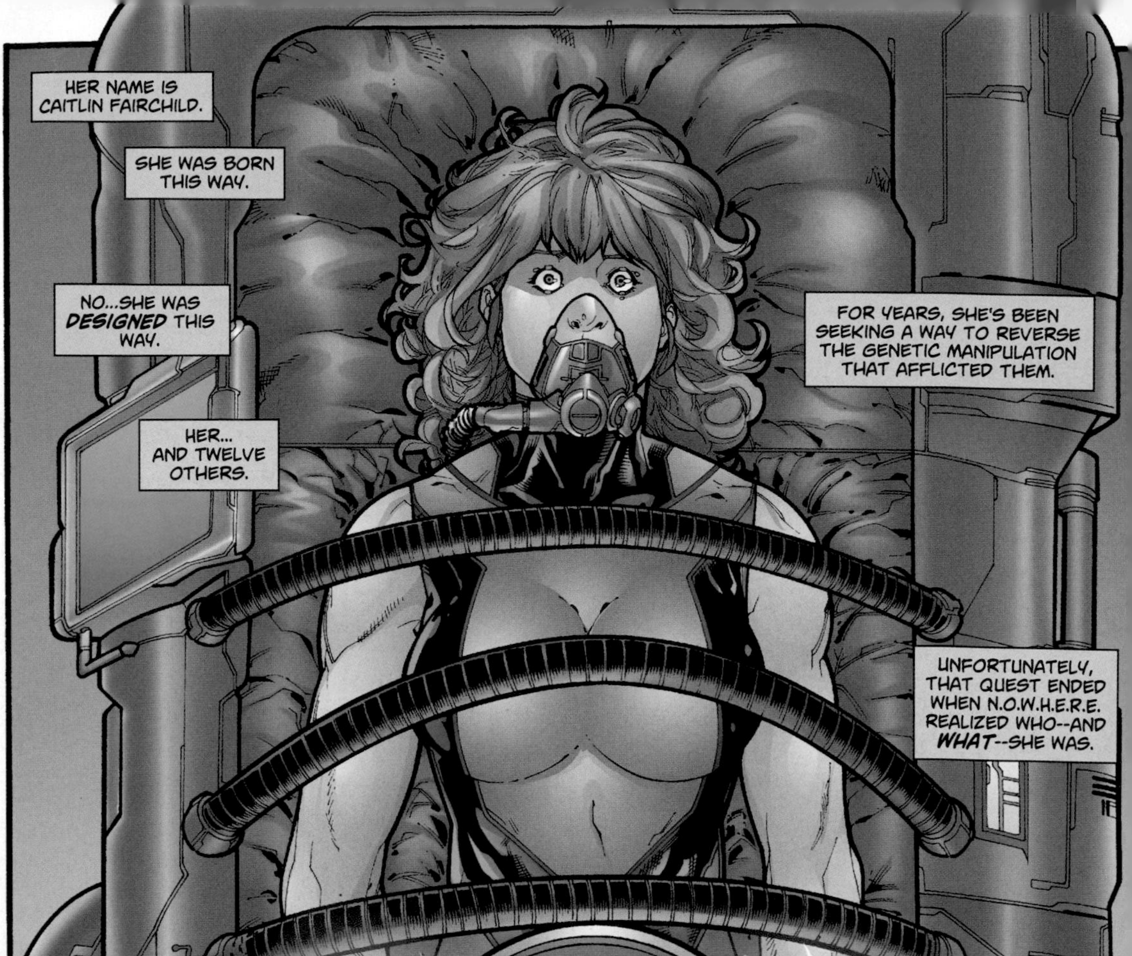
HER NAME IS CAITLIN FAIRCHILD.
SHE WAS BORN THIS WAY.
NO...SHE WAS *DESIGNED* THIS WAY.
HER... AND TWELVE OTHERS.
FOR YEARS, SHE'S BEEN SEEKING A WAY TO REVERSE THE GENETIC MANIPULATION THAT AFFLICTED THEM.
UNFORTUNATELY, THAT QUEST ENDED WHEN N.O.W.H.E.R.E. REALIZED WHO--AND *WHAT*--SHE WAS.
CAREFUL, CAREFUL...

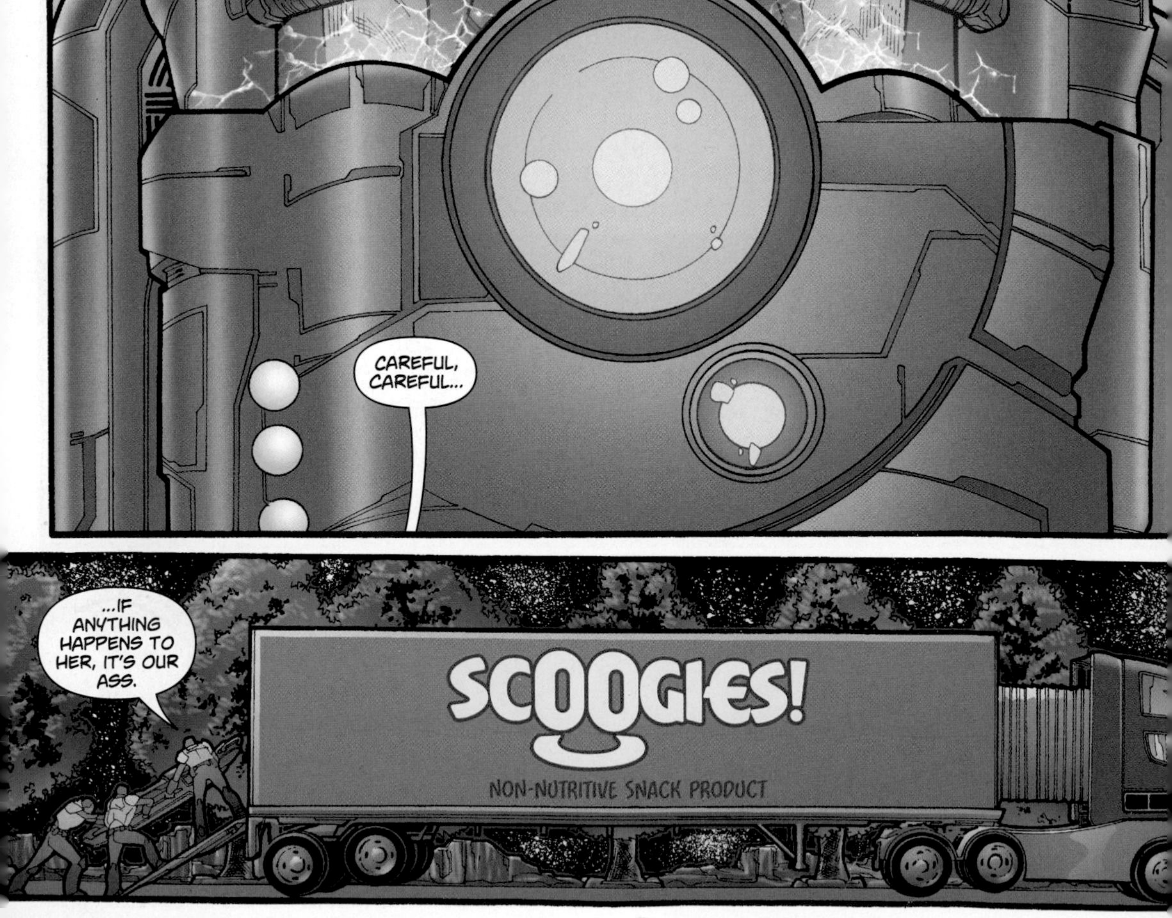
...IF ANYTHING HAPPENS TO HER, IT'S OUR ASS.
SCOOGIES!
NON-NUTRITIVE SNACK PRODUCT

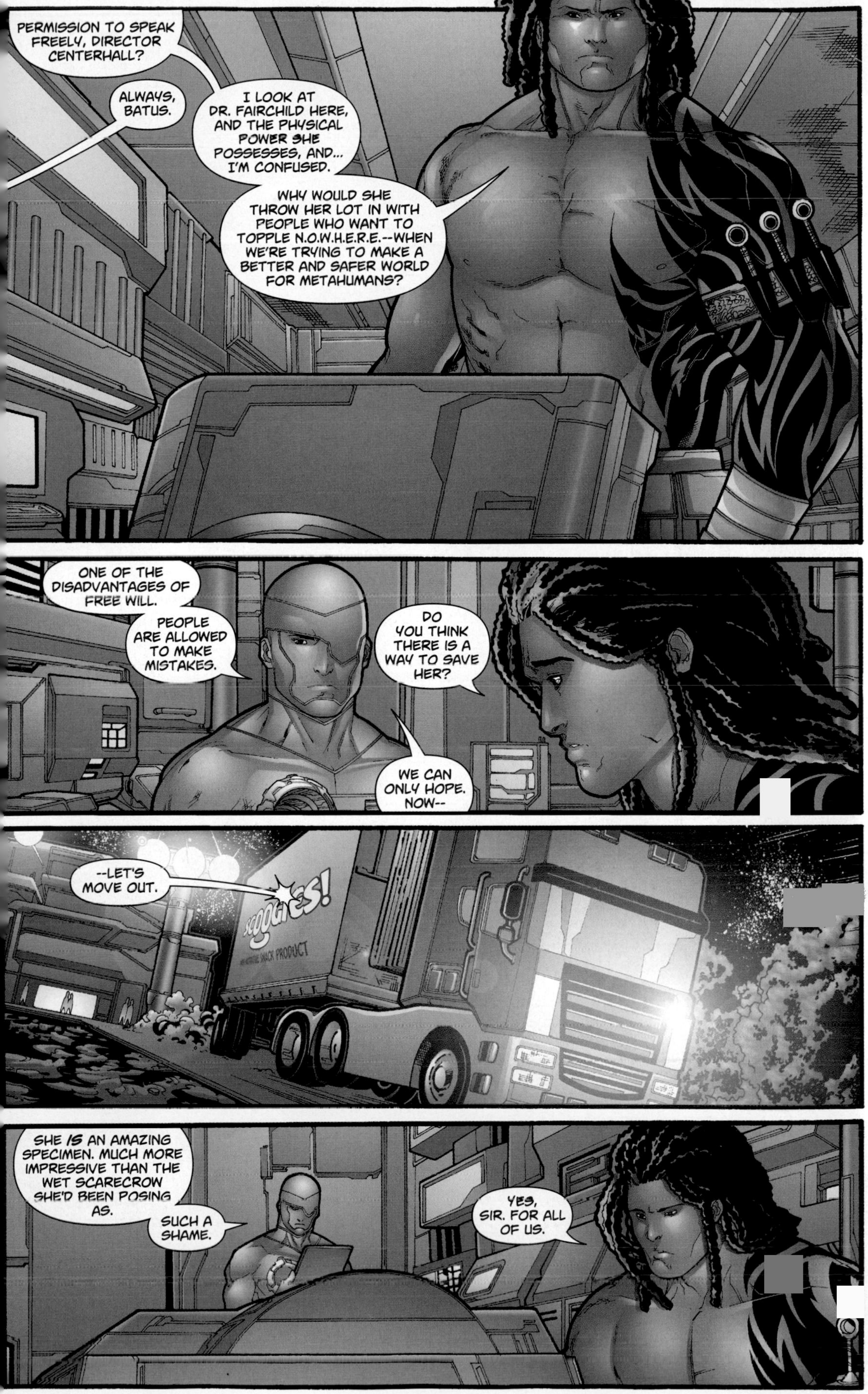
PERMISSION TO SPEAK FREELY, DIRECTOR CENTERHALL?
ALWAYS, BATUS.
I LOOK AT DR. FAIRCHILD HERE, AND THE PHYSICAL POWER SHE POSSESSES, AND... I'M CONFUSED.
WHY WOULD SHE THROW HER LOT IN WITH PEOPLE WHO WANT TO TOPPLE N.O.W.H.E.R.E.--WHEN WE'RE TRYING TO MAKE A BETTER AND SAFER WORLD FOR METAHUMANS?
ONE OF THE DISADVANTAGES OF FREE WILL.
PEOPLE ARE ALLOWED TO MAKE MISTAKES.
DO YOU THINK THERE IS A WAY TO SAVE HER?
WE CAN ONLY HOPE. NOW--
--LET'S MOVE OUT.
SCOOGIES!
SNACK PRODUCT
SHE *IS* AN AMAZING SPECIMEN. MUCH MORE IMPRESSIVE THAN THE WET SCARECROW SHE'D BEEN POSING AS.
SUCH A SHAME.
YES, SIR. FOR ALL OF US.

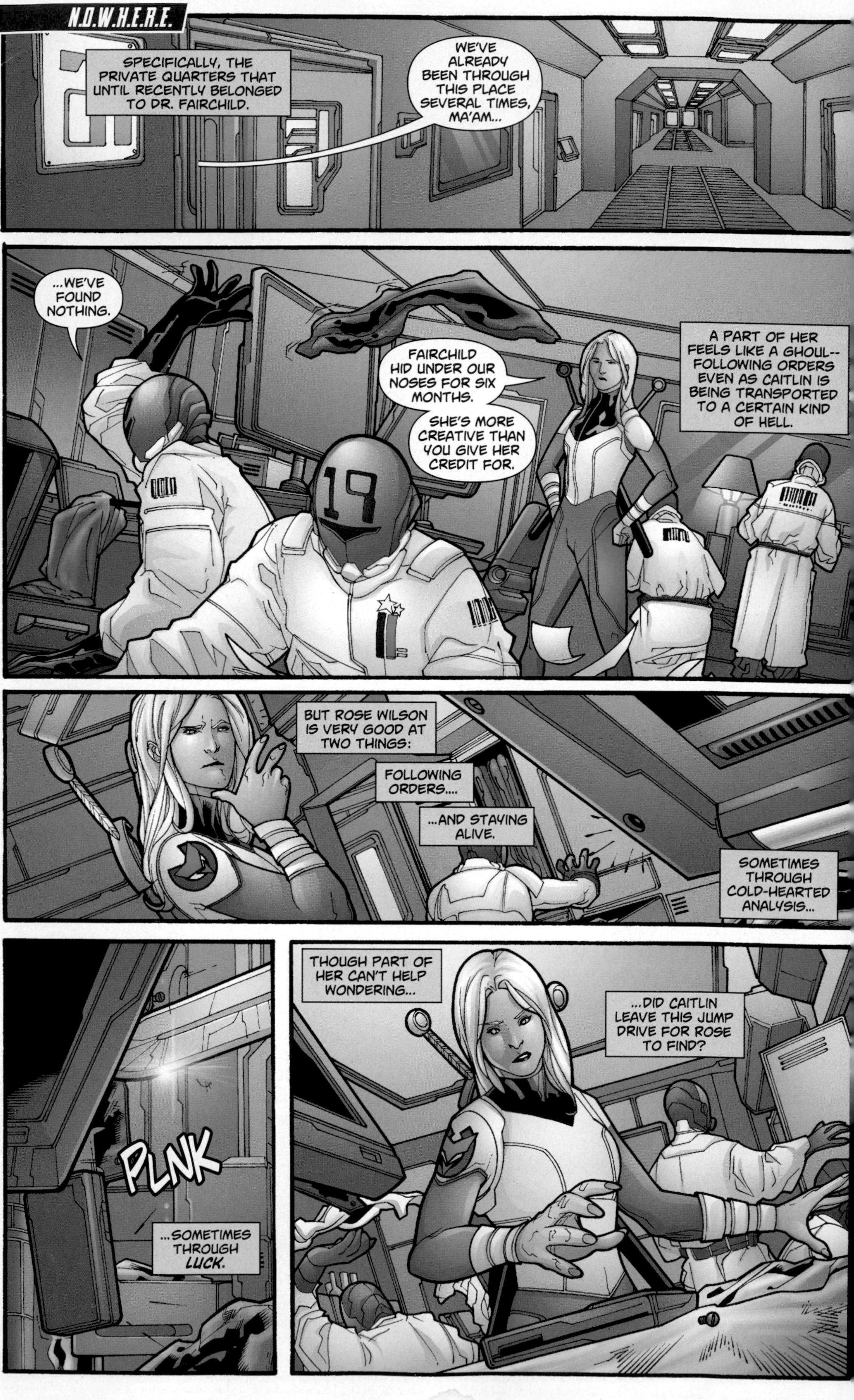
SPECIFICALLY, THE PRIVATE QUARTERS THAT UNTIL RECENTLY BELONGED TO DR. FAIRCHILD.
WE'VE ALREADY BEEN THROUGH THIS PLACE SEVERAL TIMES, MA'AM...
...WE'VE FOUND NOTHING.
FAIRCHILD HID UNDER OUR NOSES FOR SIX MONTHS.
SHE'S MORE CREATIVE THAN YOU GIVE HER CREDIT FOR.
A PART OF HER FEELS LIKE A GHOUL--FOLLOWING ORDERS EVEN AS CAITLIN IS BEING TRANSPORTED TO A CERTAIN KIND OF HELL.
19
BUT ROSE WILSON IS VERY GOOD AT TWO THINGS:
FOLLOWING ORDERS....
...AND STAYING ALIVE.
SOMETIMES THROUGH COLD-HEARTED ANALYSIS...
PLNK
...SOMETIMES THROUGH LUCK.
THOUGH PART OF HER CAN'T HELP WONDERING...
...DID CAITLIN LEAVE THIS JUMP DRIVE FOR ROSE TO FIND?

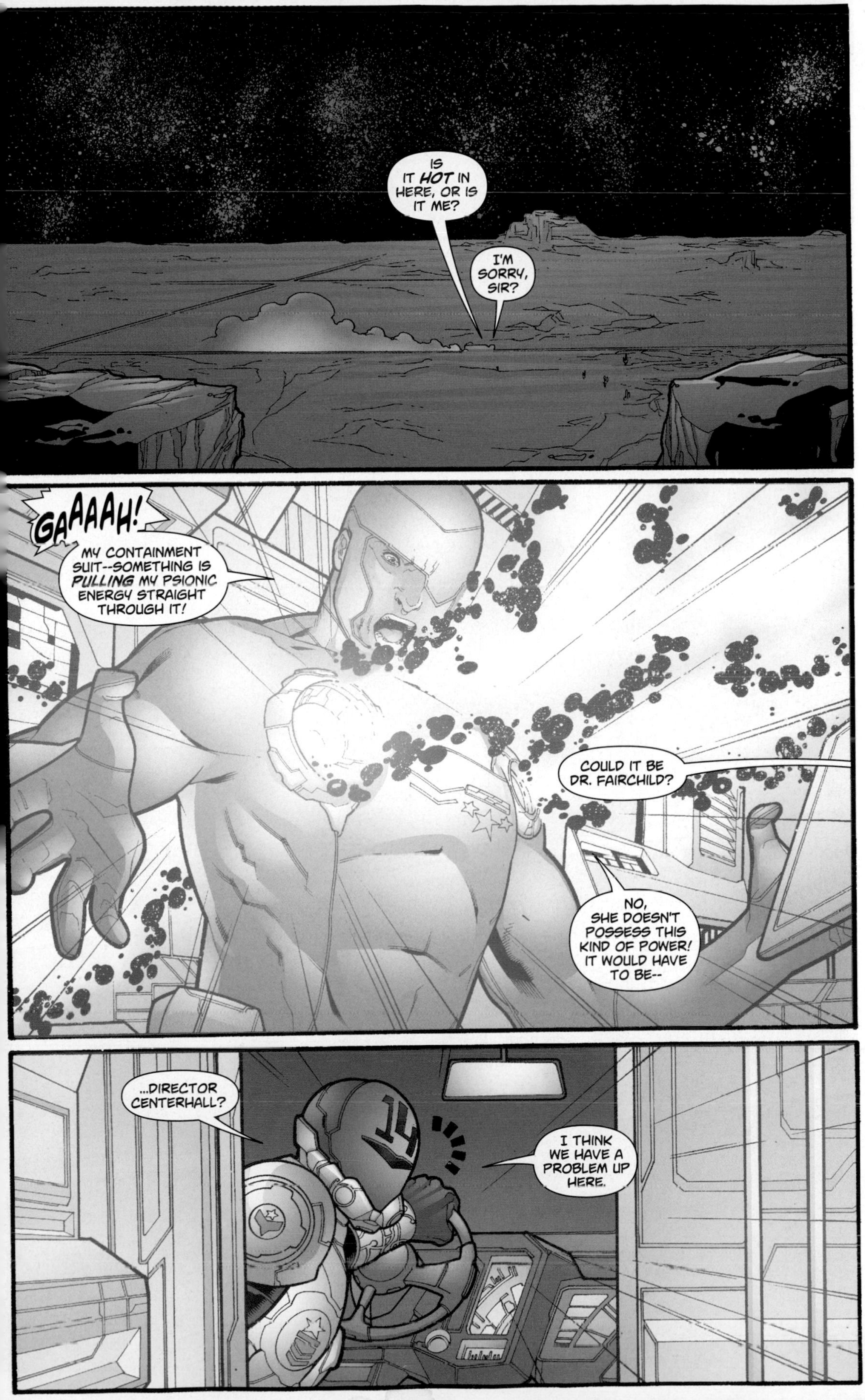
IS IT HOT IN HERE, OR IS IT ME?
I'M SORRY, SIR?
GAAAAH!
MY CONTAINMENT SUIT--SOMETHING IS PULLING MY PSIONIC ENERGY STRAIGHT THROUGH IT!
COULD IT BE DR. FAIRCHILD?
NO, SHE DOESN'T POSSESS THIS KIND OF POWER! IT WOULD HAVE TO BE--
...DIRECTOR CENTERHALL?
I THINK WE HAVE A PROBLEM UP HERE.

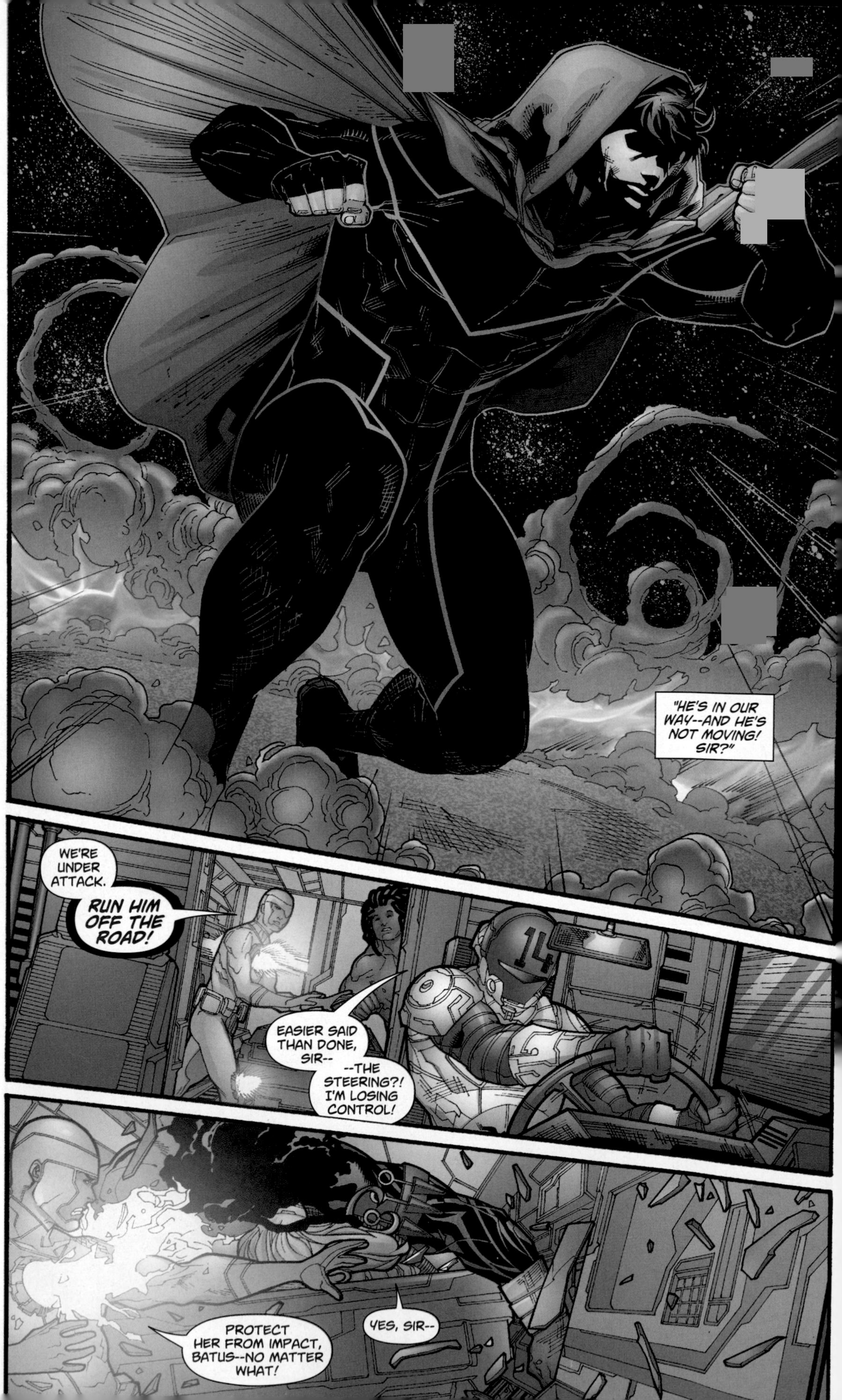
"HE'S IN OUR WAY--AND HE'S NOT MOVING! SIR?"
WE'RE UNDER ATTACK.
RUN HIM OFF THE ROAD!
EASIER SAID THAN DONE, SIR--
--THE STEERING?! I'M LOSING CONTROL!
PROTECT HER FROM IMPACT, BATUS--NO MATTER WHAT!
YES, SIR--

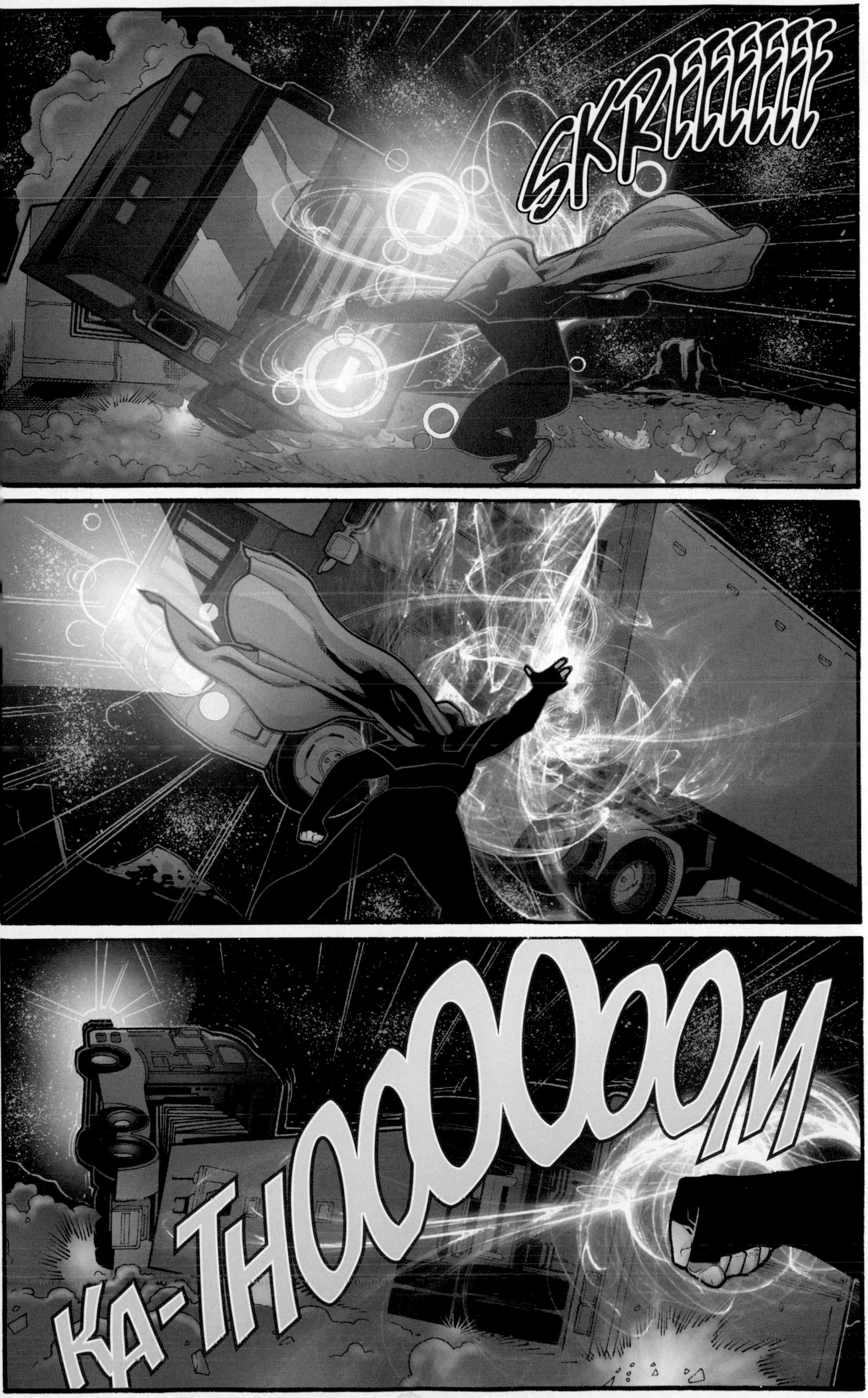
SKREEEEEEE
KA-THOOOOOOM

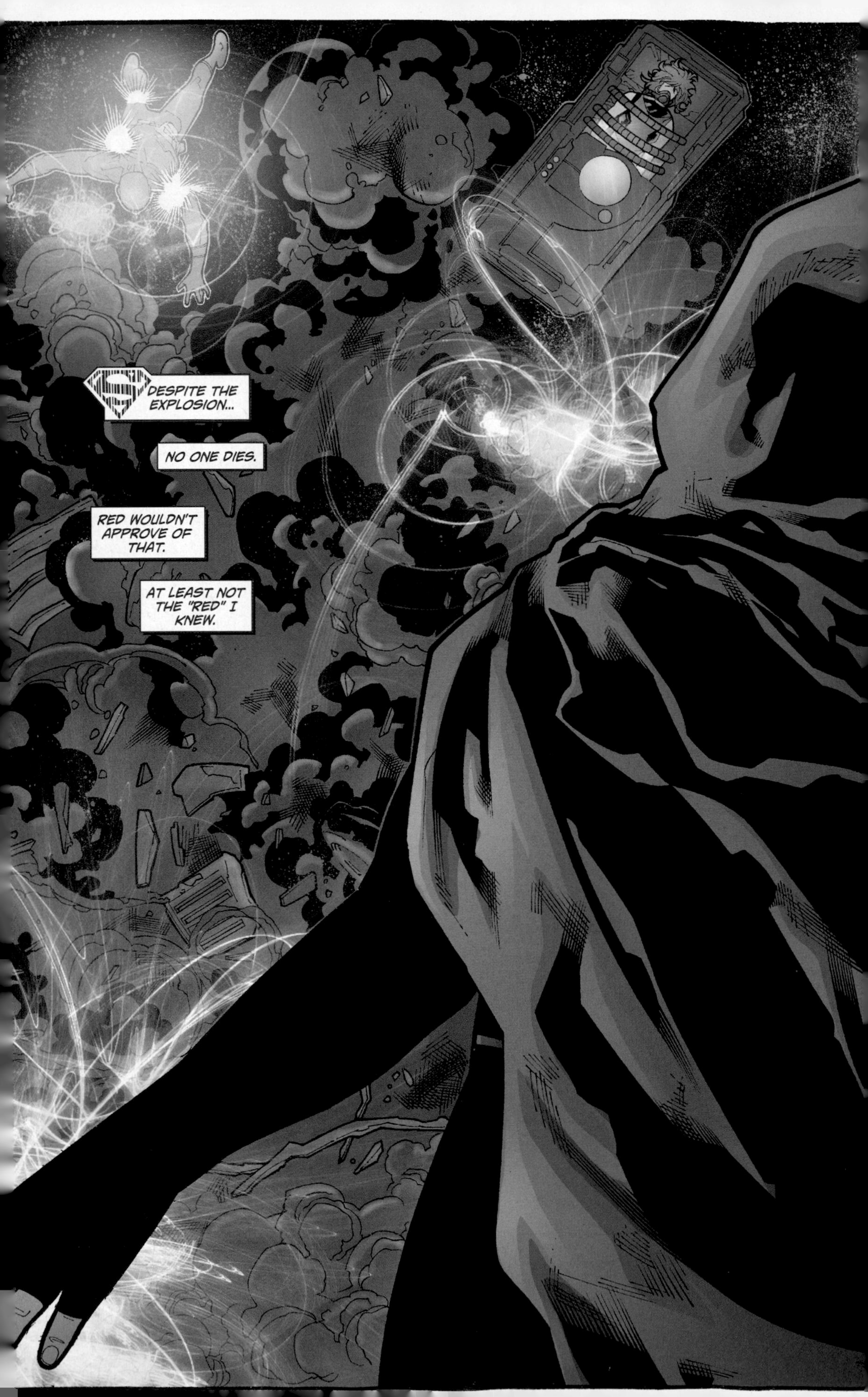
DESPITE THE EXPLOSION...
NO ONE DIES.
RED WOULDN'T APPROVE OF THAT.
AT LEAST NOT THE "RED" I KNEW.

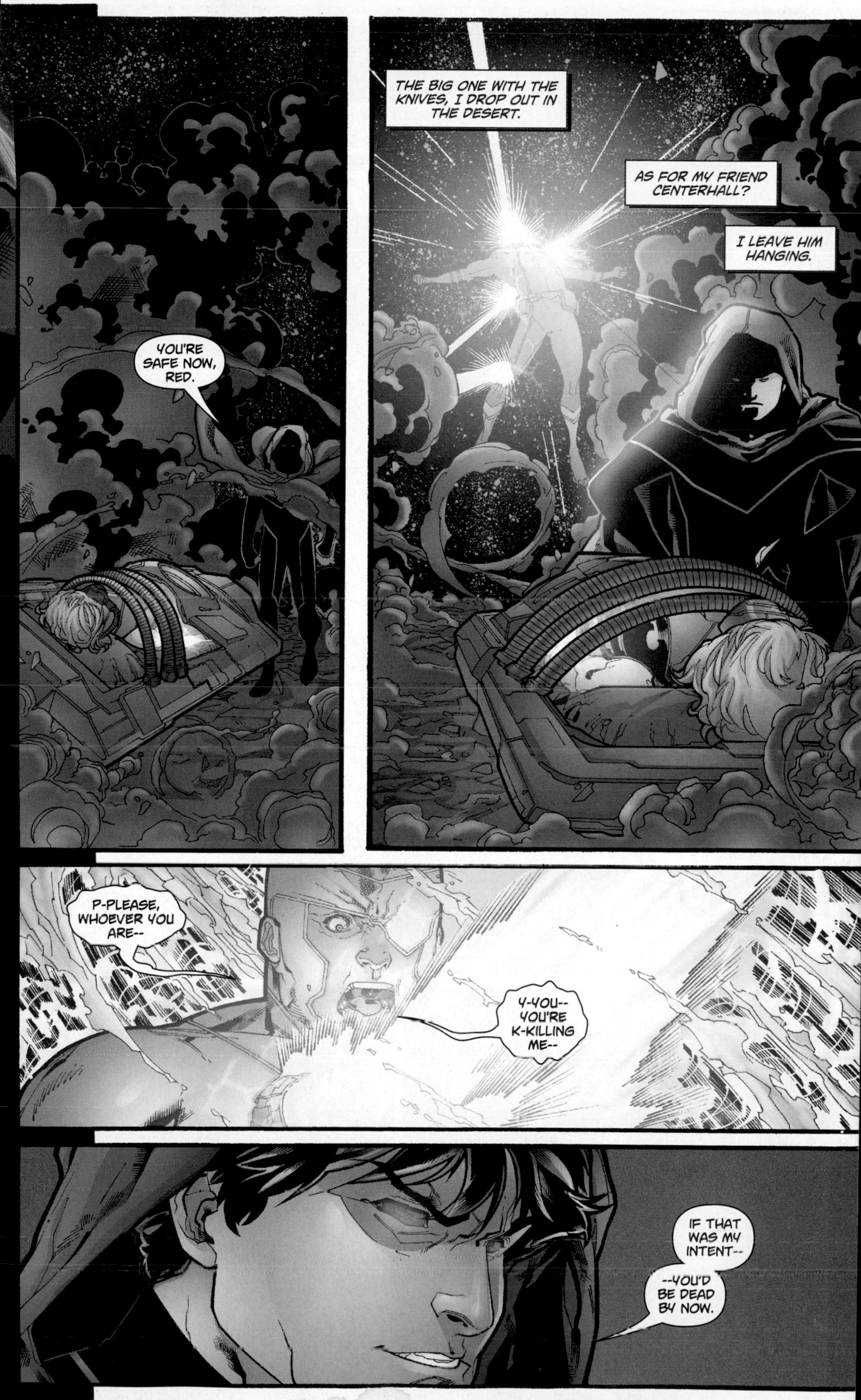
YOU'RE SAFE NOW, RED.
THE BIG ONE WITH THE KNIVES, I DROP OUT IN THE DESERT.
AS FOR MY FRIEND CENTERHALL?
I LEAVE HIM HANGING.
P-PLEASE, WHOEVER YOU ARE--
Y-YOU-- YOU'RE K-KILLING ME--
IF THAT WAS MY INTENT--
--YOU'D BE DEAD BY NOW.

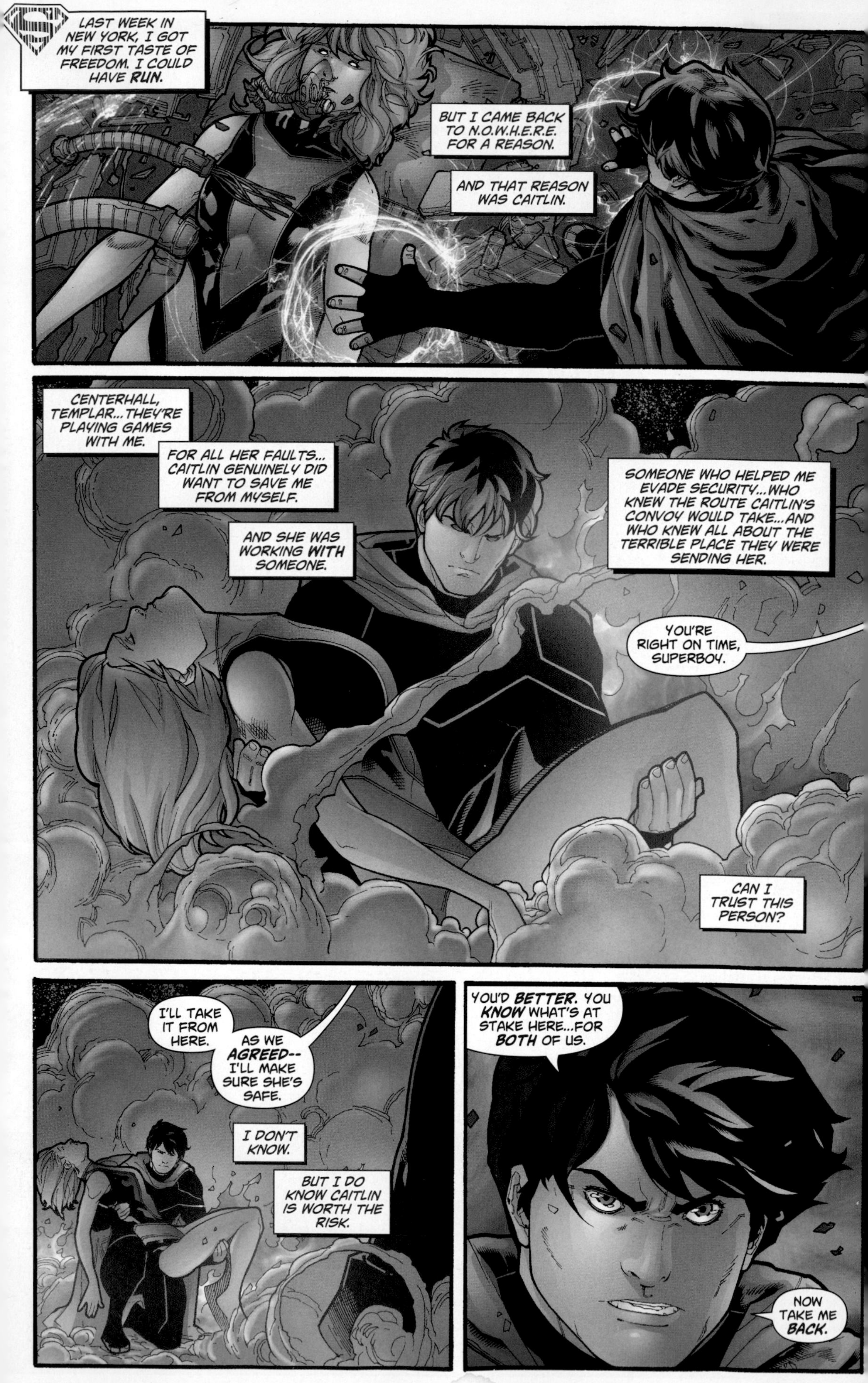
LAST WEEK IN NEW YORK, I GOT MY FIRST TASTE OF FREEDOM. I COULD HAVE RUN.
BUT I CAME BACK TO N.O.W.H.E.R.E. FOR A REASON.
AND THAT REASON WAS CAITLIN.
CENTERHALL, TEMPLAR...THEY'RE PLAYING GAMES WITH ME.
FOR ALL HER FAULTS... CAITLIN GENUINELY DID WANT TO SAVE ME FROM MYSELF.
AND SHE WAS WORKING WITH SOMEONE.
SOMEONE WHO HELPED ME EVADE SECURITY...WHO KNEW THE ROUTE CAITLIN'S CONVOY WOULD TAKE...AND WHO KNEW ALL ABOUT THE TERRIBLE PLACE THEY WERE SENDING HER.
YOU'RE RIGHT ON TIME, SUPERBOY.
CAN I TRUST THIS PERSON?
I'LL TAKE IT FROM HERE.
AS WE AGREED-- I'LL MAKE SURE SHE'S SAFE.
I DON'T KNOW.
BUT I DO KNOW CAITLIN IS WORTH THE RISK.
YOU'D BETTER. YOU KNOW WHAT'S AT STAKE HERE...FOR BOTH OF US.
NOW TAKE ME BACK.

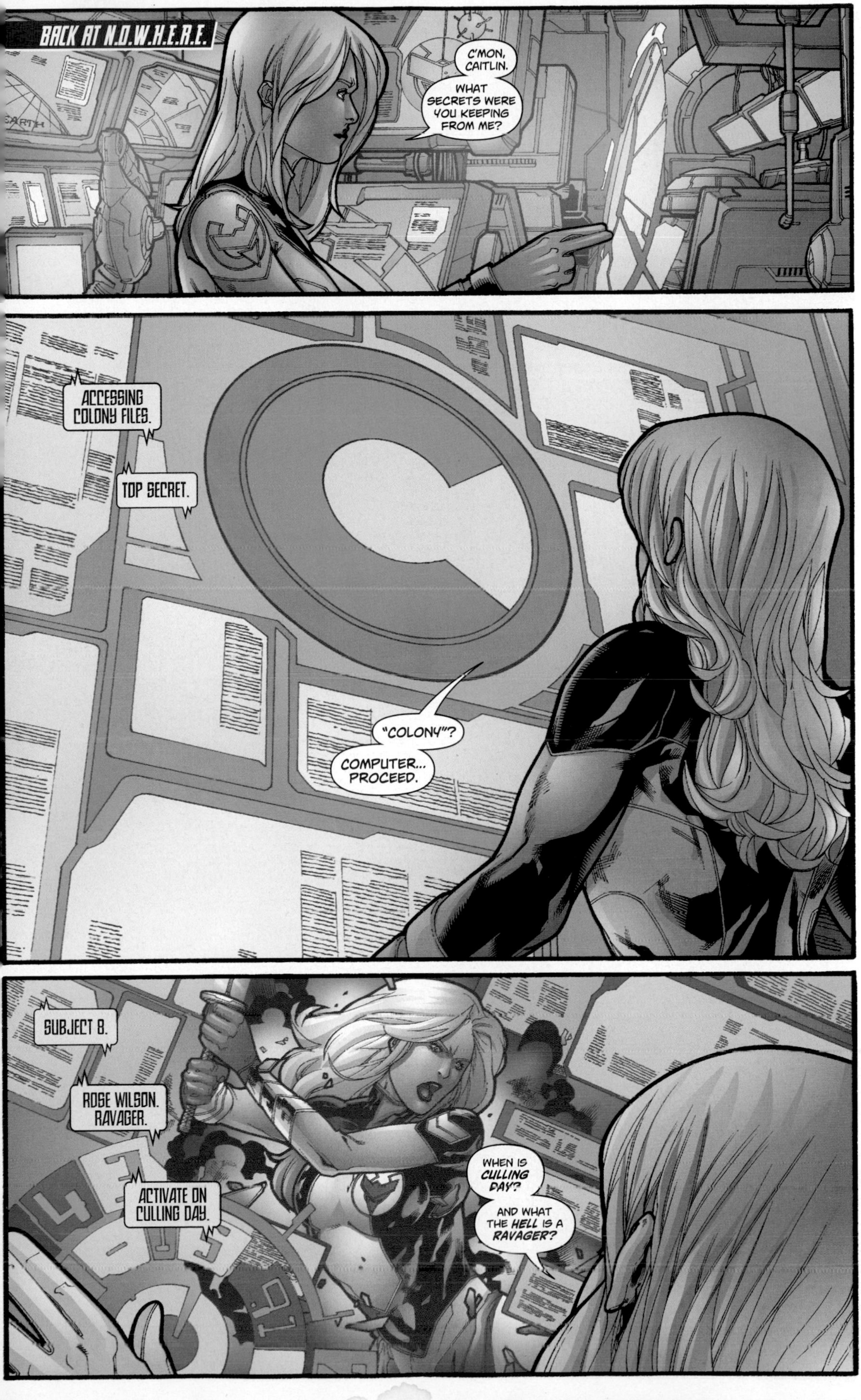
BACK AT N.O.W.H.E.R.E.
C'MON, CAITLIN.
WHAT SECRETS WERE YOU KEEPING FROM ME?
ACCESSING COLONY FILES.
TOP SECRET.
"COLONY"?
COMPUTER... PROCEED.
SUBJECT 8.
ROSE WILSON. RAVAGER.
ACTIVATE ON CULLING DAY.
WHEN IS *CULLING DAY?*
AND WHAT THE *HELL* IS A *RAVAGER?*

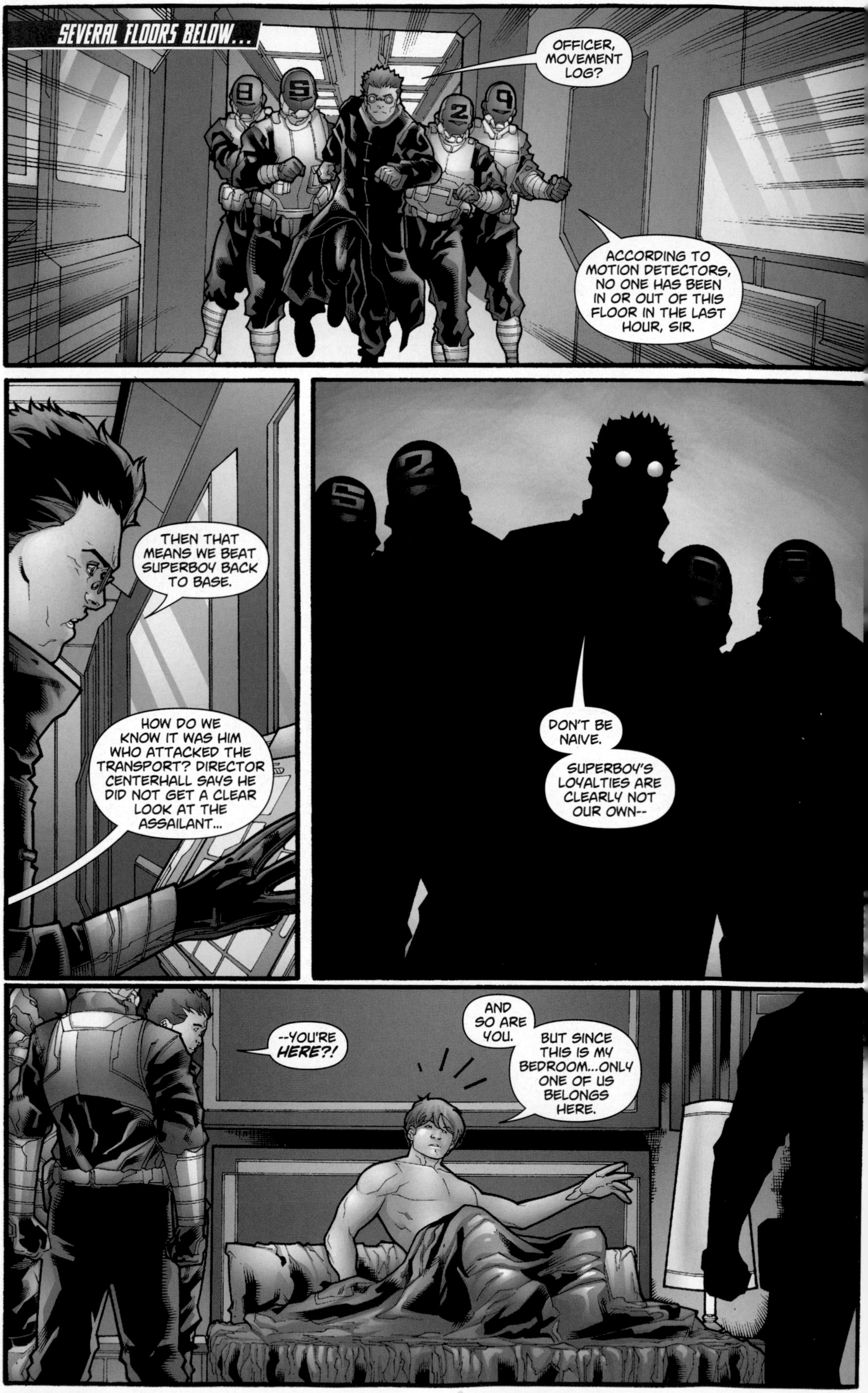
SEVERAL FLOORS BELOW...
OFFICER, MOVEMENT LOG?
ACCORDING TO MOTION DETECTORS, NO ONE HAS BEEN IN OR OUT OF THIS FLOOR IN THE LAST HOUR, SIR.
THEN THAT MEANS WE BEAT SUPERBOY BACK TO BASE.
HOW DO WE KNOW IT WAS HIM WHO ATTACKED THE TRANSPORT? DIRECTOR CENTERHALL SAYS HE DID NOT GET A CLEAR LOOK AT THE ASSAILANT...
DON'T BE NAIVE.
SUPERBOY'S LOYALTIES ARE CLEARLY NOT OUR OWN--
--YOU'RE HERE?!
AND SO ARE YOU.
BUT SINCE THIS IS MY BEDROOM...ONLY ONE OF US BELONGS HERE.

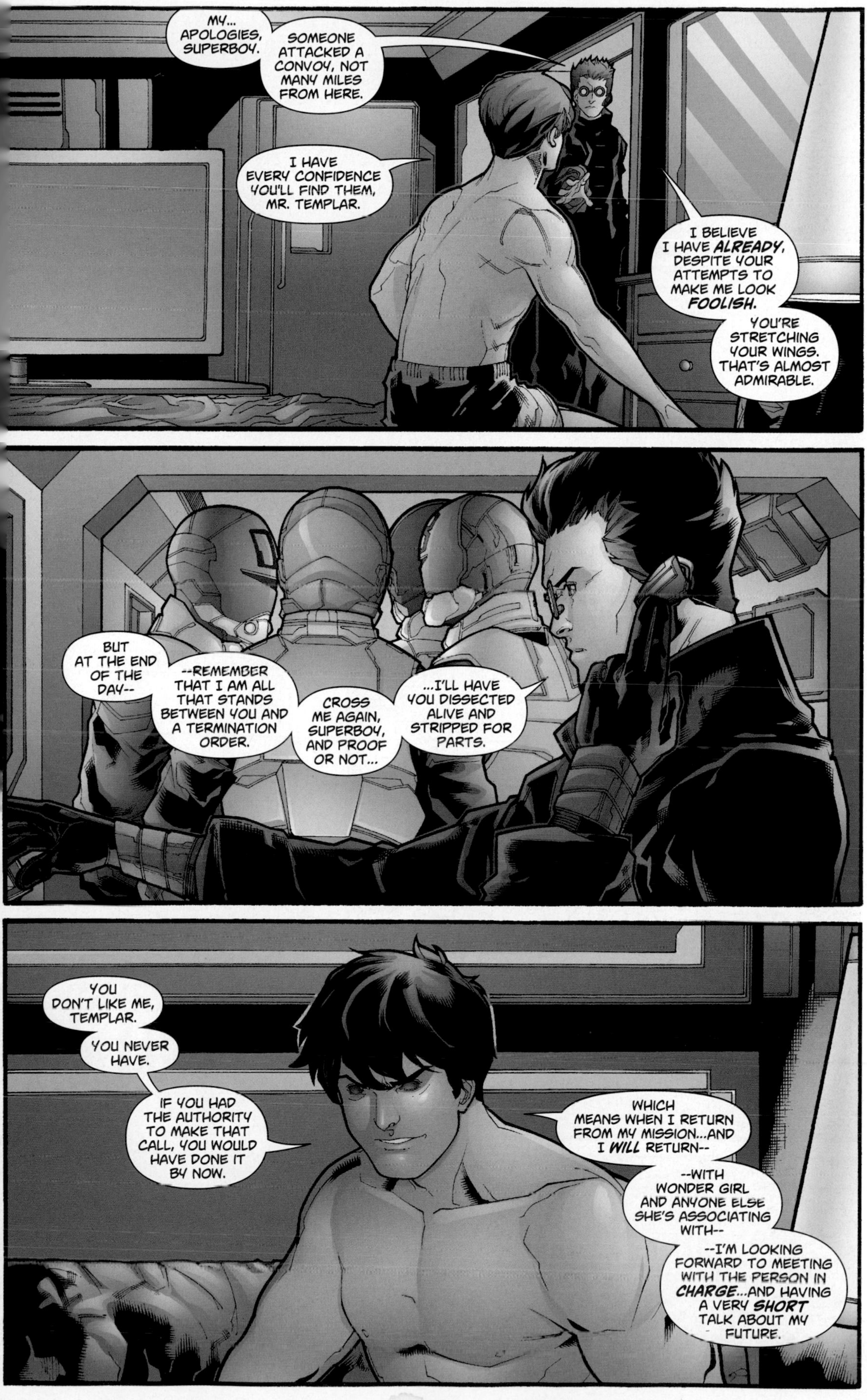
MY... APOLOGIES, SUPERBOY.
SOMEONE ATTACKED A CONVOY, NOT MANY MILES FROM HERE.
I HAVE EVERY CONFIDENCE YOU'LL FIND THEM, MR. TEMPLAR.
I BELIEVE I HAVE ALREADY, DESPITE YOUR ATTEMPTS TO MAKE ME LOOK FOOLISH.
YOU'RE STRETCHING YOUR WINGS. THAT'S ALMOST ADMIRABLE.
BUT AT THE END OF THE DAY--
--REMEMBER THAT I AM ALL THAT STANDS BETWEEN YOU AND A TERMINATION ORDER.
CROSS ME AGAIN, SUPERBOY, AND PROOF OR NOT...
...I'LL HAVE YOU DISSECTED ALIVE AND STRIPPED FOR PARTS.
YOU DON'T LIKE ME, TEMPLAR.
YOU NEVER HAVE.
IF YOU HAD THE AUTHORITY TO MAKE THAT CALL, YOU WOULD HAVE DONE IT BY NOW.
WHICH MEANS WHEN I RETURN FROM MY MISSION...AND I WILL RETURN--
--WITH WONDER GIRL AND ANYONE ELSE SHE'S ASSOCIATING WITH--
--I'M LOOKING FORWARD TO MEETING WITH THE PERSON IN CHARGE...AND HAVING A VERY SHORT TALK ABOUT MY FUTURE.

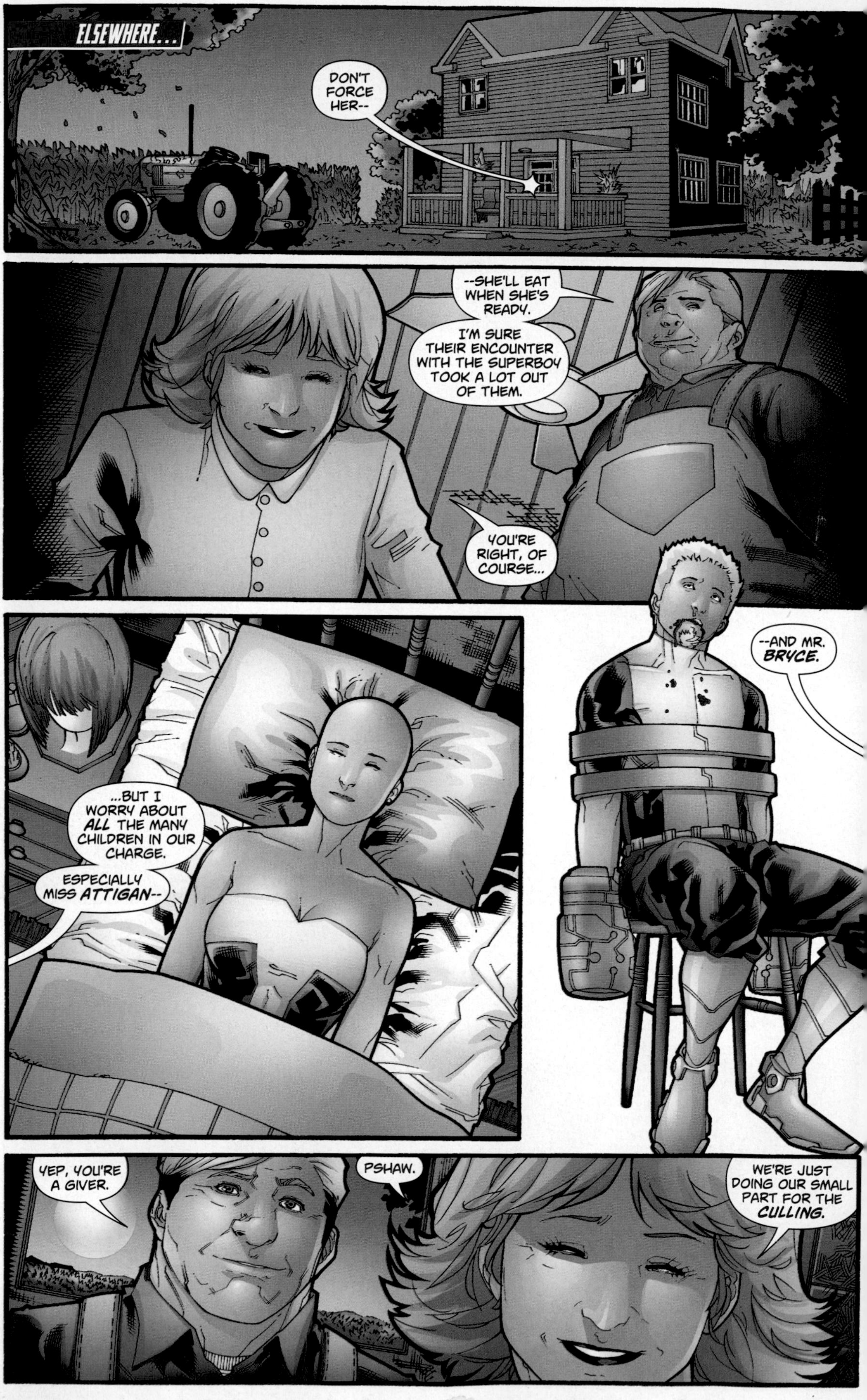
ELSEWHERE...
DON'T FORCE HER--
--SHE'LL EAT WHEN SHE'S READY.
I'M SURE THEIR ENCOUNTER WITH THE SUPERBOY TOOK A LOT OUT OF THEM.
YOU'RE RIGHT, OF COURSE...
...BUT I WORRY ABOUT ALL THE MANY CHILDREN IN OUR CHARGE.
ESPECIALLY MISS ATTIGAN--
--AND MR. BRYCE.
YEP, YOU'RE A GIVER.
PSHAW.
WE'RE JUST DOING OUR SMALL PART FOR THE CULLING.

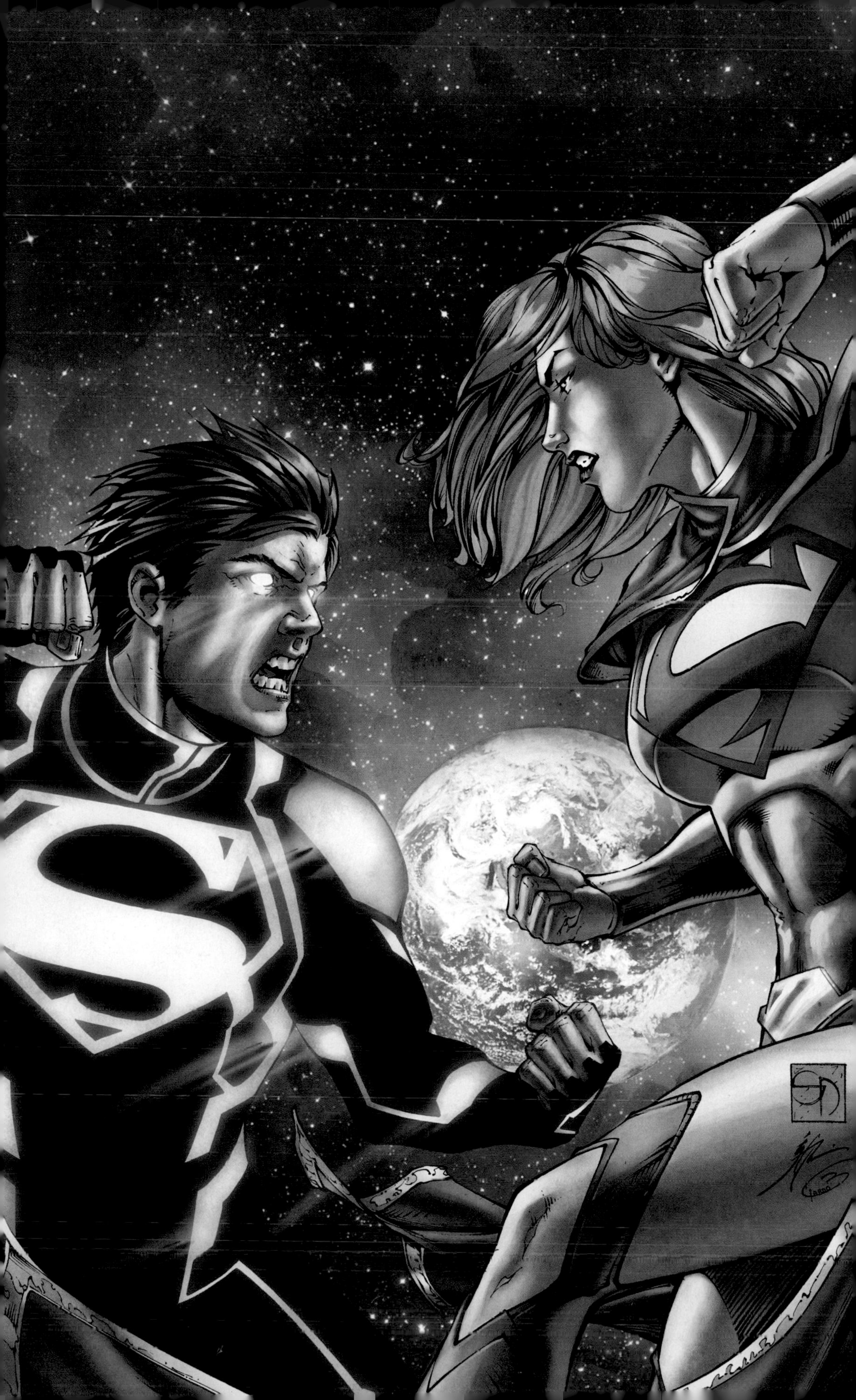

Cover by SHANE DAVIS, JONATHAN GLAPION & BARBARA CIARDO

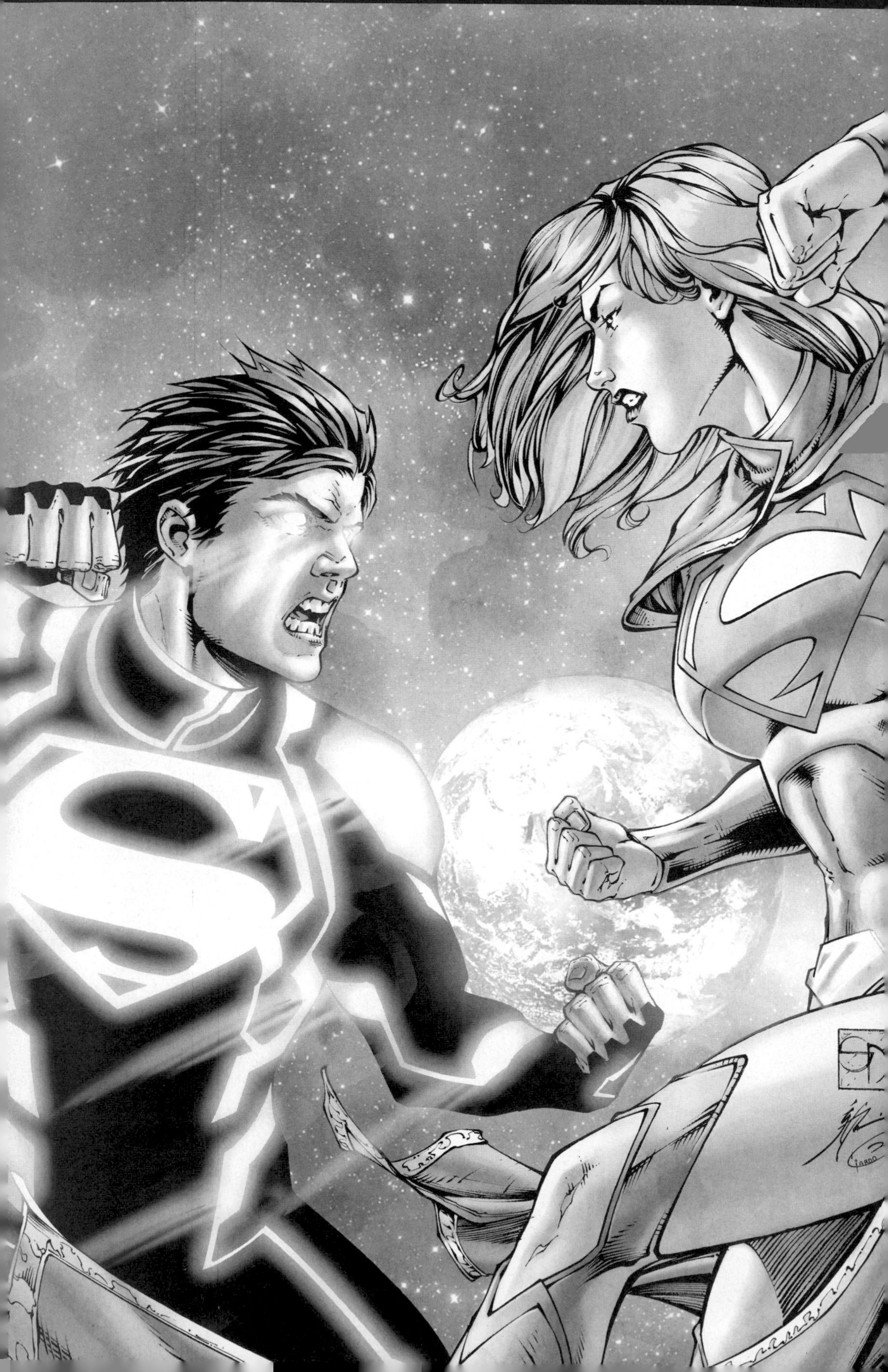

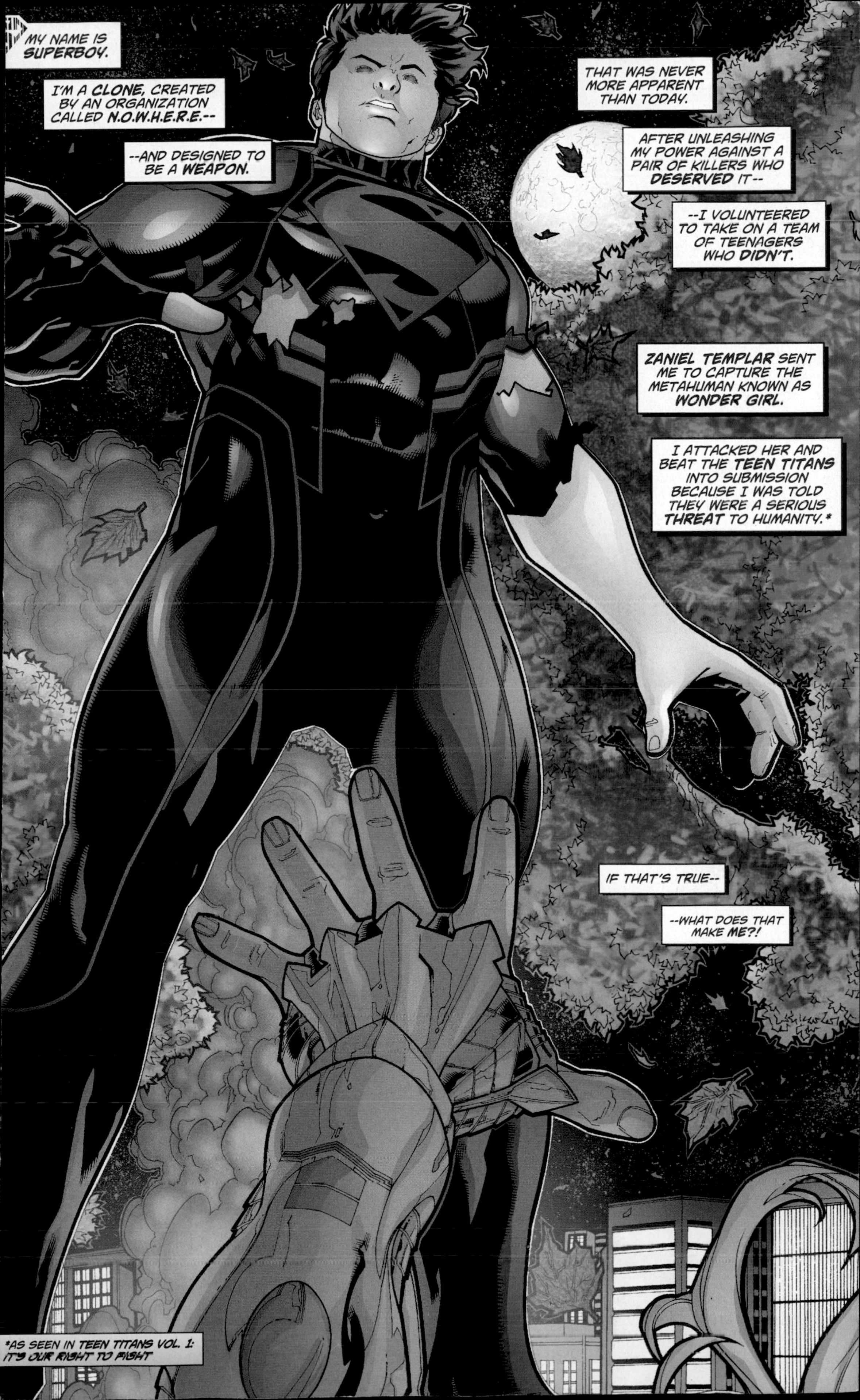
MY NAME IS SUPERBOY.
I'M A CLONE, CREATED BY AN ORGANIZATION CALLED N.O.W.H.E.R.E.--
--AND DESIGNED TO BE A WEAPON.
THAT WAS NEVER MORE APPARENT THAN TODAY.
AFTER UNLEASHING MY POWER AGAINST A PAIR OF KILLERS WHO DESERVED IT--
--I VOLUNTEERED TO TAKE ON A TEAM OF TEENAGERS WHO DIDN'T.
ZANIEL TEMPLAR SENT ME TO CAPTURE THE METAHUMAN KNOWN AS WONDER GIRL.
I ATTACKED HER AND BEAT THE TEEN TITANS INTO SUBMISSION BECAUSE I WAS TOLD THEY WERE A SERIOUS THREAT TO HUMANITY.*
IF THAT'S TRUE--
--WHAT DOES THAT MAKE ME?!
*AS SEEN IN TEEN TITANS VOL. 1: IT'S OUR RIGHT TO FIGHT

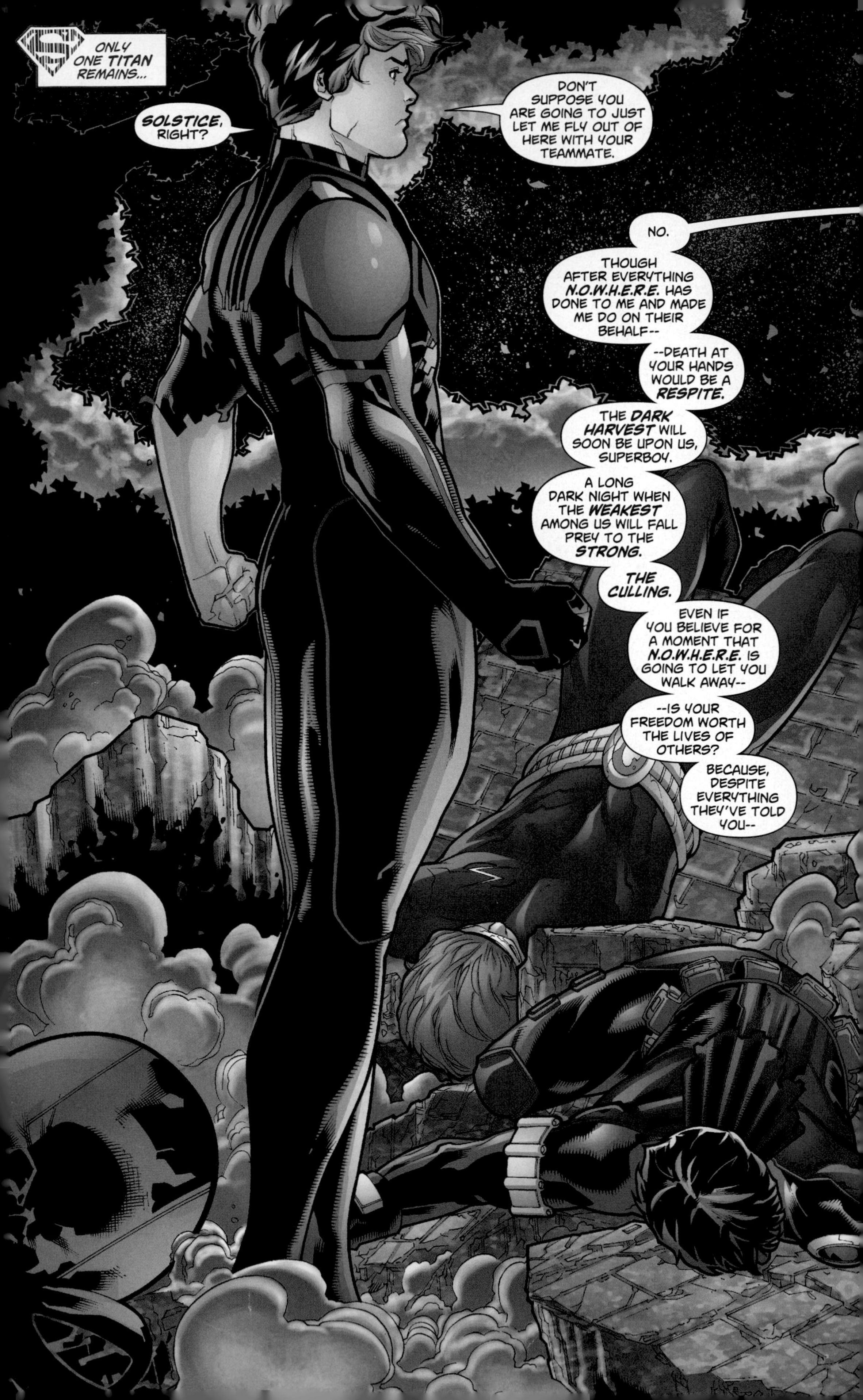
ONLY ONE TITAN REMAINS...
SOLSTICE, RIGHT?
DON'T SUPPOSE YOU ARE GOING TO JUST LET ME FLY OUT OF HERE WITH YOUR TEAMMATE.
NO.
THOUGH AFTER EVERYTHING N.O.W.H.E.R.E. HAS DONE TO ME AND MADE ME DO ON THEIR BEHALF--
--DEATH AT YOUR HANDS WOULD BE A RESPITE.
THE DARK HARVEST WILL SOON BE UPON US, SUPERBOY.
A LONG DARK NIGHT WHEN THE WEAKEST AMONG US WILL FALL PREY TO THE STRONG.
THE CULLING.
EVEN IF YOU BELIEVE FOR A MOMENT THAT N.O.W.H.E.R.E. IS GOING TO LET YOU WALK AWAY--
--IS YOUR FREEDOM WORTH THE LIVES OF OTHERS?
BECAUSE, DESPITE EVERYTHING THEY'VE TOLD YOU--

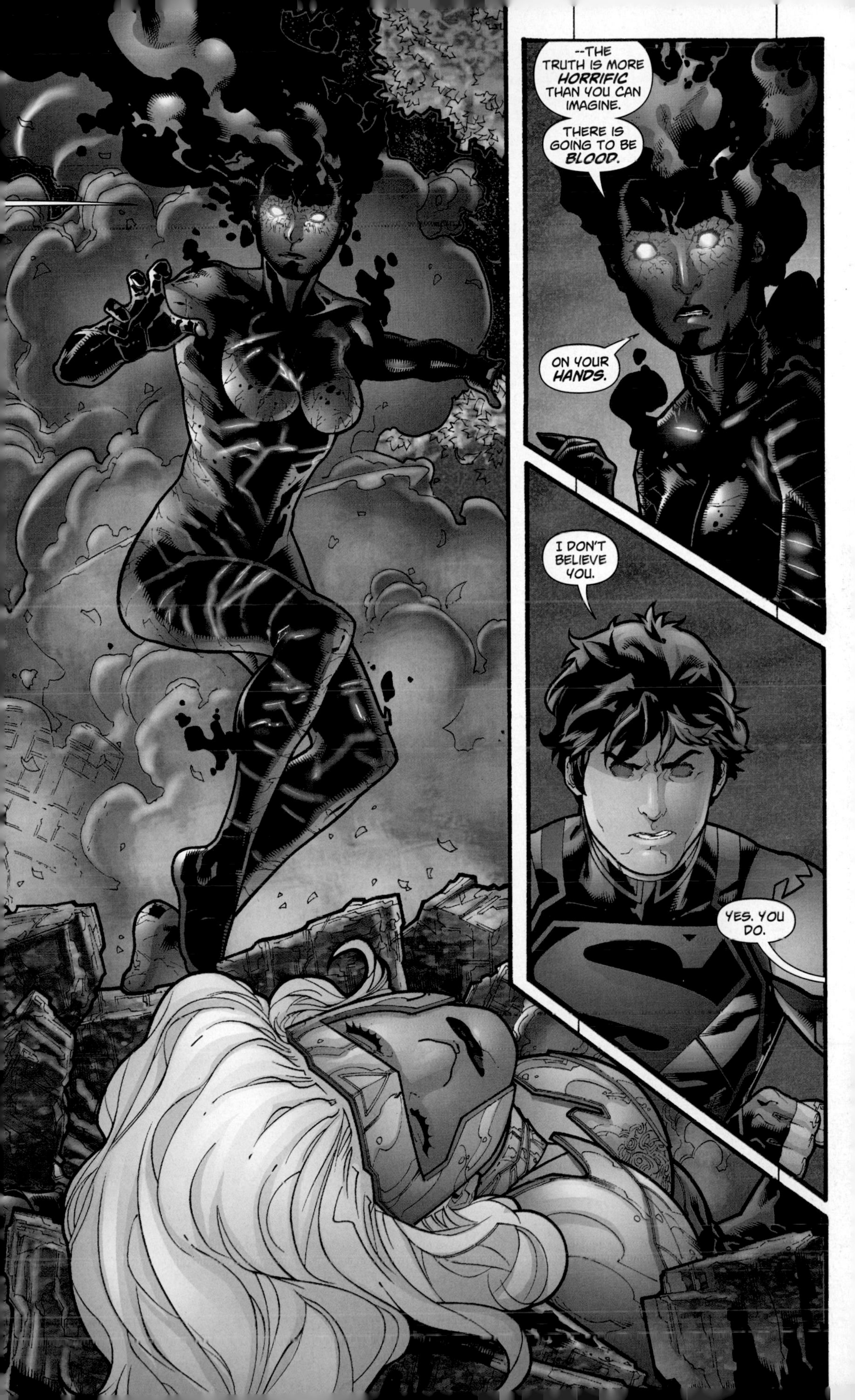
--THE TRUTH IS MORE HORRIFIC THAN YOU CAN IMAGINE.
THERE IS GOING TO BE BLOOD.
ON YOUR HANDS.
I DON'T BELIEVE YOU.
YES. YOU DO.

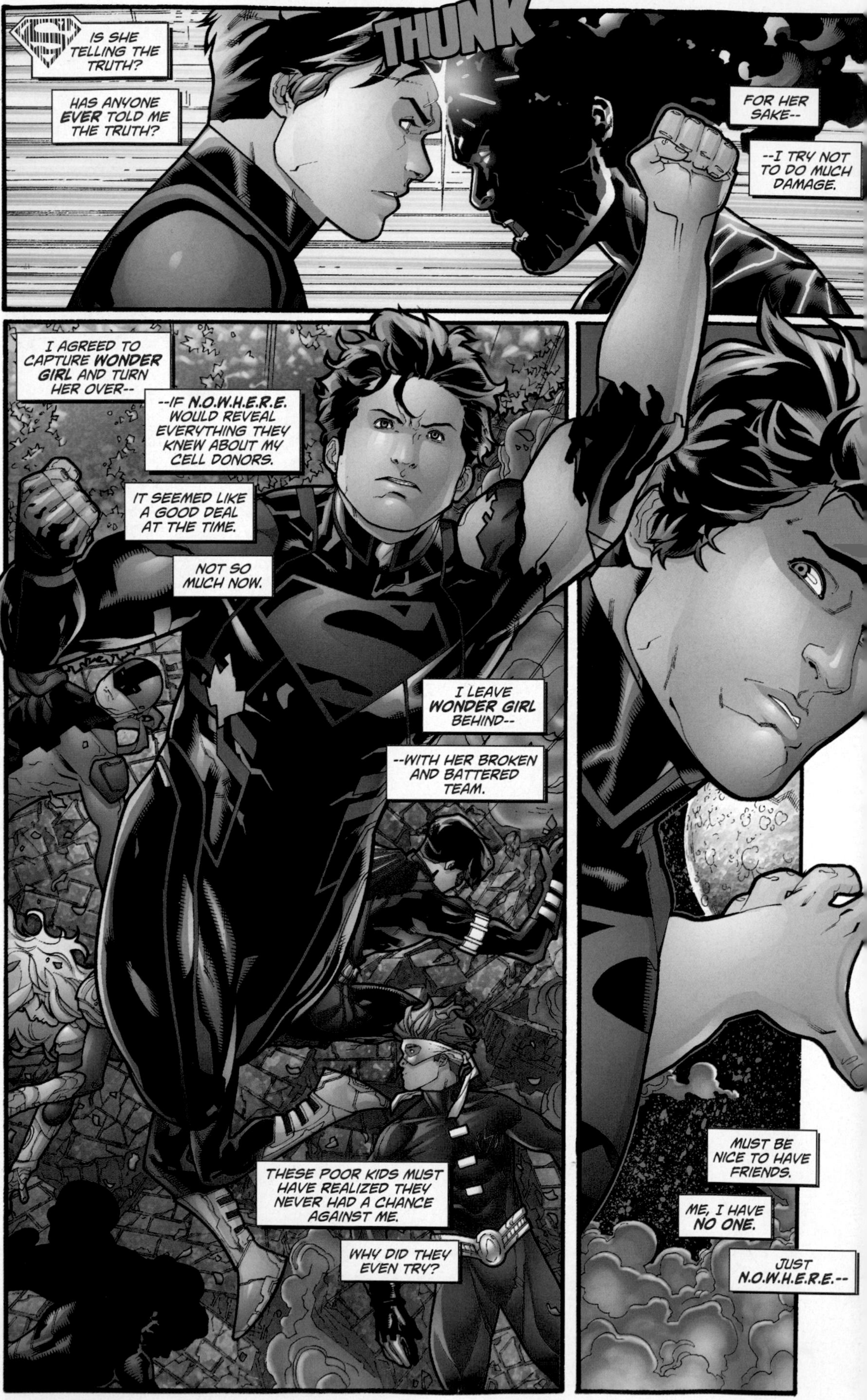
IS SHE TELLING THE TRUTH?
HAS ANYONE EVER TOLD ME THE TRUTH?
THUNK
FOR HER SAKE--
--I TRY NOT TO DO MUCH DAMAGE.
I AGREED TO CAPTURE WONDER GIRL AND TURN HER OVER--
--IF N.O.W.H.E.R.E. WOULD REVEAL EVERYTHING THEY KNEW ABOUT MY CELL DONORS.
IT SEEMED LIKE A GOOD DEAL AT THE TIME.
NOT SO MUCH NOW.
I LEAVE WONDER GIRL BEHIND--
--WITH HER BROKEN AND BATTERED TEAM.
THESE POOR KIDS MUST HAVE REALIZED THEY NEVER HAD A CHANCE AGAINST ME.
WHY DID THEY EVEN TRY?
MUST BE NICE TO HAVE FRIENDS.
ME, I HAVE NO ONE.
JUST N.O.W.H.E.R.E.--

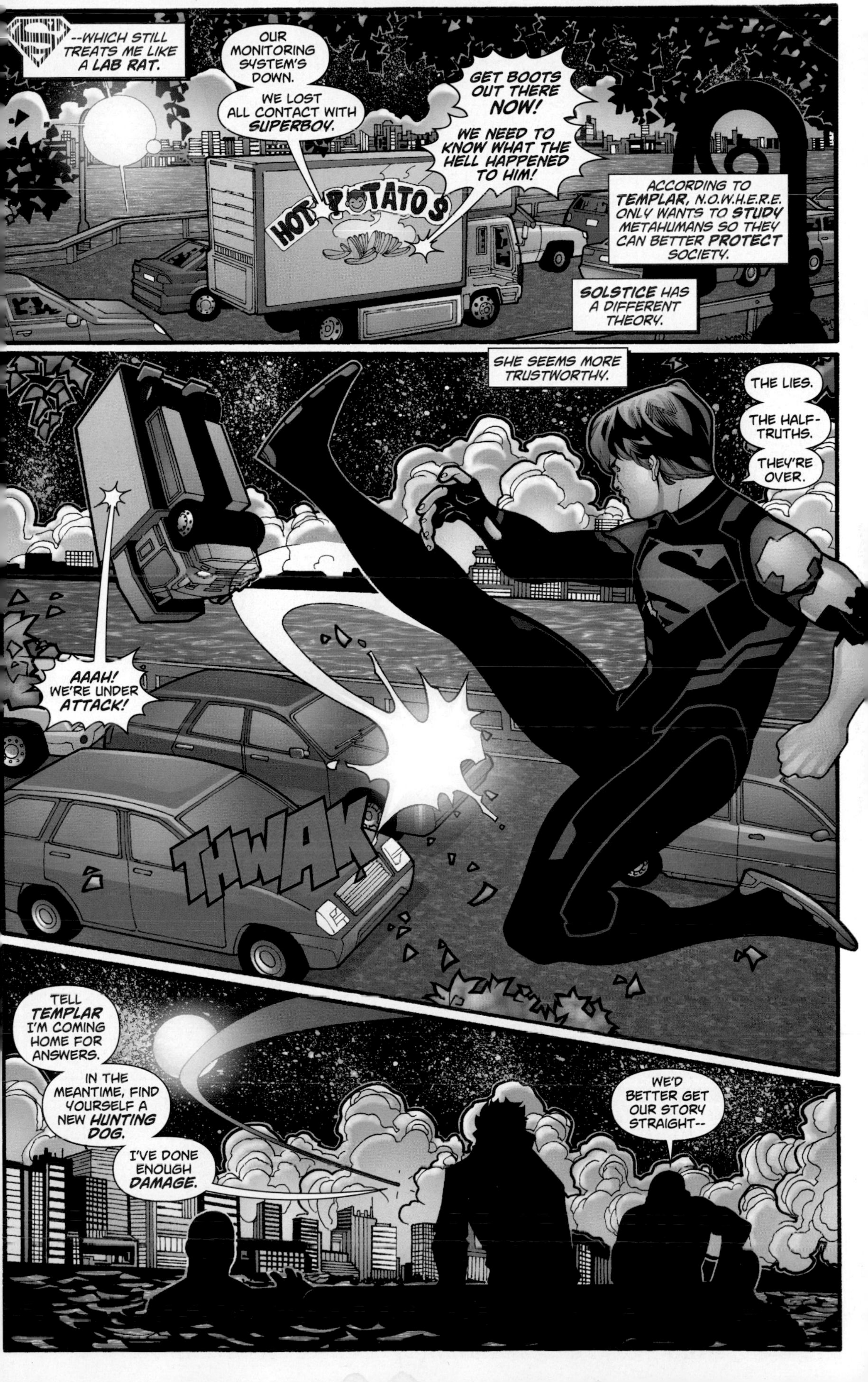
--WHICH STILL TREATS ME LIKE A LAB RAT.
OUR MONITORING SYSTEM'S DOWN.
WE LOST ALL CONTACT WITH SUPERBOY.
GET BOOTS OUT THERE NOW!
WE NEED TO KNOW WHAT THE HELL HAPPENED TO HIM!
HOT POTATOS
ACCORDING TO TEMPLAR, N.O.W.H.E.R.E. ONLY WANTS TO STUDY METAHUMANS SO THEY CAN BETTER PROTECT SOCIETY.
SOLSTICE HAS A DIFFERENT THEORY.
SHE SEEMS MORE TRUSTWORTHY.
THE LIES.
THE HALF-TRUTHS.
THEY'RE OVER.
AAAH! WE'RE UNDER ATTACK!
THWAK
TELL TEMPLAR I'M COMING HOME FOR ANSWERS.
IN THE MEANTIME, FIND YOURSELF A NEW HUNTING DOG.
I'VE DONE ENOUGH DAMAGE.
WE'D BETTER GET OUR STORY STRAIGHT--

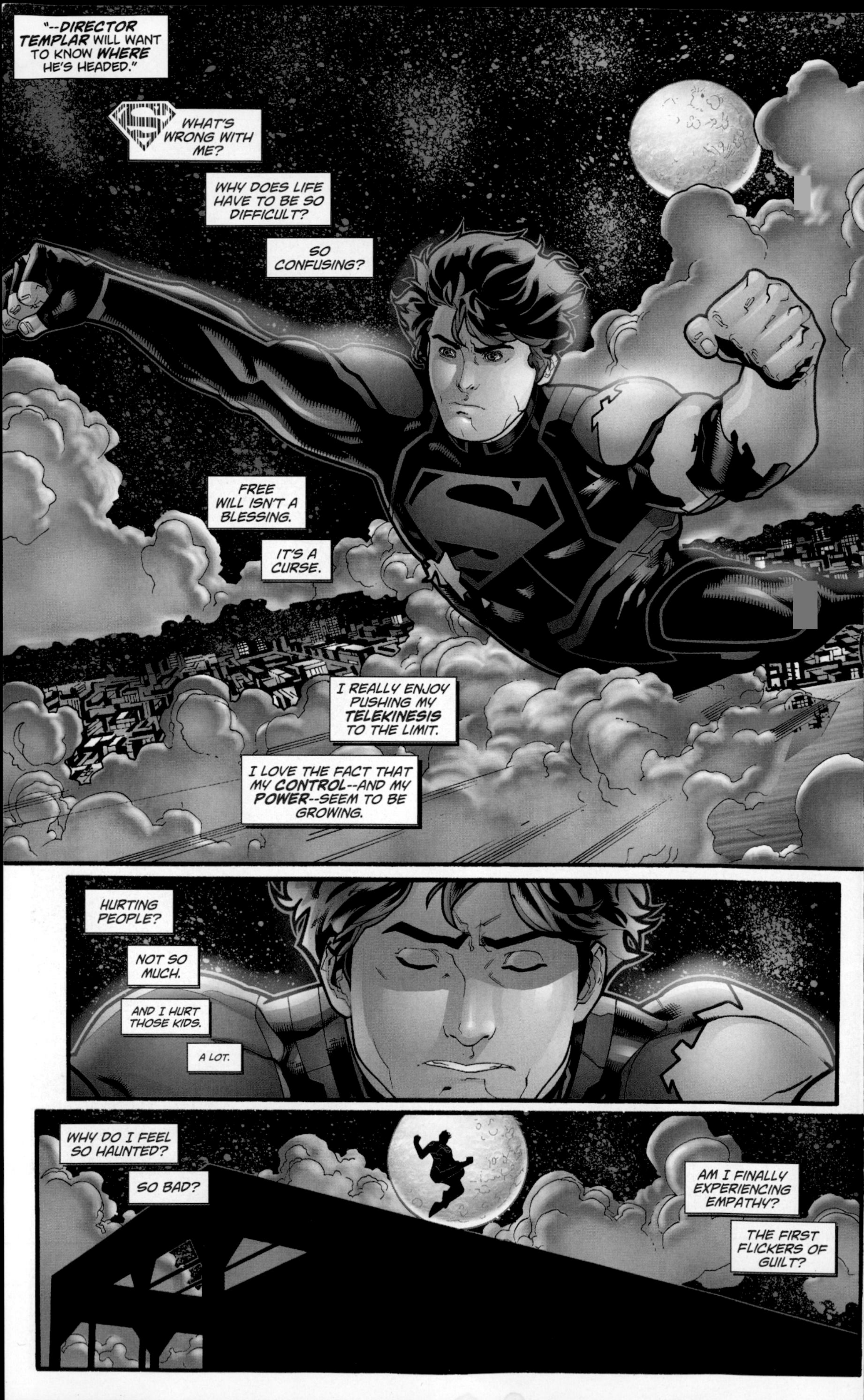
"--DIRECTOR TEMPLAR WILL WANT TO KNOW WHERE HE'S HEADED."
WHAT'S WRONG WITH ME?
WHY DOES LIFE HAVE TO BE SO DIFFICULT?
SO CONFUSING?
FREE WILL ISN'T A BLESSING.
IT'S A CURSE.
I REALLY ENJOY PUSHING MY TELEKINESIS TO THE LIMIT.
I LOVE THE FACT THAT MY CONTROL--AND MY POWER--SEEM TO BE GROWING.
HURTING PEOPLE?
NOT SO MUCH.
AND I HURT THOSE KIDS.
A LOT.
WHY DO I FEEL SO HAUNTED?
SO BAD?
AM I FINALLY EXPERIENCING EMPATHY?
THE FIRST FLICKERS OF GUILT?

IS THIS THE PART WHERE I'M SUDDENLY HIT BY A BLINDING REALIZATION?

WHERE PINOCCHIO TRANSFORMS INTO A REAL BOY?

NOPE.

PROBABLY NOT.

REAL LIFE JUST DOESN'T--WAIT A SECOND. LOOK AT THAT.

MY COSTUME. OR AS THEY PUT IT, MY CONTAINMENT SUIT. (GREAT JOB IT'S BEEN DOING.)

I-IT REPAIRED ITSELF.

IS THIS SOME WEIRD N.O.W.H.E.R.E. TECHNOLOGY--

--OR IS IT ANOTHER PERK CONNECTED TO MY TELEKINETIC--

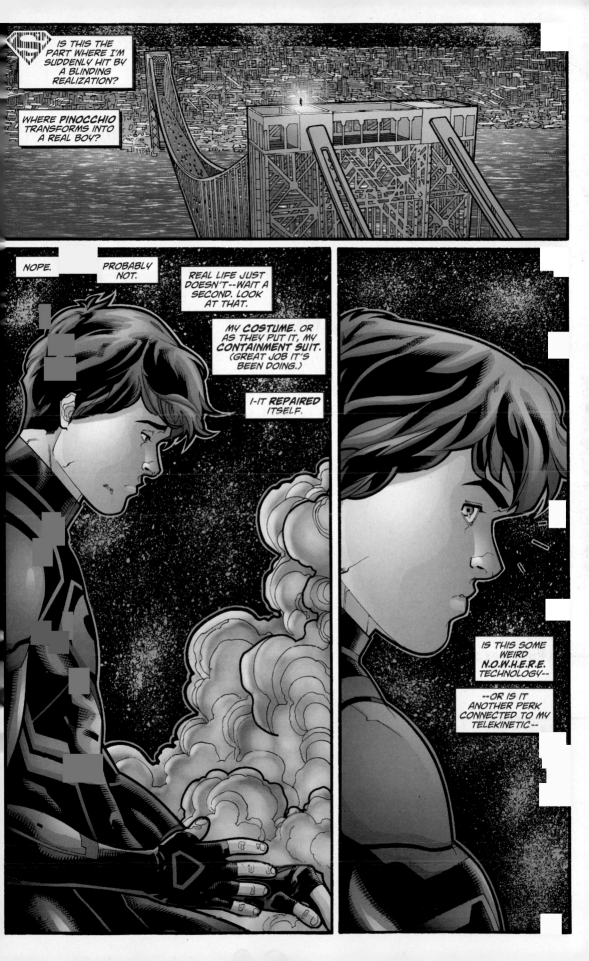

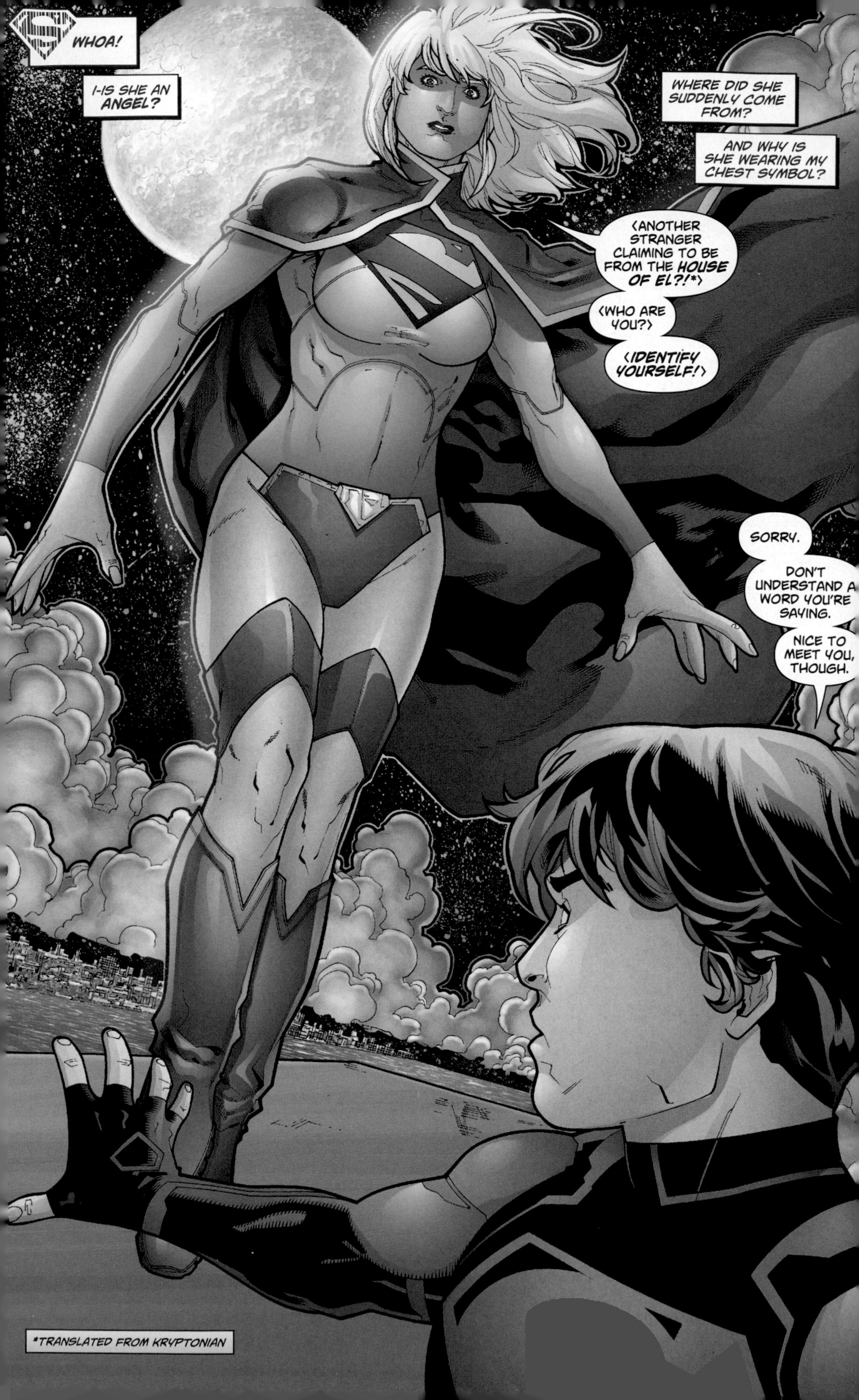
WHOA!
I-IS SHE AN ANGEL?
WHERE DID SHE SUDDENLY COME FROM?
AND WHY IS SHE WEARING MY CHEST SYMBOL?
‹ANOTHER STRANGER CLAIMING TO BE FROM THE HOUSE OF EL?!*›
‹WHO ARE YOU?›
‹IDENTIFY YOURSELF!›
SORRY.
DON'T UNDERSTAND A WORD YOU'RE SAYING.
NICE TO MEET YOU, THOUGH.
*TRANSLATED FROM KRYPTONIAN

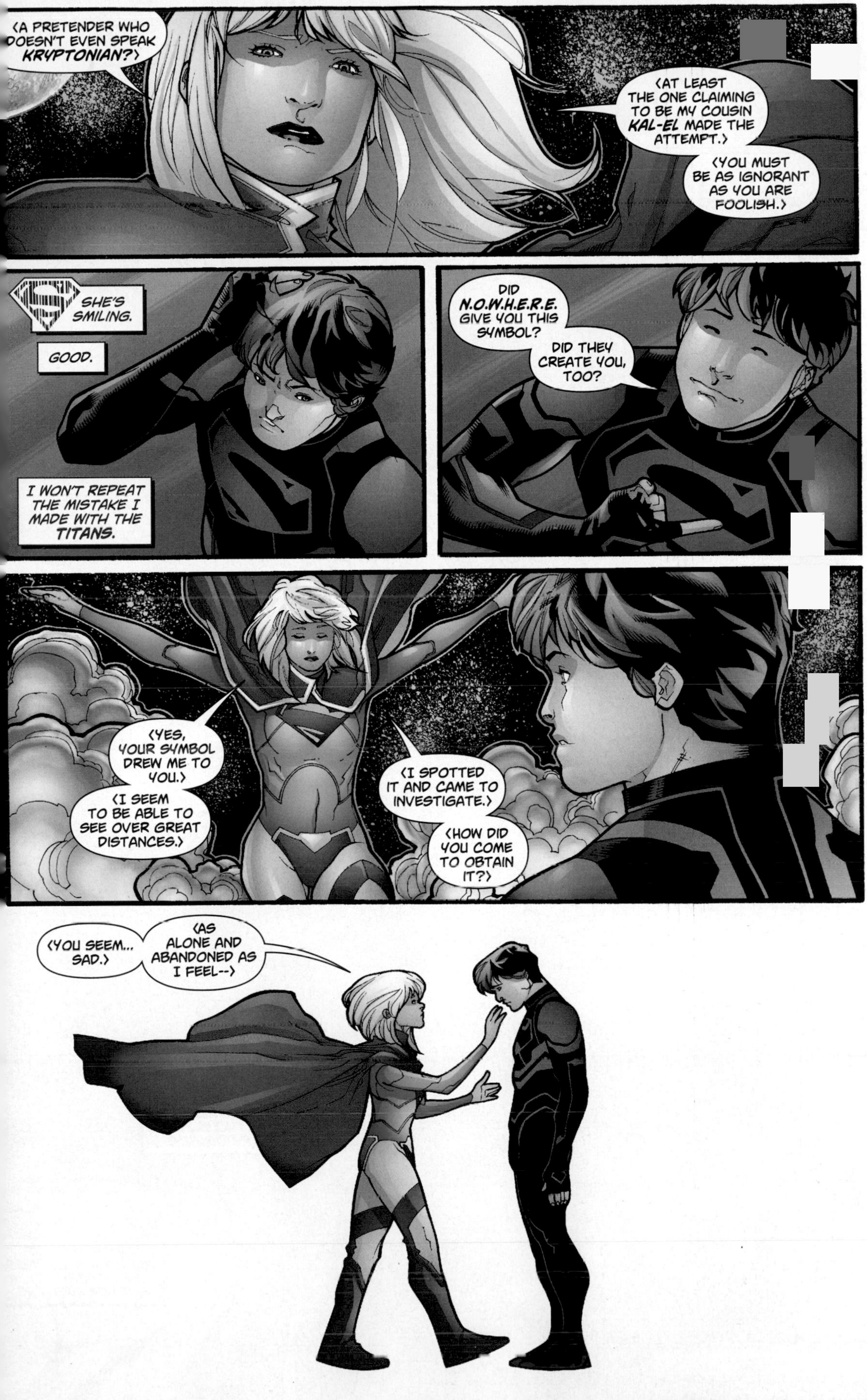
‹A PRETENDER WHO DOESN'T EVEN SPEAK **KRYPTONIAN?**›
‹AT LEAST THE ONE CLAIMING TO BE MY COUSIN **KAL-EL** MADE THE ATTEMPT.›
‹YOU MUST BE AS IGNORANT AS YOU ARE FOOLISH.›
SHE'S SMILING.
GOOD.
I WON'T REPEAT THE MISTAKE I MADE WITH THE **TITANS.**
DID **N.O.W.H.E.R.E.** GIVE YOU THIS SYMBOL?
DID THEY CREATE YOU, TOO?
‹YES, YOUR SYMBOL DREW ME TO YOU.›
‹I SEEM TO BE ABLE TO SEE OVER GREAT DISTANCES.›
‹I SPOTTED IT AND CAME TO INVESTIGATE.›
‹HOW DID YOU COME TO OBTAIN IT?›
‹YOU SEEM... SAD.›
‹AS ALONE AND ABANDONED AS I FEEL--›

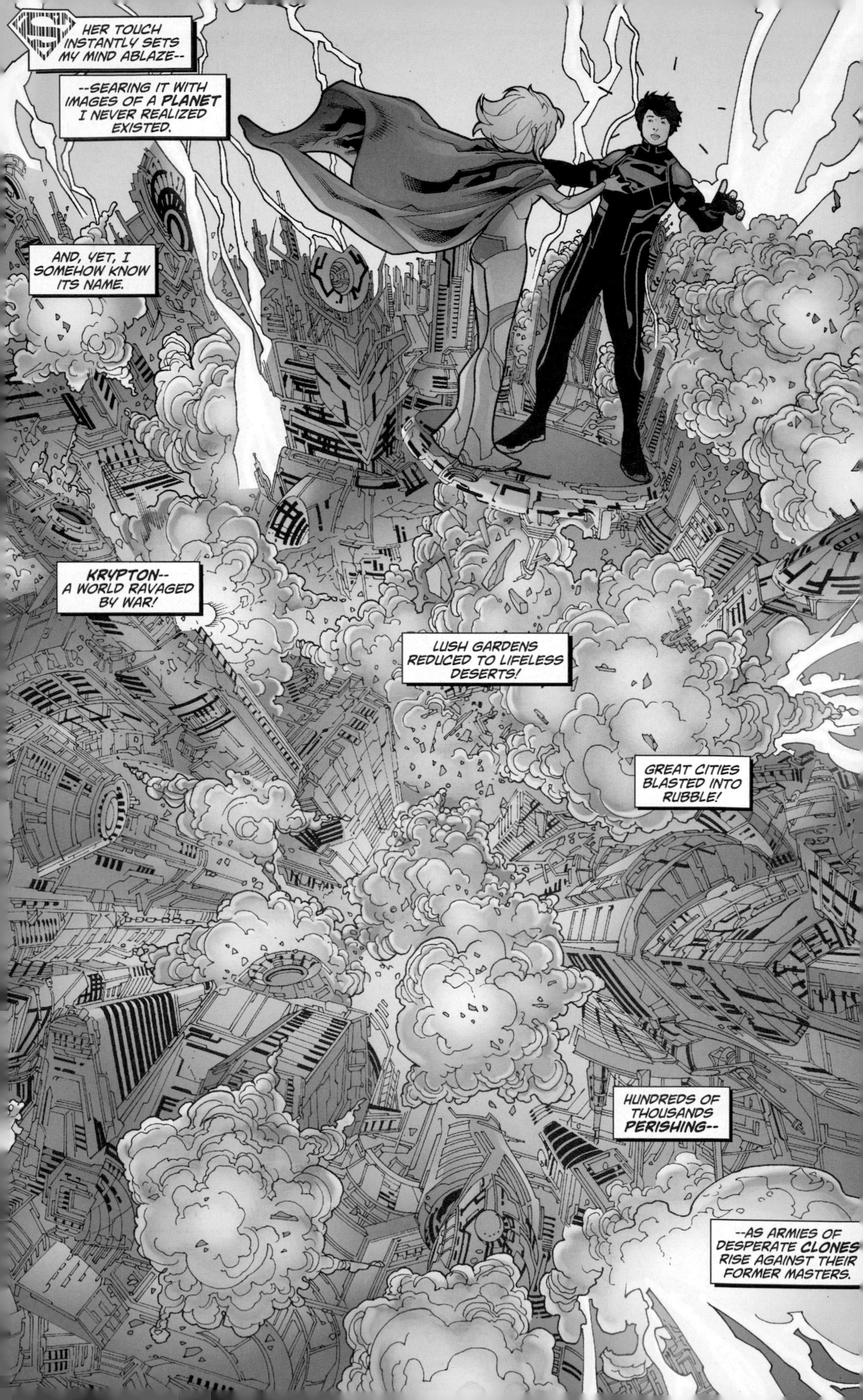
HER TOUCH INSTANTLY SETS MY MIND ABLAZE--
--SEARING IT WITH IMAGES OF A PLANET I NEVER REALIZED EXISTED.
AND, YET, I SOMEHOW KNOW ITS NAME.
KRYPTON-- A WORLD RAVAGED BY WAR!
LUSH GARDENS REDUCED TO LIFELESS DESERTS!
GREAT CITIES BLASTED INTO RUBBLE!
HUNDREDS OF THOUSANDS PERISHING--
--AS ARMIES OF DESPERATE CLONES RISE AGAINST THEIR FORMER MASTERS.

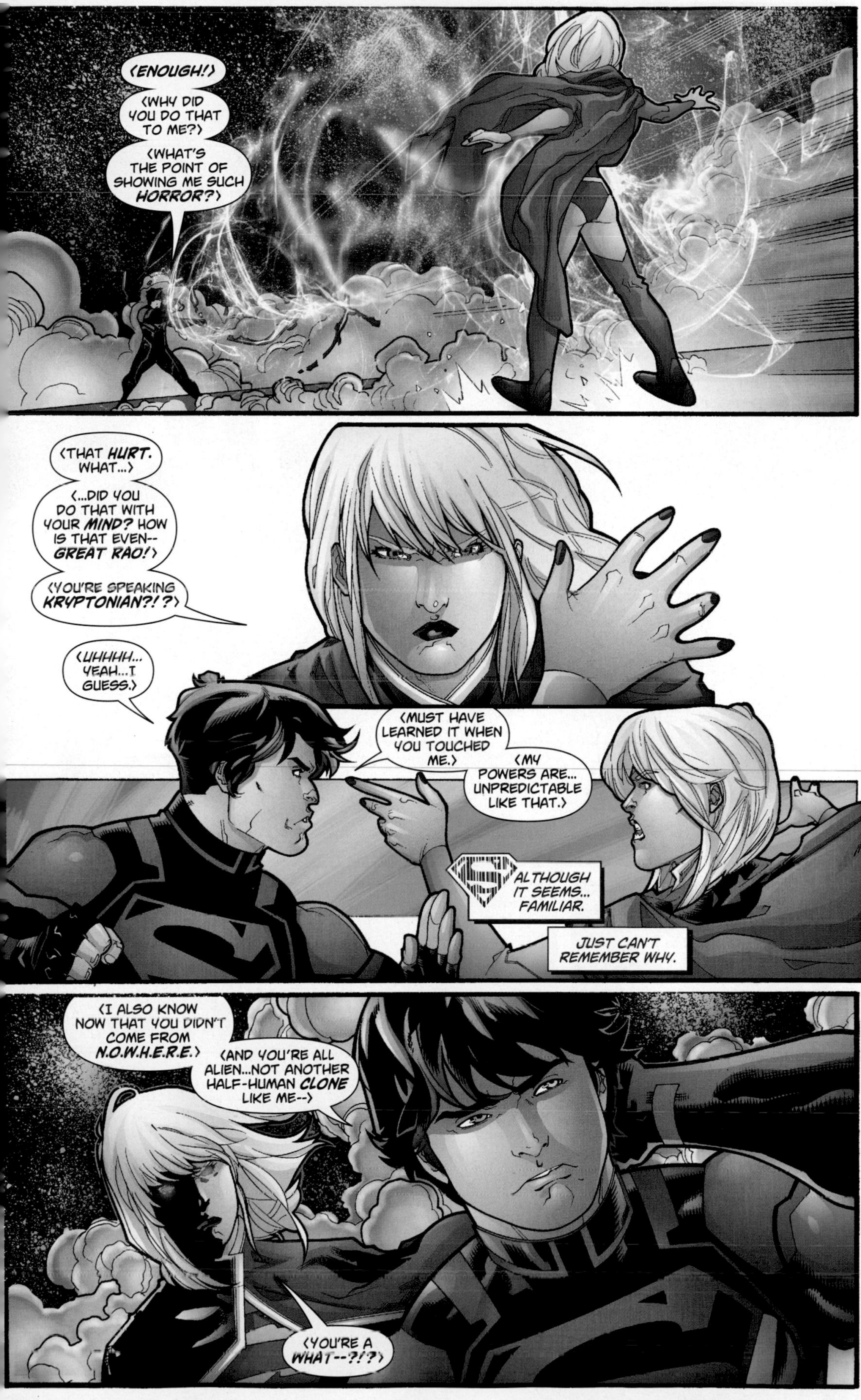

‹ENOUGH!›
‹WHY DID YOU DO THAT TO ME?›
‹WHAT'S THE POINT OF SHOWING ME SUCH HORROR?›
‹THAT HURT. WHAT...›
‹...DID YOU DO THAT WITH YOUR MIND? HOW IS THAT EVEN-- GREAT RAO!›
‹YOU'RE SPEAKING KRYPTONIAN?!?›
‹UHHHH... YEAH...I GUESS.›
‹MUST HAVE LEARNED IT WHEN YOU TOUCHED ME.›
‹MY POWERS ARE... UNPREDICTABLE LIKE THAT.›
ALTHOUGH IT SEEMS... FAMILIAR.
JUST CAN'T REMEMBER WHY.
‹I ALSO KNOW NOW THAT YOU DIDN'T COME FROM N.O.W.H.E.R.E.›
‹AND YOU'RE ALL ALIEN...NOT ANOTHER HALF-HUMAN CLONE LIKE ME--›
‹YOU'RE A WHAT--?!?›

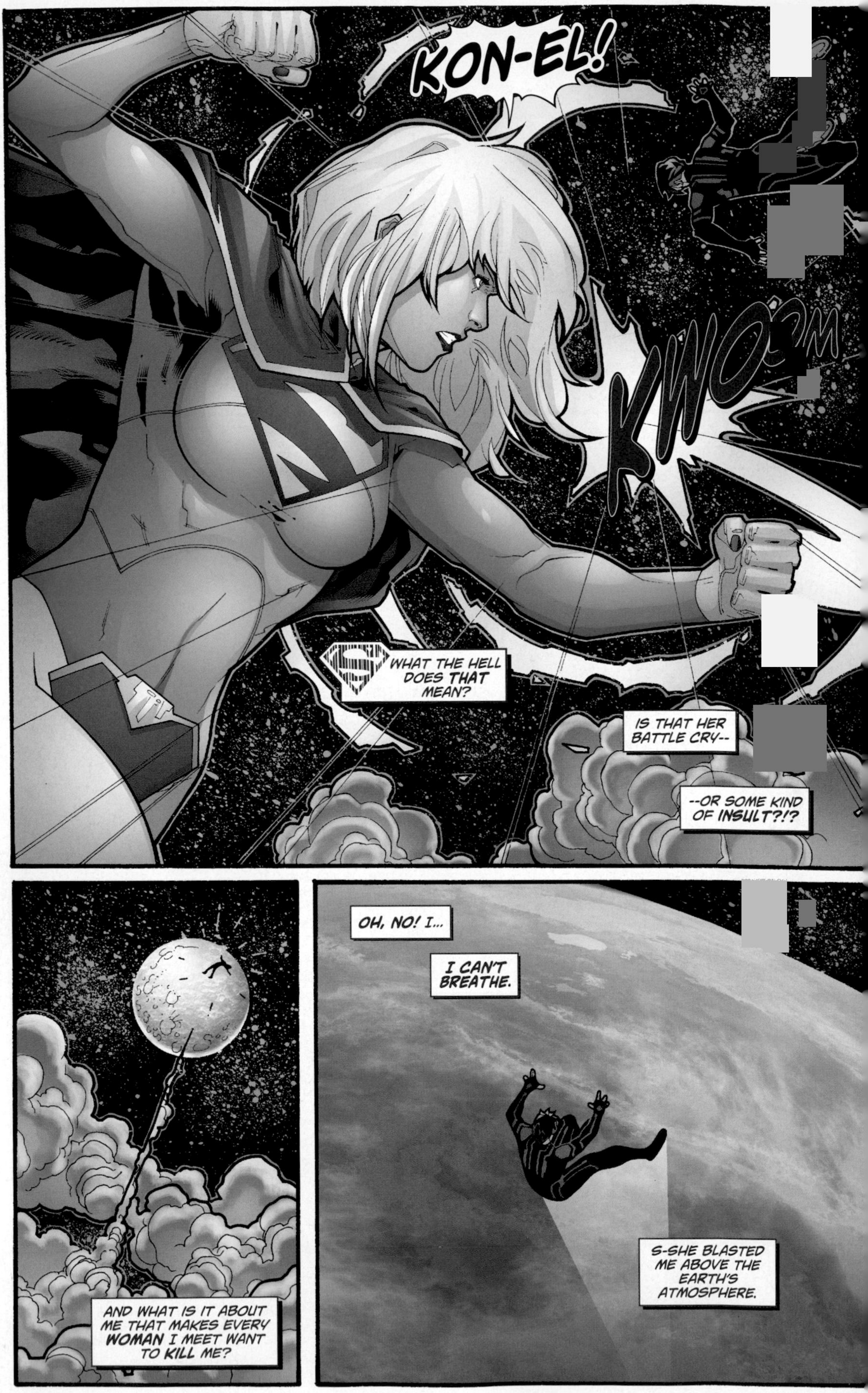
KON-EL!
WHAT THE HELL DOES THAT MEAN?
IS THAT HER BATTLE CRY--
--OR SOME KIND OF INSULT?!?
AND WHAT IS IT ABOUT ME THAT MAKES EVERY WOMAN I MEET WANT TO KILL ME?
OH, NO! I...
I CAN'T BREATHE.
S-SHE BLASTED ME ABOVE THE EARTH'S ATMOSPHERE.

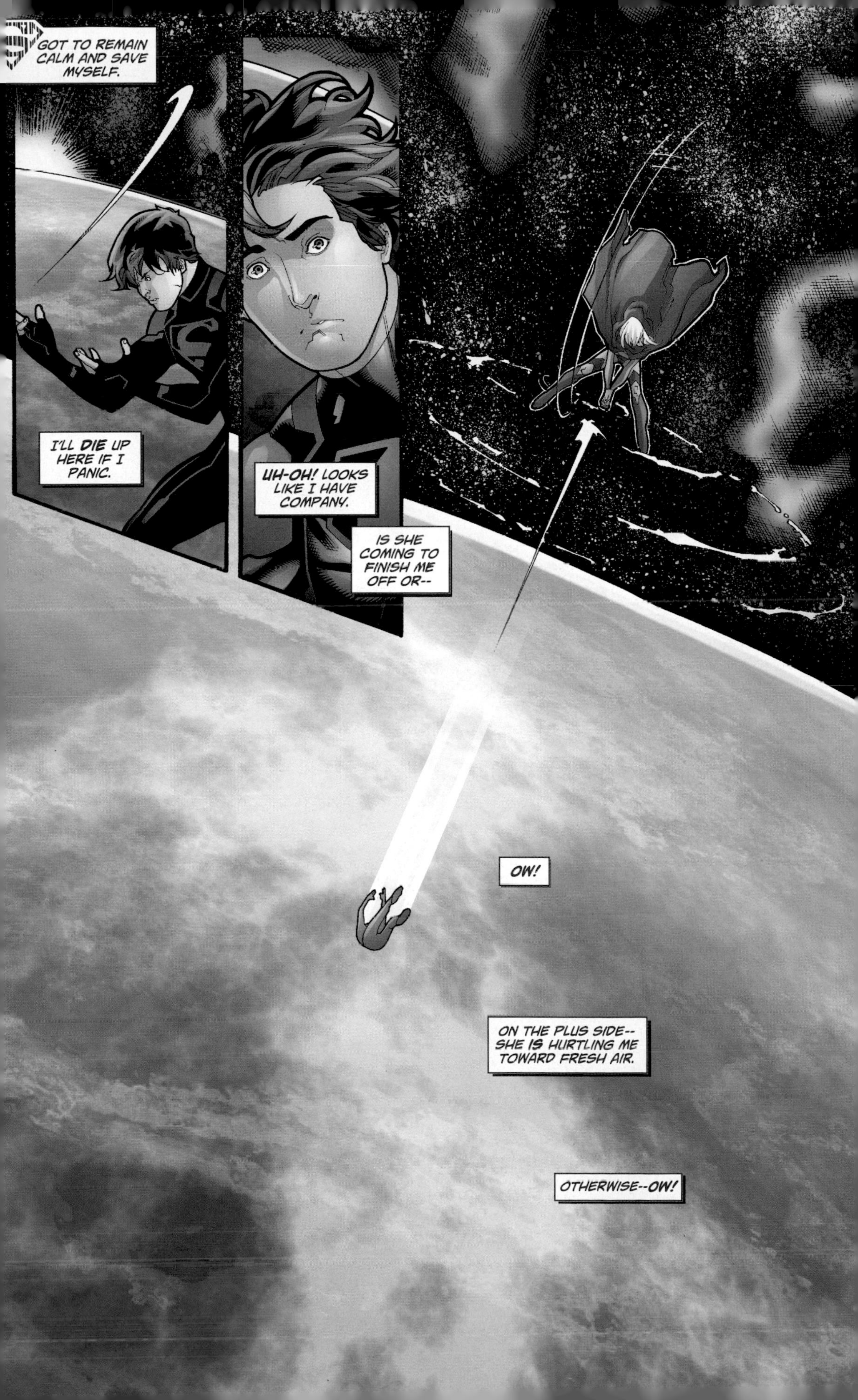
GOT TO REMAIN CALM AND SAVE MYSELF.
I'LL DIE UP HERE IF I PANIC.
UH-OH! LOOKS LIKE I HAVE COMPANY.
IS SHE COMING TO FINISH ME OFF OR--
OW!
ON THE PLUS SIDE-- SHE IS HURTLING ME TOWARD FRESH AIR.
OTHERWISE--OW!

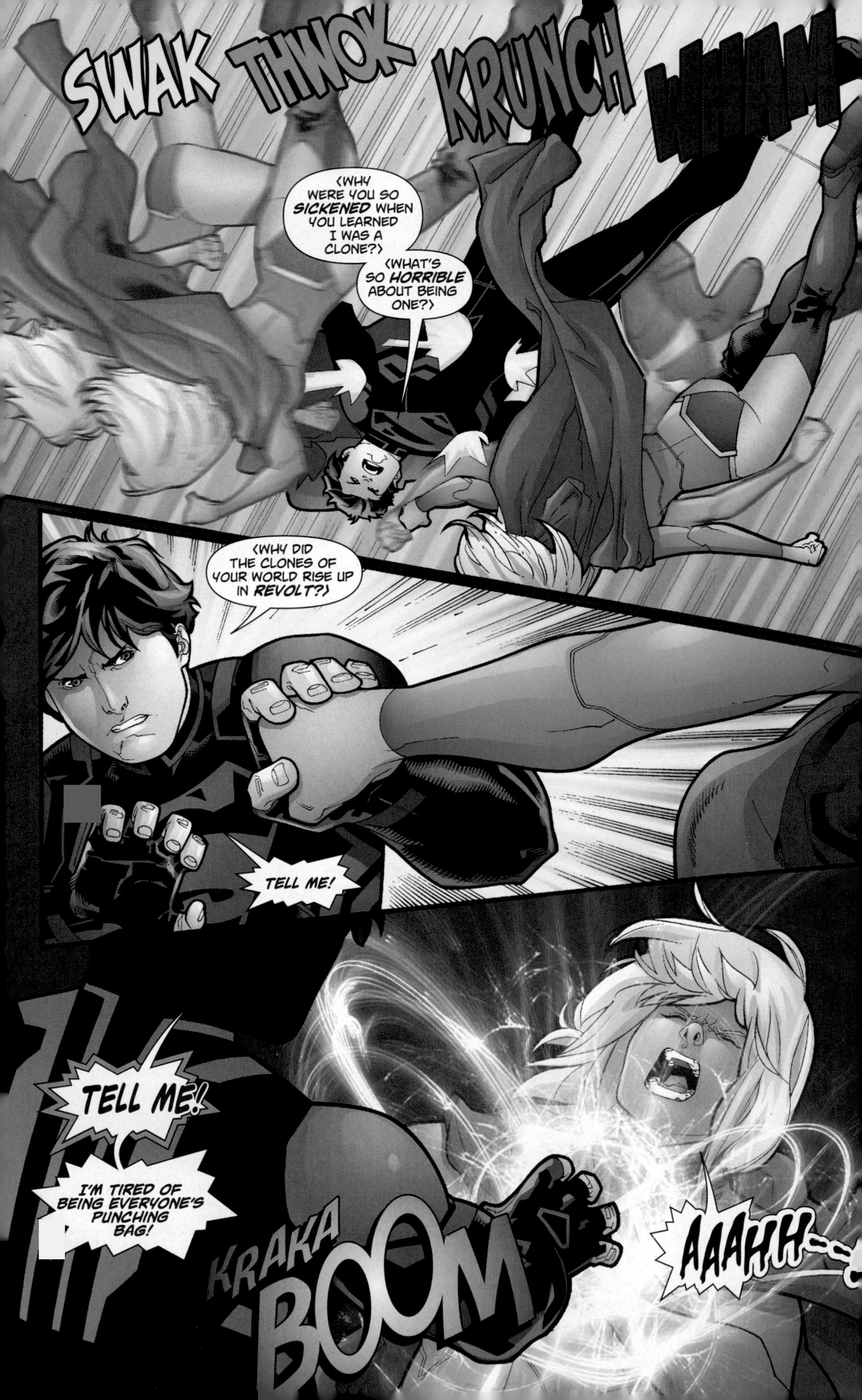
SWAK
THWOK
KRUNCH
WHAM
⟨WHY WERE YOU SO SICKENED WHEN YOU LEARNED I WAS A CLONE?⟩
⟨WHAT'S SO HORRIBLE ABOUT BEING ONE?⟩
⟨WHY DID THE CLONES OF YOUR WORLD RISE UP IN REVOLT?⟩
TELL ME!
TELL ME!
I'M TIRED OF BEING EVERYONE'S PUNCHING BAG!
KRAKA BOOM
AAAHH--

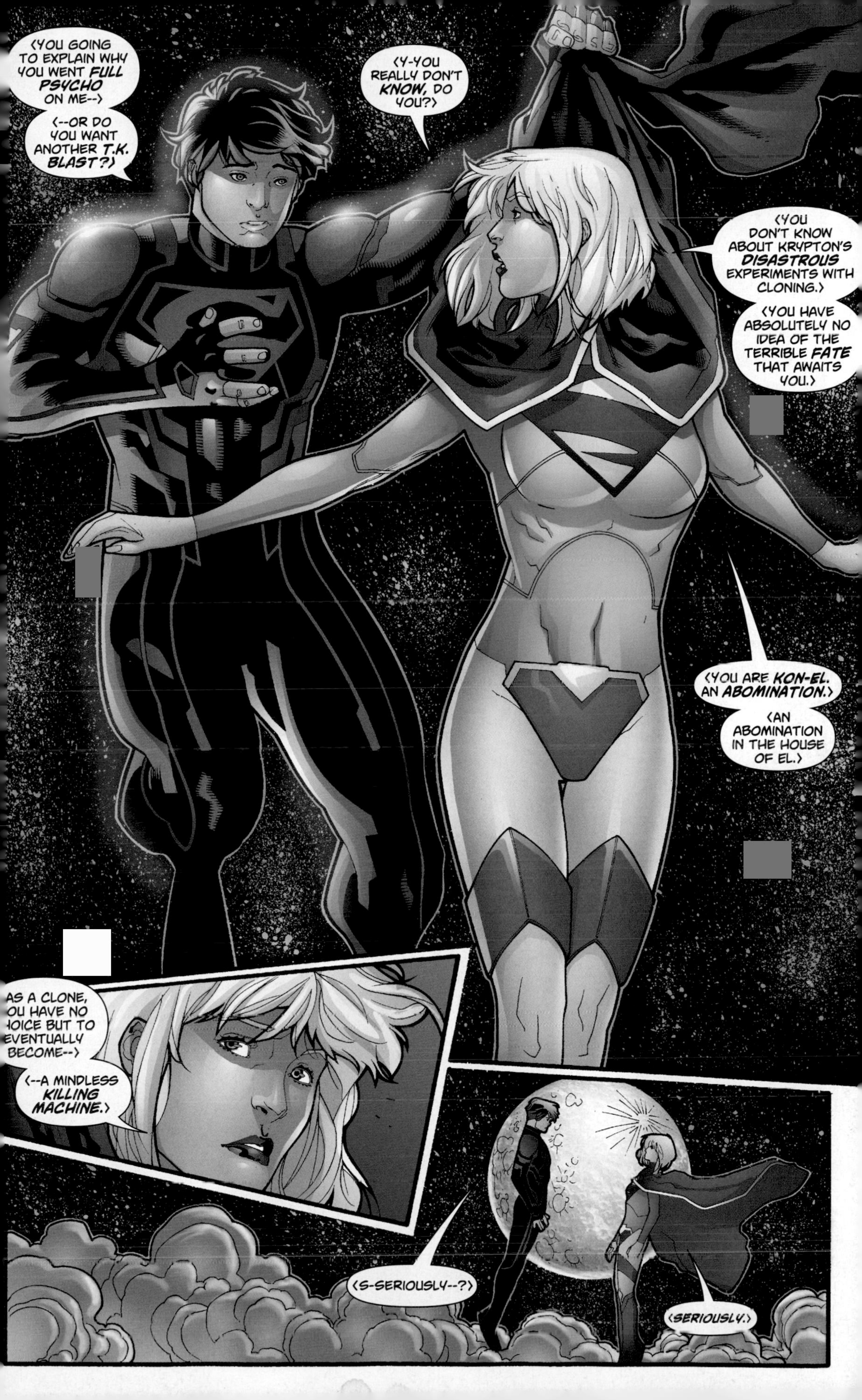
‹YOU GOING TO EXPLAIN WHY YOU WENT FULL PSYCHO ON ME--›
‹--OR DO YOU WANT ANOTHER T.K. BLAST?›
‹Y-YOU REALLY DON'T KNOW, DO YOU?›
‹YOU DON'T KNOW ABOUT KRYPTON'S DISASTROUS EXPERIMENTS WITH CLONING.›
‹YOU HAVE ABSOLUTELY NO IDEA OF THE TERRIBLE FATE THAT AWAITS YOU.›
‹YOU ARE KON-EL. AN ABOMINATION.›
‹AN ABOMINATION IN THE HOUSE OF EL.›
AS A CLONE, OU HAVE NO HOICE BUT TO EVENTUALLY BECOME--›
‹--A MINDLESS KILLING MACHINE.›
‹S-SERIOUSLY--?›
‹SERIOUSLY.›

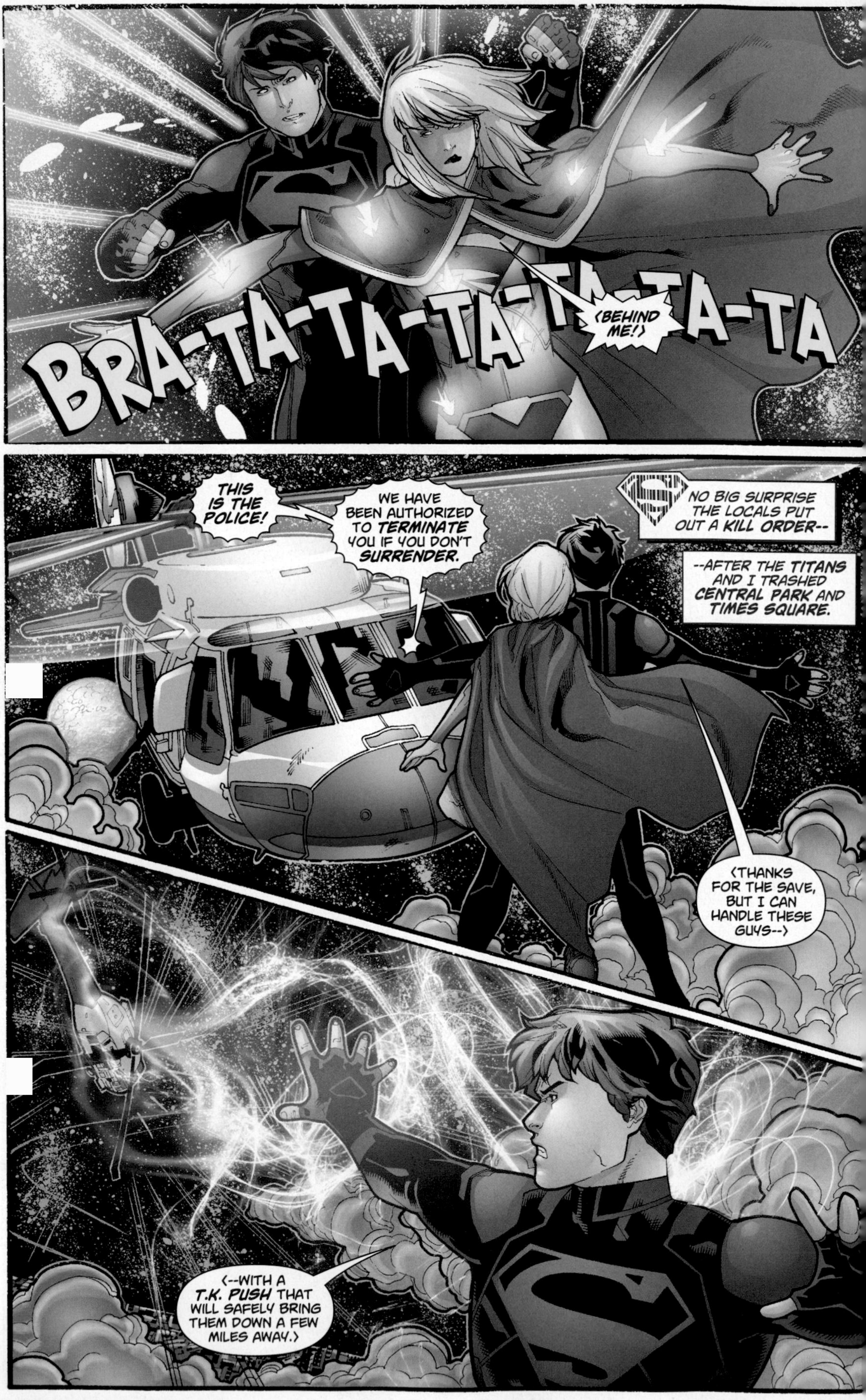
BRA-TA-TA-TA-TA-TA-TA
⟨BEHIND ME!⟩
THIS IS THE POLICE!
WE HAVE BEEN AUTHORIZED TO TERMINATE YOU IF YOU DON'T SURRENDER.
NO BIG SURPRISE THE LOCALS PUT OUT A KILL ORDER--
--AFTER THE TITANS AND I TRASHED CENTRAL PARK AND TIMES SQUARE.
⟨THANKS FOR THE SAVE, BUT I CAN HANDLE THESE GUYS--⟩
⟨--WITH A T.K. PUSH THAT WILL SAFELY BRING THEM DOWN A FEW MILES AWAY.⟩

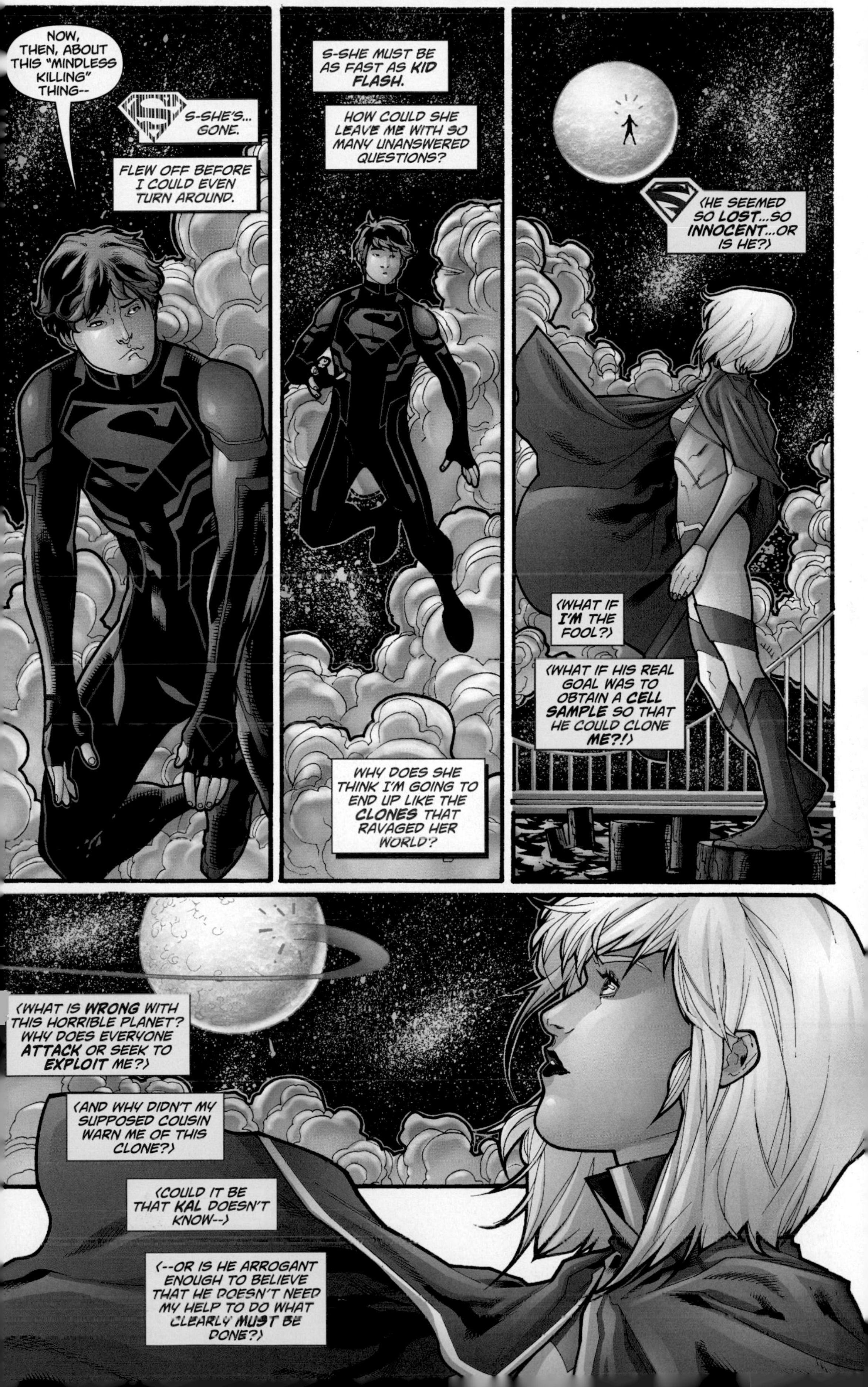
NOW, THEN, ABOUT THIS "MINDLESS KILLING" THING--
S-SHE'S... GONE.
FLEW OFF BEFORE I COULD EVEN TURN AROUND.
S-SHE MUST BE AS FAST AS KID FLASH.
HOW COULD SHE LEAVE ME WITH SO MANY UNANSWERED QUESTIONS?
WHY DOES SHE THINK I'M GOING TO END UP LIKE THE CLONES THAT RAVAGED HER WORLD?
<HE SEEMED SO LOST...SO INNOCENT...OR IS HE?>
<WHAT IF I'M THE FOOL?>
<WHAT IF HIS REAL GOAL WAS TO OBTAIN A CELL SAMPLE SO THAT HE COULD CLONE ME?!>
<WHAT IS WRONG WITH THIS HORRIBLE PLANET? WHY DOES EVERYONE ATTACK OR SEEK TO EXPLOIT ME?>
<AND WHY DIDN'T MY SUPPOSED COUSIN WARN ME OF THIS CLONE?>
<COULD IT BE THAT KAL DOESN'T KNOW-->
<--OR IS HE ARROGANT ENOUGH TO BELIEVE THAT HE DOESN'T NEED MY HELP TO DO WHAT CLEARLY MUST BE DONE?>

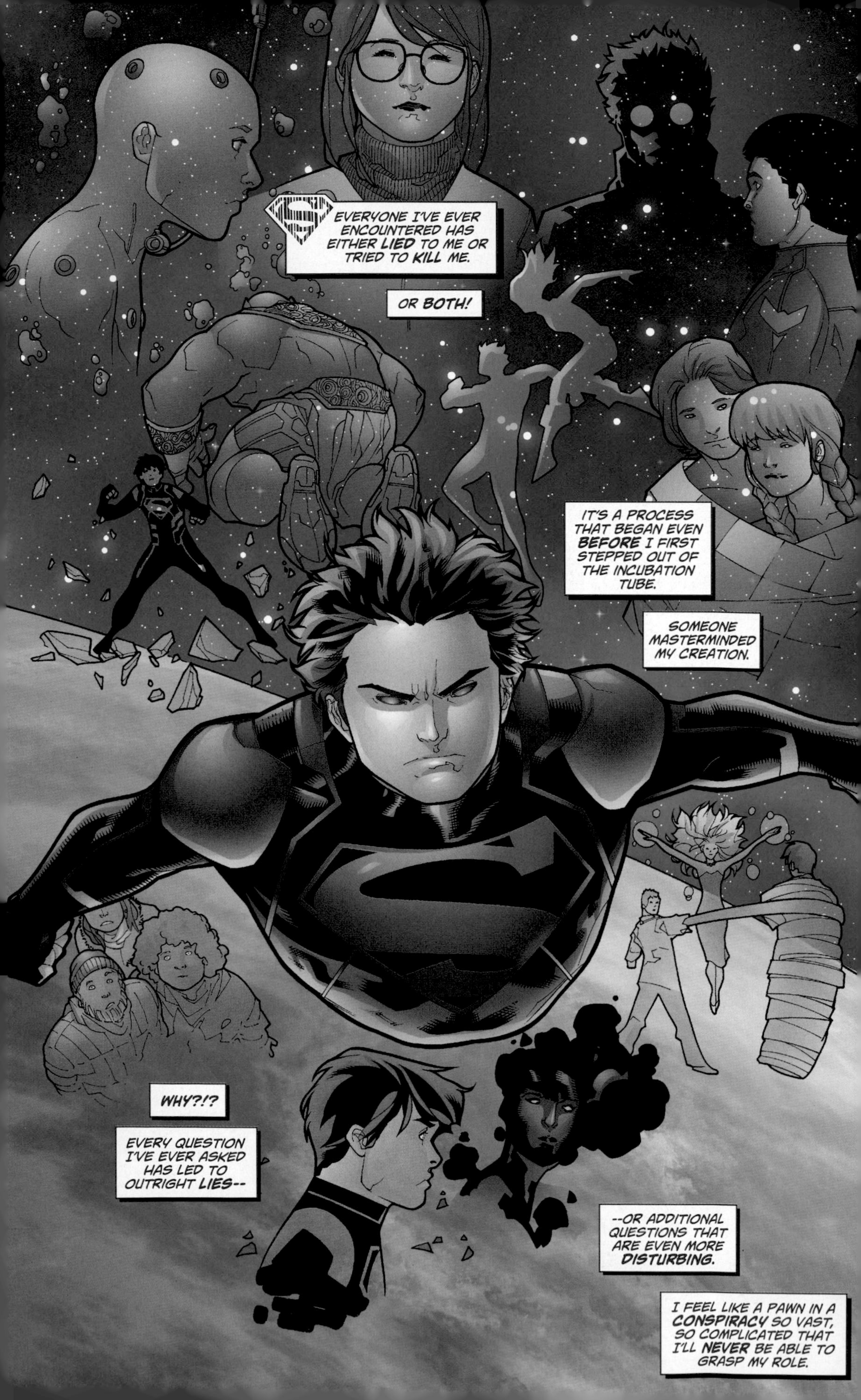
EVERYONE I'VE EVER ENCOUNTERED HAS EITHER LIED TO ME OR TRIED TO KILL ME.
OR BOTH!
IT'S A PROCESS THAT BEGAN EVEN BEFORE I FIRST STEPPED OUT OF THE INCUBATION TUBE.
SOMEONE MASTERMINDED MY CREATION.
WHY?!?
EVERY QUESTION I'VE EVER ASKED HAS LED TO OUTRIGHT LIES--
--OR ADDITIONAL QUESTIONS THAT ARE EVEN MORE DISTURBING.
I FEEL LIKE A PAWN IN A CONSPIRACY SO VAST, SO COMPLICATED THAT I'LL NEVER BE ABLE TO GRASP MY ROLE.

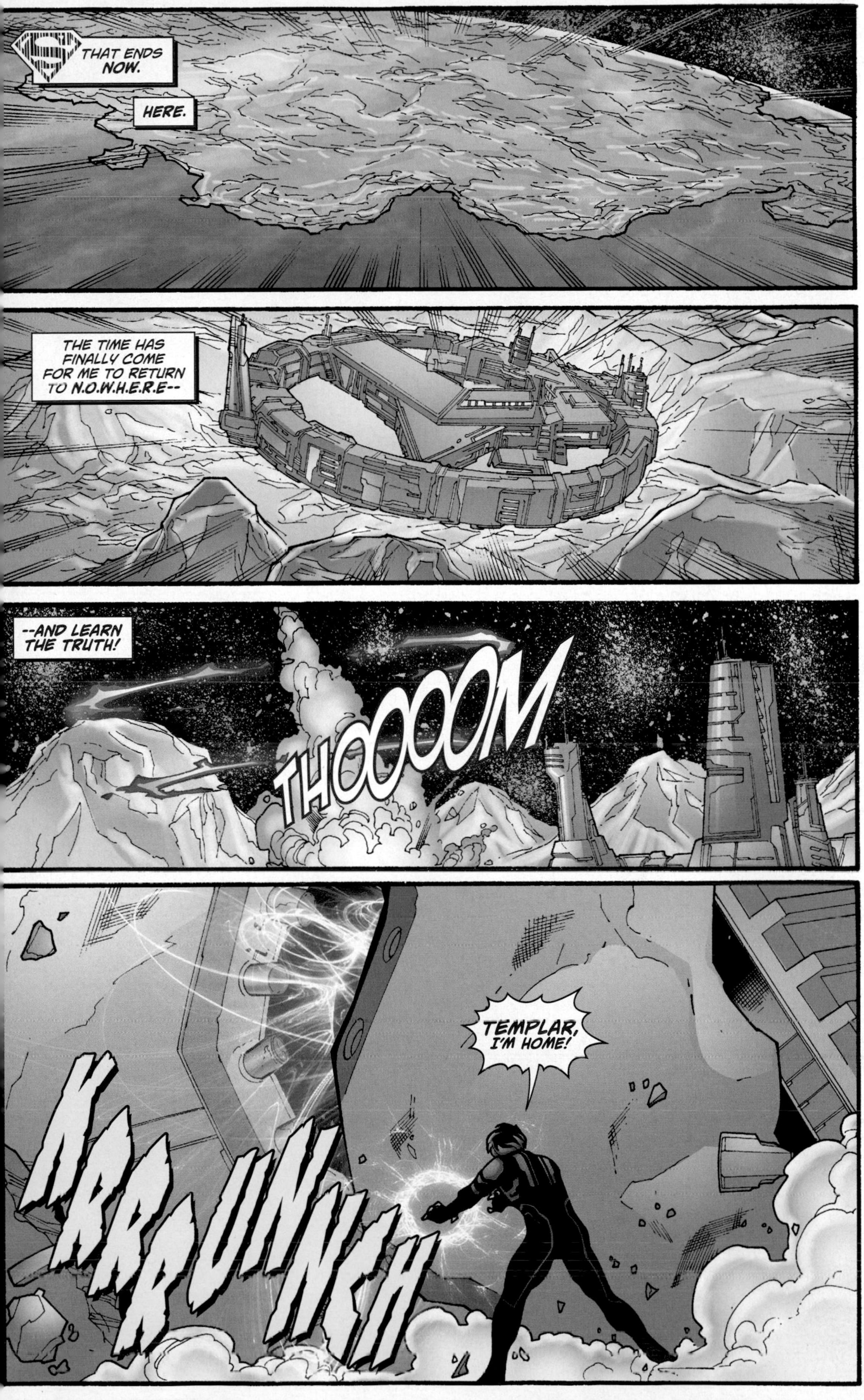
THAT ENDS NOW.
HERE.
THE TIME HAS FINALLY COME FOR ME TO RETURN TO N.O.W.H.E.R.E--
--AND LEARN THE TRUTH!
THOOOOM
TEMPLAR, I'M HOME!
KRRUNCH

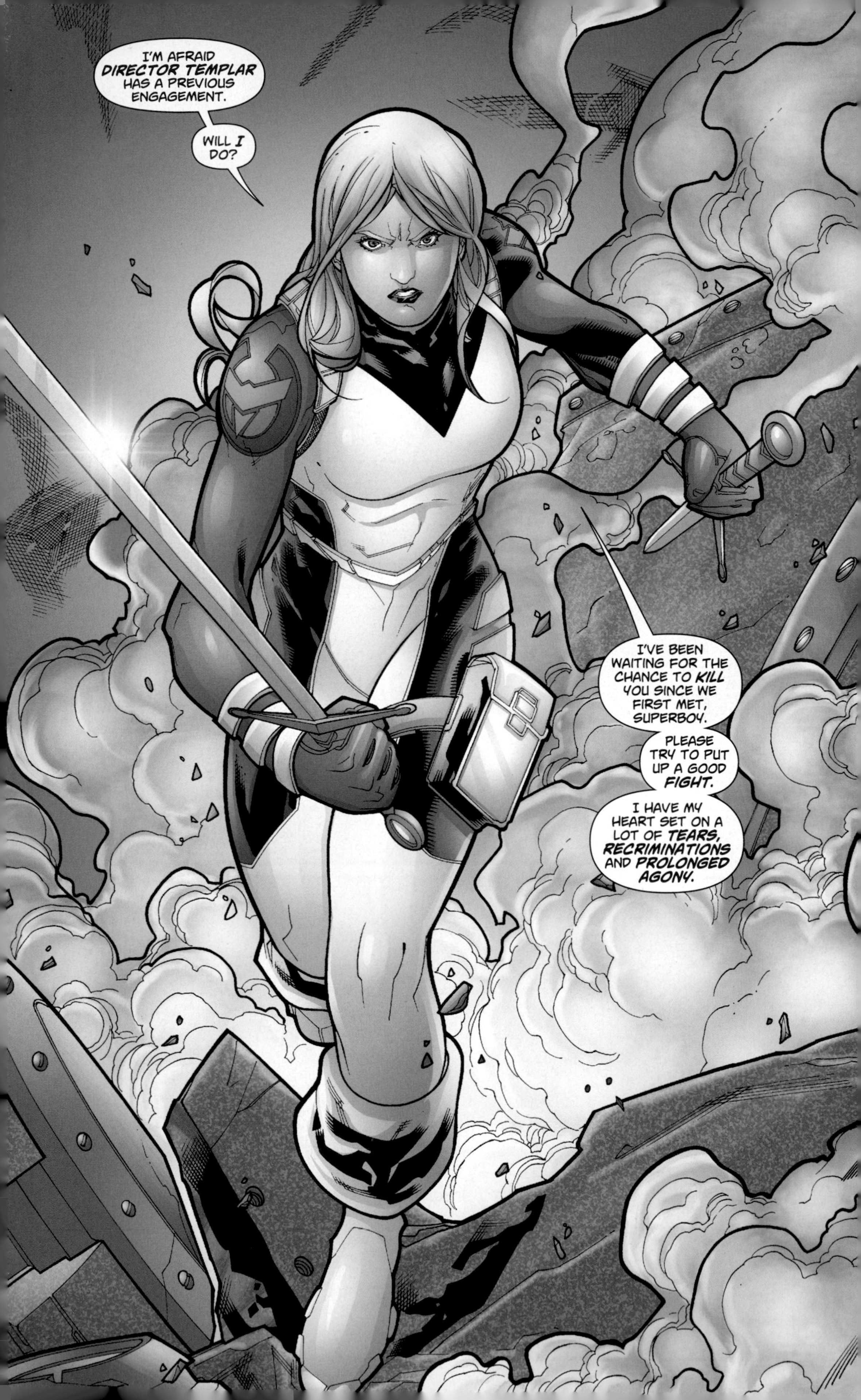
I'M AFRAID DIRECTOR TEMPLAR HAS A PREVIOUS ENGAGEMENT.
WILL I DO?
I'VE BEEN WAITING FOR THE CHANCE TO KILL YOU SINCE WE FIRST MET, SUPERBOY.
PLEASE TRY TO PUT UP A GOOD FIGHT.
I HAVE MY HEART SET ON A LOT OF TEARS, RECRIMINATIONS AND PROLONGED AGONY.

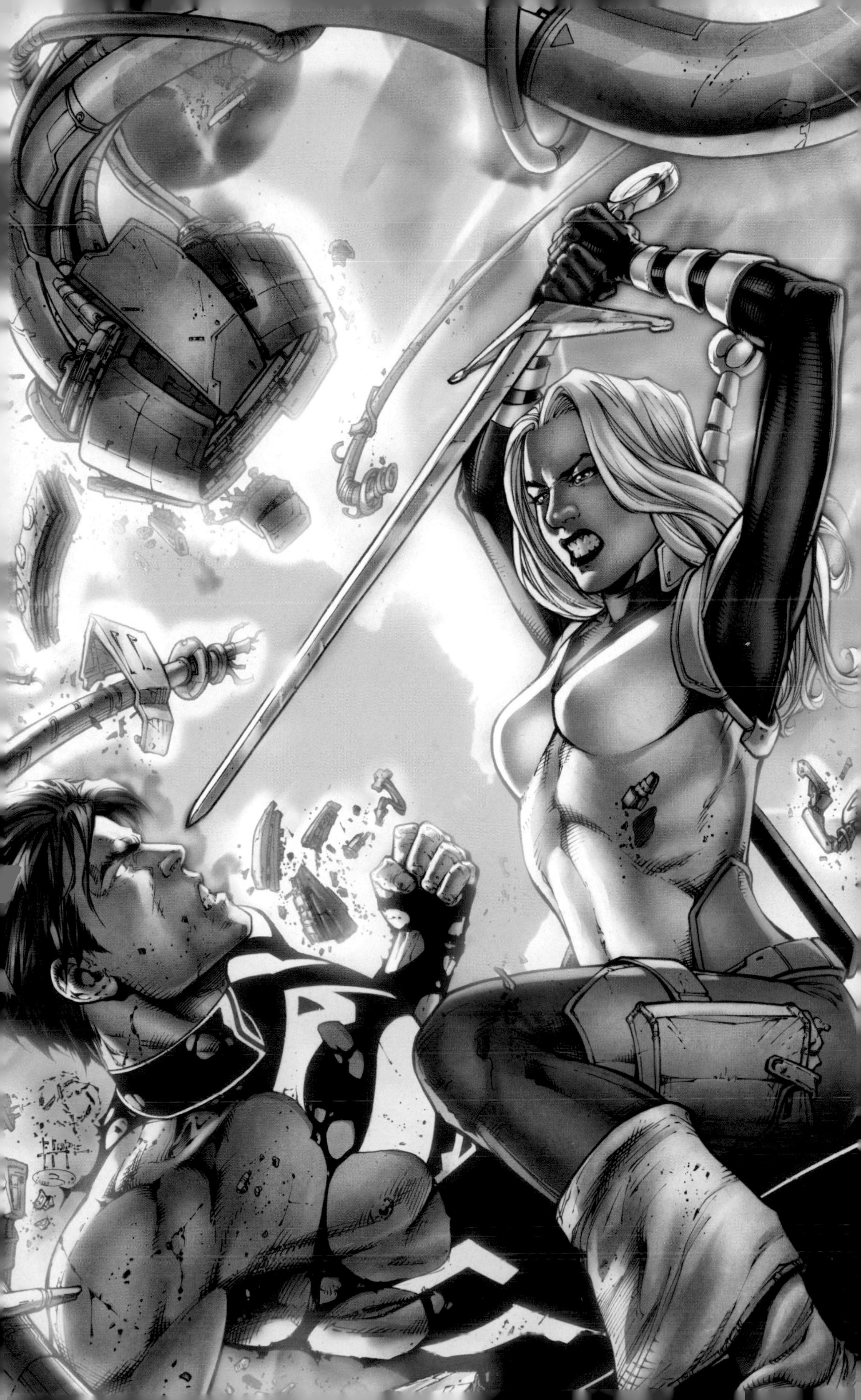

Cover by SHANE DAVIS, SANDRA HOPE & BARBARA CIARDO

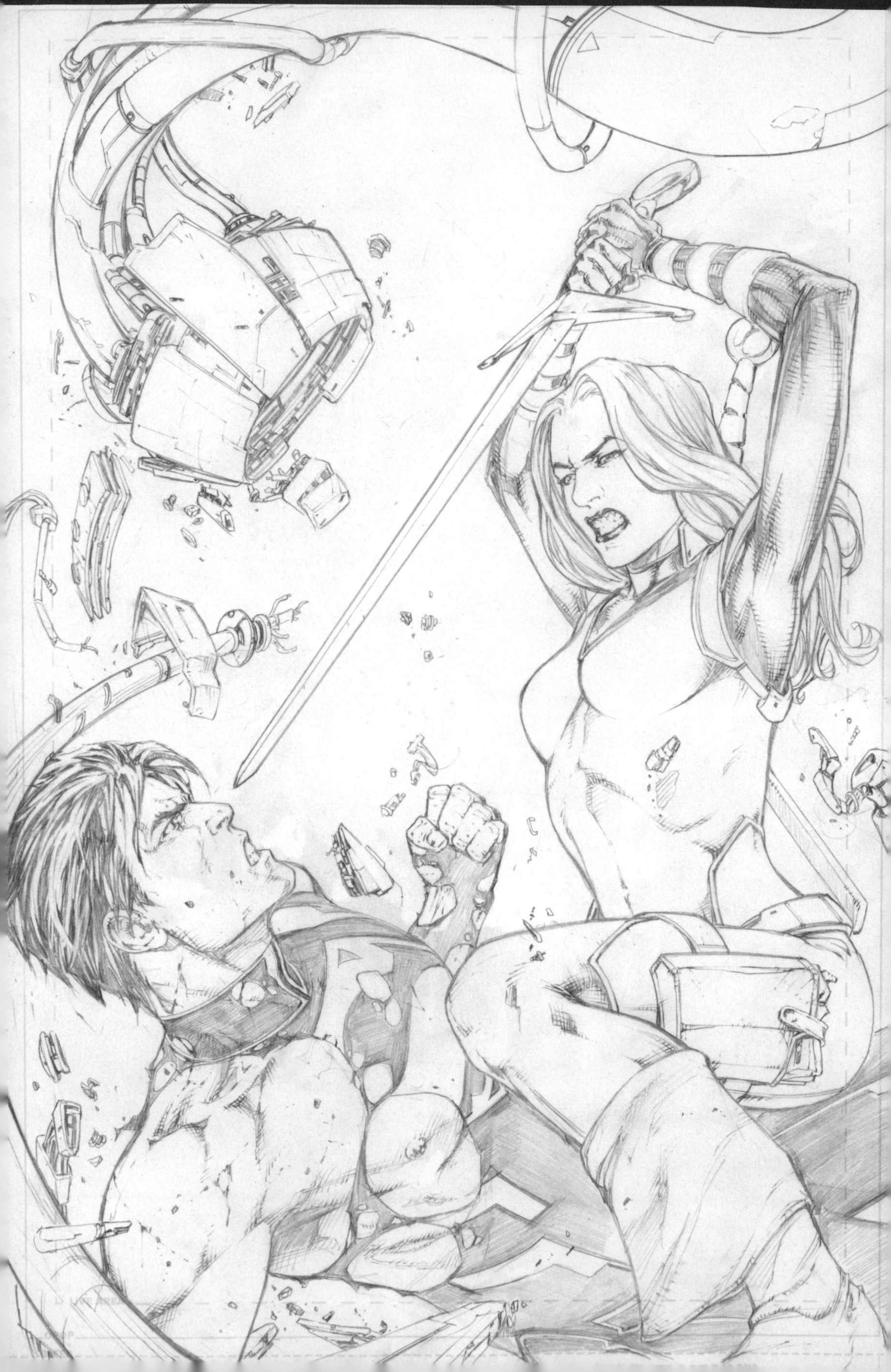

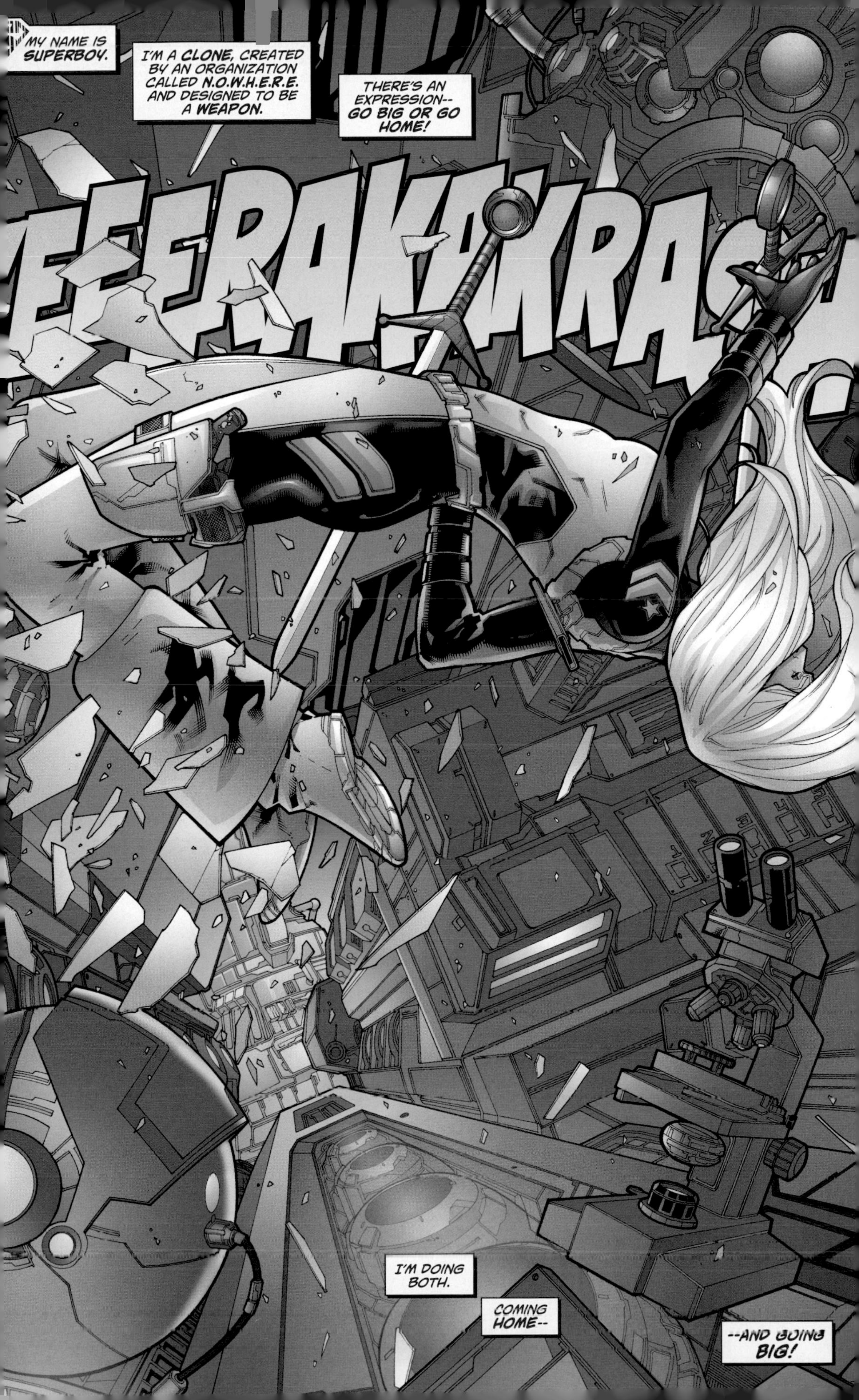
MY NAME IS SUPERBOY.
I'M A CLONE, CREATED BY AN ORGANIZATION CALLED N.O.W.H.E.R.E. AND DESIGNED TO BE A WEAPON.
THERE'S AN EXPRESSION-- GO BIG OR GO HOME!
I'M DOING BOTH.
COMING HOME--
--AND GOING BIG!

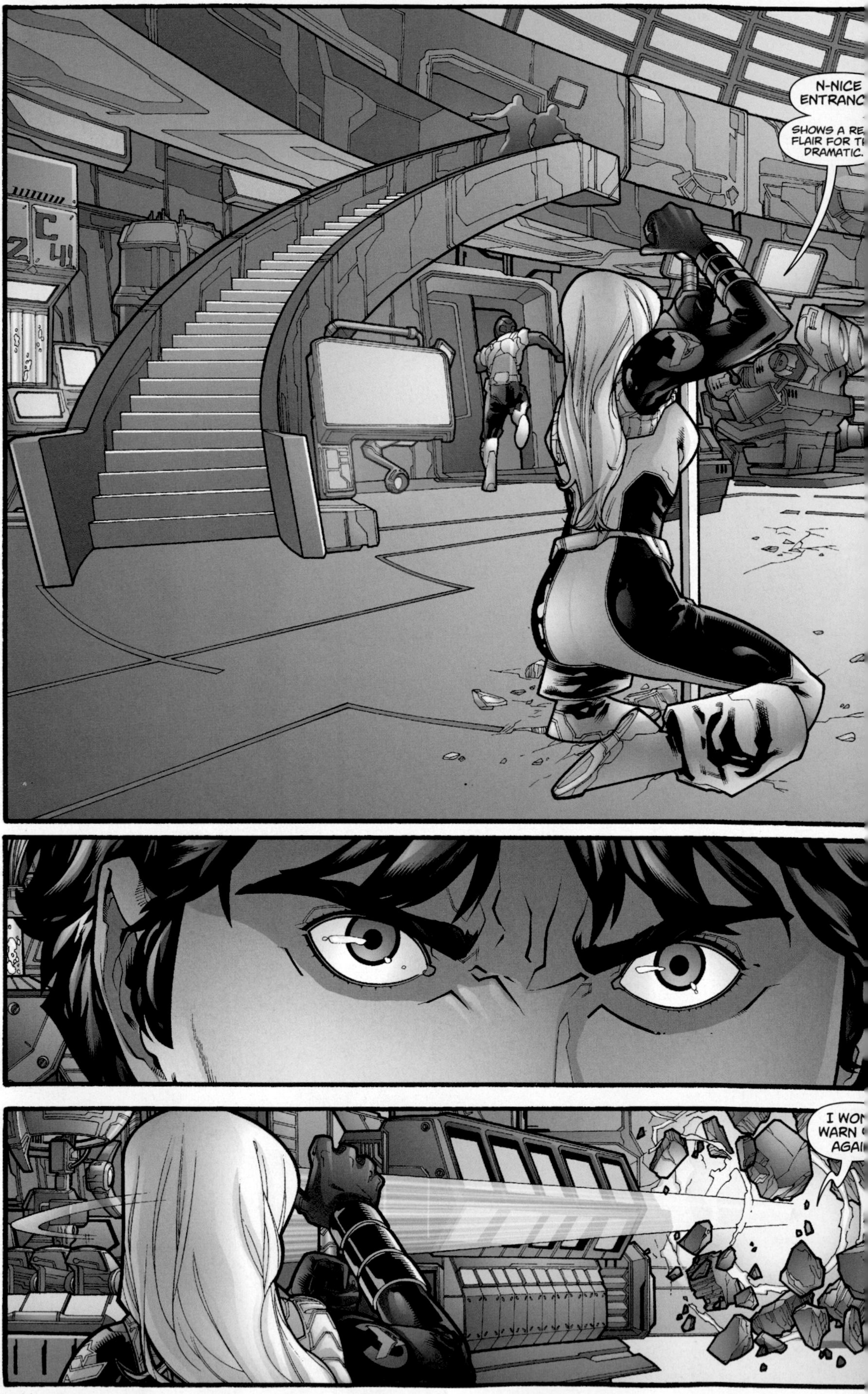
N-NICE ENTRANC
SHOWS A RE FLAIR FOR TH DRAMATIC.
I WON WARN AGAI

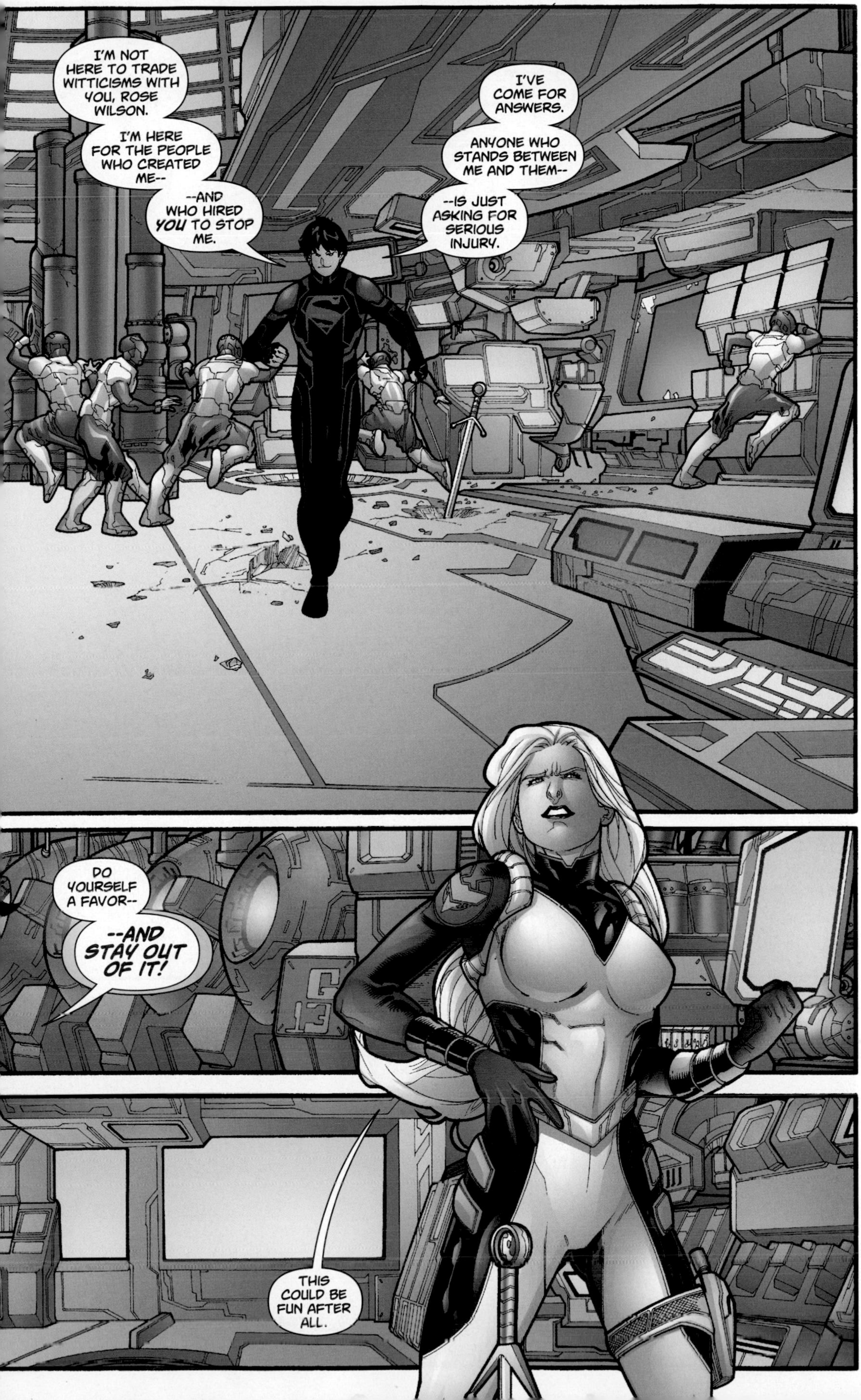
I'M NOT HERE TO TRADE WITTICISMS WITH YOU, ROSE WILSON.
I'M HERE FOR THE PEOPLE WHO CREATED ME--
--AND WHO HIRED *YOU* TO STOP ME.
I'VE COME FOR ANSWERS.
ANYONE WHO STANDS BETWEEN ME AND THEM--
--IS JUST ASKING FOR SERIOUS INJURY.
DO YOURSELF A FAVOR--
--AND STAY OUT OF IT!
THIS COULD BE FUN AFTER ALL.

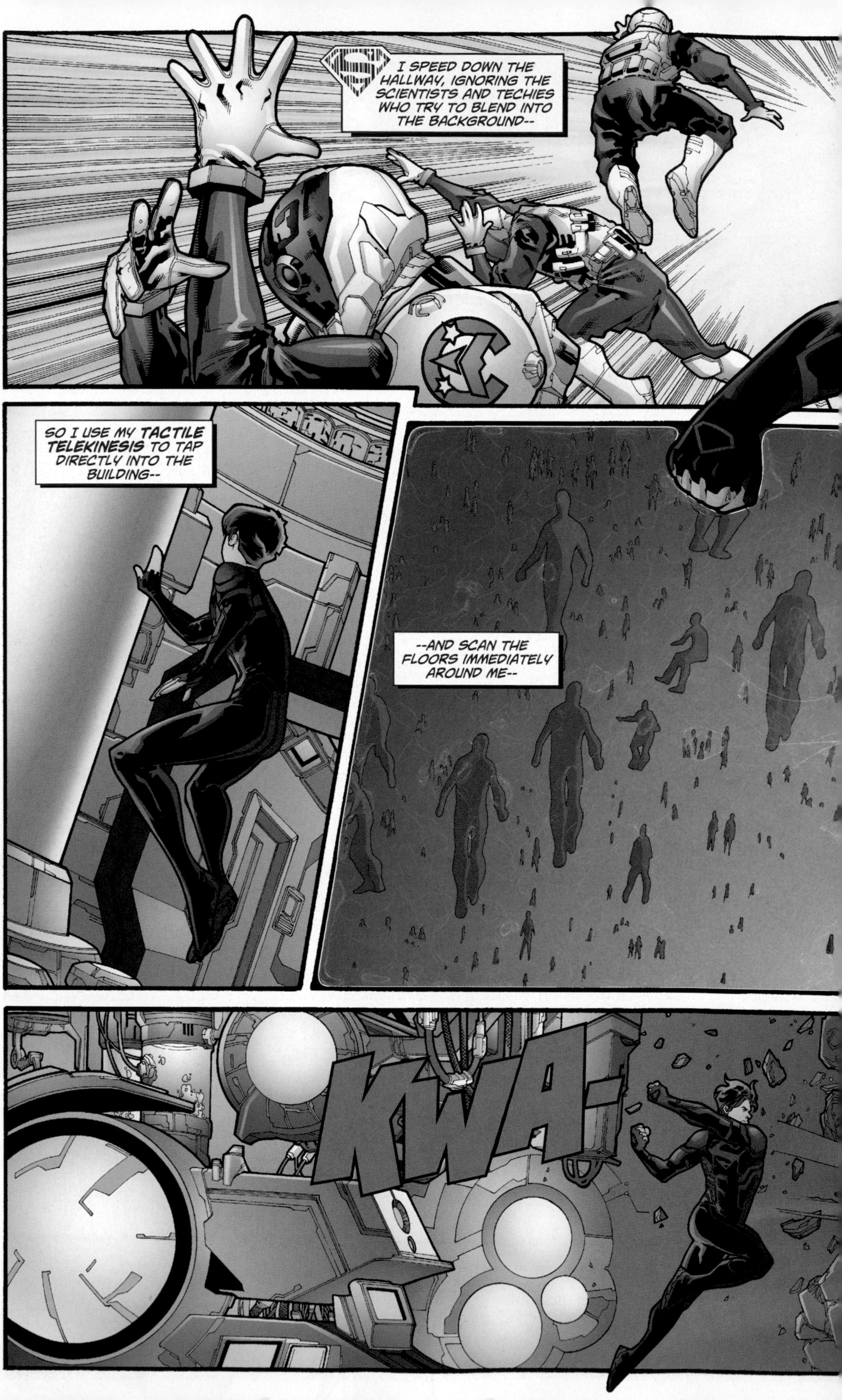
I SPEED DOWN THE HALLWAY, IGNORING THE SCIENTISTS AND TECHIES WHO TRY TO BLEND INTO THE BACKGROUND--
SO I USE MY TACTILE TELEKINESIS TO TAP DIRECTLY INTO THE BUILDING--
--AND SCAN THE FLOORS IMMEDIATELY AROUND ME--
KWA-

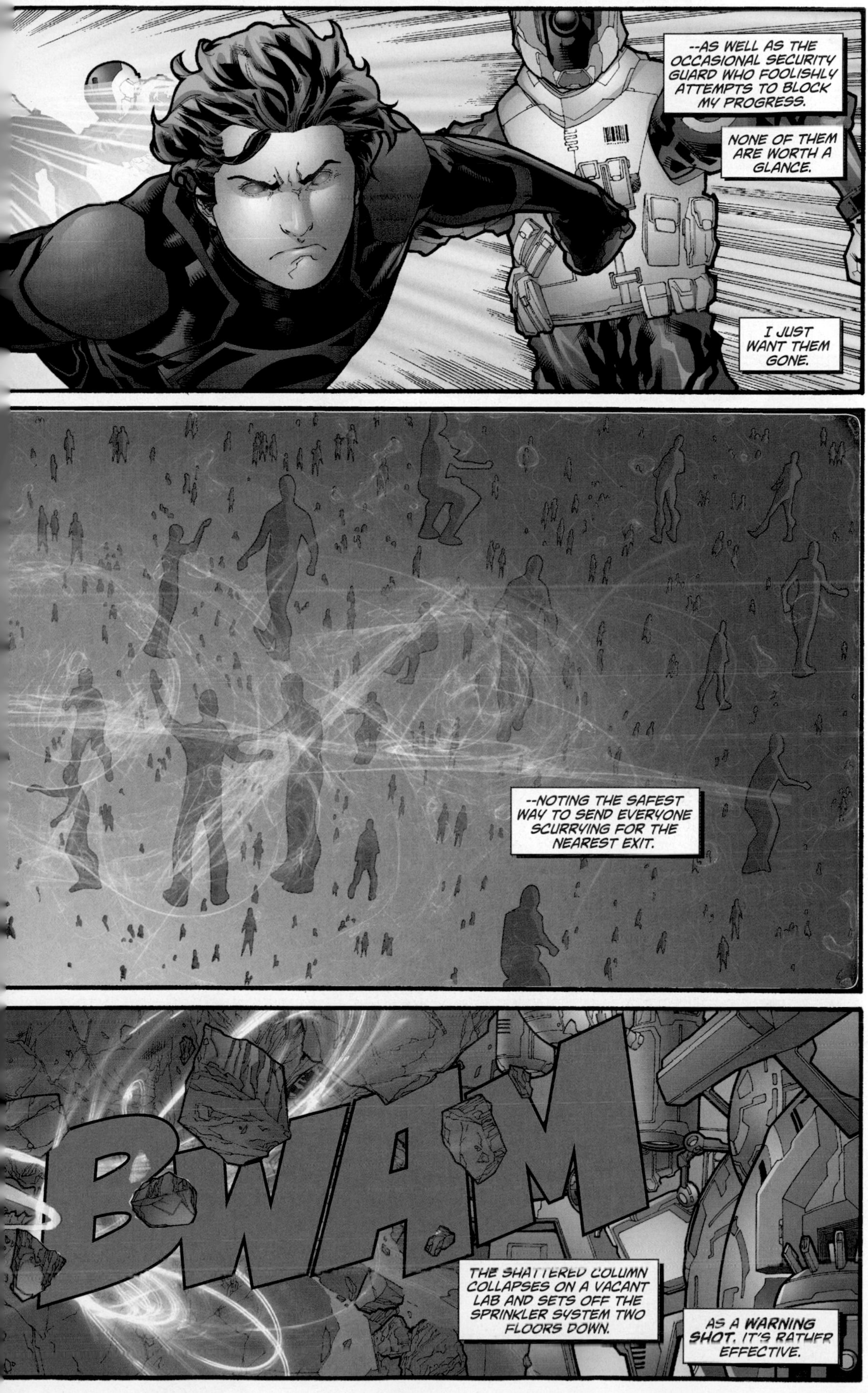
--AS WELL AS THE OCCASIONAL SECURITY GUARD WHO FOOLISHLY ATTEMPTS TO BLOCK MY PROGRESS.
NONE OF THEM ARE WORTH A GLANCE.
I JUST WANT THEM GONE.
--NOTING THE SAFEST WAY TO SEND EVERYONE SCURRYING FOR THE NEAREST EXIT.
BWAM
THE SHATTERED COLUMN COLLAPSES ON A VACANT LAB AND SETS OFF THE SPRINKLER SYSTEM TWO FLOORS DOWN.
AS A WARNING SHOT, IT'S RATHER EFFECTIVE.

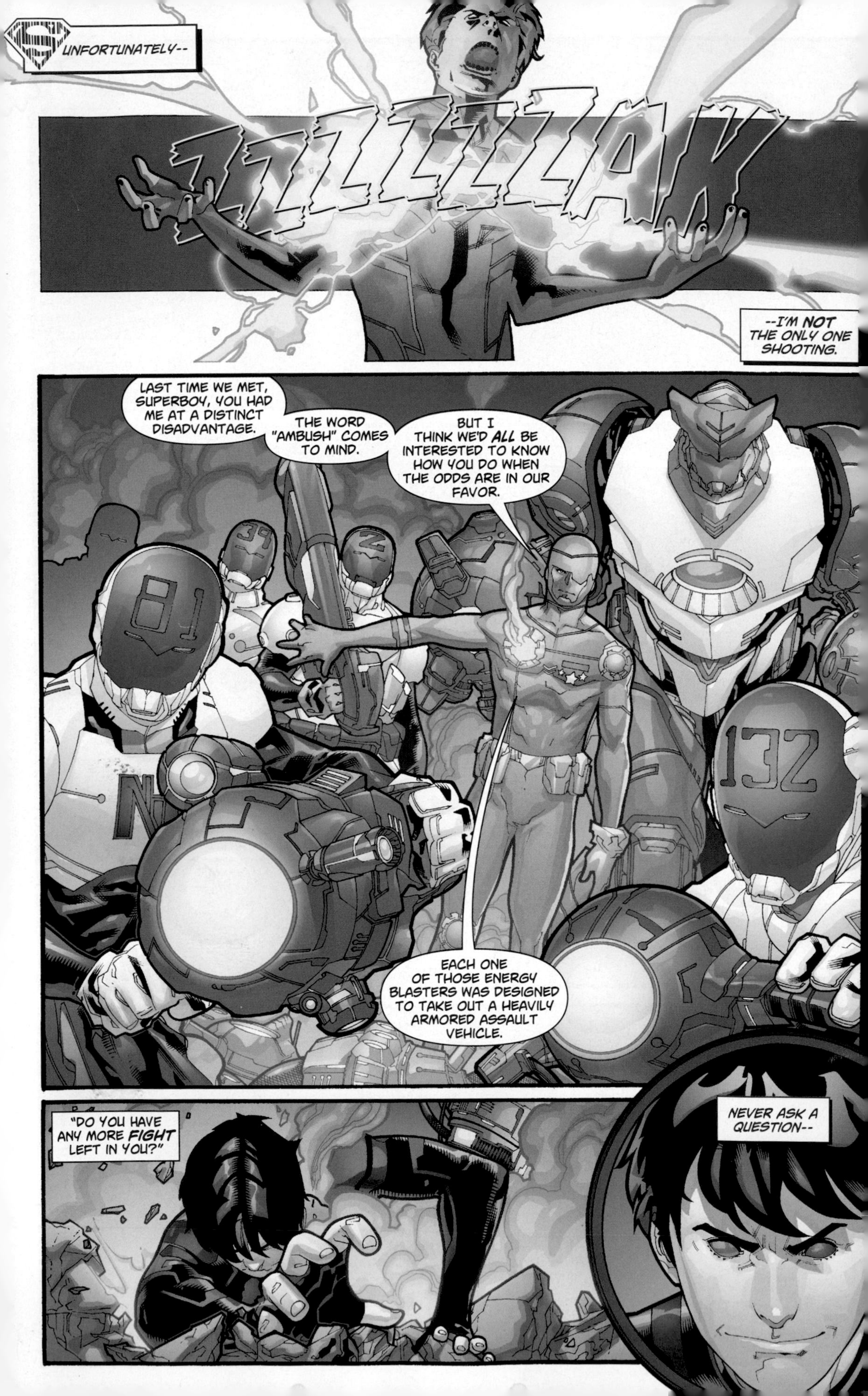
UNFORTUNATELY--
ZZZZZZZAK
--I'M NOT THE ONLY ONE SHOOTING.
LAST TIME WE MET, SUPERBOY, YOU HAD ME AT A DISTINCT DISADVANTAGE.
THE WORD "AMBUSH" COMES TO MIND.
BUT I THINK WE'D ALL BE INTERESTED TO KNOW HOW YOU DO WHEN THE ODDS ARE IN OUR FAVOR.
EACH ONE OF THOSE ENERGY BLASTERS WAS DESIGNED TO TAKE OUT A HEAVILY ARMORED ASSAULT VEHICLE.
"DO YOU HAVE ANY MORE FIGHT LEFT IN YOU?"
NEVER ASK A QUESTION--

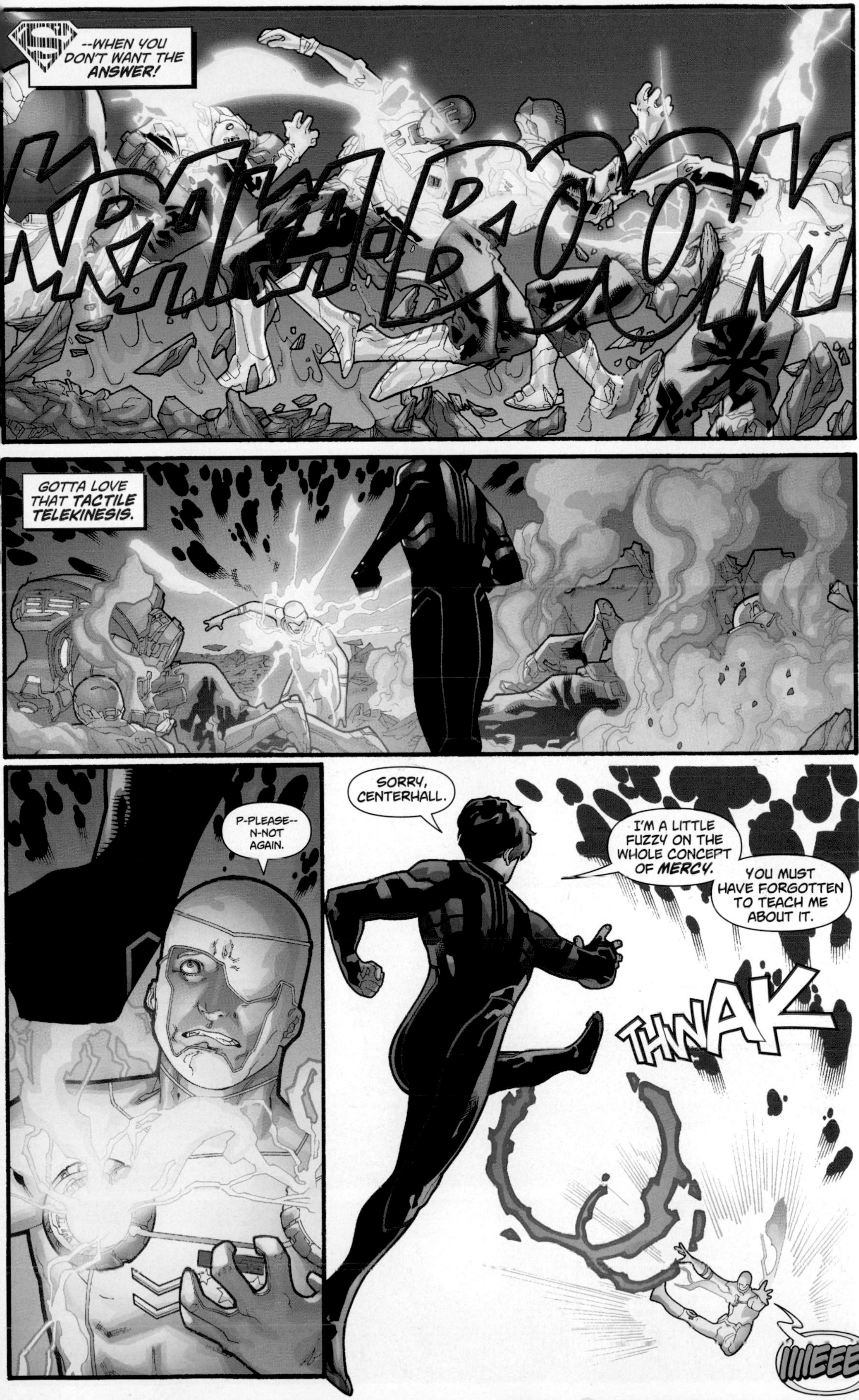
--WHEN YOU DON'T WANT THE ANSWER!
GOTTA LOVE THAT TACTILE TELEKINESIS.
P-PLEASE-- N-NOT AGAIN.
SORRY, CENTERHALL.
I'M A LITTLE FUZZY ON THE WHOLE CONCEPT OF MERCY.
YOU MUST HAVE FORGOTTEN TO TEACH ME ABOUT IT.
THWAK
IIIIEEE!

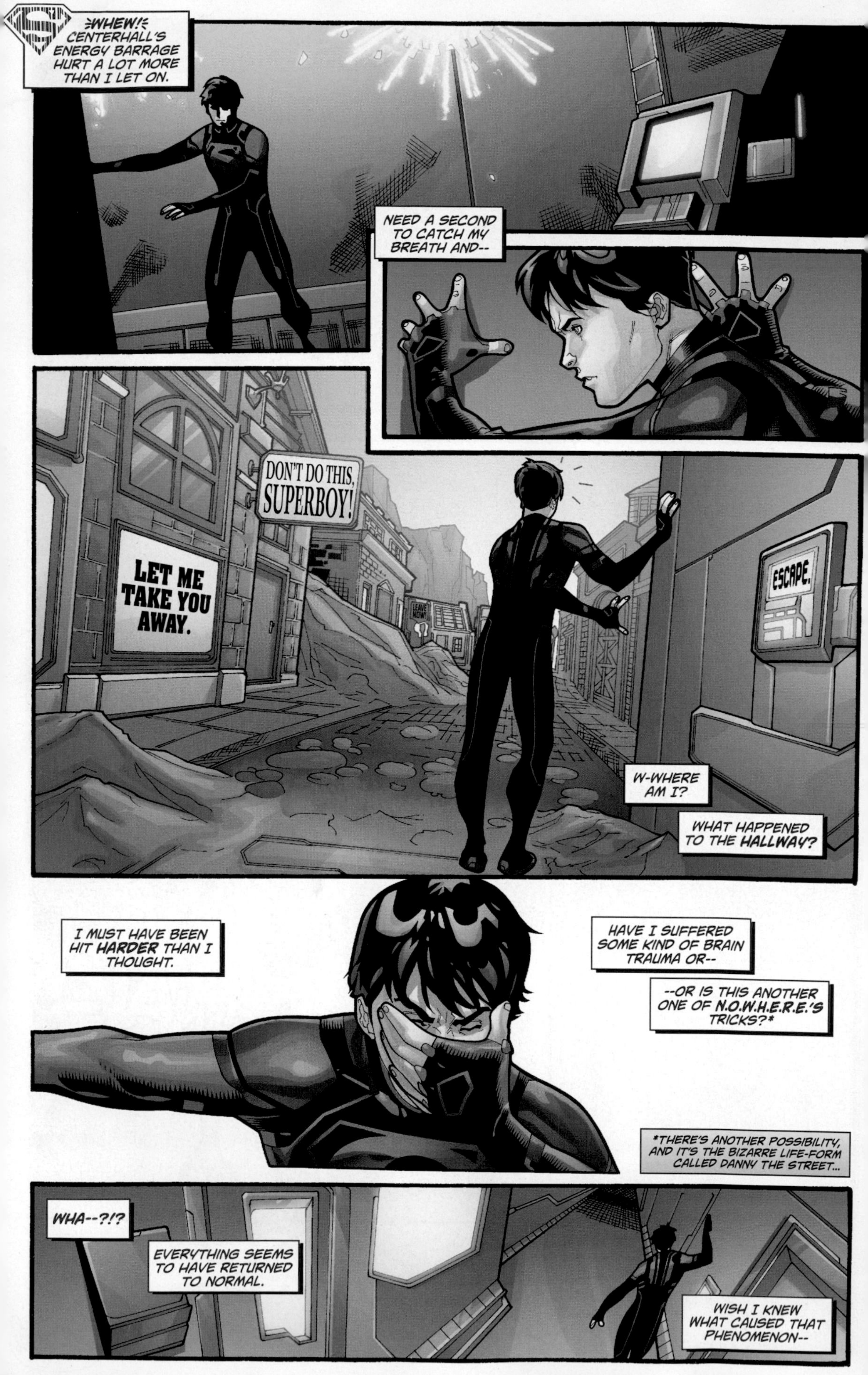
WHEW! CENTERHALL'S ENERGY BARRAGE HURT A LOT MORE THAN I LET ON.
NEED A SECOND TO CATCH MY BREATH AND--
DON'T DO THIS, SUPERBOY!
LET ME TAKE YOU AWAY.
LEAVE NOW!
ESCAPE.
W-WHERE AM I?
WHAT HAPPENED TO THE HALLWAY?
I MUST HAVE BEEN HIT HARDER THAN I THOUGHT.
HAVE I SUFFERED SOME KIND OF BRAIN TRAUMA OR--
--OR IS THIS ANOTHER ONE OF N.O.W.H.E.R.E.'S TRICKS?*
*THERE'S ANOTHER POSSIBILITY, AND IT'S THE BIZARRE LIFE-FORM CALLED DANNY THE STREET...
WHA--?!?
EVERYTHING SEEMS TO HAVE RETURNED TO NORMAL.
WISH I KNEW WHAT CAUSED THAT PHENOMENON--

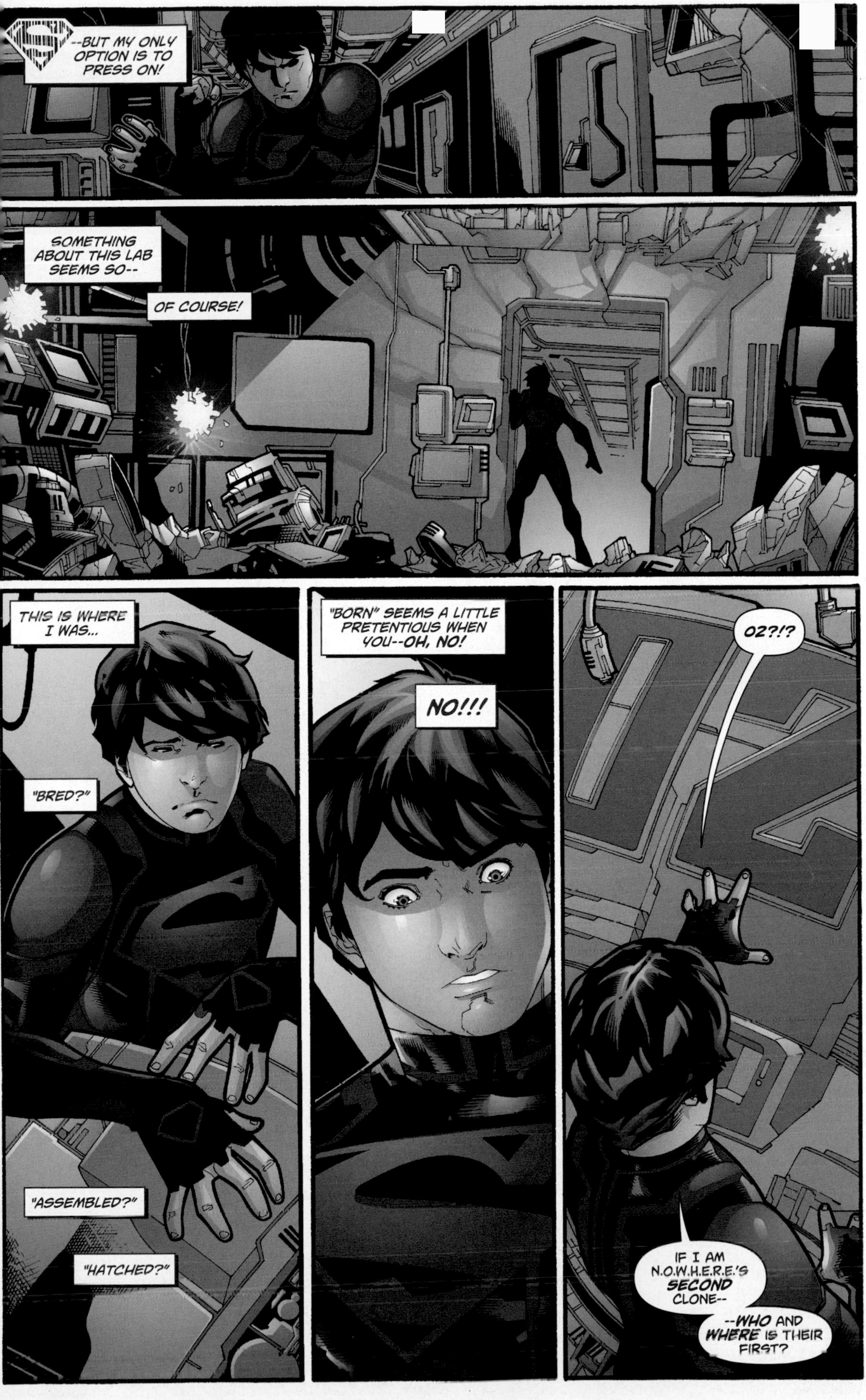

--BUT MY ONLY OPTION IS TO PRESS ON!
SOMETHING ABOUT THIS LAB SEEMS SO--
OF COURSE!
THIS IS WHERE I WAS...
"BRED?"
"ASSEMBLED?"
"HATCHED?"
"BORN" SEEMS A LITTLE PRETENTIOUS WHEN YOU--OH, NO!
NO!!!
O2?!?
IF I AM N.O.W.H.E.R.E.'S SECOND CLONE--
--WHO AND WHERE IS THEIR FIRST?

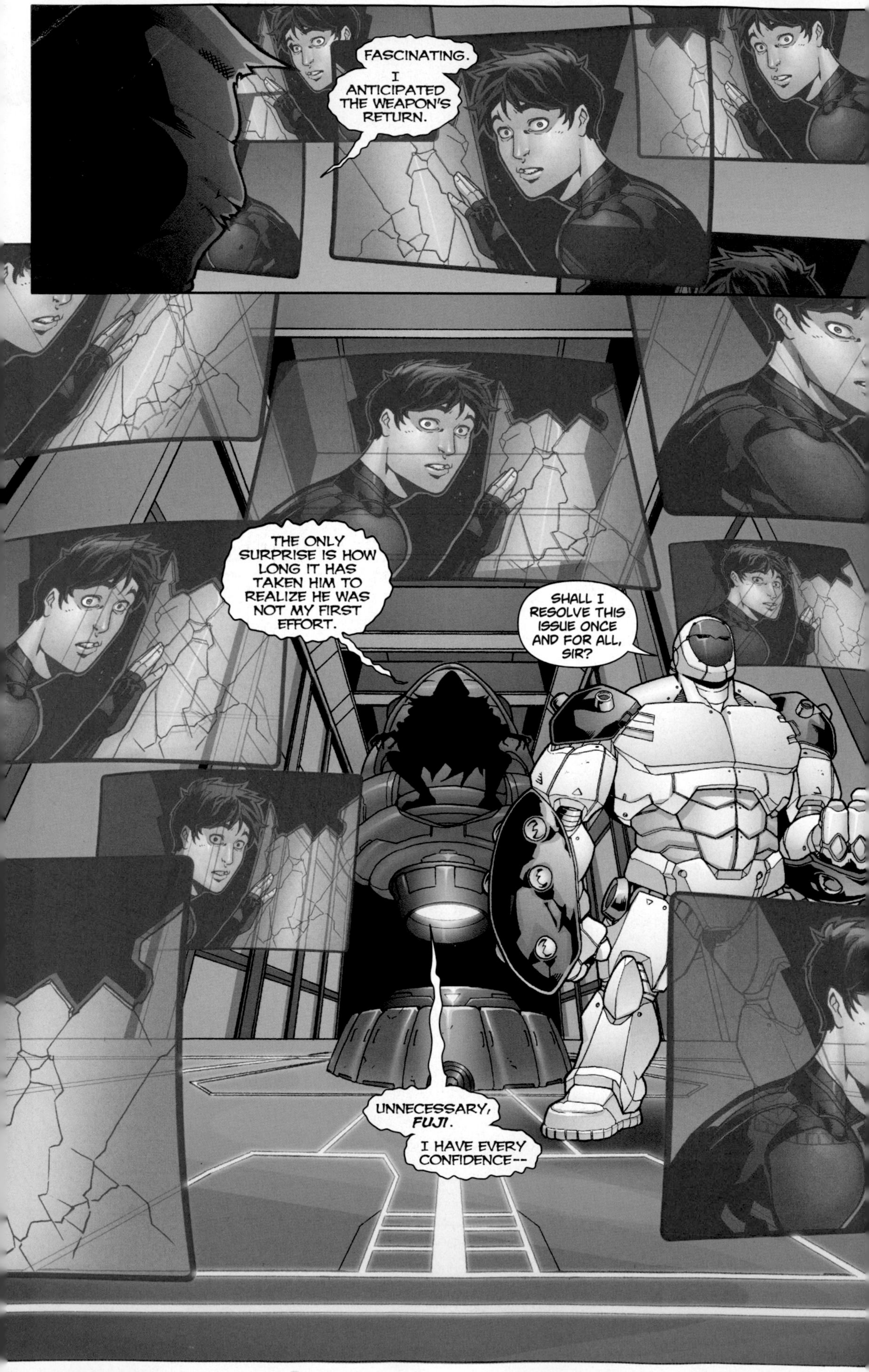
FASCINATING.
I ANTICIPATED THE WEAPON'S RETURN.
THE ONLY SURPRISE IS HOW LONG IT HAS TAKEN HIM TO REALIZE HE WAS NOT MY FIRST EFFORT.
SHALL I RESOLVE THIS ISSUE ONCE AND FOR ALL, SIR?
UNNECESSARY, FUJI.
I HAVE EVERY CONFIDENCE--

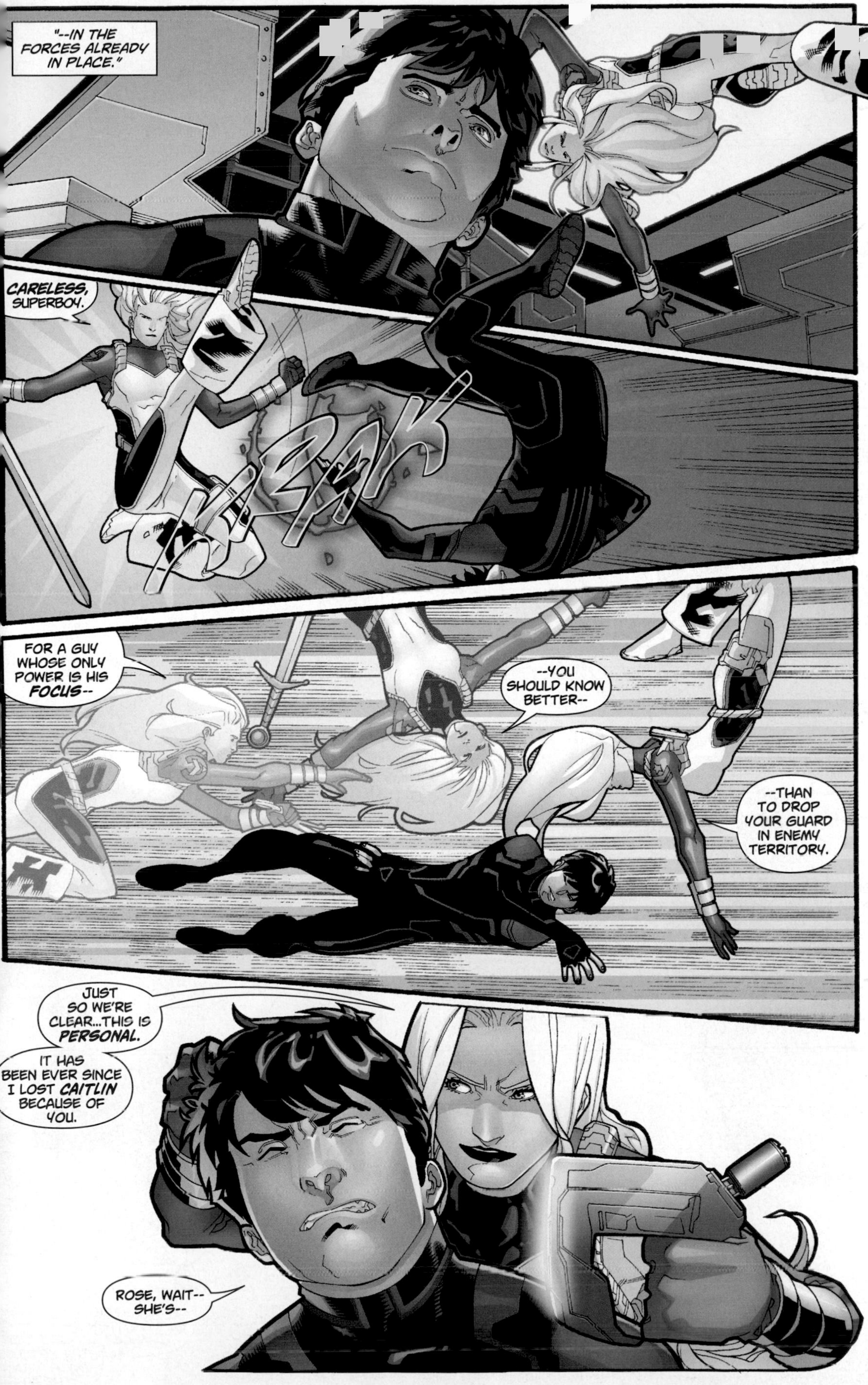
"--IN THE FORCES ALREADY IN PLACE."
CARELESS, SUPERBOY.
FOR A GUY WHOSE ONLY POWER IS HIS FOCUS--
--YOU SHOULD KNOW BETTER--
--THAN TO DROP YOUR GUARD IN ENEMY TERRITORY.
JUST SO WE'RE CLEAR...THIS IS PERSONAL.
IT HAS BEEN EVER SINCE I LOST CAITLIN BECAUSE OF YOU.
ROSE, WAIT-- SHE'S--

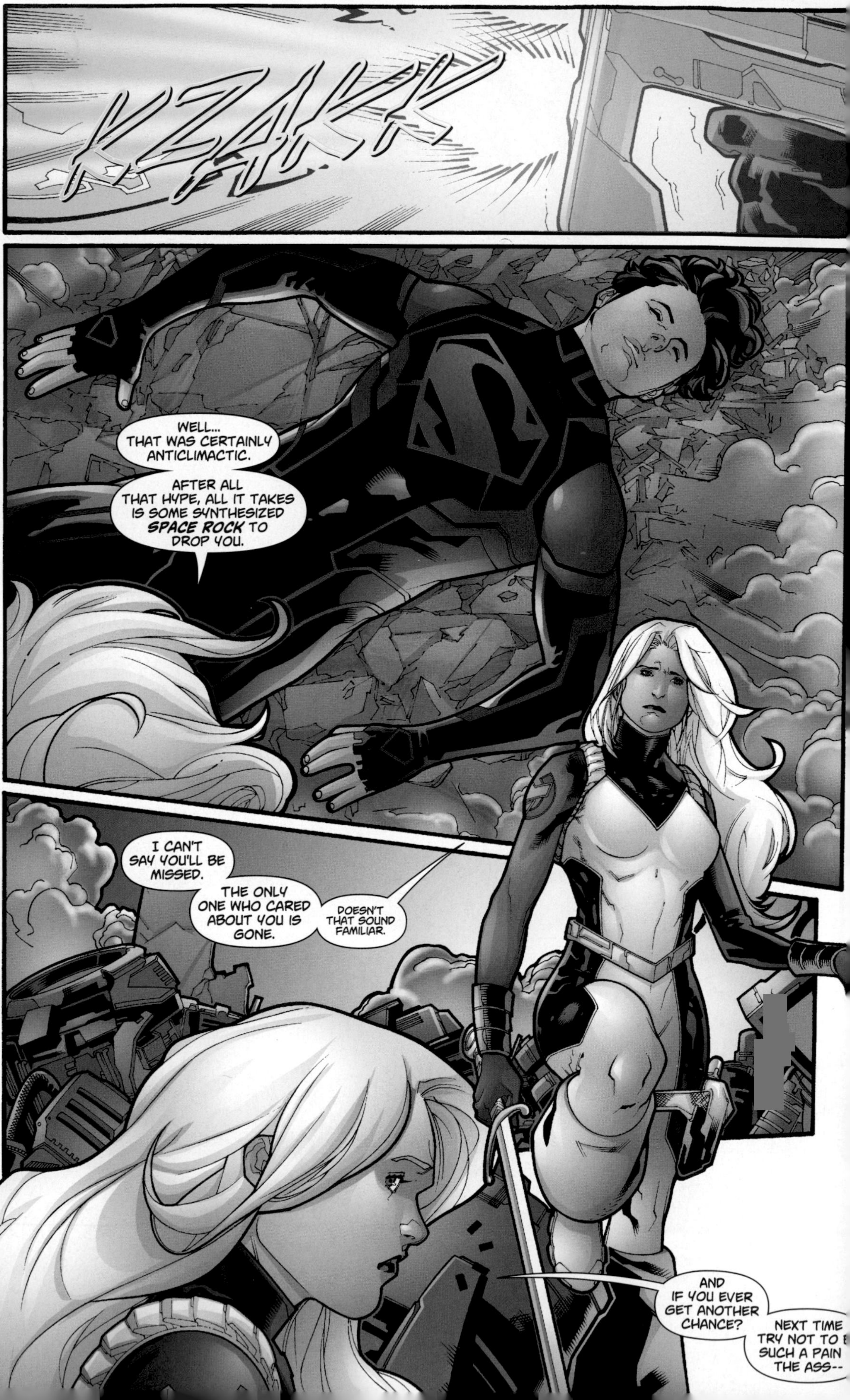
KZAKK
WELL... THAT WAS CERTAINLY ANTICLIMACTIC.
AFTER ALL THAT HYPE, ALL IT TAKES IS SOME SYNTHESIZED **SPACE ROCK** TO DROP YOU.
I CAN'T SAY YOU'LL BE MISSED.
THE ONLY ONE WHO CARED ABOUT YOU IS GONE.
DOESN'T THAT SOUND FAMILIAR.
AND IF YOU EVER GET ANOTHER CHANCE?
NEXT TIME TRY NOT TO B SUCH A PAIN THE ASS--

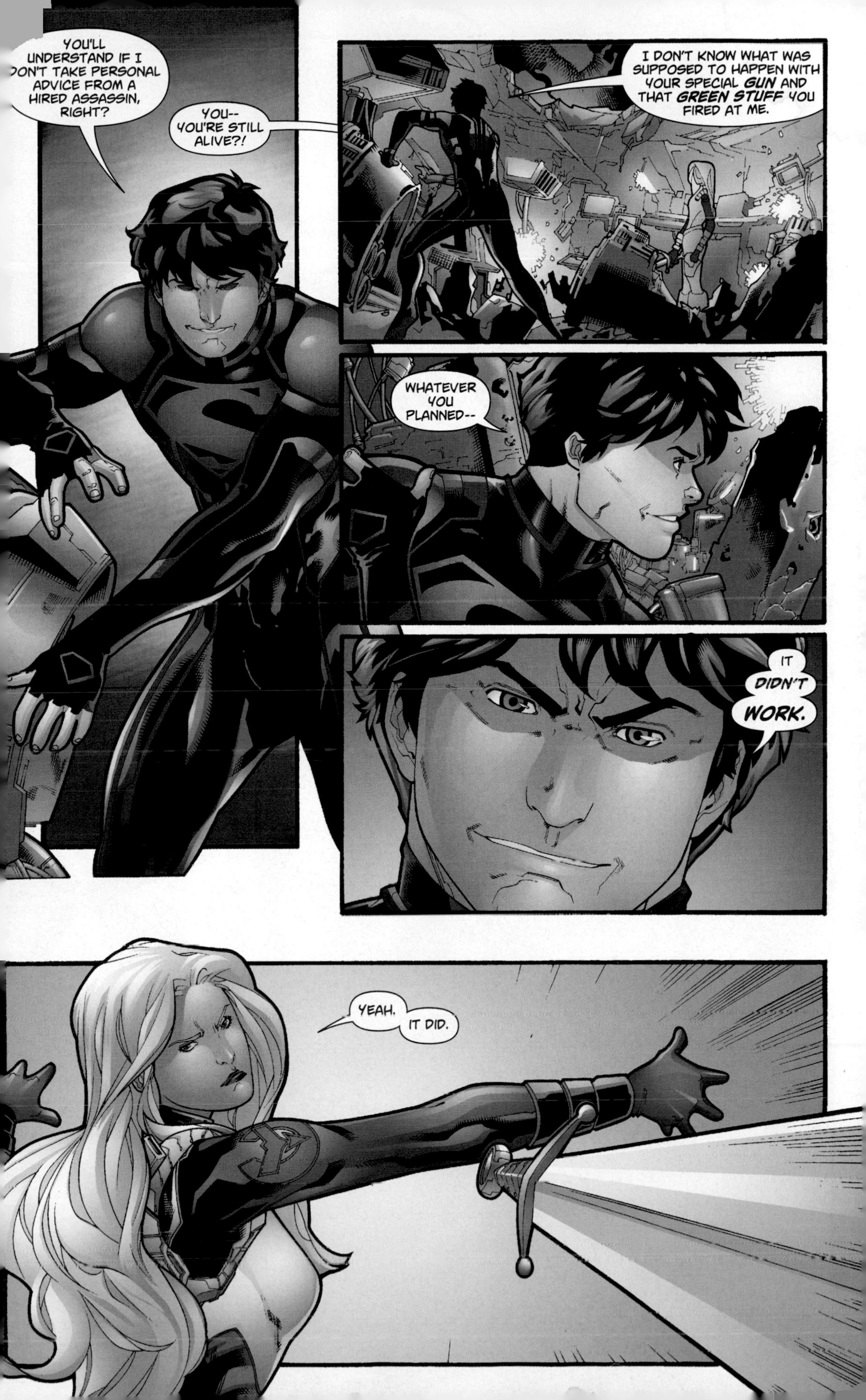
YOU'LL UNDERSTAND IF I DON'T TAKE PERSONAL ADVICE FROM A HIRED ASSASSIN, RIGHT?
YOU-- YOU'RE STILL ALIVE?!
I DON'T KNOW WHAT WAS SUPPOSED TO HAPPEN WITH YOUR SPECIAL GUN AND THAT GREEN STUFF YOU FIRED AT ME.
WHATEVER YOU PLANNED--
IT DIDN'T WORK.
YEAH.
IT DID.

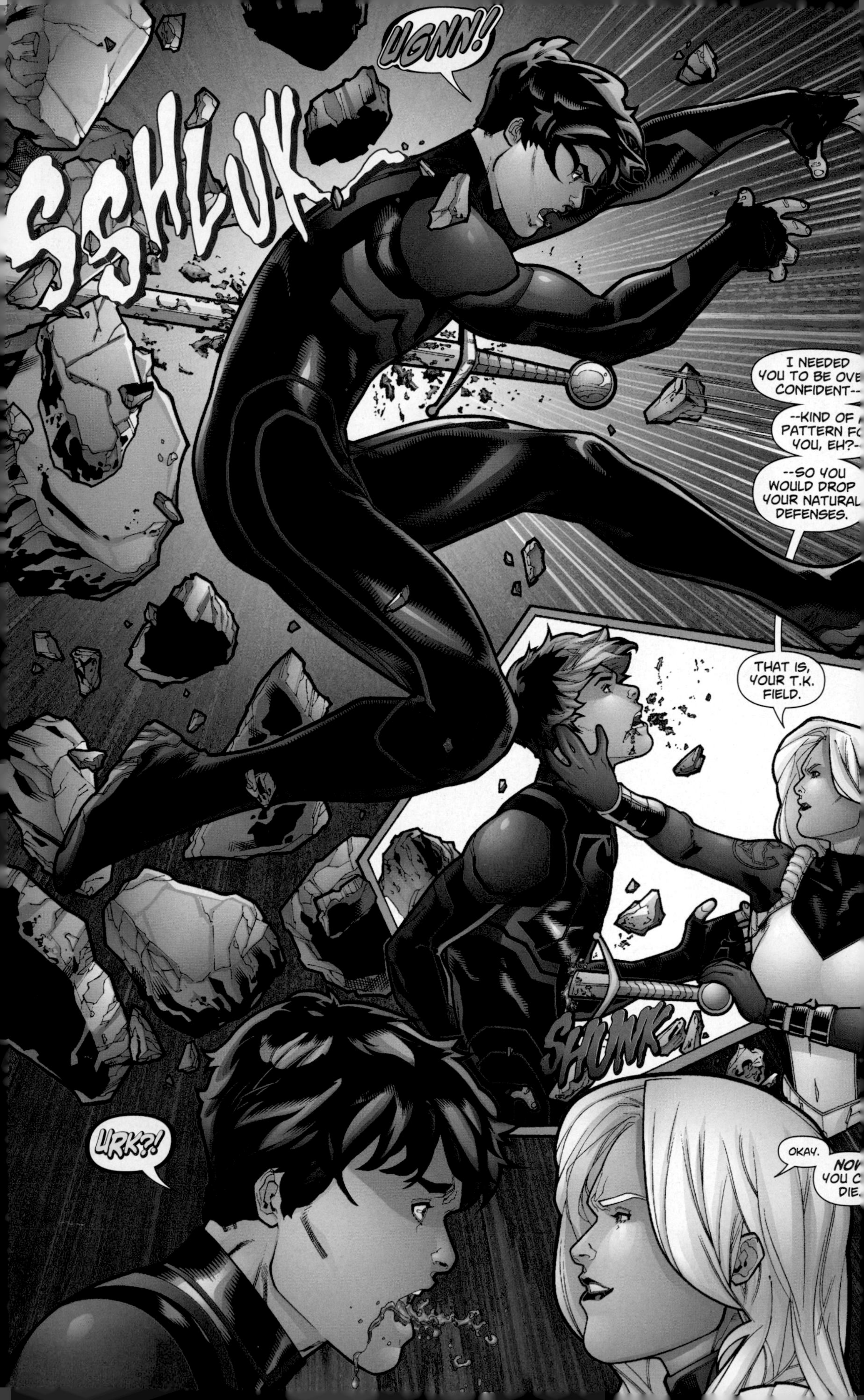
UGNN!
SSHLUK
I NEEDED YOU TO BE OVE CONFIDENT--
--KIND OF PATTERN FO YOU, EH?--
--SO YOU WOULD DROP YOUR NATURAL DEFENSES.
THAT IS, YOUR T.K. FIELD.
SHUNK
URK?!
OKAY.
NOW YOU C DIE.

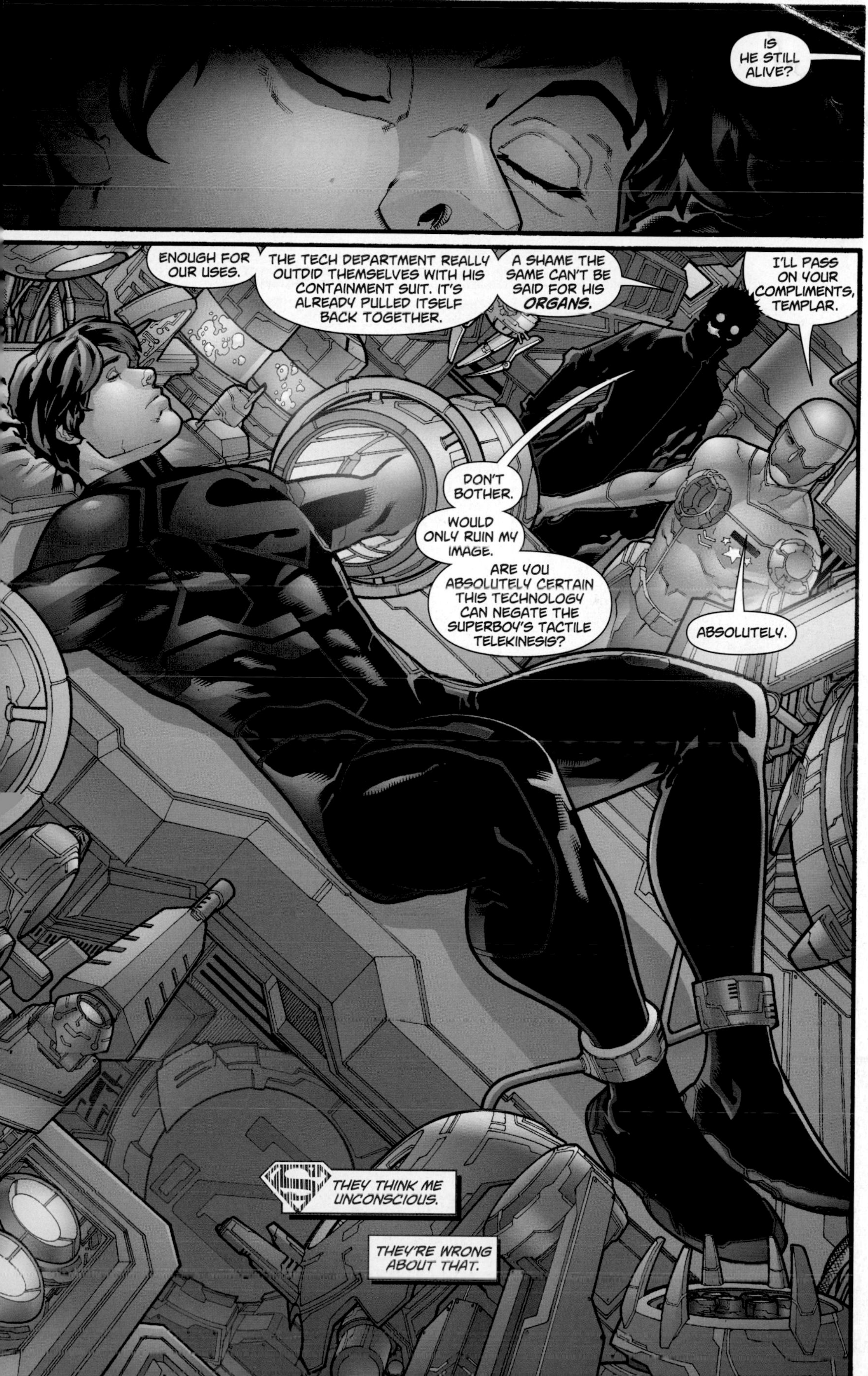
IS HE STILL ALIVE?
ENOUGH FOR OUR USES.
THE TECH DEPARTMENT REALLY OUTDID THEMSELVES WITH HIS CONTAINMENT SUIT. IT'S ALREADY PULLED ITSELF BACK TOGETHER.
A SHAME THE SAME CAN'T BE SAID FOR HIS *ORGANS*.
I'LL PASS ON YOUR COMPLIMENTS, TEMPLAR.
DON'T BOTHER.
WOULD ONLY RUIN MY IMAGE.
ARE YOU ABSOLUTELY CERTAIN THIS TECHNOLOGY CAN NEGATE THE SUPERBOY'S TACTILE TELEKINESIS?
ABSOLUTELY.
THEY THINK ME UNCONSCIOUS.
THEY'RE WRONG ABOUT THAT.

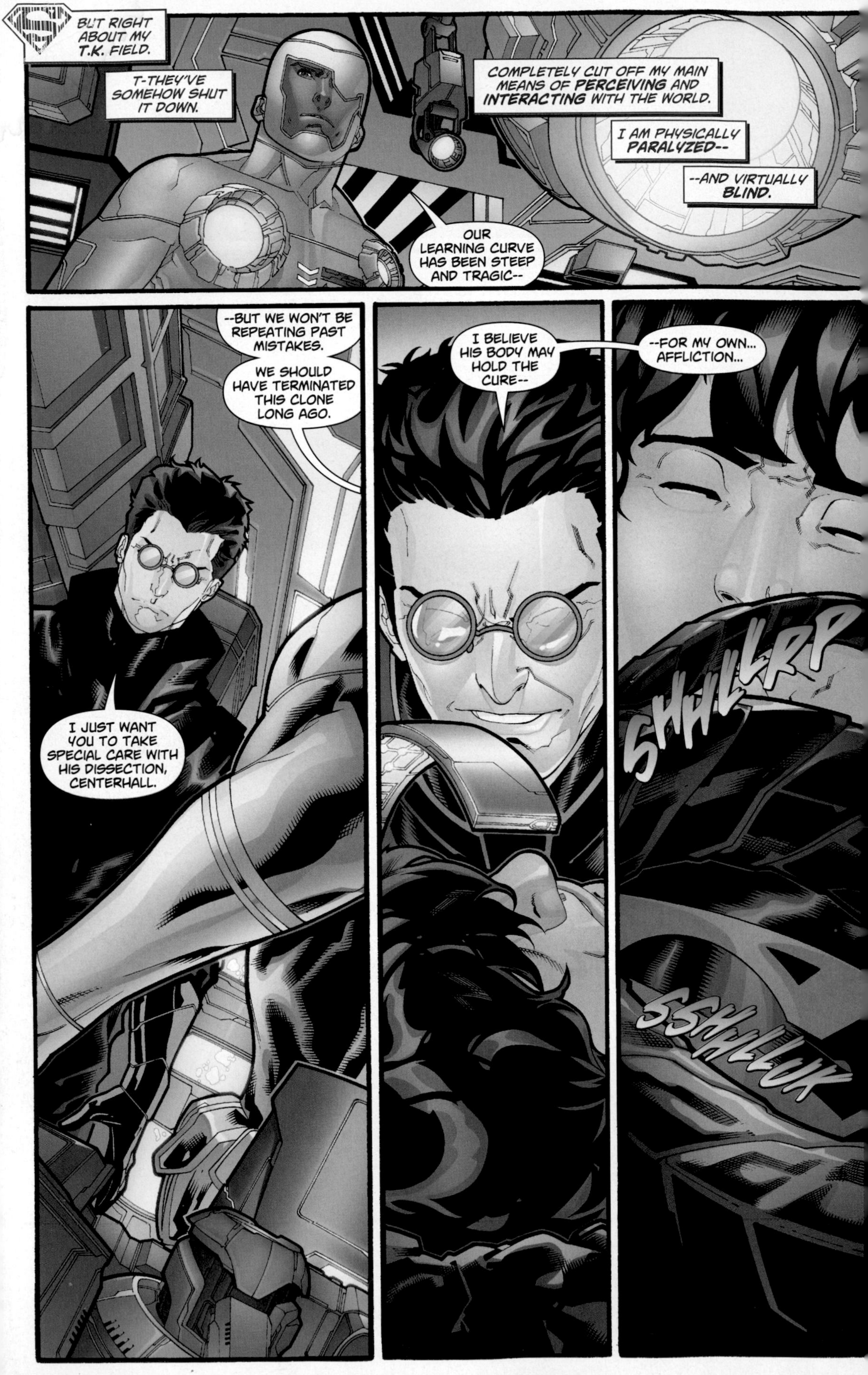
BUT RIGHT ABOUT MY T.K. FIELD.
T-THEY'VE SOMEHOW SHUT IT DOWN.
COMPLETELY CUT OFF MY MAIN MEANS OF PERCEIVING AND INTERACTING WITH THE WORLD.
I AM PHYSICALLY PARALYZED--
--AND VIRTUALLY BLIND.
OUR LEARNING CURVE HAS BEEN STEEP AND TRAGIC--
--BUT WE WON'T BE REPEATING PAST MISTAKES.
WE SHOULD HAVE TERMINATED THIS CLONE LONG AGO.
I JUST WANT YOU TO TAKE SPECIAL CARE WITH HIS DISSECTION, CENTERHALL.
I BELIEVE HIS BODY MAY HOLD THE CURE--
--FOR MY OWN... AFFLICTION...
SHHLLRP
SSHHLUK

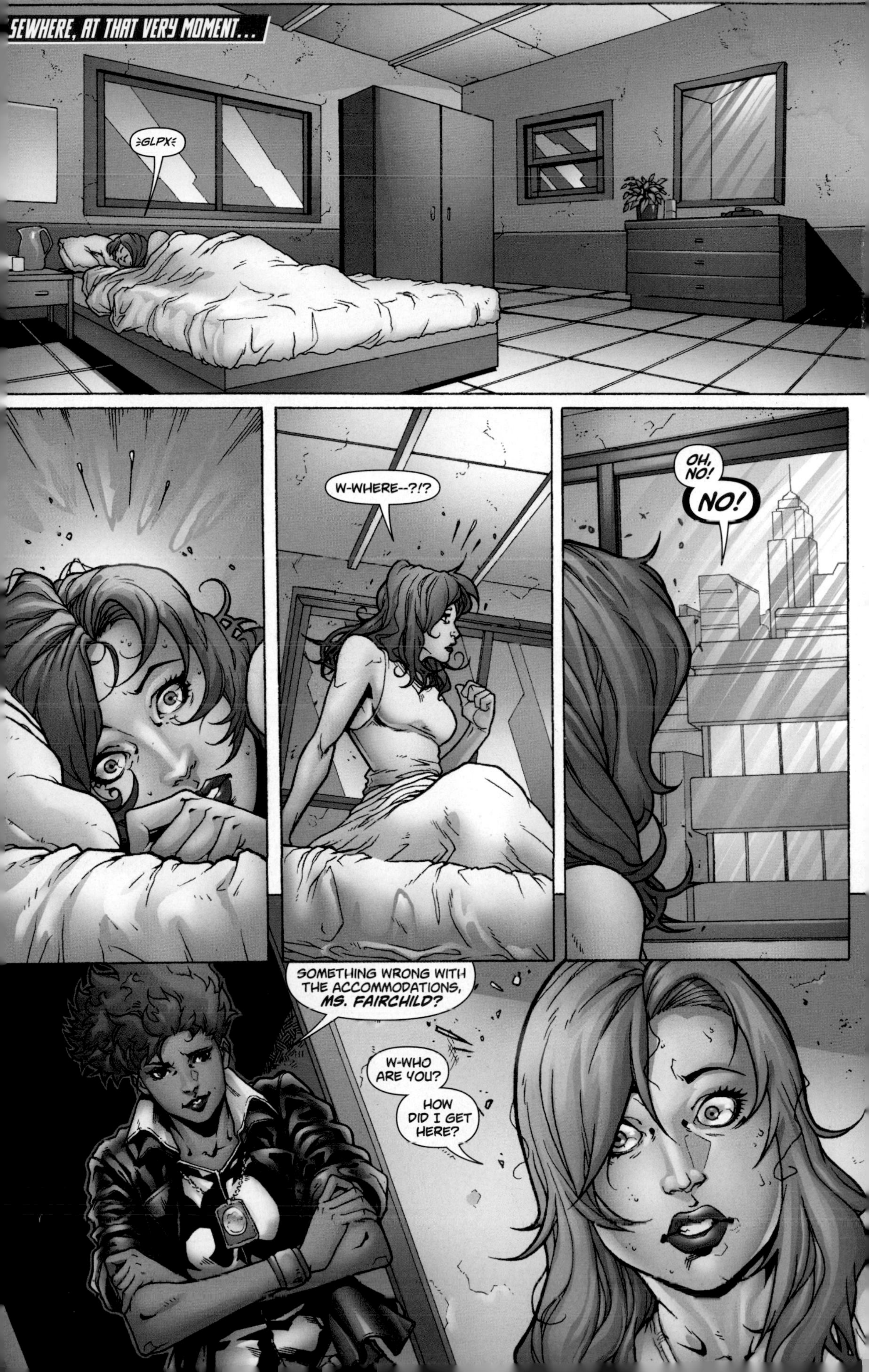
SEWHERE, AT THAT VERY MOMENT...
GLPX
W-WHERE--?!?
OH, NO!
NO!
SOMETHING WRONG WITH THE ACCOMMODATIONS, MS. FAIRCHILD?
W-WHO ARE YOU?
HOW DID I GET HERE?

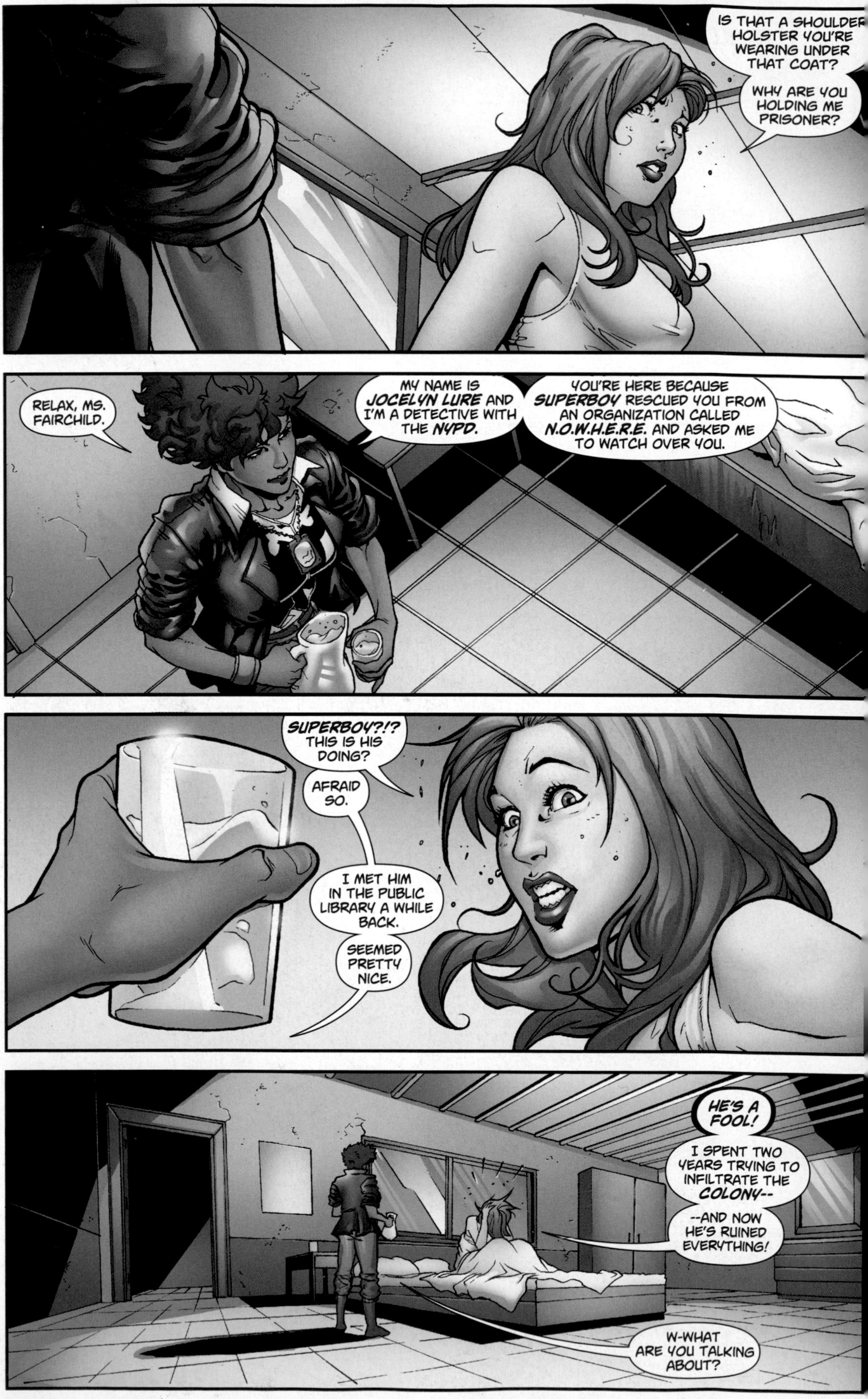
IS THAT A SHOULDER HOLSTER YOU'RE WEARING UNDER THAT COAT?
WHY ARE YOU HOLDING ME PRISONER?
RELAX, MS. FAIRCHILD.
MY NAME IS JOCELYN LURE AND I'M A DETECTIVE WITH THE NYPD.
YOU'RE HERE BECAUSE SUPERBOY RESCUED YOU FROM AN ORGANIZATION CALLED N.O.W.H.E.R.E. AND ASKED ME TO WATCH OVER YOU.
SUPERBOY?!? THIS IS HIS DOING?
AFRAID SO.
I MET HIM IN THE PUBLIC LIBRARY A WHILE BACK.
SEEMED PRETTY NICE.
HE'S A FOOL!
I SPENT TWO YEARS TRYING TO INFILTRATE THE COLONY--
--AND NOW HE'S RUINED EVERYTHING!
W-WHAT ARE YOU TALKING ABOUT?

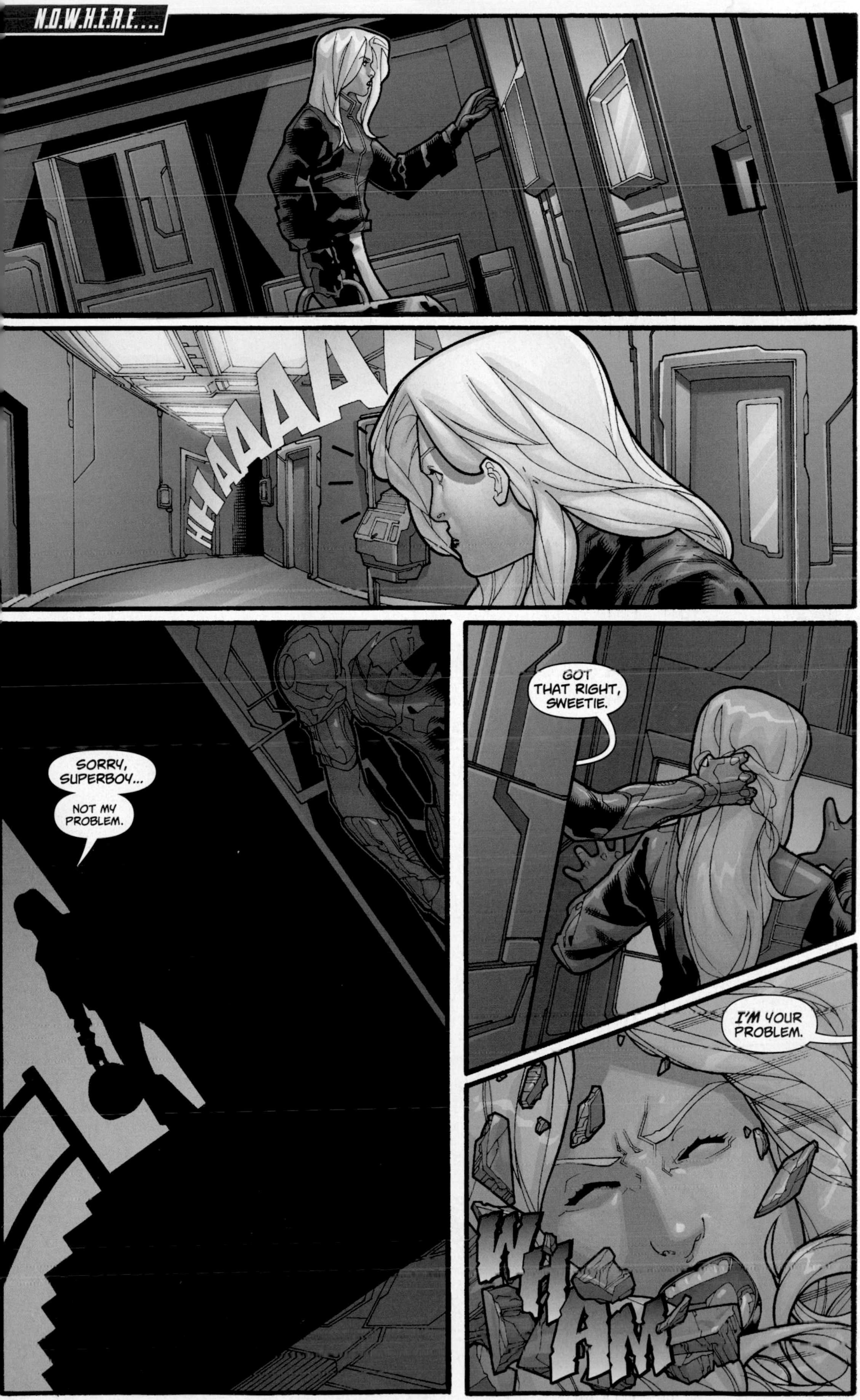
N.O.W.H.E.R.E....
WHAAAAA
SORRY, SUPERBOY...
NOT MY PROBLEM.
GOT THAT RIGHT, SWEETIE.
I'M YOUR PROBLEM.
WHAM

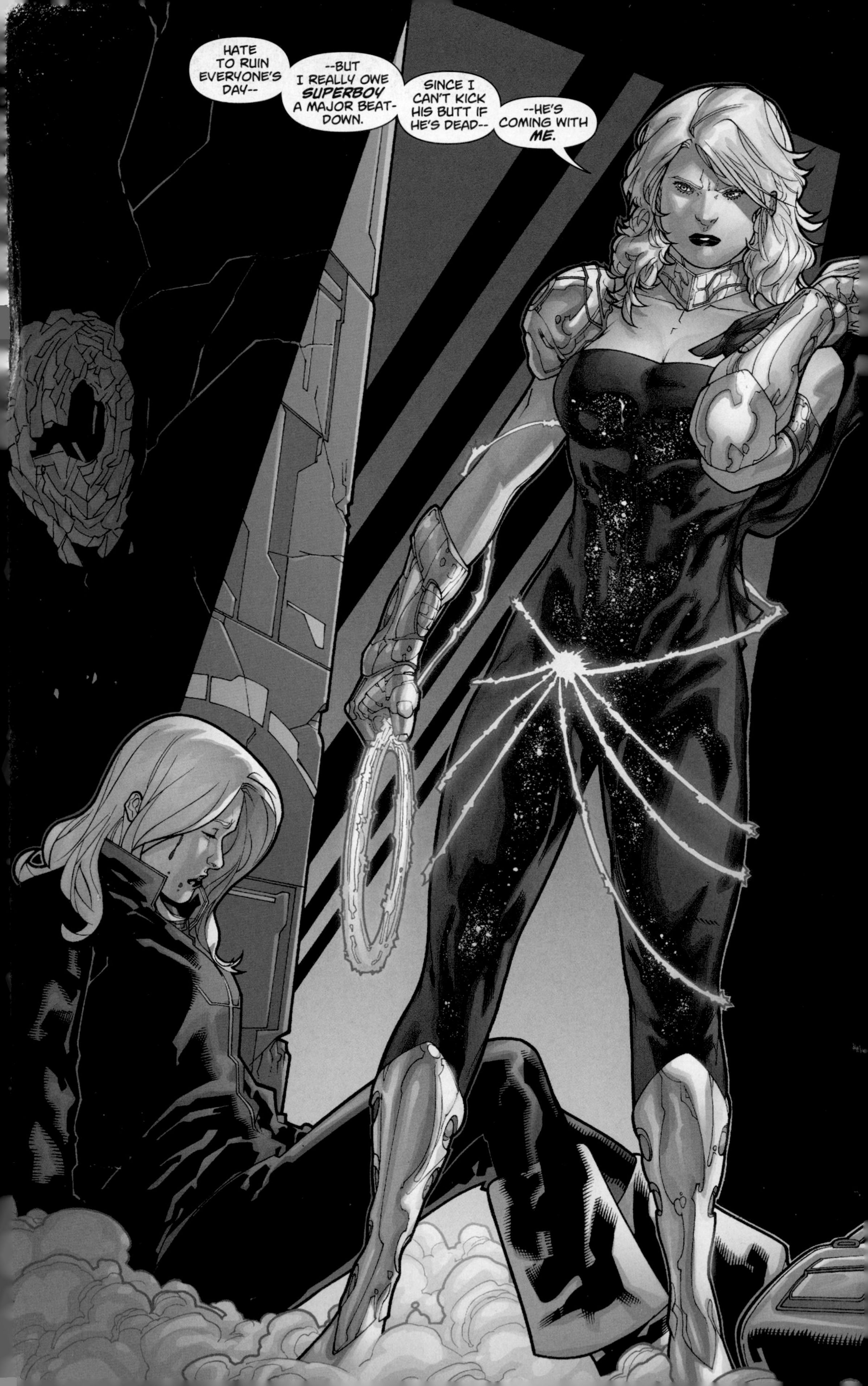
HATE TO RUIN EVERYONE'S DAY--
--BUT I REALLY OWE SUPERBOY A MAJOR BEAT-DOWN.
SINCE I CAN'T KICK HIS BUTT IF HE'S DEAD--
--HE'S COMING WITH ME.

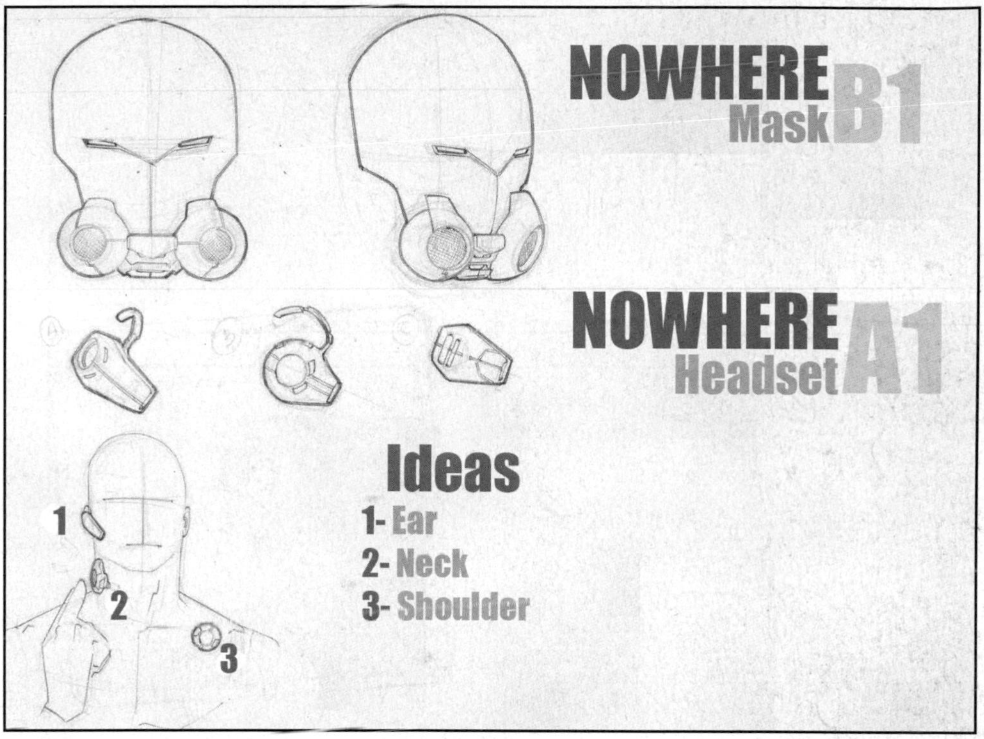
NOWHERE
Mask B1
NOWHERE
Headset A1
Ideas
1- Ear
2- Neck
3- Shoulder
1
2
3

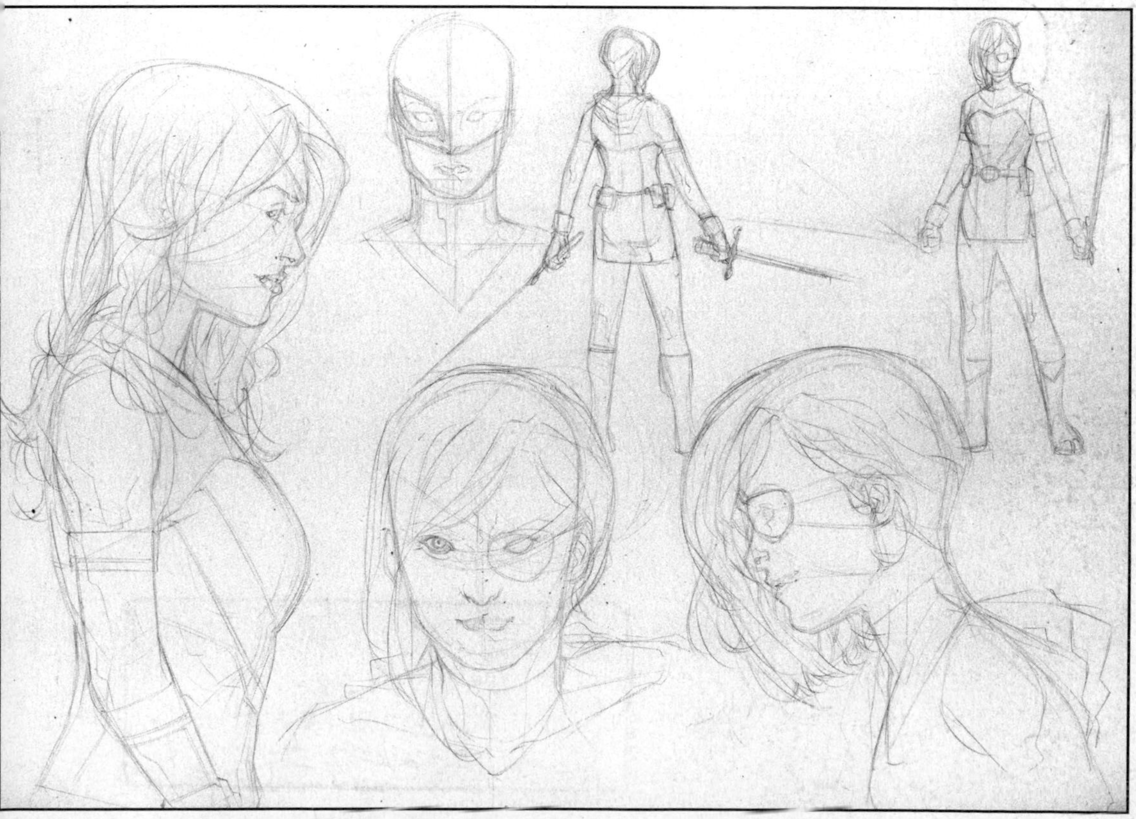

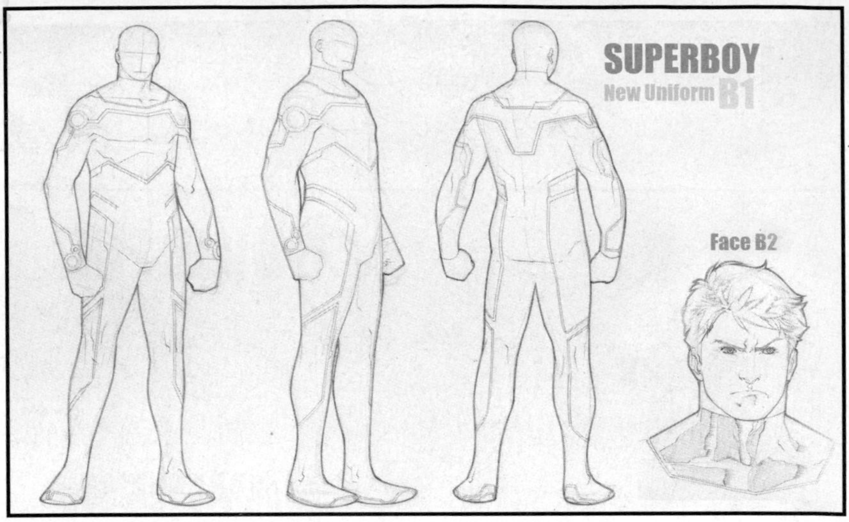
SUPERBOY
New Uniform B1
Face B2

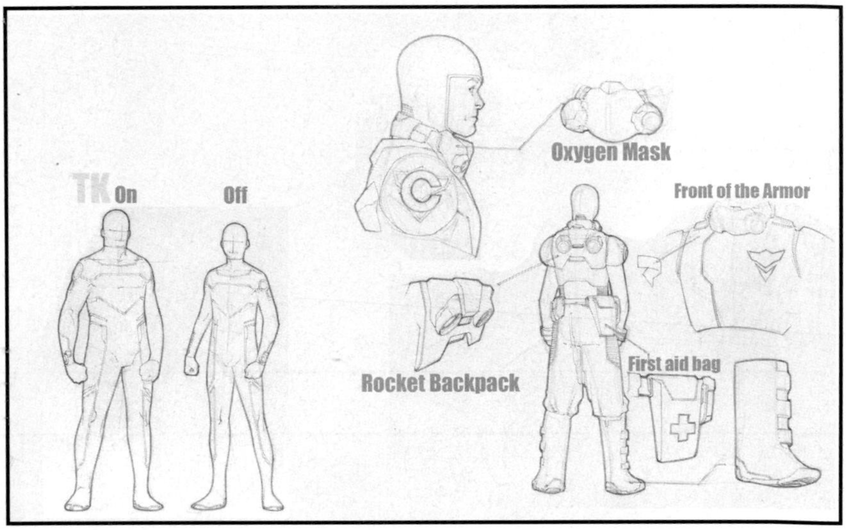
Oxygen Mask
TK On
Off
Front of the Armor
Rocket Backpack
First aid bag

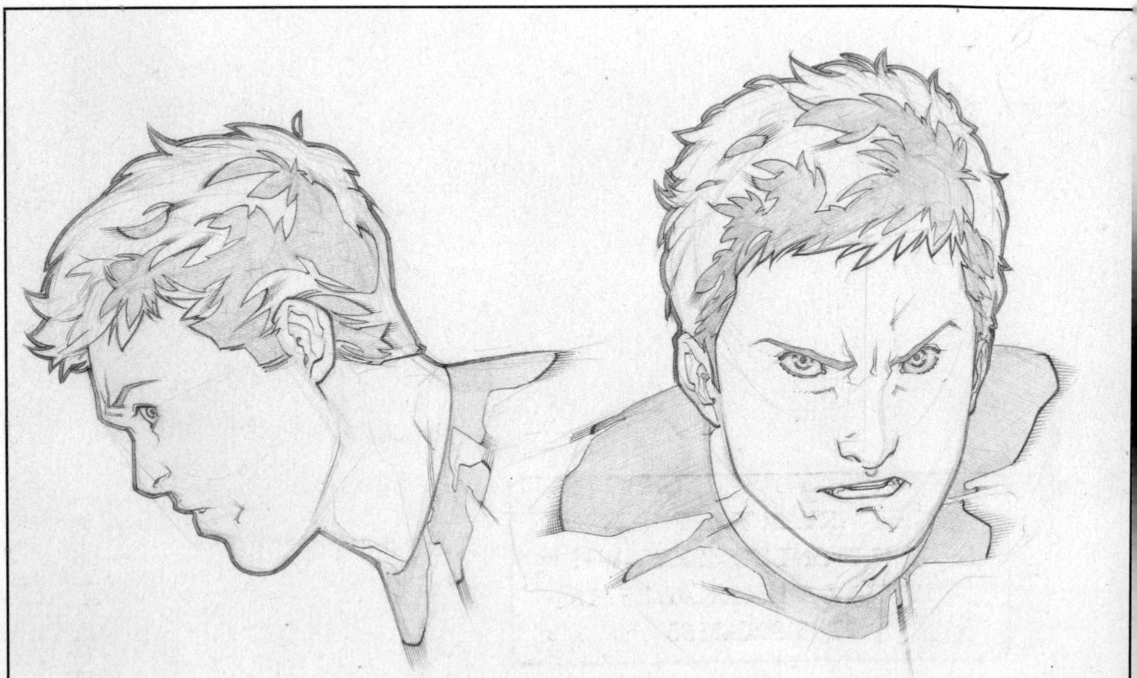

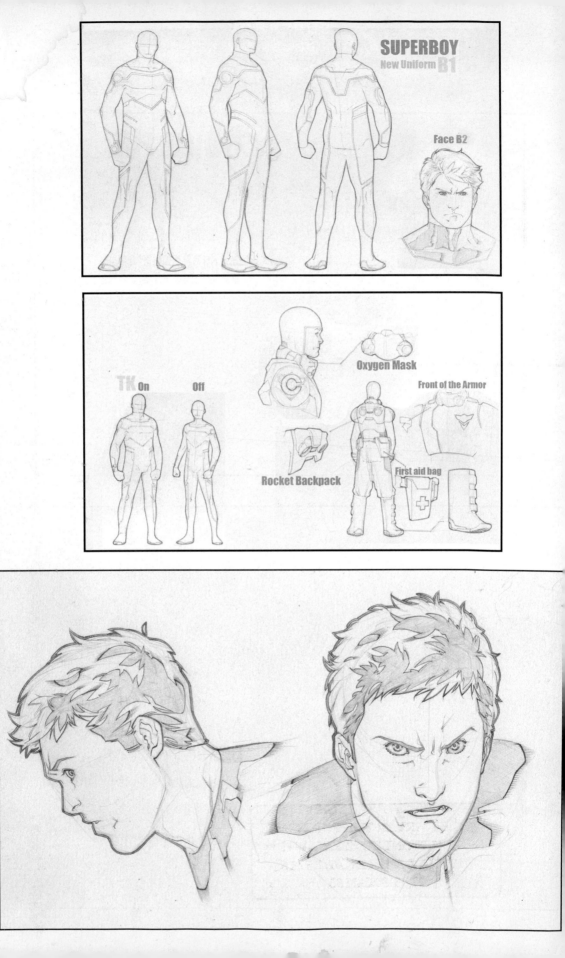